QUESTIONS

OF THE

DAY:

ECONOMIC AND SOCIAL.

BY

DR. WILLIAM ELDER.

PHILADELPHIA:
HENRY CAREY BAIRD,
INDUSTRIAL PUBLISHER,
406 Walnut Street.
1871.

Entered according to Act of Congress, in the year 1871, by

WILLIAM ELDER,

in the Office of the Librarian of Congress, at Washington, D. C.

RINGWALT & BROWN, PRINTERS,
Press Building, S. W. corner 7th and Chestnut Sts.,
PHILADELPHIA.

PREFACE.

THE purpose governing in the composition of this treatise was not so much the discussion and settlement of the questions involved in the matters now occupying the people of the United States, and awaiting solution by the thinkers and voters of the day, as a desire to help the *popular* investigation, by suggesting the underlying principles which must, at last, solve all the problems of public policy. Aware of the difficulties of my task, I intended, at the beginning of my work, to give it the unassuming title of STUDIES in Political Economy. I intended nothing else or more, and felt that I must avoid the pretentious claim of a comprehensive or conclusive treatment of all the subjects, or all the principles promised by such a title as "The Causes of the Wealth of Nations," or those more frequently adopted by the higher authorities, "Principles, or Elements, of Political Economy;" and I must be allowed, also, to say, in the personal confidence which a preface allows between an author and his readers, that under terror of the failures made, and in sight of the wrecks that strew this uncharted sea of speculation, and the disrepute into which the writers on Political Economy have fallen, I felt anxious to avoid even the most mitigated form of the old reproach. This feeling drove me upon the choice of a title less appropriate, but chosen because it is less alarming to the common sense of the reading public. I would not cheat the reader by the label upon the back of my book, but I would not deter him from opening it. My purpose is to provoke and assist inquiry in matters of such practical importance as those herein discussed, and the title page must not be allowed to scare away the reader.

This book is, nevertheless, in spirit and purpose, a series of studies in the principles which rule the questions of the time—the practical questions, which the people are engaged in settling into the policy of their social and economic conduct. It is an outlook upon public affairs, taken from an *American* observatory, and its discussions are "calculated," as astronomers say, for the Western Hemisphere.

Holding that Political Economy is *National* in its purview and range, as opposed to abstract, general, or cosmopolitan, I am content that my thoughts shall be understood to proceed from so narrow a stand-point of observation; nor would it embarrass me in the least if my doctrines should be pronounced not only American, but even Pennsylvanian, in spirit and inspiration, for I would have them something certain, settled, and actual, rather than the general and universal that comprises everything, and belongs to nothing in particular. For the reason that in the study of man, I would take for examination a completely representative individual—neither a giant nor a dwarf, an idiot nor a genius, but an average well-rounded and well-balanced man, I adopt what I take to be a community whose forces, functions, and attainments best answer as a standard of societary policy; and the reader may as well be apprised in advance, that this book is written under the conviction that the United States is the field of inquiry which, better than any other, promises the whole truth in matters of political, economic, and social speculation; and, that Pennsylvania, by its eminently representative character, is the focal point of the great facts which the nation offers for instructive study. This State is neither eminently commercial, agricultural, nor manufacturing. It is neither so near the sea as to lose its nationality, nor so far from its coast as to be injuriously separated from the outside world. Its climate and soil do not arbitrarily determine or restrict its industries, but it has, in all things, that happy balance of economic interests, and such a diversity of nationalities in its population, as assures it a condition and position of equilibrium; or, let me say, in my vernacular, American

English, enables her to carry her head "level" in economic and political questions.

There is more meaning than appears at first sight in her sobriquet, *the Keystone State.* Such a claim as this will doubtless be disputed by every other State in the Union. Perhaps, not one of them would concede her this rank as against itself, but if the point were submitted to the arbitration of a general vote, she would carry the majority handsomely, as the majority has voted with her in every Presidential election since the formation of the Federal Union.

It is not preëminence in any special excellence that we are here insisting upon, but, on the contrary, it is the very absence of anything like such unevenness in her characteristics that gives her the position of an exemplar in economic policy. If there is anything in a complete diversification of resources and of industries, and in the resulting perfect division of productive labor, she has it. It is this that makes her a model for the study of economists, and it is from this rounded entirety of her character that her distinguished Political Economists, Frederick List, Henry C. Carey, and Stephen Colwell derived the data and drift of their studies. Upon the system of the first named, who confessed that he learned here all that he afterwards taught, we have the verdict of Germany's acceptance and practical adoption, and that verdict, besides, vindicated by the astonishing achievements which have recently resulted from a long-continued and persistent conformity to its principles and policy. Such has been the influence of Professor List upon the policy and destiny of Prussia, that it is safe to say that if he had not guided its industrial system, a Bismarck, a Moltke, and an Emperor of Germany would have been impossible to-day.

Northern Europe has already recognized Mr. Carey (named second here only because later in date), as the Authority of the new time, and Interpreter of its new necessities; and I venture to predict that the last in the order of date and labor, Mr. Colwell, will, in due time be recognized as one of the greater lights in the firmament of the science when the fermentation of the problems of Finance shall come to take a settled and certain form.

The inconvenience and the labor of assigning to the several authors, who have been my teachers and helpers in the study of my subjects, their respective shares in the matter that I have used, and the overloading of my pages with such frequent acknowledgments as are due to them would have compelled, determined me to decline the task. But I had another reason or reasons for so doing; promiscuous reading and study through many years, renders it quite impossible for me to trace home to its sources the information obtained and used; besides, I would not willingly assume to settle the claims to originality for even the principal matters borrowed from them. Moreover, I would hesitate to make my authorities responsible for my use of their facts and doctrines by quoting them in foot notes.

Here, however, I am bound to say that my indebtedness to Mr. Carey is so great that only those who are intimately acquainted with his works can duly estimate it. I believe that no future writer upon any of the subjects embraced in the wide field of his studies will be able to do much more, to any purpose, than give his doctrines some required difference of presentment and application.

In like manner, I would acknowledge the heaviest obligations to Frederick List, Alexander Hamilton, and to Stephen Colwell. To Parke Godwin, Esq., I am indebted largely for matter used freely in my second and third introductory chapters; and to Horace Greeley, and the domestic and foreign correspondents of the *Tribune*, for valuable information employed in discussing the current coöperative movements of the time.

It will doubtless occur to the reader that *Taxation* and *National Finance* are among the most considerable and pressing "questions of the day." They hold, indeed, such a place among the topics now under popular and official consideration, that all other subjects of public interest actually converge in them. I intended to embrace them, but had not advanced very far in their treatment until I found that they must be reserved for a separate treatise, if they were to be discussed to any purpose. There are no questions of public affairs so much debated, and none that so much need a more critical examination than they receive in the controversies maintained upon them; moreover, there are none more difficult of treatment. In my apprehension of them, I should be obliged to confront the opinions that now rule in the administration of our State and National affairs. I can neither agree with the policy of the National Treasury, nor with the most influential conductors of the public press. The discussion would be one unbroken controversy, requiring room, arrangement, and readers wholly inconsistent with the purpose and drift of the other parts of this treatise.

The closing chapters in the division entitled Guarantyism, are intended to awaken attention to the great social question of the time—the strife between labor and capital. He would be a bold man who would assume to settle this last and most difficult problem that has ever yet arisen in the progress of civilization—a question upon whose happy solution and settlement depends the general welfare in an eminent degree. Every earnest man's best help is due to it, and I have contributed what under the circumstances I could. For the faults which admit of no fair justification—those for which I am fully responsible—I have no right to offer any apology.

W. E.

1824 MT. VERNON STREET,
  Philadelphia, *June*, 1871.

TITLES OF THE CHAPTERS.

CHAPTER.		PAGE.
I.	INTRODUCTORY.—Political Economy	9
II.	" Formation of Society	14
III.	" Civilization	26
IV.	" Migration and Occupation of the Earth	33
V.	Wealth—the Laws and Conditions of its Growth	40
VI.	Sources of Advancement in Wealth	53
VII.	Population—Law of Increase	70
VIII.	Distribution of Wealth—Wages	85
IX.	Money, as an Exchanger of Values	106
X.	Money, as a Producer while acting as an Exchanger	120
XI.	Paper Money, and incidentally, of Banks	133
XII.	Commerce	157
XIII.	Trade between Nations in diverse Geographic, and Economic Conditions	176
XIV.	Free Trade and Protection	190
XV.	Doctrine and Policy of Protection	204
XVI.	The most Prominent and Plausible Objections to Protection	221
XVII.	Protection in the Historic Nations	235
XVIII.	Guarantyism	247
XIX.	Secret Societies	264
XX.	Coöperation—Survey of the Field	281
XXI.	" Stores, Manufactories, Banks	295
XXII.	" In the United States	315

QUESTIONS OF THE DAY.

INTRODUCTORY.

CHAPTER I.

POLITICAL ECONOMY.

Definition of Political Economy; its subjects.—Individuality and Association, the centripetal and centrifugal forces of society.—Their material analogues.—A man the type of a society.—Province of Political Economy limited while its bearings are unbounded.—What it teaches the Statesman, the Moralist, and the Religionist.

POLITICAL ECONOMY is the theory of human well-being, in its relations with the production, distribution, and consumption of wealth.

Its subjects are man and those external things which minister to his earthly wants. It is concerned with his mental and moral nature, so far as these are involved in his societary relations, and, with his physical necessities, and those material things which are made to satisfy them.

OF MAN AS A SUBJECT OF POLITICAL ECONOMY.

Association with his fellow-men is the first and greatest necessity of man's life. It is indispensable to his intellectual and social faculties, and equally so to his physical welfare. For the care and culture of his body, mind, and morals, and for their due enjoyments, he depends upon others from birth till death.

For the best service of his industrial powers, he requires the largest and most direct commerce with the world around him.

Every individual soul holds beneficial relations with every created thing, and is crippled in the proportion that it is deprived of interchange, possession, and enjoyment. The attractive impulses of his constitution, which answer to this large range of relations, gather men into families, communities, states, and nations, and engage them in a commerce of ideas, commodities, and enterprises with each other and with the world. Trade, travel, and correspondence spring from them, and the highest forms and richest fruits of human development are due to them. This associative attraction is analogous to the material law of gravitation, which groups the atoms of the universe in planets, solar systems, and constellations; ordering and collocating them around their several centres; the local centres by counter attraction, holding each group in its own sphere and office, and every individual of each group in its appropriate position.

This tendency to unity would produce the evil of uniformity in character, and of centralization in place, if it were not counterbalanced by the equally essential provision for securing and developing his Individuality. It is the related differences of individuals which evoke their qualities and stimulate their growth. Gregarious animals are too much alike to educate each other into higher capabilities; but men, differing in tastes, feelings, and capacities, play perpetually upon each other's powers, and develop them by the mutual action and reaction of social commerce; their distinctiveness ever growing in the ratio of the number and variety of the relations subsisting between them. Savage society, even within its limited range of mutual services and dependencies, develops the individual, diversifies the character, and enriches the aggregate of the horde, by considerably multiplying the functions and modifying the faculties of its members. But it is in civilized societies that the immense number of mental and social affinities and industrial interchanges have opportunity to display their power in the development of the highest individuality through the most varied and complete association.

The operation of these two forces—Association and Individuality—are thus reciprocal and corroborative in enhancing each other and in promoting the progress of the man, the community, and the race.

It is a universal law of matter, animate and inanimate, that difference of quality, condition, or position, excites a manifestation of force and an interchange of activities. In chemistry, new combinations give new and varied powers to the atoms of matter; in astronomy, difference of position and magnitude give rise to and determine the motions of the celestial bodies. Association and individuality are exact correlatives of the centripetal and centrifugal forces which hold the orbs at their appropriate distances from their centres, and propel them in their respective orbits; they correspond also to that counterbalance of cohesion and repulsion which keeps the particles of bodies in position, and gives them freedom, while it enforces order and harmony in action. Especially and eminently, association and individuality obtain in the organism of the human body, in which a thousand different functions are secured in their specialty of character and service, while they are perfectly associated and coördinated in integral unity. A man is a society in the least form, and his structure and functions intimate the policy of the larger society, or grand man, to which a complete community conforms. St. Paul (Ephesians iv. 16) finds the analogue of a perfect Christian society in this individualism and coöperation of the constituents of the human frame, and borrows from it an argument and an illustration. He calls the church a perfect man, of which Christ is the head, "from whom the whole body, fitly joined together and compacted by that which every joint supplieth, according to the effectual working in the measure of every part, maketh increase of the body unto the edifying of itself in love" (or, in harmony). These forces decentralize and diversify the societary organism to secure individual liberty and development, and at the same time coördinate the elements and subordinate their agencies as the harmony of entirety requires. Individuality takes care of the severalties; association organizes them into unity of general uses.

It is admitted that the individual man has moral and spiritual faculties and necessities which do not fall within the province of political economy proper; and that communities have interests which in like manner lie beyond the jurisdiction of civil government. Yet it must be also admitted that all the interests of this life and, conditionally, of the next, are so far involved in the temporal welfare of man, as it depends upon material conditions, that political economy stands directly related to politics, morals, and religion. It has, therefore, something essential to teach the Statesman and the Moralist, as well as the producer, the exchanger, and the consumer of commodities.

As a system of the laws which govern society, its first principles instruct the Statesman that upon the utmost possible diversification of business pursuits depend the growth, the wealth and the strength of the State, and of the people individually; that, the worth of the infinitely varied capabilities of a people is to be secured and made available to the whole community, only by providing for them a corresponding variety of industrial and social functions.

The Moralist, who cannot be ignorant of the influence of circumstances upon character and conduct, especially upon that mass of men whose improvement he seeks—of all, indeed, except the race of moral heroes and martyrs—may learn how to change the necessities, which lead to violation of the social laws, into opportunities, which tend to induce conformity; how enforced idleness and dependency may be replaced by self-support, and the respect which grows out of it for the rights of property, and the resulting interest felt in the general welfare; how a partnership in a common prosperity takes away the temptations which have their source and provocation in the wants and necessities of poverty and privation—in a word; he will see and feel the force of the Great Teacher's injunction: Seek first the divine order of society, which He calls the Kingdom of God, that men may be delivered from a dangerous desire for what they shall eat, what they shall drink, or wherewithal they shall be clothed. (Matthew vi. 31.)

Nor can the Religionist rightly neglect the study of those first principles in the economy of human society which so deeply concern its spiritual welfare. He must not leave to political policy, to economical and philanthropic endeavor, the whole charge of reformatory enterprise. His Master, who taught self-denial as a means of spiritual discipline, never said a word in commendation of that poverty which means want, ignorance, slavery, despair and death; but, on the contrary, went about doing good to the bodies, as well as to the souls, of men. The fasting which he approved was not that of beggary or necessity, but the free well-principled restraint of the appetites. Among the beatitudes we do not find a blessing upon poverty in temporal goods, but upon the poor in *spirit*, nor are they pronounced blessed who suffer for lack of material benefits, but those who hunger and thirst after righteousness; and those only are required to renounce their wealth in whom avarice and covetousness are idolatry.

Thus all who are either teachers or governors, with all who are in any-wise responsible for the well-being of their fellow men, are deeply concerned to know the principles and order which best promote it.

CHAPTER II.

OF THE FORMATION OF SOCIETY.

Of the Formation of Society: History of its progress.—EDENISM: Conditions of the primitive race.—Communism and social harmony.—Suffering not the only source of development.—SAVAGISM: Nature in rebellion to human authority; fratricidal war.—Clans and Hordes.—Industry and Commerce narrowly limited.—Rule of the strongest.—Democracy in government.—Property rights held by possession.—No international or intertribal law.—Liberty without security.—In a true order rights and duties are commensurate, and life is a system of equitable exchanges.—Indolence, ignorance, immorality, irreligion, selfishness of the Savage.—Dwarfed individuality; association but little larger than the animal instincts prompt; Commerce, public sentiment, and general ideas of the lowest grade.—Analogy to infancy of an individual.—North American Indians probably a degenerate race.—PATRIARCHISM: The family polity extended to a larger community.—The type of all the despotisms.—An association that represses individuality.—Productive Industry begins, property in the soil recognized, commerce initiated, money used.—Men become self-supplying.—Women and children are slaves.—Monarchy and political slavery are better.—Egyptian bondage more favorable than the rule of the Patriarchs.—The system analogous to childhood.—BARBARISM: Productive industry, arts and sciences greatly advanced.—In advance of civilization of Western Europe previous to the inauguration of the new physical philosophy.—Characteristics contrasted with those of civilization.—Difference in powers of association and growth of individuality.—Correspondence of all the phases of society to ages in the life of an individual.

A THEORY of human history, embracing its known facts and supplying such as are logically necessary to its completeness, must help us in the endeavor to unfold the philosophy of societary organization. It will, at least, serve as a study, though it falls short of demonstration by induction.

EDENISM.

The primitive state of man on the earth is a matter of faith to those who believe they have the knowledge of it by divine revelation, by their authorities, however inspired, or, by accepted tradition. The record received by the Christian world from the Jewish is understood to declare that the first pair were created in the image of their Maker, and were placed in "a garden which the Lord God planted eastward in Eden, in which grew every tree that is pleasant to the sight and good for food. And God blessed them and said unto them: be fruitful and multiply, and replenish the earth, and subdue it; and have dominion over the fish of the sea, and over the fowl of the air, and over every living thing that moveth upon the earth."

The provision for life and happiness was ample. The state of the primal society was perfect innocence, or, total ignorance of evil, and the only labor was "to dress the garden of Eden, and to keep it." In their food, they were restricted to "herbs bearing seed, and the fruit of trees yielding seed," and, they were naked. Night and day and the varied seasons recurred, but they needed no defenses against the vicissitudes to which their posterity is exposed.

The necessary fecundity of nature fresh from the hand of the Creator, and the correspondent innocence and happiness of the new-made race of men for whom all things were prepared, gave the idea of the age of Saturn, the golden age, to the Greeks and Romans; the reign of the gods on earth to the Egyptians, and similar conceptions of a necessary period of peace and happiness to the cosmogonies of the other nations of antiquity, whose mythologies and philosophies have been less completely preserved, but were doubtless received as well authenticated.

The evidence, revealed, traditional, and presumptive is held sufficient to prove that man appeared upon the earth after the mineral, vegetable, and animal creatures had provided and furnished it for his comfortable residence and support—that, the race was first placed in the temperate zone, and that they there formed a primitive society wholly unlike those of all subsequent times.

In such conditions, it is obvious that exclusive property in the soil could not exist, and that an abundant provision for the sustenance of life prevented contests of interests, induced mildness of manners and pacific relations among the parties. While such a state of things continued, war and oppression would be unknown, and men, women and children would live as one family, free from suffering and care. But it is just as obvious that all their happiness would be mainly that of the senses and affections, and but little refined or elevated by the delights of intelligence.

16   INTRODUCTORY.

We cannot say that such an order of human life must have a limited period; for it is illogical to affirm that the growth of human faculties, any more than the faculties themselves, must spring from pain, privation, or the want of the conditions of well-being, for this would make evil necessary to the existence of good; but we know that the Edenic period or golden age did fail, whatever may or might have been its distinctive character.

SAVAGISM.

The greater part of modern philosophers have declared for the original savagism of men, which though it may be the second phase of human society in actual order, is necessarily the first in contemplation of strictly inductive philosophy, resting, as is its wont, upon observation and experiment exclusively, or upon history, and stopping short of the First Cause and of deductions from the necessary truths that thence proceed.

In this stage of societary history the earth is found in a state of disharmony, and the elements and subordinate terrestrial beings, vegetable and animal, in such resistance to man's dominion that life may be called a battle between the sovereign and his legitimate subjects. Then "the ground," as under a curse, brought forth thorns and thistles, the actual dominion over the fowls of the air and the beasts of the field passed away, and, instead, " the fear and the dread" of man fell upon all the inferior creatures that surrounded him, and he became the destroyer of the creatures of which, in happier conditions, he had been the governor and guardian.

The Edenic harmony of the race also gave way to fratricidal war. The invasion of ferocious beasts and the necessity of seeking subsistence in the chase, caused the invention of destructive weapons, which were as often employed by men in despoiling and destroying each other. The necessity of defense and the means of effective aggression led to the union of families, and of these the horde was formed.

The industry of savage tribes is confined to hunting, fishing, gathering the forest fruits in their season, and the fabrication of arms, offensive and defensive. Internal trade is extremely limited, productive industry being so inconsiderable, so little varied and so

FORMATION OF SOCIETY.

little skilled, that nearly every man is the fabricator of all the commodities which he uses. Among them there is no useful division of labor in adaptation to special capabilities, and, consequently, no organization and but little improvement of industry.

Women are in servitude. Man, in right of larger bones and stronger muscles, establishes the law of the strongest, and might becomes right in all the institutions of the tribe, and in its dealings with surrounding tribes. In all questions of internal order and external action, demanding the combined force of the mass, each has a voice. A rude democracy prevails in the appointment of rulers and leaders. The right of property rests in actual possession and occupancy. The common law of the horde, in accordance with this fundamental principle, recognizes the right of gathering the fruits of the forest, of taking wild animals wherever they are found, and, of fishing in all streams. The obligations of justice between tribes are unknown. They acknowledge no international law, and observe the conditions of treaties only so long and so far as they seem convenient and advantageous; and the right of taking the goods of other tribes, by force or fraud, is as clear to them as that of hunting in their forests. A larger license, or less restraint of natural liberty, marks the institutions of the savage than is at all compatible with the system of civilization; but there is less security for those that are allowed, and, in the same degree, the less real liberty enjoyed.

In the necessary order of things the largest benefits of society bring with them the largest responsibilities; duties are commensurate with rights; enjoyments are in proportion to social relations; and the greater the service obtained from others, the greater the reciprocities demanded. Social life is a system of exchanges; wrongs inflicted are echoed in injuries received; equity is a debt, and benevolence is the price of needed kindness.

Insecurity of property is naturally accompanied by aversion to productive industry which necessarily results in a degraded, ignorant, and dwarfed existence. The stimulant of hope in the future is wanting for the service of the present, and there is no progress. The moral nature of the savage ranges but little beyond the animal instincts, sharpened, but not refined, by his undeveloped intellect, which is less the director than the servant of his passions. His religion is a mixture of fear and selfishness. Having no father God he can have no brother man. He lacks the impulses that prompt to social amelioration, and his interest in posterity is limited to the instinct which centres in his immediate offspring.

The rudimentary forces of the higher forms of society are all found in the savage community, else the advancement from the lowest to the highest were impossible; but they are overlaid by the ignorance, indolence and brutality which characterize it. The sentiment of Association has no nobler reach than the animal passions prompt; that of Individuality has no greater growth than accidental advantages induce. Social commerce but little transcends the gregariousness of the irrational races in extent or value; for where there is but little productive industry and no permanent improvement of land, the exchanges of service must be small, and there can be no educational enterprise, no public sentiment, no general ideas or interests, no corporate feeling, and, neither the man nor the community can take the form which promotes the highest ends and aims of life.

The analogies of individual life affirm and illustrate this general conception. These earliest combinations of men by a just correspondence are regarded as the Infancy of human society; they are built upon the lowest, most common and earliest developed faculties of man—upon the instincts and propensities, with that modicum of intelligence which describes the life of the earliest childhood. In phrenological language the reigning faculties are acquisitiveness, combativeness, secretiveness, cautiousness, sharpness of the perceptive powers; all trained to the service of selfishness; while the corrective and directing sentiments of justice, benevolence, veneration and the higher reason are yet inactive.

There is good ground for believing that savages are in some instances degenerate races—remnants of a social and political wreck. Our North American Indians have lost their history, but they preserve the traces of a much higher social and political system than they have shown since they became known to Europe. It is, therefore, only in relative rank that they are here treated as exhibiting the first or earliest stage of societary organization. We are not considering them as subjects of successive, but of contemporaneous history, and this for the purpose of exhibiting the spirit, the forces, and the differences of societary constitutions from the simplest to the more complex forms.

PATRIARCHISM.

This is the next societary system in an orderly study of our subject. It is an advance upon the tribal organization and the economy of the savage horde. In effect it is an extension of the family polity to that of a larger community, in which the Chief has all the absoluteness of the father of a family, and an equally energetic government—a despotism, unchecked by the instinctive tenderness of immediate parentage, and marked by such abridgment of the subject's liberties as hinders the development of the individual and the progress of the clan.

As a community system it is circumscribed to a few favoring regions of the earth. The best known and in its best form is the system of the Israelites previous to their captivity in Egypt. It is of little importance, and almost impracticable in modern times. It centralized the community upon the family model, and was incapable of anything approaching a true nationality. In Palestine, after the Egyptian Exodus, it was greatly modified both in sacerdotal and political principles by the institutions of Moses. The Executive of his system held his office by delegation, and not in right of inheritance until the monarchy of Saul was established, which had arbitrary power in secular affairs; the Priesthood being at the same time confided to a single family of the nation. In pure patriarchism the head of the tribe is King, Priest, General and Judge—the type of all the various forms of despotism, and tending to all the tyrannies of government endured among men. It is an instance of Association without the conditions which favor or allow Individuality, with its attendant freedom, responsibility and progressiveness, to any considerable or worthy extent. It is, nevertheless, a form of society superior to the wild liberty of savage life. It is a more effective association. The first steps in social progress are made in it. Productive industry begins; flocks are reared; the simpler branches of manufacture are undertaken; property in the soil is recognized to some extent, and in movables, absolutely; exchange of services and values is initiated; money and other mediums of exchange come into use; men become attached to the soil which they now own, and they depend upon settled and distributed industries for subsistence. They supply their wants by skill and labor, and no longer live exclusively by spoliation of the forests and rivers.

But these ameliorating influences are too narrowly limited to provide for any considerable advance of the commonwealth. It is quite as apparent in the history of the patriarchal system of the plains of Asia, as of the Highlands of Scotland, that the head of the great family, though with less of ferocity than the savage Chief, is quite as perfidious and, in effect, as despotic, and as much an oppressor of his subjects. His wife is a slave and his children are servants for life; all women are either drudges or dishonored ministers of their masters' pleasures—a system of such inequality and so full of mischief, that the earliest necessities of growing communities require its modification. A single family of two or three generations may endure it, but a considerable population is safer and better in absolute political and personal slavery to masters or monarchs. Egyptian bondage, rigorous as it was, proved more friendly to the welfare of the Israelites than their accustomed tribal institutions would have been in Mesopotamia; for in taking care of the family groups, the patriarchal polity had too little control of the federative unity of the tribes, and utterly failed of effecting an association comprehensive and free enough to secure internal peace or external defense, or the advancement of the people either individually or collectively.

In analogy to an individual life, patriarchism was a government in its childhood, favorable to the stage of development to which it was adapted, but obstructive and repressive of all endeavor towards further advancement—an injuriously prolonged minority of the subjects.

BARBARISM.

The next well-defined stage of national growth is a large stride in the social, political, industrial, and commercial institutions of a State. Productive industry in a great variety of forms becomes the occupation of the mass of the people; and the arts and sciences receive a great development. Through the Middle Ages the Mahomedans of Asia and the Moors in Spain gave noble proofs of the capabilities and brilliant illustration to the polity of Barbarism. It proved itself capable of very great economic success. In mechanic skill the nations which we call civilized in the same age, so far from excelling did not approach them in excellence. In architecture and decorative art they fell but a little way behind Greek and Roman achievement. In agriculture they were greatly in advance of all western Europe—all the service of wealth they had at command; and in civil policy and military achievement they certainly had no superiors. Indeed, it is hard to find a quality of personal or national character in which they were transcended by the people of the Caucasian race, prior to the inauguration of the new physical philosophy and its wonder-working application in arts and manufactures.

Barbarism retained the warlike spirit of the savage system and the despotism of the Patriarchal, but it associated men more effectively for the ends of society, and brought the progress of the race to the verge of the next epoch in its civil advancement. Its characteristics are most clearly defined by its contrasts with civilization. The chief of these are:—Its stationary spirit, resulting from its doctrine of fatalism and fanatical theocracy; its directness and promptitude of distributive justice, springing from the free action of the passions and the simplicity of its political forms. Civilization in these respects being marked by its unlimited progressiveness, resulting from its confidence in the dominion of natural laws over the elements and forces of matter, and, by the logical structure of its religious beliefs. Its political institutions have a flexibility and a conformity to the exigencies of the times and to changes of international relations, of which Barbarism is entirely incapable; and its jurisprudence is rendered circuitous by its respect for individual rights, by publicity of procedure, and by responsibility of its official ministers.

Differences of societary constitutions may be traced to their roots in corresponding differences of mental qualities, and the reflex influence of institutions upon national character may be allowed; but with these questions we are not now concerned, we are only endeavoring distinctive definitions by arraying the actual contrasts between the respective systems which we are considering. Beside those already indicated others are noteworthy. They may be seen sufficiently for all that they suggest in the following tabular array:—

IN BARBARISM.	IN CIVILIZATION.
Ecclesiastical absoluteness, governing by divine right.	An appeal to reason admitted in the interpretation of revealed truth.
Literature, impassioned and imaginative.	Literature, logical and philosophical.
Opinion fixed.	Opinion free.
Doctrine indisputable.	Doctrine variable.
Parental and marital rights, absolute.	Parental and marital rights, limited.
Women and children enslaved.	Women and children guarded by municipal law.

These contrasts so rugged and bold in abstract statement are, however, much modified in effect, by the fact, which must be conceded, that the larger and better guarantied liberties of civilization under the rule of public opinion and official responsibility are much weakened by the substitution of fraud for force, the cunning of the fox for the boldness of the lion, wherever right is to be overborne, or wrong inflicted or defended.

Notwithstanding all the evasions of right, the illusions of hope, disappointments of trust, and the various oppressions of the more advanced forms of free government, the difference of operation upon private interests and on the destiny of the commonwealth, is very greatly in favor of civilized institutions. They still preserve the tendency to diffuse their benefits among the masses of the people, elevating the community as a whole, and giving a massiveness, stability, and aggregate value and force to the better order to which Barbarism can never by any possibility attain. Civilization has all that is possible of human welfare in its prospect. Barbarism is limited by its incapacity of change or growth, and is unfitted for the command of that infinite power of association which a perfect development of individuality secures.

We have indicated or intimated a certain correspondence of characteristics between the societary phases of the human race or races, and the marked stages in the life and growth of an individual. There must be such analogies if each man is a representative of the race, and the collective race is but a comprehensive abstract of the individual man. We do not, however, mean to affirm that the several kinds of societies flow or grow into each other as the successive stages of an individual life do, for it is not proved that the "varieties" of mankind are capable of such transition or development from the savage or patriarchal, or even from the barbarian, into the advanced form of that which we call the maturest state, such as civilization assumes, with its capability of indefinite progression. We mean only that there is an analogy or representative image of the one in the other. The reader will have noticed an analytic parallelism shown in the savage and individual infant. Following this thought, we have spoken of patriarchism as the analogue of childhood, or the period between the seventh and fourteenth year of individual life. Let us look for the correspondence: Childhood is distinguished from the next succeeding, as from the immediately preceding stage, by its facility of faith, its docility under authority, the dedication of its endeavors to preparation for action, and its incapability of any effective agency in the world's work. It is dreamy and inefficient. It has not reached the productive period in the useful arts. It has few or no social relations—no place in the world's life. It has not the impulse of self-assertion, nor has it caught the spirit of propagandism. Its period is marked by growth without corresponding increase of strength. It is a state of accumulation without responsive action. It has affection without friendship; culture without influence; crude, incoherent acquirement, without recognized ends or fixed aims. Its acquirements are only a stock of possibilities, which the age in advance must draw out and actualize. Is not this picture, if drawn at length, a reflex of the patriarchal polity, with which we are best acquainted? The childhood of Israel found the refuge of its feebleness, and was nursed into strength, in barbaric bondage. The oracles committed to their custody received their interpretation and realization in the system which supplanted theirs. The patriarchal got its evolution first under the institutions of Egypt, and eventually from the Gentile nations, whose conditions, at the era of the earliest practical realization, were in the state which we call barbarism, and by analogy, the youth of the race.

Barbarism fitly answers to the analogous period of youth or adolescence, which is usually bounded by the fourteenth and twenty-fifth years of the individual. It is the age of chivalry, enthusiasm, undoubting faith in its destiny, recklessness of risk and ardent devotedness to vague and unlimited enterprise. It is impatient and discontented with its inheritance; it demands a new world for its fresh new life.

Routine is as repulsive as imprisonment, and it forces circumstances with an industry that employs muscle more than mind, and is led by fancy rather than philosophy; it would achieve all that it imagines, and dreams that there is nothing beyond its compass—an insanity of aspiration barely checked in manifestation by the despotic authority of manners and opinion; the fates are its gods; it is passionate, peremptory, pitiless; its fortunes are predestinated, and it gives circumspection to the winds.

Are there not parallel points here to the history of Ancient Egypt and Middle-age Arabia? The vigor and fire, aye, the fine frenzy of youth glows in all their doings and darings, and their monuments, of all kinds, tangible, historical, traditional and fabulous, are all alike poetical.

In fine contrast with the youthlike impetuosity of barbarism, with its quick activity of imagination, exaggerated self-confidence, irreflective courage and passionate love of glory, we have the sobered thoughtfulness of manhood in advanced civilization, the circumspection that comes with experience, and the rigorous logic that law has impressed by its penalties upon willfulness; the warring spirit of enthusiasm is replaced by the serene masterdom of mind adjusted to the conditions of its subjects, and executive wisdom evades resistance and, by administrative address, secures success. Youth is in rebellion against the past; manhood makes experience its minister; and the issues register the unlike results. Barbarism ultimates itself in its achievements; its monuments are its boundaries, "the butt and sea-mark of its utmost sail;" its triumphs stand for its tombstones. But the highest attainments of civilization are fresh points of departure to higher and greater things beyond; they are only the scaffoldings of the edifice it rears, and every structure it erects for its service is also an observatory for a wider scope of aims and efforts. The works of barbarism, like the system, are arrested at the stage of success, and stand still in a completeness of fulfillment, which civilization never meets or confesses. The one declares its plan accomplished, the other indicates its own perpetuity.

NOTE.—Comte, author of the "Positive Philosophy," remarks, that every thoroughly developed individual passes through three mental stages: First, religious; second, theoretical or hypothetical; third, matter-of-fact or practical; and that nations have the same tendency, that is, a thoroughly developed race or family of men has a growth through corresponding phases. The theory which this acute observer of facts deduces from these propositions is not by any means sustained, but the facts are sound. They apply happily to the respective ages of Childhood, Youth and Mature Manhood, and the characteristics he assigns to them may be thus translated in our use of them: for "religious" read faith and obedience; for "hypothetical" read speculative, adventurous, enthusiastic; "matter-of-fact" may stand as serving sufficiently well for our apprehension of the soberly philosophical mood of the matured mind and method of advanced manhood; and, let it be noted, that only those nations who have actually entered upon the last stages are proved capable of rising through and over-passing the previous grades. The students of Ethnology can have no difficulty in applying this theory to the diverse nationalities in history.

Comte's scale of progressive development has met an universal acceptance, and has had the influence to carry with it, besides, his illogical deduction that the mind upon entering each new stage throws off the preceding—that the stage of the hypothetical discards that of faith, and is itself in turn rejected in the last, the matter-of-fact or philosophical state. This is decidedly unphilosophical in theory, as it is untrue in fact. Faith, speculation and fact, if they all have, or find, or hold the truth, harmonize, focalize, and persist in the issue that realizes them.

CHAPTER III.

CIVILIZATION.

Civilization, barbarism and savagism geographically distributed.—Only the European families have passed through all the stages of societary growth.—No instance or sign of decadence in them.—Asiatic communities culminate in barbarism.—Nations on the borders of Asia only are stationary.—Africans are not a decaying race; they cannot be classed with the American Indians.—Their character in the United States.—Not to be judged by our present standards of capability and fitness for the world's uses.—African race resembles European women.—The future must solve the problem of their societary relations.—Civilization elastic and composite.—Its late development.—India in advance of England in the fourteenth century.—The Moors superior to the Spaniards in the fifteenth century.—The Dark Ages in Europe.—Monarchy introduced order and initiated progress in the fifteenth and sixteenth centuries.—Intellectual and religious revolutions of the fifteenth century.—The age of the nascent industries, geographical discoveries, and the inauguration of man in the dominion of matter.—Progress of the sixteenth and seventeenth centuries.—The great career of the race carried forward by the people of European Origin.—Co-operative unity of diverse races.—Vicious generalities of the prevalent theory of Political Economy.—No single kindred is cosmopolitan.—The whole history of civilization is its only adequate definition.

CIVILIZATION connects itself historically with certain races of men, and is limited by geographical lines. In general statement it may be called the European form of societary life; as in like general terms Asia is barbaric, and Africa, for the want of any more exact term, may be classed as savage. These are the social, economic and political distinctions of those three portions of the globe in modern times; and in America civilization is found in different degrees of maturity, only in that portion of the continent which is occupied by European Colonists. Neither Asia nor Africa has organized a civilized government at home, nor formed one abroad within the reach of authentic history. If the Asiatic or African border of the Mediterranean Sea gave to Europe its superior races, they were exceptional peoples, and belonged to Europe by constitutional characters, as nearly as their geographic origin bordered upon the territory which they were destined to occupy and illustrate; and none of the regions that lay beyond them have shown any similar capabilities since the earliest known localities of the tribes of men. Moreover, it is of the European people only that it can be affirmed, with the assurance which experience affords, that they are capable of passing through all the stages from savage to civilized conditions, and who give indications of a progress in institutions and attainments without assignable limits in the future. Besides, none of the families or kindreds of Europe have ever yet shown any of the signs of declension which threaten the catastrophe that has already settled the fate of Asiatic and Egyptian nations, and of the aborigines of North and South America. No people found from the Mediterranean Sea to Scandinavia, or between the Ural Mountains and the North Atlantic Ocean, have within the range of history retrograded toward extinction. These people, whether German or Celtic, in Southern or Western Europe in time past, and now before our eyes, in the North and East, are demonstrating their capability of growth and culture into the highest style of human development. While, in marked contrast, Asiatic communities seem to culminate in barbarism, and are there arrested or thence decline, as if their constitutional maturity were reached at periods corresponding to the childhood or youth of the nations that now rule the world. Europe has emerged into civilization, settled America, and conquered whatever she desired of Asia, while the countries in which power and glory had their earliest sway have been retrograding, absolutely as well as relatively, from the time that the western mind seized the dominion of matter and undertook the destiny of the world.

A growth of the families of men corresponding to the epochs of individual life, and a decay like its decline toward extinction or death, has happened, and is threatened to the peoples which we style barbaric; but none of the European nations have perished; none of them are in the category of the dying. History has not set up the tombstone of a single branch of the Germanic or Celtic families, and the analogy has no true application to them. It is worth noting in connection with this fact, that the only members of this great kindred, ascertained by geographic boundaries, which are now unprogressive, are those that lie nearest to stationary Asia and unenlightened Africa; Spain, Italy and Greece, are borderers of the sea that separates the ancient from the modern world of human supremacy.

The people of Middle and Southern Africa are ranked as savages for want of a more sharply defined classification. But they do not resemble our American Indians in anything but inferiority to the foremost of the races. The latter are incapable of improved conditions. They are a dying people. The former have not yet shown any capability of self-development. In their native country they are without literature, science, and the fine and useful arts. They have organized no governments; they have no commerce, and they have no religion that can improve their life; but they have the physical health, simplicity, docility, and joyousness of childhood, and they show no signs of decay. Under circumstances the most unfavorable for any other people, they have improved among us to the utmost limit of their opportunity, and in the most tempting situations they have exhibited the kindliest qualities of character. Through the whole period of servitude, through the great American rebellion, and since, they have disappointed every unfavorable prophecy of their conduct in their changed relations to society, and have as much surpassed the hopes of the most sanguine philanthropists. We do not know this people; we have never known them. We cannot know them while we judge them by our standard, and hold that standard to be unchangeable for the future that probably lies generations in advance of us. Just as reason and experience find essential differences in the respective histories and destinies of the civilized and barbaric races, so we may suspect that the African is not measurable by the character and functions of the European. If they should after fair trial be found to be specifically different in the kind of mental power that is mastering the material conditions of terrestrial life, may they not have some other modification of mind not incompatible or incongruous, but helpful to the work of the world? Childhood and youth co-exist with and even corroborate maturity. The feminine mind and character are quite as broadly different from the masculine. These people in the mass more strongly resemble European women than they do the men of any other race, and they may weave into the web of social life well enough to vary and thus enrich it. Our judgment to be just and wise must wait for the facts—wait till we know what the future shall require of them and ourselves, and how they and we may answer the requirement. We know, *a priori*, that the noblest organisms are those which have the most numerous and most variously endowed constituents, and that the greatest possible diversity is compatible with peace and unity—that the limestone in our bones is organized into harmony of use with the finest nerves of sense and the highest organs of mind. The present dominant race of men live and move and have all their resources of power in the inductive philosophy. In this matter their own system binds them to wait for experiment and observation to supply the data of their reasonings.

We had no instance of a nation born in a day—of a people enfranchised at a blow. We could not believe it possible; above all, we could not believe them capable. Henry the Eighth hanged seventy thousand new-made freedmen of our own race and kindred during his reign. Political liberty seems impossible to Mexico after fifty years of discipline in freedom. France has gone back from Republicanism to Monarchy, and from Monarchy to chaos with such portentous facility that her varied examples taught us no hope of sudden adaptation to higher forms of social and civil life; Greece and Rome have declined for centuries in face of surrounding enlightenment and progress; and the precedents were contrary to the hope. History warranted our fears and suggested the preparation of gradualism—preparation *for* liberty, but forbade the trial *in* liberty. Yet, it is done; done so far safely, and so far as done, wonderfully. But is the trial yet over? Or, is it only in our country and in our age that the habit of history can be broken! There must be something in this, for the immigrants from all Europe, incapable of political liberty at home, immediately become sovereigns here. The negro may in a generation become an American citizen complete; for it seems that anything, that is, any next thing, is possible to us.

There must be truth in experience, for it is facts accomplished; but experience is not always directory. We never fully understand the present till it is past; till other experience interprets it; till we see it on all sides and to the core of its meaning. A great thing, surprisingly accomplished, never allows of any future thing which shall surpass it or destroy its value. This is the reason that all the new we have now was the impossible of the past; yet it is the character of this age of wonder-working to gain assurance of greater, from even the most astonishing present, success; and we are not discouragingly doubtful, however reluctant to undertake the fusion and reconciliation of all the immigrant races. We begin to believe that we can, in the United States unite, conciliate and organize the differences of the wide world.

It is apparent in the institutions and in the intrinsic qualities of savagism, patriarchism, and barbarism, that neither of them, nor any mixture of them, can accomplish the social destiny of man; but civilization, retaining whatever is available in them, and adding what it has of its own—as human nature, by reproducing all that is excellent of the inferior orders of animal life and superadding its own distinctive powers—provides for its predominant agencies and achievements. This analogy is worthy of attention for the support it gains from the unity of nature's plan of the government of all the forms of related existence in their several contributions to the chief and highest designs of the terrestrial system; rank and right of rule being graded by the character and number of the powers possessed, and by the dignity and worth of the offices to be filled and of the ends to be attained.

In the earlier stages of civilized societies they compared unfavorably with the barbaric states of the higher grades, as infancy is inferior to even a mediocre maturity. India was considerably in advance of England, even so lately as in the fourteenth century, in all that constitutes the well-being of a people—in industry, arts, and domestic and foreign policy; and the Moors were the superiors of the Spaniards for at least two centuries of the time which they held possession of Middle and Southern Spain. The courts of Cordova and Granada were the most splendid and polished in Europe from early in the thirteenth to the middle of the fifteenth centuries. Indeed, the dark ages of christendom were resplendent with the arts, arms, learning and science of barbaric Arabia, Persia, India and those European countries that were conquered and occupied by the Mohammedans. From the downfall of the Roman Empire the ensuing six centuries of the history of the races which now hold the mastery of the world, were marked by ignorance, superstition, vice, lawlessness, poverty, and weakness.

It was not until the middle of the fourteenth century that England fairly entered upon her career of manufacturing industry, although Flanders and Toulouse had made a promising beginning nearly two hundred years before. Previously, throughout Christian

Europe feudalism, which is a near approach to the barbaric polity of Asia, was the prevailing form of social and political life.

It was in the fifteenth and sixteenth centuries that monarchy centralized and organized efficient governments among them ; under the Tudors in England, and the house of Valois in France; in Germany, under the elective Emperors. In Sweden, Holland, and Hungary a like improving change occurred, and Spain and Portugal had fairly put themselves in the front of the age.

The fifteenth century was the period in which states and nations were firmly established upon the ruins of feudalism, and of the municipal republics which had failed to organize society upon principles which could secure general progress and prosperity. It was the age of intellectual and religious revolution, of great physical activity, travels, discoveries, and labor-saving and space-conquering inventions, such as the passage to India round the Cape of Good Hope, the discovery of America, the invention of printing, and hosts of cognate forces that inaugurated the modern dominion of men over their material conditions. The sixteenth and seventeenth centuries carried all these enterprises forward rapidly toward maturity, and left the eighteenth rich in accumulations of power acquired, and that knowledge which is the source of all attainable power. It was ready to replace the monarchical institutions which it inherited by representative governments, more or less beneficial, by responsible magistrates, enlightened liberty, freedom of thought, and through these, a grand advance in the mastery of the elements and forces of matter, with a prospect so much grander than all actual achievement, that the present age feels as if it were but entering upon the great career of humanity. In all that has been accomplished—the work of three or four hundred years—the people of European origin have had the exclusive agency, and they are thus distinguished from the races and nations whose careers have been run or are now running to their close.

All these considerations concerning the distinctive characters of the four or five varieties of political and social polities of human societies, and of the kindreds and peoples under them, are produced here, as well as for other purposes, to show that the unity of the families of man is not the unity of likeness or identity, but of diversity and its possible harmonies in that better order, of which they are capable, than any known in the past or the present.

The study of Political Economy has suffered more from a vicious system of generalization than from any other or all other errors of fact and opinion. The various races of men, whatever may have been their origin, or whatever the causes of those differences of character, use and destiny which now exist among them, cannot be confounded in a single class, or covered with a common description without sacrificing all the benefits of philosophic study, and all the useful guides of practical treatment; and, in keeping with this fact, is the corresponding one, that while all the families of men, in the aggregate, or in one category, may be called cosmopolitan, and destined in their adjusted varieties to the inhabitation of the whole earth, no single kindred or people are or can be so, but under a distributive impulse, each grand class has its own assigned locality with specially fitting conditions and a special fitness for them.

We are not yet prepared for a summary or complete statement of the characteristics of civilization. They can be given only in the details which are the history and the prospects of its service in the world's advancement. Upon these we shall enter after some further preliminaries are disposed of.

CHAPTER IV.

MIGRATION AND OCCUPATION OF THE EARTH.

Of Migration, and of the Occupation of the Earth: The habitats of men ruled by their natal peculiarities.—Colonization limited by isothermal lines or zones; Historic illustrations.—Climatic law of migration in the United States.—Negro population accommodated to change of temperature by change of occupation.—The march of science, literature and religions guided by climatic law.—The doctrine of descent from a single pair of progenitors not involved in the question.—The harmonies of a natural distribution of the races secured.—Special appetencies determine the destinies of the races.—Federal unions accommodate and preserve specialties in progressive consummation.—The United States a model, and a prophecy of normal free confederations elsewhere.—Three climatic zones of the United States.—Their boundaries.—This law must rule the future permanent unions of States and Kingdoms.

It is the custom of writers, especially of moralists and theologians to speak of man as cosmopolitan; that he is so much less affected by climate than plants and the inferior animals that he is almost independent of the meteorological conditions of his habitation on the earth. This notion needs correction. The species, or collective mankind, is adapted to all climates; but the varieties or races are governed by their natal habitudes in their fitness for and choice of permanent location. Artificial defenses against vicissitudes of temperature, and a considerable constitutional power of accommodation, enable the enterprising men of trade and travel to avoid the worst and most immediate consequences of a change of atmospheric conditions. The spirit of commerce and of conquest carry men all over the world, and across the zones; but colonization follows accustomed temperatures. The barbarous invaders of Rome came down upon Italy from the north, northeast and northwest, traversing perhaps five degrees of latitude, into a more genial region; but they retired, after a temporary sojourn, to their native climates. The Saxons could permanently inhabit England, for their native land lay in the same latitude; and the Normans had only to cross the English channel to change their residence without an important change of the climatic conditions to which they had been accustomed.

That a law of climate rules the migration and colonization of the natives of the diverse regions of the earth is abundantly proved by ancient and modern history. We cannot here cover the whole ground in detail, but a comparatively few instances are conclusive. The reader can readily fill up the outlines which we give with the proofs that offer themselves. His attention is invited to such as the following :—

The Mohammedan conquests in the east were in the line of temperature that corresponds to that of Medina from Arabia through Persia into India; and their western progress upon the south shore of the Mediterranean, and their occupancy of Southern Spain fall within the same isothermal lines. Mexico lies in the same belt of temperature with Spain, and Cuba touches its southern border. European conquests of countries outside of their own zones of climate are no exceptions to the law. Rome when she held the world in subjection *inhabited* Italy only. Military posts and governmental agents were all that constituted her presence in regions lying north or south of her. In this, England and France resemble the ancient mistress of universal Europe. They hold all their foreign provinces of unlike climates by their armies of occupation and officers of civil administration. There were not so many as fifty thousand white persons in the British West India Islands when the colored population amounted to eight hundred thousand. In 1861 the population of East India was variously estimated at from one hundred and thirty-five to two hundred millions, while the English people there amounted to only one hundred and twenty-five thousand nine hundred and forty-five persons, of whom eighty-four thousand and eighty-three went to compose the British officers and men of the Indian army, and twenty-two thousand five hundred and fifty-six consisted of men and boys in the civil service, the whole remainder (nineteen thousand three hundred and six) being females.

This law is found to rule in the colonies or provinces of all the European nations who have any foreign possessions lying considerably north or south of their own line of mean annual temperature. But the most remarkable exemplification is found in the settlement of the United States, whose territory, already occupied, embraces twenty-three degrees of latitude, and by its great variety of temperature may be divided into three climatic zones. In these States there has long been a constant emigration from the east or Atlantic coast toward the Rocky Mountains, and recently to the Pacific Ocean coast. These emigrants are American born and have unlimited liberty of choice as to their place of settlement upon the new lands of the West. Beside these, there is an immense influx of foreigners mainly from Western Europe, who are equally free to choose their places of habitation. Every tenth year a census of the resident population is taken, and their nativities are ascertained and noted. These returns give us these surprising results : Only one of every fourteen persons is found resident out of the belt or zone of their native temperature, whether born in Europe or in the Eastern States of the Union. That which seems to contradict or to be an exception to the law, is the presence and prosperous condition of the African negroes in the semi-tropical States devoted to the cultivation of cotton and rice, whose mean annual temperature is, say, fifteen or twenty degrees of Fahrenheit lower than that of their primitive African birthplace, and at the same time fifteen degrees above that of England, and ten above the south of France. How are these people adjusted to the difference from the natal climate of their progenitors, and fitted to a residence so unfriendly to the people of even the most southern portion of Europe? We suggest that the explanation may be found in the changed conditions of their life. In tropical Africa they did not need, and indeed could not labor in the fields under a steady heat considerably above eighty degrees the year round,* but in the Gulf States of North America they are exposed only to an average heat of about seventy degrees, in which they can work as healthfully as an Englishman or his descendants can labor in the fields of Pennsylvania in a mean temperature of fifty degrees. It is but a change from tropical to semi-tropical heat, and the exposure and the toil of the negro's new residence mediates between these points so as to qualify him for exertion which Africa would not allow, and which a constitution from much higher latitudes could not bear. The animal heat generated by labor compensates for its reduction in the changed climate.

The familiar adage—"*Westward* the Star of Empire takes its

---

* The isothermal charts found in atlases and school maps of fifteen or twenty years ago, are not reliable for such an inquiry as this question demands.

way" is literally true, and it is also true that science, literature and religion observe the same line of march, and for the obvious reason that the races who modify opinion and speculation according to their respective mental and moral constitutions, and impress themselves upon all their pursuits, enterprises, and achievements, migrate along their several lines of climate.

The received doctrine of the origin of all the varieties of men from a single pair of progenitors, and their propagation from a single centre, presents no difficulty to the acceptance or admission of the law which we are considering; for, however the existing differences of nationality in all their shades, from the tropical African to the best example of the European, were originally produced; whether by natural causes providentially employed, or by miraculous adjustment of each kind to its assigned locality, it is certain that such differences actually exist, and that an imperious law of distribution rules in the human, as in the animal and vegetable occupancy of the earth, and thus secures the ultimate subjection of the globe in all its varied regions to a harmoniously appropriated humanity.

The proper liberties of mankind are all under the government of law, and the purposes of the Creator are effected by its orderly control. The diverse inhabitants of the earth have their proper domiciles secured to them by this overruling law of migration and inhabitation. No present superiority of any race can permanently contravene it. The surviving wanderers will in good time be reclaimed to their native climates. In every zone, valley, and mountain; on every continent, island, and peninsula, this grand law of inheritance will hold the land for the natural claimants, and will expel the usurpers by constraining their return to their own. The complete subjugation of the material world, under the laws which govern it, seems to be the mission of the European families of mankind. When their proper work is well accomplished, the Asiatic and African tribes, and the natural occupants of the Pacific islands which shall survive, will enter upon their own domains and go forward to the fulfillment of their several destinies. Then comes the time when contrasts without collisions shall enrich the earth with all their fullness and force, and differences shall be ruled into perfect harmony.

The law of migration and settlement rooted in the special appetencies of the various races of men, will ever protect and maintain their primitive differences of endowment, and their diverse services in that corroborative unity which qualifies the aggregate or grand man for his manifold work in the world. Not an enforced and confused homogeneity, but a harmonized diversity is demanded to fulfill the functions of the species. The brotherhood of men is not a conglomeration of likenesses, but an orderly organization of related differences. This tendency is manifest in the modern changes in the political governments of both the old and the new world. Federal unions among the families of the nations are its expression and promise. The petty states of France, Germany, Austria, Italy, and that cluster of old-time independencies which are now included in the Empire of Russia, are striking examples. Most of these Unions were at first in a great degree effected by force, under the ambitious impulse of territorial aggrandizement; but more recently these have been conformed, more or less, to the principle of voluntary association, and the normal order of natural law, which, while it associates differences, respects them, and maintains the authority, and the duly regulated functions of local centres, at the same time that it embraces them in the larger and more general entireties which best secure internal peace, and provide external defence. In former times nations, wholly unfitted to unite, and incapable of beneficial union, were subdued into unnatural and repugnant nationalities; but more recently, federative unions are effected by the free play of natural attraction. North Germany is rapidly organizing the kindred peoples into a political union. Italy has taken some effective steps towards its proper reorganization. Austria has parted with its incongruous trans-alpine possessions, and has reconciled Hungary to such governmental relations as are for the present adapted to its specialties of character and position. The broken balances of Europe are not all rectified, but they are in process of regulation according to natural order, and the promise of a due adjustment is every year better and better assured; the time is rapidly approaching when political changes of the nations will be wholly internal; or, those reformations of national polity which remain to be accomplished, will be wholly improvements in the civil and social order of domestic affairs.

The Government of the United States of America seems to be the model and the prophecy of the policy which is to prevail, and to determine the political institutions of all peoples, who are near enough and like enough, to require and to accept common or general governments.

In North America we have at least three distinctly different zones of climate, and a corresponding difference of their inhabitants. The law which we have been considering, in free operation would, and in time will, throw New England and the States due west of it and the British provinces, into one class, with the valley of the St. Lawrence for their centre, and its waters for their easy communication and domestic commerce. The Middle States from Northern Pennsylvania to Cape Hatteras, in North Carolina, and all between these lines extended westwardly, are fitted for another class; and the semi-tropical States lying south of the isothermal line which enters at Cape Hatteras, and coincides approximately with the northern border of the Gulf States, may be taken to mark the division of the southern from the middle climatic zone of the Union.

The appropriate industries and special interests of these divisions exhibit sufficient diversity to modify their respective pursuits and policies, and to demand a conforming adaptation of domestic enterprise and regulation. Of such adaptation in promotion of special interests, and freedom of sectional tendencies, the federal and local systems are admirably capable; and under similar constitutions the peoples everywhere who are nearly related in blood and manners, may have all their specialties protected, and all their common characteristics preserved, combined, and energized. Political policies may vary the forms of union and intercourse among States naturally allied, giving them more or less intimacy of commerce, and more or less unity of civil government, in the transition age of societies, but the climatic law will constantly grow more and more effective, and will never be overruled nor long postponed.

Neither antiquity of claim, nor vested rights, nor opinions and theories, which the change of times has overthrown in the past, and will again and again modify in the future, can finally settle the relations of contiguous States of naturally allied peoples; neither can military force nor conventional forms, nor the obligations of treaties overrule the physical and moral laws of human nature. They may be postponed and evaded, but providential provisions are constantly in the endeavor to enforce them, and will ultimately prevail.

NOTE.—This law of climate in the government of human migrations, was first announced in general terms by Mr. Carey, in the Boston *Transcript*, of 26th November, 1859. It was not known to him when he published the third and last volume of his "Principles of Social Science," in February, 1859, and there are several portions of that work which require correction by his later discovery. In the Philadelphia *Press* of 22d of December, 1859, the writer of this treatise gave this newly-announced law an ample statistical elucidation and vindication, under the caption of " Pennsylvania's Position in the Union."

CHAPTER V.

OF WEALTH—THE LAWS AND CONDITIONS OF ITS GROWTH.

Wealth—the laws and conditions of its growth: Definition of capital.—Definition of Wealth.—False theories built upon a basis of disorder.—The Malthusian School.—Their "preventive and corrective checks" of Providential maladjustments!—Relation of sustenance to numbers.—Popular error.—McCulloch follows Malthus with a statistical statement of disproportion of food to population.—Ricardo's progressive exhaustion of the soil; Mill repeats and indorses them.—The order of earthly things only the road to ruin, temporary mitigations only end in despair.—British political economy confronted with British statistics.—Lowe, Levi, and Gladstone on the facts.—Data of British estimates.— Wealth doubles in GREAT BRITAIN in twenty years, population in fifty years.— Accelerated rate of enhancement of wealth in the latest decennial period.— Wealth of FRANCE increasing faster than that of Great Britain.—The figures and facts.—Her increased product of wheat, sugar and potatoes.—Food product doubled in thirty-five years, population in two hundred and seventy-seven years.—In the densest populations of Europe the supply of food greater, and growing faster than the increase of demand.—Relative supply and requirement in the UNITED STATES.—Rate of increase of population and wealth; the former doubling in twenty-three and a half years; the latter in eight and a half years.— Annual product not capital value, the measure of supply.—Decennial census reports of annual products of industry in the United States, not above two-thirds of their actual value.—The deficiency demonstrated.—Varied rates of increased production in particulars.—Increase of product of wealth in Great Britain and the United States twice as great in the decade 1850–60 as in that of 1840–50.—A *law* of increase indicated.—In the normal order of civilized industries, sustenance outgrows population in accelerating movement.

BY wealth we do not mean capital, merely in its common acceptation, though capital in this sense is embraced in it.

Capital, in business language, means an accumulation of values employed for further production or profits. In a broader and better sense, it embraces not only improved land, ships, wagons, ploughs, machinery, food, clothing, money, and the like tangible subjects of property, but ideas and credit, as much as these, because they are equally efficient and necessary to the production of new values.

Labor, whether of handicraft, skill, or superintendence, is, also, capital; but it is usually treated rather as the associate than as a component of capital.

The production of wealth employs all these agencies, and covers all the faculties and forces, moral, intellectual, and material, which it can in any way enlist in the service; and it is a finer, as well as a more practical apprehension, to regard wealth in a higher and wider light than the mere aggregate of the substantive things in which it embodies itself to the senses and are exchanged in market. Taken as the means and measure of man's power over nature, it embraces all the elements of capital, and opens up to the light of its true meaning. It cannot be restricted to the things exchangeable in trade. Whoever would understand it must follow it as it rises through material things, and all their service to the life of man, and stores its highest products in his heart and mind. Capital and Labor, with the intelligence that directs, and the aims which warrant and sanctify the ends, are tributaries to all the designs of our temporal existence. In such service they are worthy of higher consideration and better uses than we ever give them.

The appointed dominion of man over earth and air and ocean, means nothing more, nothing less, than temporal wealth raised in its uses into human welfare. The mastery of nature grows with every victory. Every new discovery in the constitution of the material things which surround us, gives us a new force to control them. It is power put at compound interest; each new product added to the principal to yield a larger interest; in consonance with that ever-enhancing power of the spirit to which it ministers in sublunary things.

This apprehension of wealth shakes the mind free from the clogs of market-house logic, and reflects the highest lights upon the laws which rule it in all its functions.

But the service of the elements requires of us their administration under natural law. Nature bestows none of her best benefits upon indolence or ignorance. The tribes that content themselves with plundering her lakes and rivers, her forests and prairies, find her austere, repugnant and niggard to their necessities. To partial and poor cultivators, she turns poor in exact correspondence—to those that have shall be given.

Disordered and misgoverned societies have, until very recently, and still in the majority of instances, afforded the data from which the standard authorities constructed their theories. These writers looking only to production, distribution and consumption of commodities in past history, and reasoning not from the intrinsic capabilities of men and things in the better order to which they are rapidly advancing, but from the data of an imperfect experience, have invented systems dreadfully discordant with divine beneficence and with human hope. Their doctrines, under correction of later and more promising facts, are now less confidently paraded; indeed, they are rather assumed than asserted as demonstrable truths, but like original sin, they break out into actual transgression upon every tempting occasion.

Mr. Malthus digested what he took to be the evidence afforded by history into a doctrine of despair, and his formulæ have been taken for aphorisms of science by all his English successors and American disciples. So far from believing in the constant growth of man's power over nature, he affirmed a constantly-increasing disproportion of sustenance to population—that, under the laws which govern the subjects, population tends to increase in a geometrical, while the means of subsistence relatively fall off to an arithmetical ratio. In figures he puts it, that population unchecked would in two centuries increase one hundred and twenty-eight times, while food under no circumstances can increase more than eight times in the same period; or, if it were possible to produce at once on the earth such a multitude, it could not afford them the one-sixteenth part of the food which they would require. The corrective checks, "war, pestilence, and famine," Mr. Malthus believes to have been necessarily provided to prevent such a wholesale catastrophe; and, that their operation is distributed by retail all along the life of the race, by way of correcting this mal-adjustment in the highest sphere of creation, which strangely enough occurs nowhere else in the Maker's works!

Mr. Malthus mistook facts logically possible only in circumstances wholly impossible, for laws arising out of the nature of things. He made the great blunder of taking the existing fertility of the human race, designed to repair the terrible waste of life during the ages of disorder, for a natural rate of reproduction, which he furthermore mistook for an inflexible measure. Upon data so shabbily stupid he used the inductive method of reasoning, and called the horrid result philosophy! It never occurred to him to look for providential adjustments of natural laws to varied conditions of their subjects, which must prevent the processes of the creation from destroying their own aims.

As a theory, relating to the earth's fitness for that highest use to which all other uses are tributary, this doctrine might be dismissed as an insanity of pretended science; but something of its mischief may be traced in popular reasoning founded upon hasty observation, and is, therefore, entitled to fuller consideration.

We live in a new country, where population does not press upon the means of subsistence; where famines never come, and where pauperism is an exotic. Within our boundaries there is yet a wilderness of fertility which tempts emigration even from its eastern regions, as yet not half occupied or cultivated, with still easier offers of livelihood, and better chances for rapid and great advancement of fortune; where labor is nearly the only form of productive power, and other capital is too scarce to monopolize the opportunity of acquiring wealth. From across the ocean a steady tide of hopeful poverty is constantly flowing from amid its mountain steeps of wealth toward our plain of better averaged competency. Under these influences it is easy to conclude, and as easy to excuse the conclusion, that there is something in the law of growth in human society unfriendly to its masses, and unduly favorable to the advanced class, of wealth and condition, and that this disparity results from the established order of things. But facts may be accidents, and results do not always indicate constitutional or permanent laws. And, notwithstanding the illusions which hang like a fog over real facts, the truth is not left without a witness in any quarter of the globe, for wherever in any country there is substantial progress, that is, wherever the true order of things is in any measure observed, in the same measure subsistence supports population and tends always to outgrow it.

Even in England itself, all the facts of experience are in direct refutation of the dismal science, yet we find such authorities as J. R. McCulloch, the popular economist and statistician of England, any time within the last twenty years, declaring that "sixty years is the shortest time in which capital in an old and densely-peopled country can be expected to be doubled," while it is in proof that population has doubled in England and Wales in the fifty years between 1801 and 1851.

Ricardo, whose work is the koran of this sect of economists, holds that the progress of cultivation by a fixed necessity, begins with the best lands first, and descends by a regular gradation to poorer still and poorer, until absolute sterility is reached, and general starvation would be the catastrophe, but that it is distributed all along the course of exhaustion, and thus keeps hungry mouths and recurring harvests in some sort of balance. Ricardo wrote so lately as in 1817, and McCulloch repeats him in effect, saying that "from the operation of fixed and permanent causes, the increasing sterility of soil is sure, in the long run, to overmatch the improvements that occur in agriculture and machinery." McCulloch wrote until 1863 without recanting. So the ghost of Malthus, who died in 1824, still haunts the highways of economic science.

But last, and therefore worst of all, John Stuart Mill, claimed to be the philosopher of philanthropy, in his chapter on "The Law of the Increase of Production from Land," published in the year of grace, 1865, reproduces these horrors in all their hideousness. The over-population theory of Malthus, and the constantly-declining productiveness of land of Ricardo, are reproduced with such a simple confidence of their truth as dispenses with any attempt at their demonstration.

He thinks that emigration—such as the potato-rot, the lack of remunerative labor, and the evictions of the small tenants in Ireland, compel, and the fresh soils of Australia and the wilds of North America invite, may occasionally check the progress and mitigate the effects of this frightful disproportion between man and food. The present pressure, he suggests, might be temporarily postponed by the substitution of American maize for the deficient vegetables of Europe, as a brief reprieve of the old world; but then, such fullness of supply would mischievously increase the growth of population, and soon overlap the increased supply of subsistence again, and the checks, preventive and corrective, of Malthus' invention be again demanded in all their vigor.

So present and pressing are the alarms of his theory to him, that he believes the emigration from the Atlantic to the Western States of America "is what enables population to go on unchecked in the Union without having yet diminished the returns to industry or increased the difficulty of earning a subsistence;" but he has no hope that emigration at even its greatest height " could be kept up sufficiently to take off all that portion of the annual increase, which, being in excess of the progress made during the same period in the arts of life, tends to render living more difficult for every averagely-situated individual in the community;" and again, in the United States, as elsewhere and everywhere in this wretchedly ordered world, comes in the hopeless preventive check of prudence in marriage, with the three reliable corrective ones in leash—War, Pestilence and Famine. Mr. Mill says of this gorgon law, "it is the most important proposition in political economy;" meaning his theory of it; and "were the law different, nearly all the phenomena of the production and distribution of wealth would be different." We may be allowed to be glad of this admission; for if the foundation of the entire system of this school of economists can be shown to be utterly false in facts and as false in its inferences, the whole fabric raised upon it tumbles into rubbish.

Our appeal from theory to facts, may be safely rested upon such as we here submit, which though necessarily limited in instances, are so selected as to be entirely conclusive.

Joseph Lowe calculated the value of the real and personal property of Great Britain and Ireland, in A. D. 1793, at seven thousand one hundred and thirty-two millions of dollars ($7,132,000,000) and the population at fourteen millions five hundred thousand (14,500,000), which gives an average of four hundred and ninety-one dollars to each person ($491.86).

Leoni Levi, for the year 1858, puts the value of the property at twenty-nine thousand one hundred and seventy-eight millions of dollars ($29,178,000,000), making an average of one thousand and six dollars per head ($1,006). Here then the accepted authorities give us an exact doubling of the population in all the British Islands in Europe in sixty-five years, with a four-fold increase of property, and a doubling of the average share of each individual in the same time, and Mr. Mill's "averagely-situated" individual, even in Great Britain and Ireland, did not find it more difficult to secure a living in this long period, but in fact had his average share of the total property of the United Kingdom doubled.

But the rate of increase in the general wealth was not uniform, and so far was it from diminishing that it increased rapidly year by year from the earliest date to that of the latest authoritative reports. According to them the *average* increase of the whole period from

1793 to 1858 required thirty-two and a half years for doubling itself, but the most reliable estimates for fourteen years preceding 1866, give an increase at the rate of doubling in the greatly shorter period of a fraction less than nineteen years in the kingdom of Great Britain, Ireland excluded. Mr. Gladstone in his speech upon the Reform bill in 1866 infers, from the increase of the income tax during the next preceding fourteen years, that the wealth of the kingdom of Great Britain, including Wales and Scotland, amounted to sixty-five per cent, or at the compound rate of three and three quarters per cent per annum—doubling in nineteen years, as already said; the population at the same time increasing a fraction over one and a half per cent per annum, or doubling in fifty years.

England takes a decennial census of its population, but does not estimate the value of the real and personal property of the kingdom by assessment or appraisement, as is done in the United States. The estimates of its statisticians, however, are probably as near the truth as the census valuations of the marshals under the last-named system. They have the rental, the income tax, the sworn value of decedent's estates, bank, fire and marine insurance and other corporation reports, the excises, and the imports and exports of the kingdom, for their data, and all these are official, and as nearly accurate as might be attained by any other means.

Mr. Gladstone's inference from the income tax is probably a little too high for the general average growth of wealth. The national funds are not expected to yield more than three and one-quarter per cent upon the investment, which, on account of their absolute security, is a little too low for a basis. Investments in lands, subject to income tax and other abatements, at four per cent, and in railroads, canals, houses, and other real property, still more burdened by risks, repairs, and charges, four and one-half per cent. When these rates are considered, about three and one-half per cent per annum may be safely taken for the average increase of wealth, which is a doubling, in the last decennial period, once in twenty years, or two and a half times faster than the present rate of the population.

England surely may be taken to be one of Mr. McCulloch's "old and densely-peopled countries" which he said could not double its wealth in less than sixty years; but we find that she has increased forty-one per cent in the ten years from 1856 to 1866, which promises a doubling in twenty years. This is at twice the rate of its growth between the years 1840 and 1850, which is explained by the advantage of the later period from the influx of California and Australian gold, the regularly enhancing wealth of all her customers, the improvement of machinery, and, by the additional good fortune that escaped the general scarcity in Europe and the famine of 1847 in Ireland.

The result of this inquiry may be thus presented : Wealth grows now in Great Britain at the rate of forty-one per cent in ten years; population, eleven and one-third per cent. The average of the total values of the property of the Kingdom were to each person :

```
In the year 1851..............................................$  827
    "    "    1861..............................................  1,074
    "    "    1866..............................................  1,239
```

being an increase of fifty per cent in fifteen years, and a doubling of the average distributive share of each individual in twenty-five and one-half years.

This is the answer that the statistical history of one old country, pretty densely peopled, and with a population increasing at a medium rate, gives to the Ricardo-Mill theory of political economy, which rests all its systematic doctrines on the fundamental proposition that sustenance and supplies are ever becoming less and less adequate to the demands of human life.

Let us now glance at the condition of a nation as old, nearly as densely peopled, but with a population almost stationary:—

France in 1836 had thirty-three and a half millions of people; in 1856, thirty-six millions. Increase in twenty years only four and three-quarters per cent, or one-quarter per cent per annum. Her aggregate domestic exports for the ten years from 1826 to 1836 were valued at five thousand two hundred and fifteen millions of francs (5,215,000,000f.); for the ten years from 1846 to 1856, at twelve thousand and forty-five millions (12,045,000,000f). Increase in twenty years one hundred and thirty-one per cent in the same time that her population was increasing but four and three-quarters per cent.

Measuring the growth of wealth in France by the growth in England, relatively to their foreign commerce, we find that in the same twenty years England and Ireland increased their domestic exports just one hundred and twenty per cent, or eleven per cent less than the increase in France. Therefore, by this standard

France was increasing in wealth at a slightly faster rate than England, previous to the year 1856. But the gains of France upon the exports of her products are much larger than those of England. Not more than one-fifth of their value is in the foreign material of which they are fabricated. The four-fifths at least being her own raw material and food converted into the commodities, while England's exports of manufactures have one-half of the value of her total domestic exports in her imports of raw sugar, flax, cotton, hides, hemp, silk, wool, and dyestuffs; to say nothing of the breadstuffs and provisions, and the hundred other articles for which she depends on foreign countries.

For these and other reasons the annual profits of industry in France are considerably greater than in England, that is, more than three and one-half per cent, while her increase of people is almost nothing—one-fourth of one per cent.

With regard to her production of food, the progress has been marvelous: In 1820 the yield of wheat was one hundred and fifty-three millions of bushels—a pro rata of five and four-tenths bushels per head; in 1857 it had risen to three hundred and thirteen millions (Dictionaire Universal, du Commerce tome i, p. 1384), affording eight and six-tenths bushels to each individual. This is three and one-half bushels per head more than the people of the United States consume, leaving one hundred and thirty-three millions of bushels for exportation. Her beet-root sugar in 1861 amounted to six and one-quarter pounds per head. (We raised eleven pounds of cane and maple sugar.) Her product of potatoes was two hundred and eighty millions of bushels. The United States, with a population equal to five-sixths of hers, produced but one hundred and fifty-two millions, or a little more than half the per capita allowance of the French.

The total agricultural production of France has doubled in the last thirty years, while at her present rate of increase it will take two hundred and seventy-seven years to double her population. With a density of one hundred and seventy-nine persons to the square mile, or two and three-quarter times that of Pennsylvania (sixty-five), she feeds all her people and has food to spare. The whole of the New England and Middle States of the United States in 1860 had but sixty-four persons to the square mile, and when the population of the entire Union shall number one hundred millions there will be but sixty eight, or they will have a density of but three-eighths (thirty-eight per cent) of that of France; it is now but one-eighth.

Population is certainly not pressing upon sustenance in France, nor threatening to do so. We speak not now of its distribution, but of the abundant and constantly increasing abundance of provision for the support of the nation.

Having seen how much faster wealth increases than population in the United Kingdom of Great Britain, the density being the greatest in Europe, except in the little Kingdom of Belgium, and the increase of population at nearly the highest rate known in Europe; and, having also seen how the wealth of France grows at a proportionately faster rate upon a population nearly stationary and of medium density,* we now turn to the like statistics of the United States, where the movement in numbers and wealth are both on a grander scale than in any of the countries of Europe.

The capital value of real and personal property, excluding that in the slaves, according to the census valuation, increased in the decade 1850–60, one hundred and twenty-six per cent, and the population thirty-five and five-tenths per cent; or the capital wealth grew at the rate of eight and one-half per cent, and the population a fraction above three per cent per annum. The former doubling in eight and a half years, and the latter in twenty-three and a half years. The average share of each individual in 1850 standing at two hundred and sixty-six dollars, and rising in 1860 to four hundred and forty-nine dollars, being an increase in these ten years of sixty-nine per cent upon the pro rata share of each individual.

But, everywhere it is the *annual produce* that measures the provision for the wants of men, and for their growth in numbers, and improvement of their condition. Especially in the United States, where the prospective value of real estate is always in advance of its present yield of profits, because it is always as certain as that already reached, the capital increases considerably faster than its current productiveness, the *product* must be taken, if we would ascertain its relation to the demand for subsistence. Much of the estimated

* In 1865 England and Wales had three hundred and sixty to the square mile; Scotland, ninety-eight; United Kingdom, two hundred and sixty-seven; Ireland, in 1861, one hundred and eighty-two.

value of fixed property here lies in expectation; it is, therefore, the product which land and other capital is made to yield that measures the nation's actual wealth. The same is true of that greatest source of wealth—labor-power. All the agents, natural and artificial, that may be used in production, depend for their effects upon the manner and measure of their employment. Land, labor, water and wind power, money, and credit in all its forms, are in the same category. Therefore, products, rather than capital, are the data for all calculations in this matter of wealth and of its service in the support and development of life.

Our decennial census reports do not nearly cover the annual products of capital and industry. For instance, they take a very inadequate account of the current consumption of their own crops by our agriculturists, their families, and employees. In 1840 this class amounted to three-fourths of the total population, and approached the same proportion in 1850; nor, are any manufacturing or mechanical products of the year returned where the annual value falls below five hundred dollars. Besides all this—which probably amounts to one-fourth of the actual production of the country—no account is taken of the labor employed in clearing new and improving old lands, in building railroads, canals, houses, factories, steamships, and other vessels; nor, of the labor employed in opening and working mines, in the fine arts, and a large portion of the useful arts. All of which omissions may be safely stated at one-third of the value of the products of agriculture and manufactures, mechanics and the arts, noticed by the census-takers. Some of these contributions to the subsistence and enjoyment of the people—those which continue their service during the period—appear in the valuation of the fixed and accumulated property at the recurring census appraisements, but in the aggregate, very far below their value in current use.

That the census accounts of the annual product are very far below the truth is apparent from the fact that they allow but $62.28 for the share of each person in 1840; $64.00 in 1850; and $86.31 in 1860.* This is not enough for the consumption in 1860 by $14.00

---

* Agricultural products ninety per cent increase upon value of 1850, $1,818,156,816; manufacturing, mining, mechanic arts, eighty-seven and a half per cent upon half the value of 1850 (half allowed for raw material), gives $857,671,664, total $2,675,828,480 ÷ 31,000,000 = $86.31 per cap.

WEALTH—LAWS OF GROWTH. 51

per capita, or nearly $450,000,000 in the aggregate; besides, the vast sum of $8,000,000,000 of increased capital value in the decade is to be accounted for, which, if we allow even ten per cent for speculative valuation above that of 1850, would leave a deficiency of one thousand two hundred and twenty millions, or $40 per capita, which must have resulted from actual production, and this addition to the sum allowed by the census would amount to $126,* average yield of the labor capital and enterprise of each person, which is surely little enough.

But our inquiry does not demand actual but comparative values at the several periods which we take for the purpose of estimating the proportion of wealth produced for the supply of the national consumption and accumulation. The errors and defects of one census are about equivalent to those of the others, and so we have the *ratio* of provision to the number of the inhabitants, and this is all that we want for our present purpose.

The increase of the products of capital and industry in the year 1860 over those of 1850 are well ascertained to have been:—

In the Mining, Manufacturing, and Mechanic Arts...	87½	per cent.
" Agriculture	90	"
" Agricultural Implements	63	"
" Books, Newspapers, and Job-printing	250	"
" Coal	170	"
" Wheat	71	"
" Indian Corn	42	"
" Potatoes	68	"
" Live Stock	100	"
" Number of Horned Cattle	40	"
" Horses and Mules	48	"
" Sheep and Swine	9	"
" Ginned Cotton	112	"
" Tobacco	115	"

We have no hesitation in fixing the actual increase of the products of 1860 over those of 1850 at one hundred per cent. This

---

* We reach this result in another way—the population in 1850 was twenty-three millions, in 1860, thirty-one millions—mean number twenty-seven millions. Their consumption in ten years at $100 a head makes twenty-seven thousand millions. Putting the products of industry at $126 a head per annum, we get the sum of thirty-four hundred millions, which gives an accumulation by labor and capital employed of seven thousand millions. The census of 1860 states the increased value at eight thousand millions, and we allow this one thousand millions of difference for speculation beyond the actual value of property.

would increase the *per capita* share of the people to forty-seven and a half per cent in ten years, or to forty per cent, if only ninety per cent be taken for the additional product.

Let us now restate our results in tabular form.

Increase of population, production, and, increase pro rata per capita in the decade 1850 to 1860.

	Of Population.	Of Annual Products.	Of Share of Annual Products per capita.
United States	35.5 per cent	100 per cent	47½ per cent.
France	2.6 "	44 "	40 "
Great Britain	11.3 "	41 "	26½ "

Among the most striking results of an extended examination of the growth of wealth in Great Britain and the United States, we find the fact that it was just twice as great in the decade of 1850–60, in both countries, as in that next preceding it, 1840–50. The previous decades of the present century were either disturbed by expensive wars, or by great commercial convulsions, which greatly affect the data that they present for estimating the normal progress of industry and trade; the two last-mentioned periods were but little affected by any injurious events in the business affairs of either; or, relatively to their respective resources, they were about equally exposed to them, and they both had the advantage in a relatively equal degree of all that contributed to immensely enhance the prosperity of the period 1850–60. That they should both double their decennial advance in wealth in the last of these periods as against the previous one, under conditions so similar, goes a great way to indicate a law of progress very uniform in its operation, and as that law is found to operate so favorably for the welfare of both, the manifestation is clearly and conclusively in favor of our proposition which may be thus stated:—In a good order of human societies—in the present state of civilization—the natural provision for the sustenance of the people is abundant and growing more and more so with whatever increase of numbers that can occur; the power of men over nature growing ever more complete in the increasing skill applied to production.

CHAPTER VI.

SOURCES OF ADVANCEMENT IN WEALTH.

Sources of advancement in wealth.—Seven general sources.—Nature's resistance.—The *super*-natural in the "Mechanical powers."—Measure of steam force in equivalents of man-power. Employed in England equal to the labor-power of one-quarter of the inhabitants of the Globe.—Europe and America supplement their human, by six times its force, in steam labor-power.— This power doubled again by machinery, and constantly enhancing, beyond computation.—*Velocity* gained equals the *force* thus commanded.—The mastery obtained over masses of matter.—Greater still over elements and atoms.—Practical application follows closely upon our discoveries in the laws of matter.— Abundance and cheapness of production supply an ample stock of provisions for the wants of men.—Effects of the growth of wealth on the products of handicraft in dead matter.—Advancement in agricultural production.—Increase in everything except food, unlimited.—Consumption of food like its possibilities of supply, limited.—The despair of the "Dismal" School.—General answer.—Famines and plagues disappear in the ratio that men *increase* in number.—Irish and Indian famines of the present centuries accounted for.— Exclusively agricultural countries alone exposed to starvation.—Why.—The provision for food products adequate, and therefore practically unlimited.— Not ten per cent of the soil's capabilities yet mastered.—Human destitution no impeachment of the providence and liberality of nature's provision for human wants.—The laws of nature tend to adjustment of man and earth.—Due cultivation does not exhaust, but increases the soil's fertility.—Contributions of *foreign commerce* to subsistence.—England draws four-fifths, in value, of the raw material of her exported products from foreign countries.—Legitimate foreign trade insures the needed supplies of the oldest countries.—Relief from emigration.—Space in the new answers to needs in the old world.— Room enough still in Europe.—Abundance in reserve for seven times the present population of the globe.—Economists, handicraftsmen, and horses getting over their scare at the prospective destitution.—Compensations in reserve when customary reliances fail.—Substitution of the abundant and cheap for the scarce and dear.—Civilization finds the means of human subsistence ever more and more abundant and accessible.—Sparseness of savage populations and failure of their supplies.—Diversified industry a sure defense against famine.—In progressive communities vegetable supplants animal food.—Proportion of their respective yield.—Economy of a vegetable diet among animals.—Progress from the animal, through the vegetable to the mineral kingdom, in the supplies of advancing civilization.—The Laborers' opportunity grows *pari passu* through all this progress.—Last of all man advances to the command of the imponderables.—Instances of the substitutions which mark human progress, and provide for it.—The Industrial liberty of nations, like the emancipation of men from the despotism of the elements, comes from, and is proportioned to, their control over nature's forces.—Industrial and political revolutions have their roots in the bosom of mother earth.

THE sources of advancement in wealth are, in general statement: 1st. Increase of labor-saving machinery; 2d. Substitution of artificial for natural labor; 3d. Improvement in the quantity and quality of commodities; 4th. Advancement in agricultural production; 5th. Improvement in transportation; 6th. Extension of foreign trade; 7th. Substitution of the cheap and abundant for the costly and scarce.

In some of these things the achievements of human art, and the prospective improvements well assured, have converted the fictions of magic, of our old story-books, into the facts of every-day experience. The magic carpet and Aladdin's lamp seem now but a prophesy of the wonders which science and art are accomplishing for us.

In the conversion and transportation of the materials which serve our needs, and which must undergo changes of form and place before they are utilized, the forces of nature stand in resistance to those of man. The earths and minerals which compose the solid globe, serve men no further or better than they do the inferior animals until they are transformed and subdued into use, and their resistance to change of place is overcome. Their unserviceable forms and properties in the natural state, and their fixity of local position, call for force and speed to establish our dominion over them. Something akin to the miraculous, something *super*-natural, must be arrayed against this natural to bring it into obedience. In the "mechanical powers" we have it in the screw, the compound pulley, and the wheel and axle. Nowhere in nature are either of these found. Nature has the lever and the inclined plane, with the force of gravitation, and that modification of it which is called cohesion, but these only in common with man and his instruments, which in a thousand instances serve as successful antagonists to the like forces of dead matter. Where the artificial lever is inadequate, the screw and the pulley win an easy victory; and with the wheel and axle, men out-run the bird on the wing, and out-swim the fish in the seas, carrying mountain-weights with a rapidity that overcomes all that is substantial in the resistance of Space; while Time in travel and transportation, for all the purposes of communication, is effectively subdued by the apparatus of the electric telegraph and the force of steam and machinery. In respect to force—the force of man against that of nature—there can be no lack when four tons of coal in a steam engine will evolve as much mechanical power as an ordinary man can exert, working eight hours a day, for twenty years, or, one ton of coal has in it a fifteen hundred man-power for their work of one day.

Great Britain raised from her mines, in the year 1864, ninety-two millions of tons; she exported to foreign countries but nine millions, and if she employed but forty of the remaining eighty-three millions in producing artificial labor-power, she got out of it the equivalent of two hundred millions of men's work in the year. Two years afterwards, in 1866, she mined one hundred and one thousand tons of coal, and if she used fifty thousand tons of this quantity in the same way, then she derived from it the labor-force of two hundred and fifty millions of able-bodied men, which, by the ordinary computation, is about equal to that of all the inhabitants of the globe. This, for an island numbering twenty-five millions of people, all told, is a stupendous *force*. And when we add to it two-thirds of this quantity, similarly used in the rest of Europe and the United States, we have an aggregate population of about two hundred and eighty millions, less than one-half of whom are in the producing class, between fifteen and sixty years of age, and the one-half of these only are males. So that considerably under seventy millions of men's labor is supplemented by an artificial force derived from coal, equal to that of about four hundred and ten millions of man-power, or, the mass of laborers in Europe and the United States had the help of six times their power added to their own in doing their allotted work. That is, they, with the aid of the steam-power of coal, were doing nearly twice the work that the whole population of the earth could do without it. Nor would it be too much to say that this force was again doubled by the intervention of machinery in steam works, and in its employment where water is the agent, and where human force is multiplied in effect through the instrumentality of the mechanical powers, as they are technically called. Indeed, estimates and computation fail to grasp the effective value of the adjuvants that human ingenuity employs to enhance its mastery of matter. And as a source of wealth to the civilized world, it will be felt that this compelling power over inanimate things is in a constant and rapid state of enhancement, growing day by day, until it outstrips the limits of calculation, and the mind no longer definitely comprehends the ever-swelling magnitude, just as it fails to comprehend the indefinite ever advancing toward the infinite.

The amount of mechanical force thus growing into the unlimited, in weight, is matched by the *velocity* of motion gained, which, while still computable, is scarcely conceivable in shuttles, hammers, rollers and wheels. Steam and machinery give us many hundred-fold rapidity in printing, spinning, and weaving over the old hand-press, wheel, and loom.* In transportation of men and commodities they have afforded us fifteen miles on the ocean, and fifty on land, to the hour; overcoming the resistance of wind and wave on the one, and the greatest mountain masses on the other. Some idea of this service is given in the railroad reports of England. In 1866 her trains on less than half (thirteen thousand two hundred and eighty-nine miles) the length of track in the United States transported a number of passengers equal to one quarter (two hundred and fifty-two millions) of the population of the globe, and carried one hundred and forty millions of tons weight of men and things, one hundred and thirty-four millions of miles—a distance equal to that from the earth to the sun, and half way back again.

These are but hints of the command we are to have over matter in *masses*, and over time and space, in the work of conversion and transportation.

Over its *elements and atoms* mind is achieving control still greater and more wonderful. The incantations of chemistry set free the hidden forces and agencies of the creation, and rehearse the miracles of incessant new creations, changing the forms and uses of all material things, and informing them with life and action in the service of the living world. The solid rocks, the winds, the waters, the latent fires of the great store-house of forces provided

---

* The increased economy and power obtained in the application of some kinds of machinery will be apparent from the following statement, the result of accurate calculation: Richard Garsed, Esq., of Frankford, Pennsylvania, manufactures, in every day of ten hours, thirty-three thousand *miles* of cotton thread—obtaining from *seven tons* of coal the necessary power. Supposing it possible for such quality of thread to be made by hand, it would require the labor of seventy thousand women to accomplish this work.

for our service, are compelled to take all shapes of use at the bidding of the spirit which masters their mysteries; and, what is most remarkable in the present age, and most promising for the oncoming generations, is the practical application which follows closely upon the heels of discovery. Franklin (in 1752) put his electric toy to duty in guarding our habitations from the thunder-bolt; and Morse (in 1832), before a generation had past after the discovery of galvanism (Galvani, 1791, Volta, 1801,) subdued this subtlest of nature's agents to service in the electric telegraph; and now, in less than thirty-six years more, it has triumphed over the last impediments which the oceans interposed to the instant communication of the whole earth.

Handicraft, which in the last hundred years has kept close company with the rapidest revelations of science fulfills its commission, "fixing firm in enduring forms the creative essence which lives and works through all time, and hovers in changeful seeming till made firm by enduring thought." (Goethe, prolog. Faust.) Material forces, under the direction of machinery, grow as light-limbed and strong-handed as the thought which they realize. Machinery becomes bone and muscle to the brain and nerve of science, and dead matter answers in all its aptitudes to the mind of man.

From the union of knowledge with practical genius, physical power has made such progress, and trained so many, and such stupendous natural forces into our service, and all this so recently and rapidly, that we still look forward to a yet further and vaster increase in the apparatus of production, and to a corresponding abundance and cheapness; and through that abundance and cheapness to an ever-broadening diffusion of benefits and blessings.

This is what best describes and defines the increase of the general or aggregate wealth: Men ever better and better provided with the commodities which sustain their animal life; with the luxuries, which refine it; with an ever enlarging release from drudgery, which liberates it, and, with the opportunities and inducements, thence resulting, for elevating it to its noblest uses and highest possibilities.

ADVANCEMENT IN AGRICULTURAL PRODUCTION.

Agriculture differs from manufactures in not being capable of absolutely indefinite expansion. This is true in the literal meaning of the words; but writers of the dismal school give the truism much more force in application than it is entitled to. The multiplication in quantity, and improvement in quality, of all things, except food, which is clearly possible, is by an allowable hyperbole unlimited. Busy as a nailer, was once a proverb, because he must hammer out a nail at a single heat, and had not a moment to spare, but now a boy may be seen making more than fifty in a minute, while at leisure to read a book held in his unoccupied hand. A hundred years ago England consumed one yard of muslin per head per annum, but before our great domestic conflict it was plenty enough and cheap enough there for the inhabitants to consume an average of thirty yards; and so of a multitude of other commodities which a better state of things in the new age has made necessaries of life. But food, unless it be of fish, is much more limited in supply and accessibility. Its production and consumption cannot be expanded in any tolerable approach to the possible of textile fabrics, or metals, in their infinitely various forms of use. This, however, must not be forgotten: though the number of consumers is the same, the quantity of food demanded, has vastly narrower limits.

Population, we are told by the Malthus school of economists, goes on increasing, in favorable conditions, in a compound ratio, and the food-yield from the soil at best only by simple addition; and still worse, after a certain stage of culture is reached, all additional product is at an increasing cost of labor and capital—the process of exhaustion all the while advancing—and these general abstract propositions are rigorously pressed into the service of unbelief in the harmonies of the things which most nearly concern the welfare of men.

As a general answer, it is to be noticed that, in point of fact, and directly to the point of this assertion, famines, and the plagues attendant on them, have disappeared in modern times and under modern civilization, in the direct proportion that population has increased. Particular and comparatively small districts sometimes suffer now, but these are always the grossly-misgoverned or barbarously-cultivated portions of the civilized world. No famine or resulting plague, and no instances of very great scarcity, have visited Europe within the present century; but in increasing numbers and severity, as we go back towards the earliest ages of Christianity, they crowd the chronological registers of important events in human history. In Ireland, indeed, with fifteen millions of arable acres, and ten millions of that in pasture, the mass of the population, confined for food to a single root, which, under the pressure of necessity, is stimulated into disease, while the flocks and herds go to a distant market for the landlord's profit, famines and deficiencies in food are still lingering long after happier lands have found a nearly complete exemption. Ireland, under the conditions which she still suffers, cannot be blamed with infertility, or failure of ability to feed her people. India is still frequently visited by famines, also; but, is it surprising, if the richest soil of the world fails to yield its harvests, when the rule of the foreigner, or whatever else the cause, has restored the jungles of tropical luxuriance to the old garden grounds of the Deccan, and tiger hunts are the pastimes in spots which still retain the vestiges of demolished cities? Shall mother earth be made ashamed that she sickens and withers under such abuses?

In the northeast of Prussia we have lately heard of scarcity approaching absolute destitution; but such instances as this, and others like it, occurring in districts surrounded by abundance, have this lesson to teach the teachers of Political Economy and the governors of states: famines now never occur except in regions exclusively devoted to the production of food; and, that a duly diversified industry is an insurance against them. The crop of one year, however abundant, never suffices for itself and the next following, and if that of the last greatly fails, starvation must follow, for *all* of the labor of the people fails of its returns, and they have no current products wherewith to purchase supplies. Nine hundred of every thousand people, in any country, must starve if a whole year's earnings are cut off.

Let us admit the limited acreage of the fertile soil of the world; let us admit even the temporary exhaustibility of the soil under destructive modes of cultivation, and, that the earth will not long bear the robber-system of harvesting its generous tribute; and then, we turn to the despondents and reply: what, though neither land nor its products are in themselves unlimited, are they, therefore, not under natural law sufficient, more than sufficient, and so, in reference to the demand, practically unlimited? The thousand millions of its human inhabitants have not yet conquered ten per cent of the earth's capabilities for their service, even if a few garden spots may have reached the limit of their strength; but what is more to the purpose: if the race is still brutal in its fecundity, resulting entirely from the domination of the animal over the moral and mental faculties, and is a nuisance among the fair and orderly works of creation, may she not reject them as she did the reptiles of the old geologic ages, without impeachment of her providence and liberality?

We are thinking of the laws, not of the abuses of human life and its dependencies; and in those laws we see a constant effort in correction of those abuses, and an assured promise of an ultimate adjustment. But this still allows much evil and suffering in the present and immediate future! Not a whit more suffering than sin; and we cannot even imagine a system of existence in which wrong shall get along as well as right. To have men live well in error and evil is a gross violation of order and law, and would require that the system of the universe should be changed from the divinely right into conformity, if that were possible, with the rebellious evil which assails and defies it.

It is well to speak strongly on this subject, for, whether any present good shall result or not, it is much to have a sound faith and confidence in the laws of Providence. If we have an eternity for thought and feeling before us, a sustaining hope will go along with the study, and there will be the good cheer of a better day coming, as the motive and the reward of benevolent endeavor.

But we can rest our argument securely upon experience and observation, seen in the light which the ends and issues of all things reflect upon the processes by which they must be attained.

In point of fact the productiveness of all the old countries which have any degree of prosperity is in a constant and rapid increase, far outstripping the demand for sustenance. They are growing rich upon their surplus.

The food of France increased three times in the eighty years from 1760 to 1840. In the period of 1820 to 1860 it doubled, that is, it is now increasing at the rate of four-fold in eighty years against three-fold in the earlier period named; and this with a population nearly stationary and in an area of the same extent. She is a very large exporter of food. Age has not lessened her fertility. Its tendency under a due system of cultivation is always in the

WEALTH—SOURCES OF GROWTH. 61

opposite direction. The Mediterranean wheat, which makes such a figure in commerce is grown on the oldest cultivated soil in Europe and Africa.

English authors of authority claim that the usual crop of wheat in the United Kingdom is thirty bushels to the acre. The United States Agricultural Bureau puts our crops at from twelve to thirteen bushels per acre. Here the oldest country considerably more than doubles the newest in its average yield.

CONTRIBUTIONS OF INTERNATIONAL TRADE.

Improvement in the methods of cultivation, and the resulting enhancement of the product of soils long under tillage in the older countries, are not the only means and sources of increasing and cheapening the necessary supplies of their people. The colonization of, and COMMERCE with new countries, and the contributions which they are made to yield, afford a grand increase of the means of subsistence to the participating communities. For instance, the exports of cottons from England grew at a two-fold rate in the decade ending in 1860 over that of 1840–50, constituting full three-eighths of the value of all her domestic exports in the year 1860 (52 m. £ of 135.8 m. £), while her iron, steel, cutlery, and other manufactures of iron and steel, of which she had at home all the raw material and agents of conversion, amounted to no more than eleven and six-tenths per cent (15.9 m. £), or less than one-eighth of the whole. Her imports of raw material used in the manufacture of cottons, silks, and woolens, that year (1860) were valued at forty-seven and a half millions pounds. Their export value reached seventy-five millions, which, with twenty million pounds' worth consumed at home, gave her quite two hundred and thirty-eight millions dollars of difference in the exchange. These three manufactures, founded upon foreign raw materials, gave employment to seven hundred thousand laborers, whose wages supported nearly three millions of her population, and yielded a profit of, say, fifteen millions of pounds to her capitalists (sixteen per cent upon the value of the products). It is probable that the United Kingdom does not supply more than the one-fifth in value of the materials (exclusive of the labor) of her usual exports. If so, foreign commerce gives her four-fifths of the raw stock of her multifarious foreign exports.

The United Kingdom has risen from one and a half to six thousand millions of pounds in capital wealth since the United States sent the first cotton to her looms (in 1790), and, as has been already stated, this single article has risen to the value of three-eighths of the exports of British manufactures.

All the older countries have in this species of commerce sources of industrial profit, and supplies of sustenance before them, for as long a period as philanthropy or patriotism need wish. Even when international exchanges shall be limited to trade in the unlike products of differing climates, as it eventually must be, the reciprocities natural and, therefore, stable and enduring, will still be ample in their contributions to the welfare of all parties.

While the social disorder and misgovernment of the nations of Western Europe continue to bear hardly upon the mass of the peoples, the colonization of new countries will, in an important degree, abate the evils of disproportion between men and their current means of support, at present existing. For this purpose full four-fifths of the habitable globe is still new. Europe has now less than sixty-five persons to the square mile. This number does not task the one-third of its capabilities at home; and America, that has but three and a half, is capable of an average of at least two hundred. When these two quarters of the globe shall have their highest probable population in A. D. 1900, there will be ample room in them for nineteen times as many as they will have, or for seven times the total present population of the known world. Without calculating the waiting capabilities of Asia, Africa, and Oceanica for the multitudes which they can and will, in the advancing order of the earth's occupation and use, entertain and sustain, there is in the vacancies of Europe and America ample room and verge enough for a future so extended, that we might as well undertake to forecast the arrangements of the millennium, as to concern ourselves with the provision for the existence of the men that shall come after the globe is averagely inhabited and tolerably well subdued to the dominion of man.

Distressing apprehensions for the future of mankind are not new; but it is comparatively new for science to become hypochondriacal. It must be because political economy is itself so new that it breaks its heart over the foolish fears of infancy; it has not yet cut its wisdom teeth.

WEALTH—SOURCES OF GROWTH.

In the memory of the present generation, the general and rapidly increasing substitution of machinery and steam power for hand-labor, threatened the displacement and the starvation of the toiling multitudes, and good people stood aghast at the prospect when they saw one man doing the work of fifty. The laborers themselves looked upon the wonder-working machines, much as an untrained horse regards a locomotive engine, frightened by the apprehension that his "occupation's gone." The results, however, seem to be reconciling both man and beast. They have both improved greatly in quality and numbers, and they both in some vague way are beginning to understand the situation. In like manner, our grandmothers looked forward to dreadful things, before fossil coal came into use for fuel, for the time rapidly advancing when the forests should be utterly exhausted. Even John Stuart Mill gave voice in parliament in the spring of 1866, to a statistical scare over the near exhaustion of the English coal mines, and urged the early payment of the British debt in anticipation of the utter bankruptcy of the nation; that they might be able when the worst should come, to say, all is lost but honor. When the American Rebellion cut off the Northern States from the turpentine supply of North Carolina, and the whale fisheries were showing signs of decay, trade in all its branches which had depended upon these resources, gave signs of woe; but then the petroleum rivers overflowed, and the lubricated wheels of business rolled smoothly again; and one other world's catastrophe was escaped.

By way of a short cut to the conclusion, we may be allowed to suggest that, if England and France have survived their crimes and follies; if they are recovering from the insanities of centuries, and have taken a fresh start in business, no other people need fear the fates. The decadence of the civilized nations that are disposed to behave themselves as well as they can, is sheer nonsense.

SUBSTITUTION OF THE ABUNDANT AND CHEAP FOR THE SCARCE AND DEAR IN THE SUPPORT OF MEN.

Besides the increase of labor-saving machinery; the substitution of artificial for natural labor; improvement in travel and transportation; a vast increase in the quality and quantity of manufactured commodities; the rapidly growing yield of agriculture, both by improved cultivation and extension of territory for such use; the abundant aid of commerce in distributing the materials and the products of skilled industry legitimately exchanged; and the almost miraculous helps of the natural sciences in extending the dominion of man over the subordinate creation on which he depends for his earthly welfare, there is still another source of prosperity worthy of as much weight in the scale of our argument as either of these.

Within a few years gas of mineral origin has been substituted for animal oil for producing artificial light in all the cities, and in every thriving borough in the country; beet sugar and sorghum, which grow abundantly in the temperate climate, for the product of the cane, which requires a semi-tropical temperature; roots which yield by the ton, for grain that multiplies only by the bushel for the food of men and the feed of domestic animals; mineral oils have opened up from the interior of the earth in rivers, to replace vegetable and animal oils requiring so much of the surface soil to afford an adequate supply; and manufactures have by their ever growing abundance and cheapness come to supply and displace a very large percentage of food, which a greater waste of animal heat formerly required: aye, all the modern defenses against atmospheric cold are the equivalents of so much food in sustaining human life. Our clothing and our better habitations are worth half the food consumed in ages gone by for the maintenance of a comfortable temperature and health of body. By these ameliorations the average life of a generation has been extended from thirty-three to forty years since the beginning of the present century.

In another and broader view, our proposition may be seen in convincing clearness, thus: In savage conditions men are robbers of the earth, and victims of the elements. They gather the forest fruits in their season, hunt the air and earth and waters for their food, and suffer all the privations of improvidence. A thousand acres scarcely suffice for the support of one man, and these he soon exhausts, and is soon exhausted in his turn. When William Penn landed on the Delaware, there were not more than twenty-five thousand Indians from the Potomac to the chain of the northern lakes, and from Connecticut to the Allegheny River. There are eleven millions of men now, or four hundred and forty times that number. In the pastoral state the culture of cattle commences, and some sort of agriculture is introduced; but famines frequently occur, and the children of Israel must go into slavery in Egypt for an assured supply of corn—a barbarous civilization purchases the birthright of Jacob for a mess of pottage, as he had bought Esau's at the same price. Low as it is, this stage is an advancement in the supply and security of life. Semi-civilization becomes so far forth master of its own fortunes, and owners of the service of their inferiors. This results necessarily from the law that determines the conditions of society in every stage of progress. " Be fruitful, and multiply, and replenish the earth, and *subdue* it," is the commission and the means of securing the promise it contains.

Let us look, briefly, at the workings of the policy, in the processes employed for obtaining command of the earth's services in progressive improvements of human life.

The vegetable kingdom, which yields, some thirty, some sixty, and some an hundred-fold, is first drawn upon for its supplies. Animal food begins to be supplanted, immensely reduced in the temperate regions, and dispensed with in the tropical, with gains proportionate to its reduction. Exclusive animal food, where pasturage and feed must be used in its production, requires ten or twelve acres cultivated land to grow the flesh diet of one man for one year; one acre of wheat will support three persons—affording thirty-six times as much sustenance. One acre of potatoes will support nine persons—equal to one hundred and eight times the food yielded from the same extent of soil in flesh meat. In this ratio, advanced agriculture multiplies the means of subsistence, by this process of substitution, and in proportion, by all mixtures of these substances used for food. Even in the inferior races we have a good illustration of the economy of a vegetable over an animal diet. The lion, tiger, bear, and other carnivorous beasts multiply slowly, while the vegetable eaters—the horse, ox, and buffalo multiply immensely; they go in herds, while the ravagers of the living things roam alone in the solitudes which they make.

In apparel, as necessary to the life of the more advanced classes of men as food itself, and equally expensive, the vegetable flax and cotton displace a vast amount of wool which would otherwise be required. One acre of ground will produce as much of value in textile fabrics made of these, as a hundred acres will yield in the wool of sheep.

But it is not only from the animal world to the vegetable that man proceeds in the multiplication of his means of life—from the beasts that roam over the earth, through the cereals that grow above it, to the roots nourished in its bosom, with increasing plenty at each stage in the descent. He stops not here, but deeper still he finds the richest repository of his resources in the bowels of the planet. The mineral kingdom, with its exhaustless stores, are next opened for his use. And it is a striking fact that labor, the only capital of the masses, who most need that their condition shall be leveled up to competency, and thence forward toward the luxuries that refine, enlarge, and ennoble the life of man, through all this progress from the scarce and costly, to the abundant and cheap, shall be more and more in demand for the work of the world, and will derive from it an ever increasing share of its products. In agriculture nine-tenths of the product goes to the share of the capitalist, but in mining three-fourths of the yield is in the reward of labor—another instance of the adjustment of means to ends in the system of Providence, and a sure advancement of the changes that are to carry the world from the savage to the millennial state of the human race—another proof that all the movements in human history are tending and tiding to better things and better still, in infinite progression.

In the order of human advancement to complete dominion in the earth, we thus find the race going from the animal to the vegetable, and finally to the mineral world, for their subjects and their best services—from the narrowly-limited and the precarious animal supplies, to the more abundant and more secure vegetable, though subject to the caprices of the seasons; and thence, at the last stage, to the body of the solid earth, whose stores depend upon neither time nor climate nor season, nor any of their changes. In the successive kinds of mineral contributions, it is curious to observe that gold and silver are found by savages in the sands of the water courses, while they are yet using implements of stone and wood in handicraft; that along with these, barbarous nations employ copper and iron, which they contrive to smelt and mould for use with fuel of wood, and in architecture they utilize stone and clay made into bricks; while civilization not only avails itself of the all-compelling power of heat prospectively provided for this use in the fossil coal that at present is the greatest agent in the world's work; yet further: just as modern geography has added a fifth-quarter to the old world, so modern science has begun to annex another kingdom to the three that compassed the realm of man's subjects before the birth of chemistry. We are already familiar with the use of the imponderables, which have their pavilion in the clouds and their amphitheatre of exposition in the recesses of the globe.

These successive stages of substitution stand in the following order, and the instances given will serve to illustrate it.

First. From the animal to the vegetable kingdom:

Vegetable food	*substituted for*	Animal food.
Cotton	"	Skins and wool.
Flax and cotton	"	Silk.
Hemp	"	Skins in sails and cordage.
Gutta percha, caoutchouc	"	Leather.
Wooden canoe	"	The wild horse.
Paper of rags	"	Parchment.
Alcohol and vegetable oils	"	Animal oil.

Second. From the vegetable to the mineral kingdom:

Steel and gold pen and metallic types *substituted for* The goose quill.
Iron, stone, brick, slate, in ships and architecture, " Timber.
Coal, gas, mineral oil " Wood as fuel.

Third. From animals and vegetables to minerals:

Iron Engines	*substituted for*	The horse, ox, and camel.
Steel springs	"	Feathers and hair.
Glass	"	Skins.
Mineral gas	"	Animal oil and wax, as light.
Mineral manures	"	Animal and vegetable manures.
Metal gun	"	Wooden bow and animal string.
Wood and iron carriages	"	Animal transportation.
Wooden and metallic machinery	"	{ Human bone and muscle in manufacturing.
Steam machinery	"	Animal power.

Fourth. From animal, vegetable, and mineral to the imponderables:—

Electricity *substituted for* living messengers and vegetable sails.
Galvanic heat " vegetable and mineral heat.

Beside these transitions from kingdom to kingdom of the material world, there is a constant substitution proceeding from the scarcer and costlier and poorer in each division to something better and easier of attainment within its own class, which we need not stop to specify; but there is one instance which, being less familiar, or generally unknown, though already proved, deserves to be noticed here for its surpassing importance in the world's business affairs.

This is gas for fuel made from water, and with the addition of carbon to answer the purpose of giving artificial light as we have it now from coal. Water largely supplies the combustible substance, and the required gas can be produced from it at about the tenth of the cost of the manufacture from coal. It is to her coal more than to all the other agents of industrial production, that England owes her supremacy in manufactures, and in their transportation to the world's markets. The promise of a substitute that will replace her coal when it shall be either exhausted or become over expensive in the mining, saves her from an utter failure of her industries; but, as the supply of material for this service is common and exhaustless in all climates all over the earth, there can be no monopoly by any nation, and the industrial despotism of England will come to an end. Germany, France, Russia, and the United States are even now fast approaching independence of the "Workshop of the World." Some of these have coal fields that will furnish them for a few thousand years to come. These coal beds will be for generations easily worked, and the labor cost of their product will be light, while that of England will be continually increasing with the depth and distance to which the long-worked veins must be pursued. The natural growth of capital and labor in these favored regions will, at an early day, make their rivalry successful; and if our expectations from water gas shall be realized, the end of British domination in the world's market will be the sooner and the more surely reached.

This "Old Man of the Sea" has rendered good service in guiding the nations in their forward pathway, but it has been at the expense of carrying his weight till it has grown over-burthensome. The younger nations are coming of age, and the mother country must let go the leading strings. When pupilage becomes vassalage, resistance is compelled. Children that do not in due time reach maturity are unworthy of their parents. Australia, Canada, and the West Indies are already near the end of their political dependence, and they will soon strike effectively for economic freedom after the example of the United States. "The better day coming" cannot come till all this is done and well done. Mere political sovereignty over her colonies never was her aim. It was achieved, and has been held in all her provinces for the one purpose of securing their markets. In the course of events the little islands of Great Britain which can be covered with a thimble on any middling sized map of the habitable globe, have lost the military preëminence among the nations that once could hold them in check, and her own territories in subjection. And they are fast losing that mastery in production, for which all England's wars were made, and which all her invasions were designed to secure. England must ere long descend from her pre-eminence, and take her befitting position among the rank and file of the nations. The world owes her much—a balance still after all the heavy payments made in return. But the patent right in discoveries must run out some time; and in the things for which the rest of mankind are in her debt, that time arrives when the principal of the obligation is lost in the enormous interest which it has returned.

CHAPTER VII.

POPULATION—LAW OF INCREASE.

Population : Rate of increase in United States, England and Wales, Prussia and France.—Great difference between peoples nearly alike in origin.—Malthusians hold a *constant quantity* in the reproductive function.—Variant death rate of earlier and later dates; Greatest in the sparsest populations.—Death rate nearly the same in communities which greatly differ in rate of total increase.—A constant quantity in the reproductive function, with relatively constant diminution of sustenance, held by the British authorities.—The protest of Philosophy and Philanthropy; submission of Theologians, the reason why.—The primal curse contains a promise of sufficiency.—The facts of history.—The sources of the dismal philosophy.—Contradictions of these theorists.—Analogies forced upon differences.—Different data and method of the inquiry.—Arithmetical measurement of possible quantity of life and of food, indifferent.—Sufficiency, the issue.—Possible productiveness of man and earth unknown.—The question, one of principles and not of estimated numerals.—The strictly inductive sciences assume adjustment of means to ends.—The *a posteriori* method.—Limits of its province.—Does not apply to life united to liberty and responsibility.—All the facts not within the range of observation and experiment.—Their focal point and interpretation, in the design of the Creator.—The *a priori* or deductive method alone capable of the problem of man's relations to his material conditions.—*A posteriori* method, the vice of metaphysics and political economy.—The past and future in the physical sciences rest upon the *a priori* system of reasoning.—A sound faith must be corroborated by facts as far as they go.—The power of vital reproduction in an inverse ratio to the power of maintaining life—an universal law.—No *corrective* checks in the inferior animals—Viability and fecundity proportioned to each other, and adjusted to the intention of the life.—The intention is to provide for the continuance of kinds, and to meet the casualties to which they are subject.—Transfer of this law from different species, to equally varied conditions of the human species.—Justified by the historic changes in the human death rate, and the explanation it affords of the almost fabulous populations of ancient times.—The supply answers the demand, and the demand rules the supply.—The results afforded by the argument of analogy.—The law tried by the inductive method.—Its physiological basis contained in three propositions or general laws of the human organism.—Disease a broken balance of functional activities.—Unequal distribution of action among the several organs in health.—Effect of habitual concentration.—Actual action of organs not measured by their possibilities.—Nervous functions antagonize the reproductive.—Remedy for excess in balanced activity.—The excess meets the losses of disordered life.—Improvements in the forms of labor, the self-acting corrective.—The remedy most active just where it is most needed.—The promise in intellectual improvement.—Advancement in agriculture will diminish demand and increase supply.—Moral improvement will bring with it greater production of sustenance and greater economy in consumption.—Tendency of progress to restore equilibrium of functions and harmony of relations between earth and man.—Apparent exception.—Indian chivalry.—Activity of the nervous functions in the Hunter tribes; their infertility falls within the rule of our law.—Physiological ignorance checks criticism in special cases.—Consideration due to exceptions.—The present emigration from Western Europe.—Summary of conclusions.—Great mortality results from abuses.—Waste of life not a blunder of the Creator.—Excessive fertility designed to repair abnormal loss.—The remedy in the evil.—The law works to good.—Happy results, the marks and tests of Nature's laws.

The distribution of wealth would fitly follow the examination we have given to the laws governing its accumulation; but our inquiries have a drift that requires the preliminary investigation of a subject intimately involved in the question of sustenance adjusted to numbers—the law of the relation of Population to supply. We begin with the facts that we may have the field fairly before us. In the sixty years preceding 1860, the population of the United States increased very nearly three per cent per annum (compounded), or, at the rate of doubling every twenty-three and a half years. The native white people, after deduction of the immigrants, may be put at two and seven-sixteenths per cent per annum, at which rate they duplicated once in twenty-seven years. Great Britain (Ireland excluded) doubled its numbers in the last fifty years, but allowance for emigration would reduce the period to forty-six years, or one and one-half per cent per annum. Prussia increased very nearly at the same rate, while France, almost stationary, has been increasing no more than one-fourth of one per cent per annum, requiring two hundred and seventy-seven years to double her population.

These are enough to exhibit the varied rates of actual increase occurring among nations nearly enough alike to be classed together for comparison. Men differing from each other constitutionally no more than the German and Celtic stocks in Europe, and their mixed descendants in America, are thus found to vary in rate of natural increase as the numbers twenty-seven, forty-six, and two hundred and seventy-seven do from each other. It must be understood of these figures that they express the present current movement of population in the countries named; and, throwing out of consideration, for the present, the difference of conditions that may be supposed to affect the results, we note the fact that, so far, we have found nothing to support the doctrine that the reproductive function in the human race is a constant quantity, as the school of Malthus assumes and asserts it to be.

Neither has the law of mortality any greater constancy or universality. The death rate varied in London in one hundred and sixty years (from 1685 to 1845) from one in twenty-three of its inhabitants at the former date, to one in forty at the latter. The ordinary mortality of London, in the seventeenth century, says Macaulay, was as great as a visitation of the cholera would make it in the nineteenth. Thus a main element in the population theory, imposed upon us by the authorities, is affected by difference of time and attendant circumstances. One of these circumstances, whatever may be said of the others, is particularly unfortunate for the over-population theory. The inhabitants of London, when its death rate was at the highest, were not more than one-twelfth of the number that the city contained when their mortality was reduced to one-half the proportion of the earlier date.

But in contemporary history we have a record that is every way irreconcilable with the theory of a constant quantity in the function of procreation. In the year 1860, England, whose population grows at the rate of doubling once in forty-six years, shows one death to every forty-four living persons. The United States, which double their numbers by natural increase once in twenty-seven years, had one death to every forty-five inhabitants; France, which scarcely grows in numbers at all, had one death in forty-four. Here the proportion of deaths to the living people is almost the same, notwithstanding the immense disparity in the movement of population in these three countries; and Prussia, which increases its people not a whit faster than England and Wales, had one death, to thirty-two of its people in that year. The inference, not to be escaped is, that a difference in the proportion of births to population, in nations so nearly alike as these are, must be the cause of the vastly variant increase of the people.

But this "constant quantity" of the pretended law encounters still more embarrassment, and more emphatic contradiction, when its application is tried upon very widely different races, or families of mankind, which we will notice when we come to explain it in the light of what we take to be a true theory of the subject.

Only the Malthusian economists and the utterly unschooled public hold a fixed rate, and natural predetermined proportion of births to adults, without respect to conditions, or, if the school prefers it, a determined possibility of procreative power inherent in the human constitution. These theorists are also distinguished from all other thinkers by holding the inference from their premises, that there is in the constitution of earthly things a positive, natural and ever-increasing disparity between the production of human life and the capability of the earth to support it.

The best known British authorities are of this party. Their systems of political economy are built upon it, and can stand on no other ground.

The over-population theory, presented at the beginning of the present century in the imposing form of a scientific demonstration, did not pass without protest. It is impossible in this age to allow philosophy to justify war, pestilence, and famine, as the necessary correctives of mischiefs resulting from the laws of nature. The support and apology for despotism, which the doctrine affords, is just as abhorrent to the sentiments of charity and philanthropy. Theologians, it would seem, strangely enough, were less offended. The doctrine in its scientific array sprang from a clergyman of the Church of England, and was early and eagerly indorsed by Dr. Chalmers, of the Free Church of Scotland. The strong tendency of the religious sentiment to regard the present life as under a curse, and the disorders of the terrestrial system, as the reign of punitive justice, with a necessary suspension of providential beneficence, perhaps, accounts for the submission of the pulpit to this revolting philosophical heresy. The "thorns and thistles" of the primal curse, and all the resistance of nature to the dominion of man, which it signifies, is, indeed, abundantly fulfilled, yet there is a reassuring clause in the doom pronounced: "In the sweat of thy face *shalt thou* eat bread, until thou return unto the ground." The condition being performed, there is here not only no threat of famine, but a promise of supply. Laymen, while they admit that the earth is "a vale of tears," may be allowed to press the mitigating promise, and urge the proper measures of relief upon the faith and hope of the world. In the more cheerful understanding of the earth's economy, there is no need of "justifying the ways of God to man," and, what is still more to the purpose, there is no necessity for justifying the ways of man to man. It insists that better ways of administering the affairs of earth would improve the terrestrial condition of her children. But where is the use of beneficent endeavor if it must necessarily fail—if in the settled order of sublunary things population increases faster than the supply of sustenance can any way be made to meet?

But the facts of human history in all places and times down to the present: Do they not support the doctrines of the dismal school? We answer that so far as they can support anything, they do; and we take leave to add, that the disorders of misgovernment and the ill-distribution of the products of industry, the pauperism, the potato rot, and the enforced emigration of Europe, are the puddles from which her philosophers draw all their data, and fabricate their principles; grounds about as good for a system of providential laws as a street riot affords for constructing a philosophy of societary organization. How these people philosophize upon the facts which disorder supplies!

Of the host of writers upon this subject, some hold that abundance of food increases human fertility in a direct ratio; as if, because deficiency of sustenance induces disease and death, sufficiency must run to *excess* of life! Others are of a directly opposite opinion. According to them, fecundity is in the inverse ratio of sustenance. This direct antagonism is about equally well supported by such facts as the respective parties select and use in their demonstrations. Some think that vegetable is a stronger stimulant than animal food; for which they cite the greater productiveness of herbivorous than of carnivorous animals; forgetting that the fishes literally fill the seas, yet live for the most part upon other fishes and insects; and, above all, forgetting that they are carrying over such facts from that world of animal life, whose destiny is limited, and whose creatures are incapable of the liberties of progressiveness, which is the distinguishing ingredient of responsibility, to the world of man, whose fortunes and fate are not bounded by his instincts, but who is made master of the conditions on which his well-being depends, and must, therefore, in his constitution and capabilities, be adjusted to his destiny.

The assumption that man is only a beast, as to the laws of his life and his relations to surrounding things, is not a safe starting-point for a philosophy of his nature and fortunes. So far as his constitution exactly corresponds to that of inferior creatures, and, so far as his functions are bounded by the like limits and uses, the argument from analogy is legitimate; but from the point of departure where his endowments begin to look to a totally different use and end, all analogous reasoning must stop, because it no longer serves for interpretation.

The method here to be adopted in discussing the law of the relation of population to the means of subsistence will greatly abridge, as well as greatly change, the process of inquiry. For reasons that a little further on will be seen, we abstain now from considering either the historic or the possible fertility of the race, or of the capabilities of the earth as a means of measuring their adjustment to each other. The quantity of effect in either is obviously indifferent, provided they are, under an overruling law, adapted to each other. Not the actual numbers of the one, but the sufficiency of the one to the other, is the point at issue. In fact, the quantity of the possible products of neither is known. Neither the possible productiveness of the earth, of the soil, the waters, and the air, nor the future or ultimate rate of increase in the numbers of men, are, or can be, now ascertained. These problems cannot be brought within the range of arithmetical estimate. The question rests not upon numerals, but upon principles.

The chief of these principles belongs to the province of final causes—a rule of reasoning by no means unknown or unused in the cultivation of the strictly physical sciences. The Inductive System, itself, is compelled to *assume* that the means are provided in the constitution of things for the accomplishment of the ends clearly indicated. It cannot advance a step in any path of discovery without postulating the principle that the prophesy of the end, in all the realms of nature, is the pledge and proof of provided means. There is no other basis for any science of created things. An orbit, with an apparatus of vision, found in a fossil skull, means a provision of light, or it means nothing. A skeleton chest, with a slight twist in the ribs, proves conclusively the coexistence of respirable air—the structure of a tooth implies the contemporaneous existence of a particular kind of food; so, natural science builds its certainties as much upon the harmonies of the creation, and as confidently, too, as upon any observations of events or any results of experiment. Thus far the matter-of-fact philosophy extends itself into the domain of the deductive or *a priori* system of reasoning; unconsciously, perhaps, but actually and effectively.

The rigid *a posteriori* method traces the facts of observation from the simplest, up through successive and enlarging generalizations, till the most general fact is found, which is taken to be the law of the whole series. This is the rule of inquiry into the laws of unmixed materialism, and it is legitimate and successful only in the department of physics; in general terms, it rules among the phenomena of celestial and terrestrial mechanics.

But it has never had any success in mental philosophy, ethics, civil government, or social science, or any remedial system of either animal or societary life; that is, in any department of human knowledge concerned with the errors and abuses of liberty. Moreover, the phenomena of life united with liberty or will acting upon motives, and accompanied by responsibility, are not complete enough in range, nor clear enough in their meaning, within the limits of experience, to indicate their central or supreme truths; for the reason that the ends and aims lie all out of the reach of observation and experiment. They centre not in the midst of the known, but away beyond all its measurable lines. The drift and tendency of the facts may be seen, indeed, but their focal point is in the design of the Creator.

Water may be resolved into its constituent gases, and may again be recomposed of them. The circuit of its possibilities is thus known, and the relations of its elements to each other are revealed in kind and measure. But of man we know but little, either of his past or present, that can serve to prophesy his future. Our knowledge of his relations to the things around him is so incomplete, and, withal, so uncertain, that the inductive philosophy is warned by its own principles not to reason from a part, as if it were the whole, and inquiry is of necessity remitted to the method which assumes the means required for expectant ends.

The misuse of the *a posteriori*, or inductive method, in matters to which it does not apply—of which it is wholly incapable—is the vice of our metaphysics and of our political economy; and it is owing to this that neither of them is truly a science, or even capable of rendering safe service throughout their respective realms of study.

The most rigid of the Baconian philosophers who thinks it unsafe to venture beyond the circuit of his five senses, cannot object to our assuming just what he must assume, before he can reason at all on anything of the past that has left only its vestiges, or anything of the future which affords only its hints of the un-arrived. He believes, and he assumes, the harmonies and adjustments of means and processes to their obvious ends, and he interprets those processes and agencies by the ends in which they centre and ultimate themselves. We only use his license, and follow his example in believing that, whether the earth was made for man, or man for the earth, they must mutually suit and serve each other, and that there cannot exist a war of design in the relations of either to the other.

I would not, however, intimate that our theory of the matter in hand rests alone upon our faith in providential adjustment of the earth to human needs; for a sound faith must be corroborated by facts as far as they go. Such corroboration is plainly found in the facts of observation, and in analogies which partially measure and cover the ground which we take.

Among the various species of animated beings we find one invariable and universal fact: The power of reproduction of life is in an inverse ratio to the power of maintaining it. The insects of a day are produced in myriads; the lower animals, whose span is limited to half a dozen years, are reduced and limited to hundreds of offspring; while the higher grades, who live a score or more years, are in due proportion less prolific. This is the law as it obtains among *various* species of the animated creatures inferior to man, and it has this analogous bearing upon our problem: It provides for the necessary numbers and continuance of kinds, and meets the casualties to which they are respectively subject.

Did any one ever imagine that the abridgment of the term of life in these creatures was designed to correct a natural fertility beyond the provision for their subsistence?

Now, can we carry over this law and its plain intention, as far as correspondence exists, and apply it to the varied conditions of the human race? May we extend a principle which rules among distinct species of beings, to as large a difference of conditions occurring in a single race or species, having seen, as we believe, the intention of the principle, and found in the various conditions of that species the like necessity for the analogous working of the principle? Let us see how the application will justify itself:

In the savage and barbarous states, and in the earlier stages of civilization—in all the periods of disorder, past and present—the mortality of the race in early life is frightfully large. The power to maintain life is low, and the rate of reproduction is, as the principle we are borrowing requires, very large. This is seen in the drudges of civilization everywhere in Europe. The proposition is accurately supported by the whole history of the past which is definitely known. The average term of life has been lengthening, since the earliest authentic records, step by step with the improvements, social, sanitary, and economical, that have been progressively ministering to its preservation; and it is just as true that to the extent to which famine and pestilence have been abated or abolished, fecundity has been proportionately diminished. The almost incredible populations given in ancient history are explained on our theory by the proportionately briefer term of average life. The supply answers the demand; and our inference is, that the supply will, in the future, be limited and determined by the demand. We have the prospect of a continual improvement in the conditions of men. We expect still better and better sanitary regulation of societary life; better support by food, clothing, and lodging; better morals, and better and broader conformity to the laws of mental and bodily health—all the happy influences of spiritual and material progress; that is, in the terms of our proposition, a greater power to maintain individual life, and with it a proportionate reduction in the rate of reproduction. These results the argument from analogy affords us. These we take to be the mutual adjustments which the providential law secures.

Giving their due weight to the arguments offered, and asking for them no more than they may logically claim, we propose now to meet the question directly after the manner, and using the data, of the inductive system of the matter-of-fact philosophy which must be confronted with its own weapons, and on its own ground of faith. We turn to the well-established laws of the organism whose functions and force of action are the conditions of the problem. In the three following propositions we think the demonstration of our doctrine will be found:

1st. The nervous system in the different species of creatures varies with their respective capability of maintaining life—larger proportionately as they are longer-lived.

2d. The degree of fertility is regularly in inverse proportion to the development and activity of the nervous system; the larger and the more active nervous systems being always the least, and the smaller and less active, the most prolific.

3d. The functions of the various organic systems in the individual divide among themselves the aggregate of his vital power, being equally active in a state of equilibrium, but in all unequal distributions of activity the dominating function is sustained at the expense of one or more of the others.

The first of these propositions need not be argued, nor does it require illustration by examples. The reader is only fairly assumed to be ready to accept, and from familiar instances to confirm it, or in defect of the necessary information, he may find it in any good work upon human or comparative physiology.

The second proposition results from the third, but is entitled to distinct statement because of its eminent force among the instances of the third, and its direct relevancy to the question under consideration. Such demonstration as seems to be demanded by the last two, considered as one, is here submitted.

Disease manifests this diversion of energy from one or more sets of organs, and its concentration upon others, as in fever, where the excitement of the nervous and circulating systems is inordinately great at the expense of the muscular and digestive systems; and so in every morbid state involving the frame more or less generally. Disease has been well and pertinently defined, a *broken balance* of excitement. A similar inequality of distribution of vital power is almost constantly exhibited in conditions not incompatible with the general health; and its necessity is, in all instances of intense occupation, enforced and felt. The examples are familiar in every one's experience in his casual application of one function, or one set of associated functions. In cases of permanent concentration, where the fixity amounts to a habit, excluded offices of the body or mind fall into the incapacity of disuse; the predominant offices deteriorating or disabling those which must be robbed to enrich them.

The first deduction to be drawn for present use from facts so obvious as these, is, that no fixed and invariable quantity of action, or of results, can be predicated of any one of the distinct systems of organs in the human body; much less can the highest possibility of any one be taken as its measure of activity in all times, places and circumstances, as the "constant quantity" of the Malthusians affirms. All this is eminently true of the antagonism of the nervous and reproductive powers, as appears in the excessive fecundity of the drudges of civilization—among the former slaves of the Southern States and the correspondent toilers of Europe. There does not appear to be such incompatibility in muscular as in nervous activity. The intellectual and moral faculties of themselves, and these as they are acted upon by the external senses, seem to be special antagonists of those specially concerned in the propagation of the race. Just where the animal prevails over the mental habits of life, and in proportionate degree, fecundity is seen to increase; suggesting plainly enough that the remedy for excess of population is not in this or that kind of food, nor in artificial restraint, but in the duly-balanced development of the intellectual and moral functions of the brain and nerves. All the contrarieties of fact which every other theory encounters are found perfectly accordant with this one, as expressed in our three general propositions. The conclusion to be drawn from them is, that a harmonious culture of all the powers of body and mind will insure the equilibrium that corrects all disproportion, either of excess or of defect, in any of them. In accordance with these fundamental principles, the facts of past and present observation which seem to threaten an over population of the globe, are met and disarmed of their terrors by the obvious reflection that disorder in the vital offices, giving preponderance to the procreative powers and enfeebling the constitutional corrective of the mental and moral faculties, explains the evil and discovers the remedy. The surplus, however, is to be understood not only nor wholly mischievous, but as serving to replace the waste of life occurring in conditions that rather tend to extinction than to excessive numbers of the race.

The prospective operation of these laws—their more and more happy vindication in the future, is their most attractive claim upon our attention. They are not only explanatory of an existing disorder, but they are remedial in their operation. Through what agencies and in what conditions are they to exhibit their best efforts? How is the disturbed balance to be restored, and how are the harmonic results to be realized?

The change in the forms and kinds of human labor that are so well begun and advancing so rapidly, promise a more and more complete substitution of artificial for natural labor. This modification of agency in industrial production is characterized by an ever-increasing release from muscular toil, and a proportioned substitution of art and skill, and thought, and their associate elevations of feeling, which must, while they educate the proper human nature in its superior powers, equally develop and occupy the brain and nervous system; thus ever more and more strengthening their counter-balance of the animal functions. It is among the classes of men that are usually called the masses that the remedy is specially demanded, and here we have, in the very labor which they must pursue, the opportunity for the action of the remedial principle provided. The moral regimen prescribed is, mind mixed more and more largely with muscle in producing the commodities required for human support Reformed labor, working toward the harmony of functional activity in the individual labors.

Men look now for a better, broader, more diffusive and effective mental education in the future, growing upon a grand advancement already secured—another source of brain development, and an effective aid to its counter-balancing power.

Shall we have, resultingly, an improved agriculture; helping, on the one side to replenish the store of sustenance, while the direct operation of mental education serves to restrain the present excess of requirement?

Again: do we look for a progressive improvement in the morals of the masses, and an equally improved administration of social, civil, and international justice? This promise, also, carries the double aspect of correction at once in the relative demand of the mass of consumers, and in the economies of consumption. Moral refinement will give the required supremacy of man proper over his insurgent animalism, and it will at the same time check the waste of war, the defects and misdirection of industry. and the misuse of the means of life. In a thousand ways the future presents itself in expectation, as a restorer of that equilibrium among the various activities of the human organism on which depends a growing adjustment of the living man to the material elements appointed to sustain him, and to promote his welfare in the exact proportion that he conforms to the laws of the things created for his use, and which cannot fail in the service but by their abuse.

The principle here asserted must be familiarized before criticism is safe. Some one, for instance, may answer, "but the North American Indians have been remarkable for infertility; they are, as a race, but slightly endowed with the intersexual affections, and they are savage in ignorance and in pursuits." We answer: they are hunters, followers of Diana, the goddess of the chase and of chastity, by which the Greeks must have meant something that found its correspondence in things well known. These savages are as much distinguished from the lowest class of civilizees in their occupations as in fecundity. They have a fiery, nervous temperament, great acuteness of the perceptive faculties, willfulness, arrogance—sentiments that are the rougher half of those that constitute the chivalric among us; they are proud, desperately selfish, brave, revengeful, absolutely ungovernable, and incapable of enslavement. They are eminently the men who do die in the last ditch, and they are as eloquent as unlettered men can be. All this indicates very considerable activity of brain, and in the very direction that specially answers to the principle by which our theory would explain them.

The hunter life demands great vigilance, alertness, and sharpness of observation and reflection, which draws largely upon the nerves of sense and the coördinating power of the brain. Their perpetual warfare among themselves is another heavy drain upon the nervous system, in all the modes of action that danger, ambition, and emulation so powerfully induce. Their whole life is a rapid alternation of toil and sloth, surfeit and want, and their social intercourse, or system of society, rather represses than favors the affections. The tone as well as the character of the governing impulses is unfriendly to sexual attachments, and thus this apparent objection falls very fully into the rank of an example under the rule.

The application of this doctrine to cases not apparently accordant, which may present themselves in one of a thousand or a hundred instances, need not be considered here. Their special conditions are seldom known, and medical science is yet so far from fathoming the mysteries of the reproductive functions that nothing of force belongs to it in the investigation of the question. Besides, a prodigious array of clear examples may easily be adduced wherein unquestionable absorption of the vital forces, by the mental activities of the life, are in the fullest accord with the tenor of the law which the larger and more completely comprehensive view of facts thoroughly establishes. Exceptions are not to be ignored, because rules admit of them, or because they prove the rule, as the proverb most illogically affirms, for, in fact, they contradict the rules which should include and govern them; but because, in the inquiry in hand, they are not proved to be exceptions. The believers in a law are not bound to explain away, or to surrender to, accidental instances, which neither they nor anybody else understand.

Emigration as we see it and as it has been in past times, is compelled by the failure to carry forward the improvement of the man in conformity with the law that adjusts him to the supply of sustenance. Labor in Western Europe, so far from improving him and regulating his increase of numbers in harmonic relations to the increased productiveness of the soil, works on the contrary to the constant depression of the lowest class—these are the emigrants in the much largest porportion. The more advanced classes of European society do not migrate, and the most favored and best developed portion of the people are stationary in place, for the reason that they do not multiply in offspring; the very highest scarcely keeping up their numbers, as witness the great number of instances in which titles have become extinct in England from utter failure of heirs to inherit them.

The emigration from France is almost nothing, because there population is nearly stationary.

A summary of the conclusions to be drawn from this brief discussion of the laws of population may be compactly put in this form :—

The waste of life in the past is due to an abnormal preponderance of the animal, over the intellectual and moral faculties of the race.

That waste of life is not the corrective of a blunder in the Creator's system, but results from an abuse of the reproductive function, and its excessive activity provides for the waste incident to the disorders of human societies. It is a remedy in its nature and intention, and not a mistake or maladjustment of natural laws.

Population is self-regulative. In the organization of the human frame there is a perpetual endeavor toward the establishment of equilibrium between the demand for sustenance and the earth's supplies; so that ultimate and complete harmony awaits the conformity of man to the laws under which he has his life ; and which in the mean time is growing in exact proportion to his growing development. This is obviously the meaning of the divine promise. " Seek first the Kingdom of God and his righteousness [conform your life to the Divine Order], and all these things shall be added unto you," namely, " what ye shall eat or what ye shall drink, or wherewithal ye shall be clothed."

Despair is doctrinal infidelity, and the source of misdirection, with all the ills that attend ignorance and error in man's mismanagement of his earthly dominion.

There is something healthy, holy, happy in these conclusions, and they are for these sufficient reasons *true*.

NOTE.—Limited in plan and space, the writer cannot task himself to trace the first authorship of all the doctrines he adopts, but for fuller satisfaction in the matter of this chapter, he refers the reader to an article in the *Westminster Review* for April, 1852, since ascribed to Herbert Spencer, and to Carey's *Social Science*, vol. ii., pp. 265-306, for a more detailed discussion of the subject.

CHAPTER VIII.

DISTRIBUTION OF WEALTH—WAGES.

Distribution of Wealth—Wages: In the savage state; in barbarism; in civilization; Carey's law of "Labor Value."—Bastiat's identical.—Quality of labor improves in the ratio of quantity of coöperating capital; its productiveness increased, and price of the products lessened proportionately.—Tendency of the law to equality of benefits demonstrated.—More liberal wages secure better work—the capitalist's interest supplies the motive.—Wages the index of productiveness.—In progressive communities only land and labor increase in value —reasons.—Value, the cost of reproduction.—Rise of the laborers in history.— Wages, nominal and real; value of money must be resolved into its purchasing power.—Agricultural wages in England, A. D. 1660 to 1688.—Price of wheat at the time.—Wages in manufactures in 1680, a shilling a day.—Doubled in one hundred and twelve years.—Price of wheat the same at the end of one hundred and fifty years.—Food of the people at the end of the seventeenth century.— Wages have risen faster than the price of food.—Tropical productions declined, and manufactures reduced sixty per cent in thirty-five years (1817-1852).—Labor rises in value in the ratio that productiveness increases; statistics of the United States in proof.—Wages of skilled industry rise fifteen and one-eighth per cent in the ten years 1850-1860; doubling in forty-seven years.—Rise in the United States, in the same ratio to growth of national wealth as in England, showing a law of equable growth, but, the law of the growth of wages relatively to that of coöperating capital is not equable.—Rate of increase of wages much more rapid than that of the enhancement of profits upon the capital jointly employed.—How advance of wages is provided for without corresponding loss to capital.—Statistical demonstration.—The provision traced to its source—the substitution of machinery and artificial force for human labor, proof by the figures of the census.—Artificial labor releases men from low-priced drudgery and remits them to the higher styles of work with their higher wages.—The greater effectiveness of the natural agents enhances the fund upon which labor draws for its reward.— Wages increase and employment also increases with all improvement in the modern modes of converting industry.—*Apparent* losses of capital explained.— Both labor and capital increase their gains, but at unequal rates.—Labor gains fifteen, capital five per cent.—The laborer's share of increased productiveness increases in *proportion;* that of capital declines.—In *quantity both* increase, but the laborer's most rapidly.—The harmony of these interests working through all the unhappy conflicts of the parties.—Wages of women have tripled while those of men have been doubling.—Reasons of this different rate of advancement.—Why the year 1814 is taken as the date of the new era of wages.—The

86   QUESTIONS OF THE DAY.

liability of statistical figures to abuse.—Figures must be rectified by facts.—The capriciousness of prices.—Not fluctuations, but changes from permanent causes show the truth.—Price of iron in illustration.—Causes of unsteadiness in prices.—General results, a better guidance than figures without facts.—Women's wages in house work have increased in real value about six times, while those of skilled laborers have been doubling.—Men's real wages advancing five fold in a part of their consumption, accompanied, besides, with many gratuitous additions and cheapened uses, availing for their welfare.—Wages and food, flesh meats only increased in price.—Aggregate annual wages of 1814 and 1860 distributed in subsistence, showing actual increase.—Wages effectively doubled in the United States once in fifty-five years.—Different results of arithmetical processes from different data used in these computations.—Epochal dates in societary and economic movements cannot be precise.—Error in amounts do not affect the percentage of increase which is the subject of inquiry.—Census reports of values all too low.—Under modifications, according to the greater or less aid of capital, wages are the index of productiveness.

HAVING shown the capability of the earth to supply subsistence, and all the means of well-being abundantly adequate to the requirements of its total inhabitants, we are next concerned to see what provision is made in the constitution and order of things for an equitable and beneficent distribution of its products among the members of human communities.

In the savage state all things are so far common to all, that the allotment of property is determined by individual appropriation and the power to hold possession. Here there is no division of capital and labor; no system of progressive accumulation; no productive work, in its proper sense, there being no surplus reserved for further production; no capital and, therefore, no wages, as a share of joint production. And, if there are none of the special evils of inequality in wealth, there are, also, none of its possibilities of better things to come.

In barbarism there is accumulation with its eminent creative power, and to the freer portion of the people, that interest in production called wages, and the benefits of industrial enterprise. The many may be, under some of the forms of slavery, without capital or its reflected service, and may have no recognized property right, even in the means of subsistence. But the laws of an orderly distribution of wealth are beginning to work.

Civilization (distinguished from barbarism by its necessary exclusion of personal slavery) distributes the joint product of labor and capital in the several kinds of profits, under the names of rent, interest, and wages; but an equitable allotment of profits is not yet secured. Equity encounters hostile interests, and unequal power in the parties to assert its claims; and wrongs, with their attendant disorders and mischiefs, disturb and derange distribution in freedom, even as they do in slavery, though less in degree and less hopelessly.

Let us now see how, in these circumstances, the laws of the subject work toward their end, which we assume to be the general and individual improvement of the welfare of men in progressive communities.

In the year 1837 Mr. Carey first announced to the world his doctrine of "labor value" with such resistless demonstration of its truth, that even the highest authority of the rival school of political economy, Frederick Bastiat, adopted it in 1850, under the verbal change of "service value," but so exactly identical in substance that Professor Ferrara, of the University of Turin, says: "The theory, the ideas, the order, the reasoning, and even the figures of the 'Principles' of Carey, and of the 'Harmonies' of Bastiat, coincide perfectly."

The unskilled may derive some additional assurance from such an indorsement, but the propositions of Mr. Carey are quite independent of any extrinsic support. His most general, or fundamental, proposition takes this form: The *quantity* of capital and the *quality* of the labor jointly employed in production, are in direct relation to each other. All increase and decrease of the capital connects itself with corresponding improvement and deterioration of the labor. The passive and active agents are married "for better, for worse," which may be resolved into the following dependent propositions:

1st. Labor gains increased productiveness in the proportion that capital contributes to its efficiency.

2d. Every improvement in the efficiency of labor, so gained by the aid of capital, is so much increased facility of accumulation.

3d. Increased power of production and accumulation lessens proportionally the value of the products in labor cost, and of similar products previously existing; thus bringing such products more easily within the purchasing power of present labor. This last-mentioned consequence is also covered by the same author's definition of *value*, which, in his happy rendering, is simply the cost of *re*-production, which is only another way of saying that, nothing can command a higher price than the cost of producing a similar thing at the time, and nothing can be produced at less than the cost of producing it. (The reader will, of course, take care to distinguish *value*, or cost of production, from price or selling price, which is casually affected by sacrifice and speculation.)

The tendency of the law, as stated in the third proposition, to increase the relative share of labor up to its equitable proportion in the profits of industry combined with capital, is too obvious to need illustration, *provided* labor wages do not suffer an abatement equivalent to, or greater than the reduction in the exchange value of the commodities. The argument of this point may be put thus: The laborer must receive his share, or wages, out of the product to which he contributes. That share depends upon the quantity of such product. The larger this is, the greater the fund on which he draws. When he hires the capital, his share is the residuum after paying the capitalist his interest, or profit, upon the investment. This is certain when the laborer is his own employer; and his profit is found in the enhanced productiveness of his labor due to the aid of capital.

When the capitalist hires the labor, which is the more general state of the case, a like equitable division of profits is *possible*, or in other words the fund is created for such equitable dividend, and it is made possible for him to receive the due advantage of his coöperation in the enlarged yield of his industry. This increased productiveness results from the substitution of instruments, machinery, and artificial motor power, which is capital's share of the agencies employed; and the laborer's advantage is in his release from low-priced drudgery, and in the employment of his higher faculties—the wages of skilled industry being always proportioned to its advancement above mere animal power.

The *ability* of increased productiveness to afford increased wages is clear. What of the impelling or disposing motive in the employer of labor? To say nothing of the reserve of compelling power that there is in the laboring class, and the over-ruling force of the sentiment of justice embodied in public opinion, and corroborated by the ever-active working of providential beneficence for the welfare of the world; it is found in such considerations as these:—

The human machine, like the inanimate, and for the same reasons, yields results to the employer in the measure of its capabilities and conditions. Its highest condition is necessary to its highest working worth. But beside the food and clothing of the one, corresponding to the fuel, or other motor power, and the structural materials of the other, the human producer has his most availing force in his moral and rational faculties. The cultivation of these, up to their highest serviceableness, demands the opportunities of some leisure, the refinement of some luxury, the cordial stimulus of current comfort, and the excitement of future hope. Such development can come only from a liberal surplus of wages after provision is made for the common necessities of the mere animal life. The policy of parsimony, which denies these conditions, is as unwise as the saving of fuel which would keep a steam engine restrained to half its working power. The work of a man who is aiming at a seat in the American Congress is worth much more than that of the European drudge whose prospect is the poor-house. The ox has more brute force, the engine more mechanical power, yet these are always had at a cheaper rate in their kinds of service than the labor market gives for the use of those high human qualities on which capital depends for the largest enhancement of its profits. Hence policy induces equity, and the effective partnership of the workman secures him a growing dividend of a growing productiveness. From the reason of the thing, therefore, there is a fair inference that wages must rise with productiveness step by step, and keep pace in improvement with the yield of coöperating capital. The percentage of the labor share in the yield must be carried up with the growing value to which it is an indispensable contributor.

There is, moreover, an overruling law which secures this result—a law established by all the facts of human experience: in advancing communities nothing can increase in value except land and labor. The increasing power and worth of these reduce the labor cost and exchange value of all other things. The one being the raw material, and the other the converting agent, in the production of all commodities, their worth rises just in the ratio that the value of all other things declines. Value is simply the measure of the resistance that labor and skill meet in subduing natural objects to human use. The converting power must rise in utility in the degree of its growth, and it must also rise in exchange value in proportion to the cost of its own production, which in the case of labor is the cost of its education and training. Land necessarily rises as its elements are advanced from uselessness, or resistance to use, toward the serviceable states and forms that minister to man's requirements, and the cost of its improvement measures its value. A surface acre of ore unwrought, has no other than a prospective value; converted and carried up to its best forms, it realizes a market value of hundreds or thousands of dollars in the currency that commands all the means of human subsistence. In like manner, and for the like reasons, the labor of bones and muscles may be had at the price that barely supports life; that of the artisan commands the means of advancement; and, the highest skill, united to taste, talent, and science, brings the rewards of the highest rank of service in the finer manufactures, in the fine arts, and in the learned professions. In all possible applications the definition is true—value is the cost of production, or of reproduction at the time; and all increase of skill and competency must have its proportioned price.

The facts of history in the past, and all observation of the present, are in proof of these propositions. Ever since the system of villenage was abolished in England, the laboring masses have been rising into better conditions—very slowly in the days of the Stuarts; something faster under the reigns of the Georges; and with accelerated rapidity since the beginning of the present century. A full array of the evidence would require a separate treatise, but the pivot points of this history are entirely sufficient.

WAGES, NOMINAL AND REAL.

Wages, in report from such records as exist, are, like the prices of other things, expressed in the money of the time; but money has itself a very variable exchange value at distant periods; and, to understand its worth, we must know its purchasing power, or its command over the commodities required for consumption. Money is no more a standard of the things exchanged in the market than is any other commodity. It is the common medium of exchange, of all historic times, but it has been much more variable than anything else called, or used, as a measure in the world's business. Measures and weights—yards, bushels, and pound-weights—do not enter into the exchanges of the things which they gauge, but money does, as a thing of intrinsic value, or as representative of some valuable medium. Its variableness in value, therefore, requires a reduction to its equivalents in the commodities of the time, or, as it is usually expressed, to its purchasing power, which must be ascertained if we would understand the real under the nominal value. This equivalence must be kept in mind, and be as well ascertained as may be, in an inquiry into the relative rates of wages paid at different periods.

For our purposes we must depend upon the authorities in the statistics of labor. As it would only burden the examination to carry it back into the time of feudalism in Europe, or even to the transition from bondage into the modern condition of civil freedom of the working people, we shall take the seventeenth century for our starting point, and for the facts of that date, we may with great confidence rely upon Mr., afterwards Lord, Macaulay. He fixes four shillings a week, without food, as the average agricultural wages, at any time between the Restoration (A. D. 1660) and the Revolution (1688). In 1685 the Justices of Warwickshire, under authority of an act of Elizabeth, fixed the wages of the common agricultural laborer, during the spring and summer, at four shillings a week, without food, and at three and sixpence for the fall and winter months. In the south of England the rates were a little higher, and about the centre and near the borders of Scotland something lower. In the county of Essex and the vicinity of London, the Justices allowed six shillings in winter, and seven in summer, for the year 1661, which our author says was the highest remuneration in a period of twenty years, but it happened that in that year the necessaries of life were immoderately dear. Wheat was at seventy shillings the quarter* (eight bushels), which he adds, would even in 1848 be considered as almost a famine price.

The pay of workmen employed in manufactures is always higher than that of tillers of the soil. In 1680, a member of the House of Commons said that "the high wages paid in England make it impossible for the products of the English looms to compete with those of India. An English mechanic, he said, instead of slaving like a native of Bengal for a piece of copper, exacts *a shilling* a day. It

---

* The average of the monthly prices for 15 years, 1846–1860, was 53s. 8½d.
 "   "   "   "   9 "   1857–1865, " 48s. 4d.

is true he often works for less, but this sum is his demand." Mr. Macaulay, from all the evidence, concludes that, " in the generation which preceded the Revolution (1688), a workman employed in the great staple (woolens) manufacture of England thought himself fairly paid if he gained six shillings a week."

Coming down to a later period we find, by the register of the Greenwich Hospital, that the wages of such mechanics as carpenters, bricklayers, and plumbers, had more than doubled in one hundred and twelve years, (from 1730 to 1842),—rising very regularly from 2s. 6d. per day, to 5s. 8d., (McCulloch's Com. Dict., p. 1061).

Thus it appears by this last quoted author (whose doctrines as an economist, as we have given them in a former chapter, were directly hostile to his facts as a statistician), that the wages of all labor estimated in money were in 1730 not quite half of what they were in 1842. Meat was cheaper, in money, it is true, but hundreds of thousands of families scarcely knew the taste of it. Wheat, as early as the last twelve years of Charles II. (1672–1685), averaged fifty shillings per quarter, and during a like period one hundred and seventy years later (1843–1855), it was about the same price. But the difference, in fact, is, that bread such as is now given to the inmates of a British workhouse, was seldom seen even on the table of a yeoman or a shop-keeper. The great majority of the nation lived almost entirely on rye, barley, and oats. (Macaulay's Hist. Eng., vol. 1, chap. iii.)

Here, then, we see that in England, whose limited territory makes her dependent upon foreign countries for full one-fifth of her food, in this prime necessary of life, the wages of labor have risen largely above the prices of the required supply, while in all other things necessary to ordinary comfort, prices have gone down immensely, bringing such commodities as are the produce of tropical countries, and of the mines and manufactures of the country, within the purchase of the laborer in proportionate abundance. Sufficient proof of this is found in the fact that the prices of all the manifold exports of Great Britain declined sixty per cent in thirty-five years, from the year 1817 to 1852; that is, of all the articles of British and Irish produce now exported to foreign countries, comprised under a hundred general heads or classes in the export entries, and of a thousand specific varieties, one dollar will now purchase as much as two dollars and a half would in the year 1817. Cottons only are excepted, and even these are twenty-five per cent lower than in 1817, and will take rank in reduction of price again when the cotton supply of our Southern States shall be restored to its state before our civil war.

Now, if the wages of such a country as England doubled in money in one hundred and twelve years, and wheat and all other breadstuffs remained at about the same price, while only flesh meats became dearer, and all the multiform products of the mining, manufacturing, and mechanic arts fell sixty per cent in the last thirty-five years of the period, and all the products of tropical climates greatly decreased in price also, is it not fully established that labor rises in market value in the ratio that productiveness increases and products abound?

Tried in the United States, where labor beyond the supply is in demand, the rise of wages is proportionately greater than in countries not so favorably circumstanced.

We shall not here insist upon the arithmetical precision of the statistics which must of necessity be employed, nor need we; our aim is only to show conclusively that wages do rise in keeping with the profits yielded by labor combined with capital in the modern system of production, and in proportion to the joint productiveness. First, then, as the question stands in the United States, we have at least an approximate valuation of the elements of our problem in the census reports of 1850 and 1860. The latter being more accurate than the former, its data will be more particularly relied upon.

The total products of manufactures in 1860 were valued at $1,885,861,676. The annual cost of labor was $378,878,266, which is twenty and one-tenth per cent of the value of the products. The cost of the raw materials was $1,031,605,092, which leaves but $854,256,584, of which labor took forty-four and three-tenths per cent, leaving to capital fifty-five and seven-tenths per cent of the value of the products over the labor wages, to cover interest upon an investment of $1,009,855,715, interest of raw material until sale of the products, taxes, superintendence, losses upon sales, repairs, insurance, expenses, and net profits.

The number of hands employed was one million, forty thousand three hundred and forty-nine males, and two hundred and seventy thousand eight hundred and ninety-seven females. The proportion of wages of males to females was ascertained in 1850 to be as nine to five. We have taken the same ratio here for the year 1860. This rule would distribute the wages of the year thus: aggregate wages of all males employed $330,996,917, which is $318.16 per annum averaged to each, or $1.02 for every working day (three hundred and twelve in the year). To the women, a total of $47,881,349, giving to each an average of $176.75 per annum, or fifty-seven cents per day.

In the year 1850, according to the census, there were engaged in manufactures in the United States seven hundred and thirty-one thousand one hundred and thirty-seven males, and two hundred and twenty-five thousand nine hundred and twenty-two females. The total wages paid were $202,066,770 to the male operatives, which gave them an average of $276.37 per annum, $5.31½ per week, and eighty-eight and six-tenths cents for each working day; to the women, $153.54 for the year; $2.95¼ per week, and forty-nine and one-fifth cents per day. Comparing these rates with those of 1860 we find that wages had increased fifteen and twelve-one-hundredths per cent in ten years, at which rate they would double in forty-seven years. Wages of skilled labor in England, as we have seen, stood at double after one hundred and twelve years. Our wealth grows now at the rate of eight and one-half per cent; British wealth at three and one-half per cent per annum. Here we have a remarkable correspondence. As forty-seven years is to three and a half, so is one hundred and fourteen years to eight and one-half. In other words, if English wages grow in the same proportion to the growth of English wealth, that wages in the United States keep to their increase of wealth, they should double in one hundred and thirteen years; we have just seen that they do in one hundred and fourteen years. This looks very like the effect of a universal law, that is, a law ruling the relation of the wages of skilled labor to the *general wealth* of the nation, but it is by no means the law of the relation of wages to the *capital employing* labor in manufacturing industry. Here wages not only keep pace with the profits of capital, but gain upon those profits, at a rate of constant increase that will not be arrested until such advance shall be checked by reaching the point at which capital can yield no more of its profits to labor. Let us see whether we can find the facts that prove such a law in operation among the data afforded by our census reports:

LAW OF WAGES.

The wages paid in 1860, as already stated, were an advance of fifteen and twelve one-hundredths per cent over those of 1850, the aggregate increase amounting to $57,286,494. Did capital suffer the loss of this sum in reduction of its former profits? Or, if it neither did or could do so, how was this fifty-seven and a quarter millions provided for? The cost of material and wages in 1850 was equal to seventy-seven and seven-tenths per cent of the value of the products, but in 1860 these items of expense fell to seventy-four and seventy-nine one-hundredths per cent of the total yield. This saving refunded to capital $54,830,464 of the advance of wages, and left a loss of only $2,456,030, which is but a fraction over one per cent of the product. Whence came this fifty-four and a quarter millions? Not from an increased yield of the material, for curiously enough, the materials used in 1850 bore the proportion fifty-four and forty-seven one-hundredths per cent to the value of their products, and those of 1860 only two-tenths of one per cent more, or, we may say, exactly the same.

The following tabular statement shows the sources of the fund supplied to meet the advance of the wages:

	In 1850.	In 1860.	Decrease.
Labor took of the products	23.23 per cent	20.10 per cent	13.86 per cent
Labor took of the enhanced value of products over cost of material	51.07 "	44.35 "	13.16 "
Capital took of the enhanced value of the product over the cost of the material	48.93 "	55.64 "	Increase. 13.71 "
Capital took of the enhanced value of the products over cost of materials and wages	22.29 "	25.20 "	13.05 "

The *apparent* loss of labor and gain of capital in their respective shares of the product shown by this table, very accurately provides for the actual advance of wages in 1860 (fifty-seven and one-quarter millions) out of the actual gain of capital (fifty-four and eight-tenths millions) in the products, with the loss of the trivial difference before stated (two and four-tenths millions). This gain in products here set to the credit of capital, did not come out of an increased yield of the materials, nor could it have come out of the wages of labor, for these were greatly increased; it must, therefore, have resulted from improved machinery and methods of conversion supplied by capital, and at its expense. The sum, fifty-four and eight-tenths millions, is equal to a fraction less than three per cent of the value of the products, and that amount of improvement in the apparatus and management of the manufactures of the nation in a decade is every way probable. That we put the credit to the right account is further supported by the fact that the wages bore the proportion of forty-one and forty-one one-hundredths per cent to the cost of the materials used in 1850, but in 1860 fell to thirty-six and seventy-two one-hundredths. Thus forty-eight and one-third millions' worth of work at the rates of 1850 was transferred in 1860 from human hands to machinery, and at the advanced rates of 1860 would amount to fifty-five and seven-tenths millions, or barely nine-tenths of a million more than the sum transferred to the credit of the capitalists who supplied the machinery. Subject to the inseparable errors of statistical data, so large and complex as ours, these results may be regarded as the exactest proofs that such subjects are capable of.

The noteworthy results of this inquiry are these: the substitution of artificial labor, in the form of steam or water force and machinery, for muscular toil, relieves the laborer of so much mere muscle force, which is low priced, and remits him to the higher styles of skill, which always command correspondingly higher rates of wages, which, in every way that concerns his advancement, is so much in his favor. Again: machinery adds a rate of speed, and in many cases a degree of precision in the execution of manufacturing processes which human hands cannot command, increasing the quantity and value of the products, and so increasing the fund from which wages must be paid; which, under the operation of other laws ruling the case, insures him an increase of his distributive share.

These propositions on their face seem at first view paradoxical, but like other paradoxes, in abstract statement, opens up its essential facts in the simplest forms of truth.

We must get accustomed to look through the alarms of innovations that attend the progress of economical affairs. A wagon road displacing the pack-horse system of transportation across the Alleghenies, threatened destruction to the horse-breeders of the time. The railroads that followed, menaced a total loss of occupation to the same interest. What has followed these changes? Horses discharged from this drudgery have been advanced to work requiring higher qualities, and, behold! their numbers and individual value have been multiplied many times. In like manner, when a machine is introduced that displaces nine in ten of the laborers before occupied in the work to be done, it is hastily inferred that capital is dispensing more and more with human labor; yet all experience shows that wages rise, employment enlarges, and products cheapen at the same time, and the benefit to the poor is in the aggregate much greater than to the rich! Else why have the masses risen in condition, step by step, with all improvement in the agencies introduced into the modern industries?

Another result of the calculations here submitted remains to be noticed. We found by our figures that the capitalists in 1860 received a trifle less from the enhanced value of the products over the cost of material and labor than the increase of the wages paid—the sum of $2,456,030. To this must be added the interest upon the increased capital employed ($482,646,522), and the interest running upon the increased value of the materials ($476,481,370), from the date of their purchase until the sale of their products, with whatever of other increased expenses the extension of the business added. These items cannot be calculated from any data at hand, but they must have aggregated at least fifty millions.

Again comes the question, did the capitalists lose this estimated fifty millions, or suffer such an abatement of their former profits? Let us for the purpose of trying this question, call the difference between the cost of materials and the cost of labor together, and the value of the products, profits. It appears that such profits in 1850 were equal to twenty-eight and seven-tenths per cent of the total yield, but in 1860 they rose to thirty-three per cent. The gain in amount is a trifle over eighty-one millions, and the fifty millions additional expense here estimated, would leave to capital a clear increased gain of thirty-one millions.

Thus, on the basis of the facts and figures here used, is demonstrated the increased yield to both capital and labor of improved methods of conversion in manufacturing, mining, and mechanical industry; labor gaining fifteen and twelve one-hundredths per cent upon its smaller principal in ten years, and the capitalist upon his greatly larger principal but five per cent.

Mr. Carey's general statement of the *law* of distribution is thus verified in one grand province of its operation. It may be found supported by the context with great amplitude of demonstration in his "Social Science," vol. iii., p. 159. We here condense his formula: " With the growth of wealth and numbers, the power of "combination increases with great increase in the productiveness of "labor, and in the power of accumulation—every step in that "direction being attended by decline in the power of the already "existing capital to command the services of the laborer, and by "the increase of power on the part of the latter to command the aid "of capital."

"The *proportion* of the increased product of labor assigned to the "laborer tends, thus, steadily to increase, while that of the capitalist "tends as regularly to decline. The *quantity* assigned to both in-"creases—that of the laborer growing, however, far more rapidly "than that retained by the capitalist."

"The tendency to equality is, therefore, in the direct ratio of the "growth of wealth, and consequent productiveness of labor."

We cannot leave this discussion without calling attention to its highest and happiest result—the harmony of interests really subsisting and working toward the most beneficent issue, under the system of relations between capital and labor which are unhappily marked by so much hostility of the parties as the world still witnesses—the employer gaining larger profit from increase of the wages paid, and the laborer sharing in the product from the aid of capital coöperating, and on both sides, in proportion to all improvements in the processes attained, with the assurance that their prospective fortunes are under the government of the same law.

Let us now look at the operation of this law as it rules among different classes and conditions of laborers. That the wages of *men* have doubled as reckoned in money in the United States since the general introduction of steam and modern machinery, say in the year 1814, will be readily admitted; but it is equally true that the wages of women have tripled in the same time; and this not alone by the transfer of their industry from the household to the factory, where capital directly aids its efficiency, but domestic service has received an equal increase of remuneration, as measured by the circulating medium. The reason of this is, that a rise in value in any branch of business necessarily pulls up all related branches with it. It is plain enough that if a new demand is made for the labor of women, all are invited to accept its tempting offers, and those who remain in their accustomed engagements must be made to find their account in it. There is also a less obvious influence always at work which tends to level up all the members of a class toward the condition of the most favored. Opinion has much to do in fixing values in all things, and whatever people generally believe they must have for their work, they must get, if the employers can afford it. Those who need the best service pay its higher price, and this becomes the standard of demand, and soon regulates the opinion and conscience of the pay-masters.

But there is another reason why the lowest rank in earnings should rise faster than those more advanced. The better part of any class of laborers always have received as high prices as the employer can, or thinks he can at the time afford, and the rise of these will just keep pace with the rise in worth of their work, while those who formerly could command nothing, nor make any terms with those who gave them employment, when changed conditions come, and they begin to be wanted, shoot up more rapidly in proportion to the greater distance they must rise. For this very reason we may look for a greater celerity of progress among the lately emancipated negroes of the South, than we can expect for the people who made an earlier start—where the capital is small, accretions of the same value are a much larger per cent of increase, than where a little is added to a greater amount. The addition of one to two makes an increase of fifty per cent, the addition of one to a hundred is but one per cent.

We are as nearly correct as the nature of the question admits of, in stating that the labor wages of artisans in the United States increased one hundred per cent in money value from the year 1814 to to 1860. We take the year 1814 for the first of the new era of manufacturing industry, because the power loom was first introduced at Waltham, Massachusetts, in that year, and steam began soon after to be generally applied in the various processes of production in the mechanic arts; and for the further reason that, from and after that year the remarkable fall of prices is noticed in the reports of British exports in all the manufactures of the United Kingdom; and we take the year 1860 for our latest date, in order to avoid the general disturbance of our home markets by the war of the Rebellion, and by the suspension of specie payments at the close of the following year. Whoever will look over the lists of current prices of the principal commodities for any period of twenty or thirty or forty years within the present century, will be convinced that there are many causes of fluctuation, casual and temporary, which disturb his estimates of permanent and normal changes, and render the figures commonly quoted by partisans of conflicting theories so liable to yield support to either side of any question for which they are appealed to for confirmation. The statistics, by skill or blunder in selection of dates and periods, may be manipulated so as to prove anything that the uncandid or the incapable may choose to demonstrate. Indeed, nothing but the most general and the most comprehensive views derived from the records deserve reliance. Periods worthy to be examined for instruction, or quoted for proofs, ought to be large enough to embrace all the changes which time and chance usually can considerably modify, in order that the fluctuations of rise and fall may be embraced in all their bearings upon the question at issue.

For instance: common English bar iron in England varied from £8 per ton in 1822 to £15 in 1825; from £5 10s. in 1832 to £10 15s. in 1836; from £4 10s. in 1843 to £10 in 1845; and, from £9 10s. in 1847 to £5 5s. in 1849. In such an up-and-down flutter as this, specialties run into contradictions, and deductions are confused and false. But such facts as these broader ones are not doubtful: in 1783 mineral coal was substituted for charcoal in the manufacture of bar iron, and in the following year the rolling mill was invented. Previously, for many years, the price of iron had been steady at from £17 to £18 per ton. In 1829 the hot blast was used, effecting a great saving in fuel, and the price went down to £7 10s. for the next six years; and a succession of improvements through the ensuing fifteen years marks the tendency downward by rates running as low as £7 5s. in the first half of the period, and an average of £6 in the closing year 1850.

Iron has been, perhaps, subject to greater and more rapid vicissitudes of price than any other article, for the reason that it was put under constantly increasing protective duties by the policy of England from 1787 (about the date of the great improvement in its manufacture) until 1826. A part of this period of near forty years, its most important forms were prohibited in terms, and the duty rising through the period to full fifty per cent upon the kinds admitted, was in effect quite as prohibitory. After safety from all foreign competition was secured its price was, and is to the present day, still more wildly variable under the policy of holding its foreign markets by gorging them at losing rates, and recovering the losses again by enormous changes in price, when, and as long as it could, hold them monopolized.

But all commodities are influenced more or less by the policy of the mercantile and manufacturing nations. Such manufactures as depend for their raw materials upon the seasons, as they variably affect the agricultural products used; and, again, by the effect of the seasons upon the food required by laborers; and, again, by wars, periods of mercantile speculation, and the condition of the currency—all these causes play upon prices, and vary them from the lowest possibilities of the producer, to the highest prices that the consumer can bear.

For all these reasons we would avoid the incertitude, as well as the imposture of the arithmetic of market statistics, by choosing our data from the broadest and safest groups of facts; and, while we do not refuse the assistance and the guidance of such records, carefully examined and interpreted, we resort with still more confidence to the clearer and truer experiences which get no record except in general observation.

We have said that women's wages have risen threefold in money price since 1814. It will be recollected that fifty years ago house service did not command more than sixty-two and a half cents per week, and rose in the average to at least $1.75 in 1860. To show the value of these prices, respectively, we submit the following statement of the market values, and the quantities of certain articles of clothing required, which these different amounts of wages would command:

```
Money Wages in 1814, 62½ cents.        Money Wages in 1860, $1.75.
1 yard of dimity   at  62½ cents................. 7 yards at 25 cents.
2    "    sheeting "   31¼  "    ................14   "  12½  "
2½   "    calico   "   25   "    ................14   "  12½  "
2½   "    shirting "   25   "    ................17½  "  10   "
```

Other articles of dress, if not equally, had at least very greatly fallen in the market. With the price of food and lodging she was not concerned, in any way, except as to quality, which, with other things, was constantly improving. In general terms, we will be sustained by the memories that cover the whole period of this great change, in saying that the hired women reached in these fifty years enjoyments that would have cost them at least six times the amount of their wages at the beginning of the period.

With respect to the advance in the real wages of men, it is to be remarked that the doubling of their remuneration gives them at least a fourfold command of all that part of their consumption which has undergone the improved methods of production. Fourfold is not enough to allow when we recollect that all the multiform productions of British industry have fallen sixty per cent, which increases the purchasing power of the same money two and a half times, and the wages being doubled, we have a fivefold purchasing power as to these items. Some other indispensable things he has now for nothing, and the best of them at rates that put even the lowest rank of self-supporting people on a level with the wealthiest of fifty years ago. He has these things in a free system of common schools; in the street accommodations of light, and police security; in travel and transportation, cheapened down to his means; in the newspapers, periodicals, and books which formerly only the wealthy class could well afford; in the accessibility of other means of instruction, refinement, and enjoyment, not forgetting the general respect and its advantages, which so great an improvement in personal conditions insures.

Thus much as a hint, for it falls very short of an array, of the benefits brought to every man by the joint achievements of labor, capital, skill, and science in the last half century.

The proportion of food to all necessaries other than house rent, is, of course, a variable quantity, but it is safe to say that under the normal rates of the period previous to 1860, it did not overpass the cost of these, and that such food as was used in 1814 was as costly then as the better supply of the later date. The groceries of tropical climates had greatly declined in price; so much so, that tea and coffee had come into universal use; sugar had fallen at least fifteen per cent; flesh meats increased, perhaps, twenty-five per cent; vegetables, generally; and flour fluctuating considerably, but hovering about the same rates at the beginning and end of the period. If this is correct as to food, that is, if the improved food cost no more in the aggregate than the inferior supply of fifty years ago, that portion of the wages which must be so applied, being doubled be-

LAW OF WAGES. 103

tween the dates assumed, was, in effect, reduced to one half the real expenditure, or allowed a double indulgence. Food in the consumption of the tolerably circumstanced artisan is not the half of his consumption of commodities; therefore, for more than half his wants he has a fivefold provision in his enhanced real wages, and in respect to food, twofold. These surpluses leave a very large margin beyond the increase of his house rent.

The calculation would stand thus: as against the purchasing power of wages in 1814, that of 1860 was, after reducing the other items equally to make up for the probable doubling of his rent—

$50 worth of food in 1814.............	$ 85 47	worth in 1860.
50 worth of other commodities in 1814...	114 53	" "
58 house rent in 1814.....	116 00	" "
$158 annual wages...................	$316 00	annual wages.

This division of the excess of the wages applied to food and other commodities is not given as the determinate distribution that would be made of it. The two classes (food and other commodities) are here put at equal sums—fifty dollars each in 1814, and probably the necessity of the case arising out of the limits of the fund would oblige as great an expenditure for food, at the expense of a severe economy in clothing and the like things, but the greater stock of wages, ($200 against $100), and the greatly less cost of textile fabrics and other manufactures in 1860 would allow $100 for food, and the other hundred, as it now purchases two and a half times the quantity afforded by $50 in 1814, would permit expenditure in this direction to be pushed to this limit in this class of commodities. The ratio of appropriation would be a matter of choice, or would be determined by circumstances. We are only concerned to show that the wages of 1860 provide a surplus of $100 over those of 1814. If this is clear, then, our point is made, that the supporting or purchasing power of wages doubled in forty-six years as to all things except house rent, and including house rent, increased in real value sixty-three and one-third per cent.

We have said that wages double in *money* price once in forty-seven years. But in real value, when surcharged with the increasing value of land, and of its rent, it will take fifty-five years to double, at the rate of change in prices of rent, of commodities and labor, during the last half century. All of which accords with the primary propositions :—wages are the index of productiveness, the former enhancing, by a law of the subjects, with the increase of the latter; and, the other general principle, that in progressive communities nothing can normally increase in value but land and labor.

It will be observed by those who have a turn for the figures of statistics, and especially by those who innocently imagine that arithmetic gives its own exactitude to the measure and meaning of the facts to which it is so applied, that we have spoken of the doubling of American money wages as requiring a period of forty-six years when estimating their purchasing power over commodities other than food and lodging in the years 1814 and 1860; and, that we extend the period to forty-seven years, when we estimate the period of duplication by the rate of their rise in the decade 1850–60.

We let these differences stand. It would be easy to force a compromise agreement, and deliver a definite and, perhaps, even a more exact result. The data are in their nature elastic enough to admit of equalization; but the inexpert would only be deceived into an undue confidence in the cipherings of political economy. It is impossible to decide whether 1813, 1814, 1818, or 1820 marks the effective beginning of the new era in manufacturing productiveness. Nothing so sudden ever takes place, all over the civilized world, as will fix the precise year when some grand epoch in discovery gets itself realized in business affairs. We have taken—as we must take, some definite date—the year 1814 for the point of departure for the reason that then the products of British industry commenced that permanent drift of cheapening which has since gone forward with great uniformity in spite of all disturbing influences, until the increase of converting skill and agencies have reduced the average price full sixty per cent. If the decided change began a little later in the United States, it has progressed proportionably faster in the whole compass of the period.

Further to clear up the data adopted, it should be seen that the average expenditure of artisans, fixed for the year 1814, is exposed to cross-questioning from various positions which critics may assume. One hundred and fifty-eight dollars wages per annum is an *average*, or is intended for an average, only; though based upon the official reports of the census-takers of the time; and, as an average, will accord with the observation or experience of very few individuals. The same things are true of the average three hundred and sixteen dollars for the year 1860. Yet objections, however well taken to the specific sums allowed, are nothing against the deductions drawn from them. Though they be wrong in amounts, they are very probably right in proportion to each other, and rectification of such amounts will not affect the percentage of increase, which is the thing required in this discussion.

The distribution of the wages among the classes of necessary expenditure is more embarrassing, and more important, in reaching the actual result. Food is much cheaper in some parts of the United States than in others, while manufactures are not materially different in price. The proportions of expenditure upon these classes of commodities must, therefore, vary accordingly; and this will affect the real value of wages. Again: even in the same place, and at the same prices, the circumstances and the taste of the laborers will induce a various relative proportion of expenditure upon them, and so produce a difference of surplus to meet the enhanced charge of rent.

Moreover, the sums or amounts of annual wages allowed for both periods are obviously too low, and this must be rectified to the cases before a just judgment can be formed. Nevertheless the point to be met remains unaffected—the positive increase of wages, and that they increase in the ratio of the general increase of the national wealth, but much more rapidly than the profits of capital employing labor in the manufacturing, mining and mechanic arts; and at various rates in other industries, with a tendency in all branches to a fair equality of dividend in the fruits of labor and capital combined. Under these modifications the proposition that wages are the index of productiveness, is made good.

CHAPTER IX.

MONEY AND ITS FUNCTIONS—AS AN EXCHANGER OF VALUES.

Money and its function as an exchanger of values: Production defined.—Nature's forces in the mastery of natural substances.—Instruments employed in effecting changes of form and place.—Transportation, difficulties, and cost of; social effects; improvement in proportion to increase of population and wealth.—Improvement in distribution of products; freight the impediment.—Transportation and conversion improve *pari passu.*—Drudgery and slavery.—Emancipation by machinery.—Freedom of exchange and freedom of man.—India enslaved by cost of freight.—Abridgment of transportation and elimination of middle-men.—Simple barter the type of a true commerce.—A common representative of values required to remove impediments.—Money, the medium of exchanges.—Kinds of money.—The precious metals; their befitting qualities.—Change of exchange value in long periods, but still the best security for creditors, although it lessens the value of debts.—Small coins.—Money as an agent of transportation.—Money not a standard of value; only a conventional standard of payment.—Why.—Great change of market value in long periods.—Estimates difficult.—Prices two centuries ago, and change of nominal value in coins.—Reduced value since the eleventh century, reduced cost of production in the period.—Exchange value of silver eighteen hundred years ago.—A common and permanent standard of values impossible.—The labor cost of precious metals not ascertainable; causes specially affecting cost of mining them.—Equivalence of value in the supply of money and totality of things in exchange, fallacious.—False analogy to paper money—the differences.—Excess of paper money explodes it as a currency.—No increase of coin lessens its exchange value.—Prices of other things decline under its increase—the reverse of its supposed effect.—The law of "supply and demand" at fault here.—Coin in exchange is payment; paper money only a promise to pay.—The one an existing real value; the other an anticipation of values.—Business alarms depreciate paper, but appreciate metallic money.—Value of coin fluctuates only under changes in cost of production.—Increase in Europe, in three centuries, thirtyfold.—Coinage in England before and after 1850—in the United States seven times greater.—No depreciation under so vast and rapid an increase.—Adam Smith's testimony.—Demand not fixed independently; relation to supply wanting.—Money not consumed; consumption of the things it buys quite immeasurable.—Outlets for its use.—Thousands of millions of commodities ready to absorb hundreds of millions of added money.—Cash payments in lieu of credit.—Not the value of money, but the credit system affected by its influx.—The use of money supplanted by other means of pay-

MONEY AS AN EXCHANGER OF VALUES.

ment.—Money of account.—Clearing houses pay by offset.—New York banks thus settle ninety-five per cent of their mutual claims.—Money only needed to pay profits.—Business in England done with less money, in inverse proportion to values in exchange.—Rapidity of circulation does not explain the fact.

THE power of man over matter is limited to change of form and change of place. Both these changes are necessary, in various degrees, and almost universally, in his use of the primitive substances which nature furnishes for his service. Change of form, including change of properties, and change of place, are both included in the word production. Ore or coal or lime delivered at the pit's mouth, are produced. The ore and coal and lime being put through the furnace, iron, by change of form, is produced. The iron transported to a distant market is there, by change of place, produced. By the change of form, utility is subserved; by the change of place, use is effected.

Production, whether in form or place, looks to exchange of values for all marketable commodities beyond the consumption of the producers. The whole life of man is a round of exchanges—between his body and the elements of subsistence—between the individual and his kind, in services moral, mental, and material, in their varied ministries.

Man compels nature into service, for the most part, by the use of power-multiplying instruments, thus employing the forces of nature in one form against her resistance in another. Mind is qualified for its proper sovereignty by its power of converting some of the natural agencies into *super*-natural forces, and all of them by ingenuity of application into controlling forces.

The instruments employed in effecting changes of form are such as ploughs, mills, furnaces, steam engines, and generally, all mechanical and chemical agencies of which he has the mastery. The instruments of transportation are such as horses, wagons, rail carriages, ships, currents of water, air, and electricity.

When these have performed their offices the producers are ready for exchanges of values, or, in more suggestive terms, exchange of services, as these are embodied in their commodities.

In the earlier and ruder stages of commerce the change of place is generally the greater part of the cost of production. Navigable waters abridge the expense of transportation, but inland or overland carriage absorbs nearly the whole prime value, or doubles the cost of the product. Improvement and extension of navigation in this state of trade makes princes of merchants, as in ancient Tyre, and in middle age Venice and Genoa, and producer and consumer are alike kept poor. Monopoly of transportation and of exchange have the same mischievous tendency in the most advanced states of society.

The natural process of improvement follows increase of population and wealth. The foot-path widens into a carriage road; then it is graded and paved, and finally, iron tramways diminish friction, and the locomotive engine replaces the six-horse team as it had supplanted the pack-horse. Now the transporter takes less and the producer gets more of the price given by the consumer for the articles produced at market. It must not be forgotten, however, that the cost of carriage ever remains so much dead loss to the prime producer, and an equivalent tax upon the consumer. Freight is the thing to be diminished, and, wherever it can be, entirely abolished, in the progressive improvement of necessary exchanges.

There is a corresponding progress to be effected in the work of changing the *forms* of things for use, and these two changes are found going forward in a near approach to equal measure. In the savage state the quantity of labor required to convert grain into bread is very great—it means drudgery and enslavement. The stone pestle and mortar must give way to the flouring mill; the hand-wheel and loom to the spinning-jenny and power-loom, and at last, hammers, saws, and files to steam-driven rollers, lathes, saws, and chisels. Labor must be saved in manufacturing and forwarding—in change of form and of place. Capital accumulated must work for those who have worked for it. The reluctant natural agents must be yoked to machinery in production, in relief of toil and in the elevation of labor in uses and benefits. Society must be organized; its members must be so related in industry and in commerce, that all impediments to the freest, cheapest, directest possible exchange of services may be removed.

The poverty of India, once the leading manufacturing people of the earth, is explained by the fact that the policy of British rule forces its people to send their cotton wool five thousand miles direct, or more than twice as far by the Cape of Good Hope to find the spindle, and to bring the cloth all the way back again, for such market as it may find at Bombay, Calcutta, or Delhi, at the foot of the Himalaya Mountains.

The gains of a close neighborhood of the prime producer and consumer are larger, greatly larger, than those to be expected from the greatest possible improvement of roads and conveyances; for closeness, *pro tanto*, abolishes transportation and eliminates the middle-man, and with him, his frauds and profits. It is best even in the rude stage of commerce in which services are exchanged through their representative commodities, without the intervention of the merchant class.

This simple barter is the type of a true commerce, for it is the very thing to be attained; and the best method of effecting such exchange is the aim, and remains the hope of the highest civilization.

The natural hindrance to this, the purest and best form of exchange, is that, the man who has blankets to spare may not want the venison or furs which the hunter must buy them with; and so of the miller, the blacksmith, tailor, doctor, lawyer, and preacher. They cannot take exactly the thing, or the exact quantity of the thing, which the customer has to give in exchange. Somebody else, however, wants the venison or furs, which the hunter offers for the cloth, cutlery, or other commodity or service, required; and if all the producers could be brought together, in fact, as at a fair, or in effect, by some other means, more frequently and conveniently, the needed exchanges could be made to the mutual advantage of all the parties. If some representative of values, and of all values, capable of fitting itself in amount to all desired exchanges, and always, and for all purposes, commanding them, the legitimate ends of commerce would be accomplished by such an instrument, and it would be an instrument of association as well as of barter.

This predicament instantly suggests the familiar medium which we call MONEY—money in all the senses in which the word is employed—coined metals; representative paper money; money of account, or credit money of all kinds, answering the purpose, and each in turn better than the other, in circumstances specially adapted to its use.

The necessity of such a representative of values in the business of exchange is shown by the fact that the North American Indians adopted beads, made of small and variously-colored shells; Africans and East Indians still use shells, called cowries; the ancient Romans employed cattle, and bars of copper, and the Spartans, iron. All these were money, as real as the precious metals in use elsewhere;

for they passed at their labor cost and commanded all other commodities in exchange in the communities using them as a circulation. They were just as much a measure of values, and perhaps not less constant in their own exchange value.

The necessity for some common medium of exchange is obvious. That its service, and its influence upon society is not confined to its convenience in barter we shall see as we advance. For the present we stop to consider the eminent fitness of the precious metals to supply the requirements of commerce in the range of exchanges to which they are adapted.

1st. Their scarcity and high cost of production has the effect of compacting large value in a small compass and light weight, compared with other substances anywise adapted to such use. Precious stones greatly excel them in these qualities, but in others are altogether unfit for currency. Gold and silver have also capabilities of storage and concealment which are great advantages added to their portableness.

2d. They have a certain approach to constancy of value, for their cost of production does not vary very much during the periods that private contracts for payment usually run. In long leases, carrying a money rent, and in national funds, particularly such as the English consols, standing for nearly two centuries, the pound sterling loses very largely its original correspondence to a fixed weight of pure gold or silver; but this objection is relieved by two good considerations: the value of all other commodities of the market diminish much more rapidly; and, national debts and long-lease rents and annuities have no equitable claim to an invariable exchange value more than other things. Society cannot be asked to insure a permanency of value for debts that does not and cannot attach to any other property. As coin grows cheaper the burden of debt grows lighter, which is so far a remedy for the evil to the debtor, and is no injustice in the workings of Providence upon the interests of the creditor, who, in such case, and so far as he is a creditor, is simply a sleeping partner in the world's business; and, as he supplies none of its current industry, and takes none of its risks, or of the risks of any other form of capital invested, he cannot expect to be provided or cared for by the system which governs the business of the working generations of men. Moreover, the change in the value of any other medium of payment, except land and labor, would be incalculably greater.

3d. The precious metals are, in a certain sense, indestructible, losing nothing by rust or other waste, except wear, from which they are sufficiently well defended by alloys of more durable metals.

4th. Their divisibility into very small portions, and their capability of reunion or restoration to larger bulks and values without loss, rank among the best of their intrinsic qualities. This point is made very clear when small coins are withdrawn from circulation by a suspension of specie payments. The lack of one, two, five and ten-cent pieces is a greater inconvenience than the absence of ten-dollar pieces or ten-dollar notes, or any large denominations of current money. Bankers' checks or drafts would answer for the payment of large sums, but there is no acceptable substitute for small money in daily and hourly purchases by the great mass of the people.

For a three-cent piece we obtain a required share of the service of thousands of people who build, equip, and run our railroads, in the carriage of our letters; and for a less piece or sum we have a fraction of the labor of the hundreds that produce the daily newspaper—these infinitesimal portions of the great agent, spread by minute division and "they operate unspent."

5th. These metals acting as money, may very well be classed among the instruments of exchange, with wagons, rail-cars, and ships, for they in effect transfer the property in things, and thus bring the things themselves to the consumer to an extent that dispenses with the transportation of manifold the quantity of the things which otherwise must be carried from place to place. The man who has wheat to give for iron, need not send it to the forge and bring the iron back, he can convert it into money and buy his iron at the nearest store; and so of a thousand other things, for which the whole circuit of travel and transportation would have to be traversed for the supply of a hundred wants a day, but for the service of this greatest of all exchangers.

6th. By virtue of their intrinsic value they pay, not promise to pay, all international balances of trade.

7th. They are capable of receiving and retaining such stamps, engravings, and impressions as readily and truly certify their value at sight, without chemical tests or incessant weighing. Something of their real value is in these qualities, just as paper in quires and reams, cloth in pieces of determinate length, and flour in barrels of settled weight, are worth more than without the forms of packages and ascertained quantities; provided, always, that governments honestly fix the legal quality and quantity at their real value.

All experience proves that no other substance, having in itself equivalence of value, possesses at the same time so many qualities of a good medium of exchange for universal circulation, as are found in gold and silver. It is to be noted, however, that the precious metals, in any condition, whether estimated by weight or accepted at legal-tender value, are not, in a strict sense, either a permanent standard or measure of the value of other things. They are only a conventional standard of payment. At fixed rates they cannot measure the natural price of commodities whose labor cost is varying every day; and they are not any truer equivalents of long postponed payments of debt. Such standard or measure they cannot be, so long as their own cost of production is changeable. They have not the measure permanency of the yard-stick or pound-weight, which are measures and standards, simply because they do not themselves enter into the act of exchange—the pound-weight does not pass to the purchaser of the commodity which it measures, but gold and silver are the things exchanged for the things whose value they are at the same time used to measure. In considerable periods of time their value varies so greatly that the reduction is one of the most difficult undertakings of accountants and historians. Writers usually put the intrinsic value of these metals, as measured by their purchasing power, in the reign of Henry the Eighth of England, or about three centuries ago (A. D. 1509–1547) at twelve times greater than now. But for want of a standard to measure the intrinsic value or labor cost of the metals themselves, there is no proof of any tolerable exactness in the estimates that are made, even by the most capable persons, of the change of value of an ounce of gold or silver after the lapse of centuries. And, if it is difficult for long periods, the rate of the process from day to day or year to year is no less so, though of less moment.

The price of horses in England in the year 1696 Mr. Macaulay puts at fifty shillings. The pound of silver was at that time coined into sixty-two shillings, now into sixty-six shillings, so that fifty shillings then contained within a fraction of as much silver of the same fineness as fifty-three and one-quarter shillings now, which gives us the average price of horses in England one hundred and seventy-four years ago as the equivalent of $12.92 in American gold in 1870. The horses of that day, however, were not really worth, and would not be worth more than half the price of English horses now, if so much. This estimate would put the comparative average value of horses now in England at but little more than twenty-five dollars in the money of 1696.

If the change be pursued still further back, we find that in the year 1066 the Tower pound of silver was coined into twenty shillings, equal to eighteen and three-quarter shillings of the Troy pound adopted in 1527, and, that thereafter the same quantity, or Troy pound, underwent the following striking changes: In 1527, forty shillings; in 1553, sixty shillings; in 1600, sixty-two shillings; in 1816, sixty-six shillings. Here we have the legal tender and exchange value of silver increased to more than double in five centuries, and three and a half times in eight centuries; the real value, or the labor cost of production, declining, if not regularly through the whole period, at least very greatly in those eight hundred years, and still more and more rapidly within the last twenty years.

Going still farther back into the past, a still greater change in the money value of silver may be safely inferred. The Disciples estimated the value of bread that would suffice for one meal for five thousand hungry people in the wilderness of Judea, eighteen hundred years ago, at two hundred pence (Mark vi., 37). The Roman penny, then and there in circulation, was equal in quantity of silver to seven and a half pence sterling now, or about fifteen cents of American money. Two hundred pence were therefore equal to thirty dollars. This is an allowance of just three-fifths of one cent for the bread of each person. It would probably cost thirty cents a head to supply such hungry men now. If so, money has only one-fiftieth of its purchasing power after the lapse of eighteen centuries. But there are no means of calculating the relative commercial value of gold and silver at any distances of time, either long or short, because in the intervals *all* other values are undergoing changes which are at once fluctuating and incapable of measure. The attempt is like measuring a flying cloud on a windy day with an elastic string; yet, one can be sure without such a *standard*, that the day is more cloudy than a clear one.

The general fact is indisputable that silver and gold have grown several times cheaper intrinsically than they were before the discovery of America by Columbus; and it is clear that they must have cheapened materially since the mines of California and Australia were opened—not because of their greater abundance in use, but from the reduced labor cost of their production. Yet this fact does not even help to determine their purchasing power now, as compared with three hundred years ago; because, in all that period, land and labor have been enhancing in value faster as measured by them, than the metals have been declining in cost of production; and manufactures have been at the same time cheapening certainly very much faster than they possibly could, for they are not equally under the power of cheapening processes of production with the commodities made of the useful minerals and of the raw materials of textile fabrics.

As we insist that what we call the labor cost of these metals settles their commercial value, might an estimate be made with approximate results from such data as the business of production affords? Here again great difficulties, and equally great uncertainties are encountered. Gold and silver mining is now marked by all the characters of gambling, except its fraudulent intention. It is in the main a desperate game. The risks of loss and the hopes of gain engender a recklessness that belongs not so much to an industry as to a speculation, dependent upon the incalculable changes of fortune. Success in discovery and yield must compensate for the labor in vain which so often goes before, and is always likely to follow. The expense of machinery and water-supply, the varying cost of provisions, and the capriciousness of the workmen under the constant seductions of better luck in promise, and other influences, in character with the wild speculative spirit of the enterprise, altogether put calculation at defiance. Such is the unsteadiness of the whole business that no one can calculate upon compensation or profits except the brokers in the Pacific coast cities and metropolitan money markets of the Atlantic coasts in Europe and America. The labor cost of this intractable subject is as difficult as its exchange value in the ever varying markets in which it plays the go-between of protean-priced commodities.

There is yet another way of vaguely estimating or imagining the value of the precious metals. This is by the supposed effect of their changes of quantity in use. This idea rests upon an assumed

MONEY AS AN EXCHANGER OF VALUES. 115

equivalence of the money in circulation to the whole value of the commodities in exchange; an assumption utterly unwarranted, as we shall presently see. The doctrine, or notion, that an increase of quantity must diminish value in these metals, helps itself to something mistaken for proof, in a supposed analogy to the workings of paper money. It is not questioned that paper money is cheapened by its abundance and depreciated by its excess. But if this were so, and the measure were accurate, there is this grand difference between the two currencies: the value of paper money bears reference to its redeemability, or convertibility into coin. Gold and silver have no such dependency. They are not in the category of credit. They are not convertible or redeemable in any other value upon which their own depends. We have had several experiences of excess of paper money in the United States, and it appears that, whenever its circulation exceeded the steady-going amount as much as twenty-five per cent, an explosion resulted. Now we need not say that any supposable increase in metallic money would not utterly destroy its value as money, and we may very properly and pertinently point to the fact that the whole increase of coin money between the years 1850 and 1860, which could not be less than double the amount in use at the beginning of the period, did not put up the aggregate market price of the whole range of commodities in our markets. On the contrary, the price of thirty out of sixty articles reported in New York, *declined* through a range of principal items in the list, from forty-four to twelve per cent in the five years 1855-60, when the gold influx was at the highest. The quantity of gold so greatly increased, helped, besides, by an increase of thirty-three per cent of paper circulation in the ten years 1850-60, had not the effect of depreciating the exchange value of either, and especially of the coin circulation. Whatever force there is in the law of "demand and supply" it manifestly had no application to the money conditions of this remarkable period, which can help us to measure the effect of quantity of money upon either its intrinsic or exchange value.

The argument, borrowed from the history of paper money, we must insist, has no proper application to the operations of a coin circulation in the respect now under consideration. The difference lies in these particulars: circulating notes have not any intrinsic value (beyond the cost of their production, and that only while they answer their designed use). They are merely pledges of credit—the credit of governments, or banks, and of the borrowers from them, and being, to a very great extent, mere anticipations of values not yet realized, the holders under such uncertainties of security, and especially in periods of alarm, will push off such notes for anything better secured; they will realize by investing in property more secure, willingly paying the premium of such insurance; that is, they will give higher prices for safer property, and so, paper money depreciates. Specie never depreciates for such cause. Its abundance never touches its solvency, and we must look elsewhere for the fluctuations in its value. Only one cause remains, and that has the great strength in this argument that it is the sole cause of value of all industrial productions that are exchanged among men—the cost of its production; that is, of its reproduction at the time when its value is the question. If it were as easily obtained as water, its market, or exchange value, would be only the cost of transportation from the rivers to the consumer, or the cost of sinking and working the wells, and of conveyance when it must be found beneath the service. When it is found as abundant as iron, and as easily produced in condition for use, it will be as cheap by the ton, whether it be more or less fit for like purposes.

Some idea of the increase of metallic money in circulation in Europe may be had from Humboldt's estimate, which is accepted by experts as approximately correct. He puts it at more than thirty times the quantity in the eighteenth century over that of the fifteenth. This period of three hundred years covers the comparatively vast addition derived from the American mines, which followed the discovery of the New World. The rate of increase upon the previous supplies within the present century, may be guessed at by the coinage before and since California and Australia have been opened. The British mint, in the fifteen years 1816–30, coined gold and silver to the value of fifty-five and three-fourths millions of pounds sterling. In the fifteen years, 1851–65, to the amount of ninety-six millions of pounds. Taking later and fairer periods for contrast in the United States—the mint and branches coined one hundred and six and a half millions of dollars in the fifteen years 1825–49; and in the fifteen years 1851–65, seven hundred and forty-nine millions.

It is known that such multiplication of the amount in use as these figures show has not yet depreciated the exchange value of money made of these metals. So we say again that whatever force the law of supply and demand may be allowed, it helps nothing in determining either the intrinsic value or purchasing power, or, so to speak, the market price of the precious metals in use, as they have operated in past or present times. Nearly a hundred years ago, when the matter was as well in view, and the facts of experience as strong to the point, as now, Adam Smith said that the importation of one hundred and twenty to one hundred and forty millions of francs per annum for more than a century, with all the substitutes for metallic money added in that time, had not depreciated the exchange value of the precious metals in Europe.

The source of error in the customary reasoning on this subject lies in fixing or finding a standard of supply, and making no allowance for the variance of demand which such supply induces. Even if the limit of consumption or use were ascertained, or ascertainable, or imaginable, the application of the law to money would be a mistake. A community cannot consume more than a certain quantity of food, but who can fix a limit for the use or consumption of newspapers, furniture, clothing, or of vehicles for travel and transportation? And how can a gauge be invented for the use of money? As concerns the present and probable supply of the precious metals, the possible requirement is the subject of such conditions as these :—

The wealth of Great Britain is growing at the rate of a thousand millions of dollars a year; France and the United States, together, twice as much, without embracing the rest of the continents of Europe and America. These three thousand millions of added property in their markets can easily make room for an addition of two or three hundred millions a year without altering prices, or producing a relative depreciation of a farthing in the hundred pounds worth. Nay, they may employ, besides, double their ordinary amount of bank paper, keeping it sound the while, and by adopting cash payments in lieu of the usual run of credits for sixty, ninety, or one hundred and twenty days, or for six months or a year, such increase of circulation would be all "demanded" and the medium would not depreciate, whether metallic, or paper, or mixed. Furnish the money in any increase of quantity that the market will absorb and, not its value, but the credit system among buyers and sellers will be proportionately affected.

But a metallic money and its representative, convertible circulating paper money, together are not the only mediums of payment in use. There are other agencies working in their stead, and toward their exclusion from this office and service, which greatly affects their supply, and their sufficiency relatively to the requirement or "demand" in the business of exchange. This is money of account in ledgers, checks, drafts, bills of exchange, negotiable notes of hand, or, in whatever form private and bank debts and claims are evidenced. These, to a great extent are settled without the use of anything that is called money or circulation. Clearing houses strictly so called, in the principal cities, and banks of discount and deposit everywhere, perform this office—they settle debts and claims by the process that in law is called set-off. During a year ending in October, 1869, the banks of New York settled mutual claims of debtor and creditor, occurring among themselves, which amounted to one hundred and twenty-five millions dollars per day; the balances paid on these transactions averaging about four per cent, seldom rising to five per cent of the whole amount of the claims so adjusted by set-off. In other words, they paid to each other about one hundred and twenty millions every day without using a dollar of money of any kind, other than this money of account expressed in drafts, checks, and bills.

Country banks do exactly the same thing for their customers which the banks of the cities do for each other—they balance debts against each other by charges and credits on their books, and to the extent of such balances, no *money* of coin or bank notes, whatever, is paid by or to any body. Wherever business is well organized all credits may be liquidated without the use of more money than the profits of business which may vary from five to ten or fifteen per cent, and for the amount of such profits only can any one need money of any kind where any form of the clearing house agency is employed. Accordingly currency is in greater demand, relatively to the business done, where no such set-off system is available, and, where it is employed money is proportionately eliminated.

By virtue of this agency of the clearing house in England, the necessity for money of any kind is diminishing relatively to the amount of business transacted. For example and proof: the ex-

MONEY AS AN EXCHANGER OF VALUES.   119

ports of British and Irish products, in the year 1840, were valued at fifty-one and a half millions of pounds; the note circulation of the United Kingdom in that year was thirty-six and a half millions of pounds. In 1865, the like exports amounted to one hundred and sixty-six millions, and the note circulation stood at thirty-seven and a half millions. Taking the exports of 1865 to indicate the general increase of business, and the necessarily equal increase of some or all the methods of payment, we find this result: the business of the Kingdom increased in these fifteen years two hundred and twenty-four per cent; the circulation only two and three-quarters per cent. Evidently the service of money in exchanging values, is totally misunderstood when its quantity is supposed to be the equivalent of the values exchanged. People confuse themselves with the fact that the same piece of money may be used in a dozen, a hundred, or a thousand payments in the year. But here the same, or within a fraction of the same amount of money served the business of producing and purchasing more than three times the quantity of goods after a lapse of twenty-five years. Did it circulate more than three times faster? The goods bought and sold with money, change ownership, or circulate just as often and as fast. A dollar's worth of goods passes with every dollar paid for them, and one dollar cannot do the exchange work of three in cash sales. But we will understand the subject more clearly, when we shall have ascertained and considered those other functions of money which are not seen in its simple office of exchanger of commodities in market.

CHAPTER X.

MONEY—A PRODUCER WHILE ACTING AS AN EXCHANGER OF VALUES.

Money—a producer, while acting as an exchanger of values :—How money stimulates production.—It is not dead capital.—Money in civilized labor—the *primum mobile* of industry.—Production proportioned to capital employed.—Productiveness not in arithmetical, but in geometrical proportion to the money impulse.—Error, vulgar and scientific, of the equivalence of value of circulating money to the things exchanged in commerce.—Hume.—Mill.—Money the pendulum of prices, Mill's formula, contradicted by obvious facts.—Not one dollar of money in any country to sixteen or twenty in value of commercial exchanges. Increase of circulation does not *pro tanto* increase prices.—In nothing else do gluts and deficiencies affect prices in simple arithmetical proportions.—Prices of wheat in excess and deficiency of supply.—Ratio of money to prices in sixteenth, seventeenth, and eighteenth centuries, by Arthur Young.—In the nineteenth century prices have fallen as money increased in quantity—in England, sixty per cent in thirty years—in New York, in a range of from forty-four to twelve per cent in five years, under an increase of the currency of twenty-two per cent.—Land and Labor have risen by increase of their intrinsic worth.—Prices of manufactures fall—food remains stationary, because the vital laws are less understood than the mechanical.—Land and Labor rise, and their products fall in price.—What is meant by land—what by labor.—Without capital, land, labor, and people worthless.—Sparseness and poverty of savage populations.—Causes of Indian extinction.—Without property in the land, no labor; without labor, land worthless.—Nature subdued through her own agencies, man and land enriched.—Renovation of the earth conditioned upon obedience to the Creator's laws.—Money embodies all forms of capital, and is efficient in proportion to its amount and movement.—It employs wasting labor, and raises prices of commodities and wages to par, but never higher.—Afterwards reduces prices by increased production.—Par value of money defined.—The assumptions of Mill's theory are impossibilities.—Money of account—its equivalence to values exchanged precise, because it is itself their ideal measure.—Results of the argument.—The supply of money and labor always hitherto short of the service required from them.—All increase of both beneficial, except in its effects upon creditors.—These effects, nevertheless, not inequitable.—Debt-holders have no right to a perpetual release from the labor of self-support.—Effect of lessened cost of their production upon the precious metals.—Their use till they have performed their uses.—How they widen their sphere of use till their service is fulfilled.

MONEY AS A PRODUCER OF VALUES.

"In every Kingdom into which money begins to flow in greater abundance than formerly," says David Hume, "everything takes a new face; labor and industry gain life; the merchant becomes more enterprising, the manufacturer more diligent and skillful, and the farmer follows the plough with more alacrity and attention." This statement is true, and the reasons for it are especially worthy of attention. We must understand why money is such a stimulant of industrial production and of activity in trade. Labor is capital, unless the cause is lost in the effect. Labor power is the result of the consumption of other capital in the form of food, clothing, and other means of support and development. But labor power, like that generated in steam, perishes instantly upon coming into existence. If not instantly employed it is lost. Money is in the same predicament. Its productiveness is in its activity—it must yield interest or profit, and it must be made to yield profit in order to pay interest. "Time is money" to money itself, as it is to labor. It solicits employment, and prompts, while it aids, industry. It is a motor power to labor of all kinds; heads and hands, men and things are put to use, that otherwise must remain idle, and while idle, useless and wasting, though life and its necessities go on with their demands through poverty to destitution.

The conditions of human life are such that its indispensable supplies, comforts, and luxuries must be drawn by perpetual new creations from the elements of the earth. Labor, in its largest sense, is the cost of these supplies. Among civilized men in advancing conditions these necessities are ever increasing in extent and variety. Civilization is progress, and progress means growing control of material things, and this, again, means a growing demand for them. Money stimulates, promotes, and assists the production that meets the enlarging wants, and is far from being passive in its use—a sign, a counter, or a mere measure of the values of other things.

Capital in the form of money, or credit representing money, is the yoke-fellow, the coöperator of labor in all production in advancing stages and conditions of society. Men cannot work without implements; they cannot work profitably or availably without all sorts of machinery; and they cannot work at all without current subsistence. They cannot wait a day for the conversion of their special products into the clothes they must wear, and the food they must eat. And above all, they cannot wait, without loss and suffering, for the labor by which they live. Capital is thus the prime condition with labor, just as labor is the first consideration with capital. Married they are, for better or worse, in mutual and equal dependence; and on that marriage depends their issue for its existence, quantity, and quality. A certain amount of coin or credit money is indispensable to adequate production. It may, indeed, be called the *primum mobile*—the first cause of motion in all civilized industries; for here, as in the Ptolemaic system of the planetary circulation, it is the outermost revolving sphere which gives motion to all the rest.

Money (coin and credit) is the power which puts all the wheels of the great machine of business into motion, and, accordingly, their velocity and force correspond to the force of the propelling current, or to the force of the currency. Hume states the effect of an abundance in general terms sufficiently descriptive; but it should be understood that the measure of increased activity in business is not an arithmetical ratio, or a dollar's worth of increased effect for every dollar added to the sum of the force. The proportion of increase in the motor power is not a dead numeral multiplier. It is an impulse generating force by its own action, and producing a movement best described as accelerated velocity. To this character or quality of its law of increase corresponds the action of its deficiency, which, with constantly and rapidly growing effect at every stage, tends to fall below the power of moving the machinery at all; the stand-still being anticipated long before the supply is totally expended. Nothing is so sensitive to prospective changes as money capital. The apprehension of diminished exchange value puts it to unwonted activity of productive effort. It quickens its movement just as its use cheapens, until at last it goes begging for work. On the other hand, under the prospect of a rise in its exchange value, it tightens its outgoings; its interest rises; debtors, to escape bankruptcy, and non-capitalists, who cannot afford to be idle, must have it at whatever sacrifice they can bear; and accordingly its rate of hire, and its purchasing power, rise relatively to all other capital, including labor, in far more than the arithmetical ratio of its own scarcity.

This is all so plain that no argument is required to establish its abstract truth; but we want the force of this truth for most important and greatly-needed uses in considering the functions and

MONEY AS A PRODUCER OF VALUES. 123

influence of money at large. Just here we have to meet a prevalent error of the unskilled, backed by the authority of a school of economists, who hold the popular ear by the easy terms of furnishing logical formulæ for the verification of acceptable notions.

Money is a mystery—enough so in itself, but all the more that the mystery is muddied with a parcel of aphorisms which are allowed to obstruct the light that might clear up some of the fundamental principles of its true theory.

For instance, it is currently held that the amount of money in circulation represents the value of all property in exchange; that, no matter whether the quantity be great or small, it is equally, and in all cases, the measure of prices. Hume made this mischievous blunder seventy years ago, and J. Stuart Mill repeats it in the last edition of his "Political Economy." He says, "the doubling of the money in use would do no good to any one; would make no difference except having to reckon pounds, shillings and pence in greater numbers. It would be an increase of values only as estimated in money, a thing only wanted to buy other things with; and would not enable any one to buy more of them than before." And he goes on to say, "this ratio would be precisely that in which the quantity of money had been increased. If the whole money in circulation was doubled, prices would be doubled. If it was only increased one-fourth, prices would rise one-fourth."

How like clock-work this thing is calculated; and with what confidence the notion is delivered! Thus, if the pendulum beats two strokes for one in the second, the hands will traverse the dial-plate twice as often in twelve hours as they do, but they would measure only the same length of time. But, is money the pendulum of prices, and are its scarcity and its abundance measured by arithmetical multipliers and divisors on the price-current dial-plate of the market? Or, is the whole thing an assumption—a bundle of assumptions, having nothing to recommend it but the arithmetical symmetry of its dogmatic statement?

In the first place, the money of no country in the world is either equal, or bears any constant proportion to the total values in that country's markets. The gold, silver, and bank paper of the United States never, before the great Rebellion, reached beyond four hundred millions of dollars. Nay, if the inactive specie be subtracted, three hundred millions was the extreme limit of the money in use.

But, the annual products of industry were at least worth four thousand millions, of which if but three-fourths were bought and sold, and another thousand millions worth of real estate went into market, and still another thousand millions were paid for all professional, educational, and artistic services, we have five thousand millions to be paid and received, by means of three hundred millions, or by one dollar of money for every sixteen and two-thirds of values only once exchanged!

Now, if one to sixteen expressed the proportion in 1860, at some given day in that year, would an addition of a hundred millions of currency, made the next day, being one-third of the sum existing the day before, put up all prices thirty-three and one-third per cent? or, would it certainly enhance by so much the price of any commodity whatever, by its own proper operation, that is, by the effect of such addition?

The radical error of this doctrine is in the assumed fixed equivalence of the money in circulation to the commodities in exchange, and it becomes all the more strikingly palpable as it is applied to varying quantities. There is no such ratio of effect in the excess or deficiency of any other thing, as is here assumed by the alleged principle, and expressed in the detailed statement. Gluts do not proceed in cheapening, nor deficiencies in enhancing, market values in arithmetical proportions. Ten per cent deficiency in wheat will enhance its price thirty per cent; the supply being reduced to one-half, the price will go up to a four hundred and fifty per cent increase. Mr. Mill is himself aware of this fact, and formally states and affirms it elsewhere. The like variance of price with difference of supply happens when the market is overstocked—the decline in price of that which is anxiously seeking purchasers, is not measured evenly by the percentage of surplus.

The proposition which affirms a constant equivalence of money with the market values of other things, is answered in its own terms, thus: Arthur Young estimates the increase of money in the sixteenth, over the amount in the fifteenth century, at two hundred and eighty-two per cent, and of general prices in the same time at forty-two per cent; in the seventeenth century at seven hundred and seventy-five per cent of money, and ninety-six per cent of prices; and in the eighteenth over the fifteenth century at one thousand and nineteen per cent of money to one hundred and ninety-two per cent of prices. Here we have money increased faster than prices rose six and three-quarters times in the sixteenth, eight times in the seventeenth, and five and one-third in the eighteenth century.

Since the epoch of modern improvement in industrial production we find that prices fall, and fall immensely in the face of a vast increase of the money supply, just as on our theory they should fall in inverse proportion to the force of the great agent affecting them. Take, for example, the thirty years between 1817 and 1848: in this time England retained for use an average of ten millions of dollars per annum of the precious metals which she imported; in the whole period, adding three hundred millions to her stock. Did prices go up in proportion? Were her traders put to counting pounds, shillings, and pence in greater numbers for the same quantity of goods? On the contrary, the prices of all the multiform products that enter into the British exports fell sixty per cent, fell from a dollar to two-fifths of the dollar! In the presence of this three hundred millions of increase in the precious metals, the exports, which at the prices of 1817 would have cost three thousand two hundred millions, were valued at only one thousand two hundred and eighty millions in 1848.

The notion tried again at a later period and nearer home—in the United States: the bank notes in circulation and the bank deposits, which also perform the functions of credit money, together amounted to three hundred and seventy-seven millions of dollars in the year 1855, and in 1860 they had risen to four hundred and sixty millions —twenty-two per cent. Were market prices twenty-two per cent higher on this account? As before stated, thirty of the sixty principal articles on the price-lists of New York had in those five years actually fallen some forty-four per cent, others twelve per cent, and others more or less between these rates. On the other articles, the changes were too slight to have any bearing upon the point at issue, and they were, besides, generally such articles of foreign supply as would be affected by many other causes.

The history of prices in England of manufactured goods such as she exports, under the influence of a doubled quantity of gold and silver in the country ought of itself to be conclusive.

With respect to labor, it is admitted that its wages rise as money increases; not, however, because more pieces of an aggregate equal value must be counted as the equivalent of an equal amount of work, but because the money added to the employing capital increases the productiveness, and with it the rewards of the laborer. In the like circumstances, land also appreciates, but not more than the real increase of its productiveness made by the industry of the period— by improvement in cultivation and convenience of market; both being effected by the employment of increased capital and labor. The general statement is, that, under an influx of money, the prices of all the commodities commonly called manufactures fall rapidly and greatly. Food remains nearly stationary, with a natural tendency to fall in price, but is subject to a slower and less certain reduction, for the reason that its production depends upon the laws of vegetable physiology in which but little advance of knowledge is yet made; while those laws which are concerned in the arts of conversion, generally having dead matter for their subjects, are more and more mastered day by day; leaving land and wages as the only things that naturally enhance in value under the stimulus of capital applied in their employment and development.

Have we fallen upon a paradox here? Meaning, by a paradox, a proposition seemingly absurd or self-contradictory, but true in fact. Probably. And this apprehension warrants an attempt at a fuller exposition of the principles and facts involved. We take the ground that land and labor, and only land and labor, can and must enhance in value under the appliances of capital in their employment, and, that their products, in forms of use, must as continually decline in value. Baldly stated : land increasing in value lowers the cost of its products; wages growing in cost, their products decline in price; always supposing that both the one and the other are intrinsically improved by the aid of capital. By land, we mean all primitive substances belonging to the material globe—timber, water, soil, minerals, and the like, with all their spontaneous products; by labor, the muscular power of man, the intelligence which directs it, and the moral qualities which contribute to its efficiency.

Now let us see how the argument runs:

The gold of the Rocky Mountains was as useless as their iron ores or their fossil coal, or the latent electricity of the earth and air to the savage Indians; and the Indians were as worthless to the world and to themselves, just because their land was as nearly good for nothing as they were. Land and labor are bound together for good or ill. The soil, indeed, gave them a little maize, the waters a few fishes, and the forests fire-wood, wild fruits, and game ; but the brute elements and spontaneous food starvingly maintained a declining human stock, tending constantly to extinction. The richer soils of the Mississippi valley and of the Atlantic slope did scarcely better for them. In all that region which now supports eight millions of people, reaching from Connecticut to Lake Erie, and from the chain of the Lakes to the Potomac river, Colonel Parker, the best authority we have on the subject, says, there were not more than twenty-five thousand Indians when Columbus discovered the Continent. The maize culture was deficient ; the wild herds failed them ; they had no commerce, either in furs or manufactures ; and famines, diseases, and the wars of hungry rapacity were rapidly destroying them. Earth and man worthless to each other ; poverty, sterility, despair and death, described them both. Making no accumulations of the means of subsistence, they had no capital. Having no capital, they had not the indispensable agent for the subjugation of nature's forces to their service.

In this state of things there was nothing in land worth claiming in individual ownership, except for temporary occupation, and the fee simple of the territories was not worth more to the tribes collectively than the powder, blankets, and glass beads for which they sold it ; nor was the whisky, which acted so largely in the extinction of their title, much more insalubrious than the untamed forces of nature to which they were exposed.

But change the scene—the coal becomes fuel, the fuel becomes power. A ton of it does the work of fifteen hundred men for one day ; three hundred tons are equal to their work for a year. The capable soil, the power of the running streams, the mines, with all else which the earth holds for human use are all utilized, and the desert becomes the property and the home of millions of men. The thorns and thistles of the primal curse are displaced, and the soil, baptized in the sweat of the face of labor, brings forth bread in abundance, and, behold, it is once more " very good," even as when the approving smile fell upon the first garden. The recreated in its degree, approaches the new created earth. The original conditions of human sovereignty are observed ; the command is fulfilled—" Be fruitful, and multiply, and replenish the earth, and *subdue* it." How striking the mutuality subsisting between land and labor, with this appropriate advantage that the human agent is much more improved than the material things joined with, and subject to his advancement. The earth has physical and vital properties for his service; man has these and moral, intellectual, and religious endowments, besides, to spread a world-wide distance between his savage state and his highest possible earthly development. All that there is great and happy in his destiny is conditioned strictly upon the application of his powers to the capabilities of nature, and is achieved in proportion to the agencies employed. These agencies are all comprehended in the signification of the word capital. Money represents them all, and its efficiency is in the measure of its amount and activity.

Is there a man in the nation idle—idle for want of capital to employ him? Are there a million of men and women thus unoccupied? Is half the available time of all, in the average, thus wasted? Why? Do they answer as they stand in the labor market, "No man hath hired us?" Then double the capital; put them all to work; and will a dollar of the required increase of capital then be acting only in reduction of exchange values? No; under the quickening touch of invigorated industry, rendering the whole people able to obtain and consume the added products, instead of starving and economizing, prices will not rise further than to restore from depression the natural values of labor and commodities. The first effect will be that the minerals, which before lay idle, will come into market; the commodities, that gorged the markets before, will find purchasers, and all prices will rise to the level of general prosperity, until cheapened processes of production and conversion shall reduce them, but without abating the remuneration of either capital or labor, now made capable of larger results by the employment of the same forces through better means and instruments.

Money coming into larger and more active service, and setting idle hands and minds to work, by finding employment for all, will give wages to the unemployed, and raise the wages of those who have been underbidding each other for work, and so, will raise the labor cost of industrial products and their raw materials to living prices—to par. In its scarcity money was at a premium and man and property at a proportionate discount. An adequate supply gives a resumption of values. Money has not depreciated, but returned to its normal value, by regaining its proper producing operation; its par value being determined by its ability to put all hands to work and fairly reward them for it.

If metallic money were nothing else than a medium of exchange, and at the same time the only medium of exchange, or, in the language of Mr. Mill, "a thing *only* wanted to buy other things with," and if, as he holds, it had such elasticity of exchange value as to be always equal to all varieties of quantity of other things, it must, of necessity, rise and fall in value in the ratio of its supply relatively to the property exchanged by it; and the same thing would be true of its convertible representatives. Its scarcity and its abundance would then work like an elastic measure, and be always equal to all quantities of things exchanged by it. These *ifs*, however, cover just as many absurdities and sheer impossibilities.

Even confined to its office as an exchanger of values, it is not the only medium in use; and so far as it does serve in this office, it also acts at the same time as a producer of the values to be exchanged, thereby furnishing the increase of subjects upon which it is to operate as an exchanger in the market, and thus maintaining its own equiponderance.

There is one sort of money—the money of account—that, expressed in the ledgers of traders, which has an exact equivalence to the total value of the commodities which they deal in. Such equivalence it has because it is an ideal money only, and not in itself a valuable thing or substance. When such accounts are settled by set-off, the exchanges are effected by simple indirect barter, in which circulating money has no place, and the nominal values are wholly indifferent to the question in hand. But money having the value of its labor cost in itself, or in the thing which it represents, is subject to the general law of value, which is the cost of reproduction, and has no other equivalence than its comparative labor cost; in other words, it is no more, nor otherwise, the equivalent of marketed goods and things than wheat or iron is.

It results from the examination of the whole subject that only ideal money, such as the money of account, employed in indirect barter by set-off, is the sliding-scale equivalent in exchanges; and that all other money, having in itself intrinsically or representatively, a value of its own, and having, besides, the functions of capital in production, is not a simple exchanger, even when acting in this one of its offices, and for these reasons, is subject to varying price in exchange only as all other commodities are.

Thus far we have been considering money as it is and has been. A history marked by this conspicuous fact—there never yet has been enough of it. Let this fact have its due force. Its assigned office is to put the whole world of men to work upon the whole world of matter. This it has by virtue of its universal acceptance as the representative of all accumulations of wealth, which accumulations are the instruments and agents of all civilized industry. In the hitherto, and present state of human industry, neither labor nor capital have even tolerably approached the full performance of their duties—each defective, in lack of the aid of the other. Insufficiency and inefficiency of labor argues insufficiency and inefficiency of money. Therefore, no casual, or fluctuating, or steady increase in the whole of the medium ever could hitherto have had the character or force of an excess, or overplus supply.

The growing quantity has never done anything but good, tending always towards better and better service to the world. An exception—the only one—might be taken to its effects upon the contract value of debts, to which it is a sufficient answer, that in this, like all other valuable things, the precious metals follow the law of labor value. The original creditor gave something—services or goods, or lands, in exchange for the obligation. If he had kept these properties till the maturity of the debt, they would have been worth no more than the like things produced at the time, and he must take just the quantity of gold or silver that he bargained for, though at the end of the term it is produced at half, or any less, labor cost, and will command only the same or some other proportion of property and service. Moreover, it is well that the burden of old debts—annuities and national debts—lose much of their burden in the progress of human affairs. If it were not so, the coming generations would be wofully oppressed by the debts of the present and past. The interest of some of these debts has already supported several successive lives, and no harm will be done in equity if their successors shall have to do something for their own support. All things else "perish with the using;" why should debts remain intact perpetually?

But the supply of the precious metals has always heretofore been

MONEY AS A PRODUCER OF VALUES.

below the requirement, because of the difficulty of their production, or, what is the same thing, their scarcity; and this has been the cause of their high value in exchange, as it must necessarily be. If ever they shall become as plenty as iron, will they not be as cheap, and thereby be depreciated in value till they exchange by the ton instead of by the ounce troy, as now? We answer, that their labor cost will always be their standard of exchange value, and when they lose their convenience as a medium of payment, they will cease to be so used, and then there will be no question of the effect of their abundance upon the value of other things.

But they will never be produced in excess of the demand for such uses as they can serve; for beyond the point of paying, as well as other things, for the labor employed in their production, it must cease; and in the mean time, while advancing toward such point, they will be more and more dispensed with, by the growing use of those other kinds of money, which are already carrying the world of business towards the type form of exchange, simple barter, by the intervention of credit money, which is so much better, cheaper, and more convenient than gold and silver. Except in international dealings, and the small change of daily expenses, these are now but little used, and are destined to a continual process of elimination, as business is better and better organized.

Until metallic money and its convertible representatives shall have reached the point of increasing by their active agency the production of commodities to their utmost amount and utility, they cannot decline in permanent value, so as to require the counting of more pieces in payment for the same thing in market, for they are found to cheapen such products much more rapidly than their own value declines by added quantity. They of course will not be multiplied in the payment of debts; for the debt-dollar stands unchanged through all changes in other things; and nothing remains to take the effect threatened by the theorists of equivalence, but land and labor. These, indeed, will require larger amounts as they improve; not because money is cheapened, however, but because they have become worth more of it than they were while it was scarce, or comparatively scarce, and was therefore less efficient for their advancement to a higher real value.

The necessary action of its growing quantity is the opening of new industries, and improvement of the old. While there remains a useful substance in the earth, or sea, or air, not utilized to its highest worth—while an improved apparatus of production is still wanting—while a brain requiring the means of sustenance, and the command of opportunity, and of implements, has yet a latent thought capable of human service—capital in the form of money will have ample scope and verge enough to spread without weakening its value. It will go on constantly cheapening the ultimate products, but its own accretions will all be demanded in calling into existence additional values, greater quantities, and better qualities; and this work will absorb it all without a depreciating remainder of supply.

What remains to be said on this subject will be considered in the chapter upon banks of discount, deposit, and issue.

CHAPTER XI.

PAPER MONEY; AND, INCIDENTALLY, OF BANKS OF DEPOSIT, DISCOUNT, AND ISSUE.

Bank paper, not banks, the subject: Banking, an instance of coöperation.—Money an exchanger and producer of values.—Exclusive metallic money and barter.—Hoarding.—Depositing at interest in early times.—English bankers of the seventeenth century.—Negotiable certificates of deposit, their service.—Convenience of metallic money increased in its substitutes.—Basis required for representative money.—Limited analogy of the circulating medium to the circulation of the blood.—Figures of speech need watching.—Plethora of money, a mischievous phrase.—No measurable ratio between quantity and rapidity of money circulation and their effects upon business.—Exchange value of money, the cost of its production, or of the things it represents, not affected by its quantity.—How deposit bankers affect the money supply and its service.—Bank of Amsterdam in the seventeenth century.—Banks of Genoa and Venice in the twelfth century.—Difference of effects between the transfer of money and of the property in it. —Representatives of money begin in deposits, and depend upon them; credit system arises.—Miracle power of faith in commerce.—Multiplying power of credit.—Faith-force over and above fact-force.—Brotherhood in business affairs corresponds to brotherhood in spiritual things.—Deposit banks, sources of profit and creators of credit.—Instances in illustration.—Concentration of capital brings credit with it.—Elements of the banking business.—General Benefits.—Credit makes capital of character.—Abuses of the credit system.—Evil is inverted good.—Civilization and liberty rest upon credit.—Bank notes, their convenience greater than that of checks and drafts.—Special adaptation to ordinary uses.—The money of the common people.—The bank note as a traveler.—Circulating notes issued by the United States Government—their amount in 1864 and 1871.—Irredeemable currency—six hundred and ninety millions in 1870, against two hundred and fourteen millions in 1857.—Extent of depreciation.—The work done by this currency.—Prosperity under its use.—Paper money the resort of nations in their days of trial.—More loyal and cheaper in its service than funded debts.—Service of deposit banks.—Exemption from runs.—Safe proportion of loans and circulation to amount of capital and deposits.—Profits upon bank capital.—Average of twenty-eight city banks.—Banks enhance the service of money three and a half times.—Development of the banking system in serial order.—Benefit, risks, and necessity of banks.—Credit system indispensable—to be amended, but not restricted.—English system unimproved in the last two centuries.—Balance of good and evil in favor of banks.—Distribution of banks.—In Scotland-average area of her bank districts—in the United States.—Excellence of the Scottish system—its popularity.—Popularity of the greenback currency.—Governments cannot administer a general banking system.—United States National Banking system requires amendment.—Banking should be as free as any other business.—Convertibility, exclusively aimed at, hinders reform.—Failure of Bank of England charter.—Safety, not convertibility, the essence of the bank note.—Inconvertible paper better than a deficient sound currency.—Loss by discount as nothing to an arrest of industry.—The mystery of money, no mystery to currency cobblers.

It must be understood that we have no room here, and no use for an exhaustive treatise upon banks and banking. We are occupied with money and its functions; and banking systems are but little more concerned in our investigations concerning bank paper money, than gold and silver mines, their geology and practical history, are involved in discussing their products, which are employed as a medium of exchange.

The pivot point of our inquiry is the service of coins and circulating notes in the world's business. This must be kept steadily in view in order to avoid distraction and confusion of thought; just as it is necessary to keep the eye fixed upon some stationary point, lest the head grow giddy, when all around is reeling in counter currents of shore and stream, as one crosses a rapid river. The policy of banking systems as one of the coöperation movements by which associations of capitalists combine and enhance their force in commerce is, however, so immediately in our track of thought, and so pertinent to the general issue of our work, that even here some of the plainer and more important features of the subject will be in place, though the treatment be an anticipation of the orderly consideration of the associative movements, growing more and more conspicuous and efficient with all progress in civilization.

Asking the reader to carry with him all the while, the steadying idea that money is at once the agent in universal use for effecting exchanges of services and of commodities, by which the results of all labor are distributed among men in fitting quantity and kind, according to their several necessities, and at the same time, that it acts as exchanger, is also the agent of capital of every kind in its office of producer of all commodities in civilized life—we may proceed to consider the means by which it is supplied for use, and by which its circulation is promoted.

Assuming a state of society in which coins of the precious metals alone are in use, as representatives of exchange values, and at the same time, assuming that they are employed only as other commodities are, in simple barter, such coins passing at every purchase and payment in business transactions, it will be immediately perceived that we are involved in a condition of barbarism of a low stage— barbarism bordering upon savagism so closely as scarcely to be distinguished from it. In such a condition of things money must be idle in the hands of the owners during all the intervals between sales and purchases. It is for such periods hoarded and useless, and so would indeed be, what Adam Smith calls, dead-stock, or rather stock in a state of suspended animation. But the holders naturally desire to have it at once active in their service and safely at their command, and for this purpose, a depository must be found in which it will yield some profit to the depositor, either directly, in the shape of interest, or indirectly, in the common benefit of the whole community. Accordingly we find a bank in which money could be deposited, so that the owner after an interval might require "his own with usury" mentioned as a well known existing institution as early as the beginning of the Christian era, (Luke xix., 23). Indeed, scarcely the earliest organization of commerce and industry can be conceived of as possible, without a money exchange or market, corresponding and proportioned to the coexisting commodity-exchange or market, which business of any sort implies and necessitates. The earlier communities had not the institutions which *we* call banks; but they had, as they must needs have had, in their place individual bankers, answering in a degree the same requirements. According to Mr. Macaulay, so lately as the date of the restoration (A.D. 1661), the goldsmiths of London kept the cash of the commercial houses, paid their drafts, and loaned balances in hand, paying themselves for trouble and risk out of the interest of such surplus as experience showed might be loaned consistently with the solvency of the bankers.

The goldsmith's note or certificate of deposit, says Macaulay, might be transferred ten times in a morning, and thus a hundred guineas, locked in his safe, did what would formerly have required a thousand guineas, dispersed through many tills. Adam Smith makes a similar estimate and statement of the advantage derived from the note of the deposit banker, as he states it, the substitution of paper is an operation by which £20,000 in gold and silver, perform all the service which £100,000 could otherwise have performed. It concerns us, however, to observe that the operation of representative paper does not actually increase the fund on which it is based just as many times as the paper is passed from hand to hand. The whole effect is no other than the substitution of a cheap and convenient medium for an expensive and comparatively very inconvenient one, with the great but not easily computed benefit of the increased rapidity of transfer, and the service rendered to so many more receivers in the same time. The fund itself is not affected by the rate of its circulation. A thousand pounds in either coin or paper is not a thing so changeable in value, so nominal, so unreal, that it can be increased or diminished at will by any of the incidents of its use. If it were so, then, indeed, any sum in coin might be made to answer in the transfer of any amount of values. London or New York, by the better organization of its circulating system, could make a million of pounds or dollars answer the purposes of a thousand or ten thousand millions. Nay, to push the proposition to the extreme, any sum, not so small as to check the circulation of its certificates or representative notes too much, would answer all the purposes of money—the whole fund of money—in any community. The effect of rapidity of circulation bears relation to the quantity of the thing circulated. A hundred making ten revolutions, is not equal to a thousand making ten or five or two, in the same time.

The idea of *circulation*, with its obvious allusion to the movement of the blood in the animal frame, may easily be pushed farther than the true analogy warrants. Blood, in the animal economy, is circulated as the conveyer of nutrient matter for the consumption of the textures, and as a stimulant of their vital functions; for which purpose constancy and sufficiency of supply, that is, a certain rapidity of movement is required, and for this a certain amount of propelling force. In greatly increased force of propulsion and rapidity of movement of the blood, mischiefs result, for which there is no proper parallel in the circulation of money in the channels of business. Momentum of the blood in the vascular circulation means, besides quantity delivered in relation to time, force of impingement, and pressure upon the vital organs. There are no such mechanical effects attending the changes in the circulation of money, nor anything corresponding to mechanical plethora or force. The dollar in great rapidity of currency does not strike its objects the harder, nor gorge its receptacles the more, nor, as a result, morbidly exaggerate or repress the activities of the things on which it operates,—there is no such disease as money apoplexy—and for these reasons, the process called contraction of the currency is not indicated as a remedy corresponding to venesection in febrile or inflammatory states of the animal body. Money circulation cannot by excess over-stimulate industry so as to mar its functions, nor can it arrest them as by an apoplectic congestion. Figures of speech must be watched, or they get themselves substituted in our reasonings for facts which do not exist. It seems to us that both Smith and Macaulay, and many another thinker upon the offices of money, have had their fancies tricked by making their parables go on all-fours in illustrations of very unlike modes of progression.

We cannot by simple addition or multiplication measure the effect of any increase in the rapidity of a money circulation. Ten times exchanged is not a ten-fold increase in the use of money, equivalent to a ten-fold quantity once moved. The effect of such increase of velocity is indeed immense, but under conditions which render it incalculable by any arithmetical process. It saves time and labor, but it does infinitely more by employing time usefully that must otherwise be wasted. It saves money by making money for money; it saves labor by employing it more productively and profitably, and all this in various degrees, from the least up to immeasurable amounts, and to effects still more inestimable in their influence upon the social life of men. Our objection is to the multiplying, squaring or cubing results that are absolutely incommensurable, because of the reflex error that is made to fall upon the management of the factors of the problem. We must take care not to say that a thousand dollars circulated ten times, is just equal in its commercial or industrial stimulus to ten thousand dollars once moved; for, by the same rule we can imagine the impulsive power of any sum made equal to any other sum for all purposes in proportioned multiples of exchanges, and thus confuse our notion of its proper inherent force. There is an ideal money, or measure, with which logic may deal at will, but there is also a substantial money which has an intrinsic value, requiring us to treat it as we do any other commodity in use. And we must, if we would think to any purpose, keep in mind that the value of this money is the cost of its production, or reproduction at the time in which it is used in exchange, and that wherever it goes, or however often transferred, it carries with it just its own inherent or representative value; and that for this reason, no particular sum of it can be thought of as equivalent to any other sum or sums moving faster or slower. And, above all, we must not ride to death the loose analogies commonly employed in the discussion.

Now let us see what modification of use and operation a banker or deposit bank produces upon the money of a community. In the first place, the depositary gathers up the unemployed surpluses from every point, as a river collects the thousand rills of its vicinity, and gives them the flow and the force of accumulation. The affluents, too feeble singly for effectiveness and direction in use, become a tide of power, ready for every diversity of productive employment. The difference is that between threads and the cable which they compose; between the rills of the hill sides and the current that turns the mills of the valley.

Money seeks profit and security. A bank or a banker offering a moderate interest or only safe keeping and prompt delivery, invites deposits by the confidence reposed in him, more than by the amount of interest allowed; and such advantages to the owner draw out the thousand little hoards into an aggregate that, well and wisely distributed from a central position, gives life and power and the best direction to the enterprise and waiting labor of the whole mass of the community. Beside the service of adepts secured by the interposition of depositaries selected for their acquaintance with the business of the country and its requirements, and with the enterprise and abilities of customers, the bankers are generally such as are themselves large contributors to the fund which they administer, and so, are in all respects qualified for the great business of turning the master wheel of the general business machinery. To secure all the requisites, many corporators are, as a rule, preferable to a single person in this function. From such combinations we have what in modern times are called banks of deposit and discount—incorporated institutions put under the general control of their stockholders, who, in other words, may be termed permanent depositors, taking profits instead of interest, and standing as joint debtors to the outside depositors upon interest, and joint creditors to those who borrow the money and credit of the institution.

The Bank of Amsterdam, established in A. D. 1609, was the earliest considerable institution of this kind which looked to the promotion of commerce among the people; its predecessors of the twelfth century, in Venice and Genoa, having been chiefly devoted to the management of *state* finances. This bank was guaranteed by, and was under the authority of, the city. It continued to serve the public, and to promote the prosperity of the city for nearly two centuries. It failed in 1790. With the particular provisions of its government and principles of its management, we are not here concerned, nor with the causes which specially led to its establishment, further than that the abrasion of the coins previously in use, and the other injuries to which they were exposed, put them as a currency at eight or ten per cent discount. These things, with all the troubles and vexations attending the exclusive use of coins in payment, drove the business community into the necessity of contriving a plan by which coins should serve as pledges for payment, while the certificates of deposit were substituted in transferring the *property in the coins*, without passing the coins themselves from hand to hand, after the manner of barbarous commerce.

A simple depository for money—not necessarily used in the smaller affairs of business, or in transactions with strangers, or persons ignorant of the security of the fund—is in its narrowest sense a place of safe keeping where the money is held ready to answer the demand of the depositor. If the identical coins, bars, or notes, so deposited, were to be returned, and must lie idle till called for, the whole operation would be merely a matter of custody, and could produce no other effect upon the money function than if the several sums were kept under the private lock and key of the owners. Security might be increased and some inconvenience avoided, and for these advantages the depositor would be justly and necessarily chargeable to the value of the service rendered to him; but there follows of course the right of transferring the property in the deposited money from the owner to others at will, without any movement of the deposited money itself. At this point the business of banking opens.

Banking, in all its kinds, rests upon this power of transferring the right to the thing without touching the thing itself, and here the representative certificate, or note, or draft, takes the place of the substance; the substance is converted from use as an active agent into a pledge; the certificate, or note, or draft, becomes a promise, serving instead of a payment, and serving just as well, but with an ingredient in it unknown to business effected by actual transfer of money in payment—the ingredient of Credit, which implies confidence and fidelity. This credit principle is the faith that removes mountains. It is the miracle power that changes water into wine; the multiplying power which feeds five thousand men with five loaves, and leaves a basket full for each of the agents of distribution.

A common note of hand, negotiable in its terms, payable to assignee or bearer, performs the function of money to its nominal amount for as many transferees as will accept it in the faith that it will be paid by the promisor to the holder. The draft of a depositor, where the like faith is given to him and to the banker, serves at every turn instead of the money which it represents, and so, the abstract property in the money of a community, gathered together and secured through the operation of market-faith, multiplies indefinitely the service of the great instrument of all production and exchange.

Faith in the fulfillment of promise, made by the substitute, is the power that moves the mass of human business, as the compound pulley lifts weights vastly disproportioned to the hand power which puts it into motion: the indirectness of action in the credit system, and in the mechanical machine, being alike evasive of the resistance to be overcome, and alike triumphant by virtue of such evasion. As a single man lifts a ton's weight, so a single dollar may move a thousand in values, by the magical power of adapted instruments.

How far faith goes in business is apparent when any medium of exchange, having no intrinsic value in itself, is employed,—whether the instrument be a draft, bank note, note of hand, or a book-of-entry charge; how much further than the actual pledge warrants, was shown by the fact that the Bank of Amsterdam carried on its immense business for full fifty years after the great bulk of its capital had been secretly loaned to the Government of the States General, to the East India Company, and to the city of Amsterdam; none of which were in condition to make instant restitution, and so the bank failed or exploded, though it had been doing a business of not less than five thousand millions of dollars a year so long as faith held in the security of the deposits or funds on which its paper rested. The treasure amassed in its vaults was estimated at not less than fifty millions, and the property in this value moved by the bank one hundred times a year makes the enormous amount of the exchanges here stated.

We do not know the amount of loss, or the amount of deferred payment, with the incident loss of the holders of its paper, when the discovery of its mismanagement was made, but for half a century faith in its solvency had maintained the commerce which it conducted without check or loss, or other disadvantage; and, if the ultimate losses could have been distributed in fair proportion among all its customers during the two centuries of its service to their business, they would have been still immensely its debtors for benefits received. After all, the Just live by Faith. The higher the truth the higher the life, and all the losses by the abuses of the principle are in the end as nothing to the issuing benefits. The principle at work here, aye, even in the banking system, is that of coöperation—the brotherhood of business, the community of risks, for the sake of the community of profits; in which, as in the things intended by the Apostle—" Look not every man upon his own things, but every man also on the things of others" (Phil. ii., 4), the policy of the secular exactly corresponds to that of spiritual life, and is put under the same laws; for, though corporations, and especially money corporations, have made themselves a proverb of selfishness and injustice, they nevertheless have hold of the miracle power, and " He maketh his sun to rise on the evil and on the good, and sendeth rain on the just and on the unjust," who alike faithfully employ the agencies which provide the harvest.

Banks serving as depositories for the spare money of those who confide in their solvency, by adding to the simple safe keeping of the fund the further function of discounting the paper of borrowers, may employ such amassed deposits in various proportions to the total on deposit, according to the range of their business, the strength of the stockholders or permanent investers, and the reputation of the institutions. There always will be unclaimed balances in the vaults of the banks, while they have the public confidence, say from one-fourth to one-third of the temporary deposits, and they may lend, besides, upon the capital paid in not only the whole amount, but a further amount equal to the capital itself in well established institutions. Here there is a source of profit, which enables them not only to hold money for safe keeping free of charge to the depositors, but to invite more investments, and for longer periods, by paying an interest upon them—less than the rates at which they lend, of course—but large enough to induce the holders of idle money to leave it with them. Certain banks in our eastern cities, dealing exclusively upon their capital and deposits are able to divide ten or twelve per cent to the shareholders. One such bank reports above a million dollars in its deposit accounts, for which it pays no interest, while the capital is no more than $400,000. It appears quite possible to make large profits above expenses, when it is seen that this bank reports loans to the amount of $1,371,592. Here its capital is twice loaned, and quite one-half of its deposits besides; and the bank is thus receiving perhaps six per cent upon nearly a million over and above its paid-in capital. But its undivided profits amount to a surplus fund of one hundred thousand dollars. Including this sum in its effective capital, it is doing business upon above two and a half times the amount that it owns.

But our business is now with the effect of credit added to capital by the operation of concentrating money, and by turning their combined forces into the channels of business. The elements of this business are 1st, the accumulation of unemployed money at centres of deposit, where all the inconsiderable and inefficient supplies are combined into effective forces; 2d, the activity given such funds in graduated portions, under the direction of adepts in business, by loans to those who will employ them as capital in production; which brings the waiting labor of the country and the raw material lying idle into the service of the community; 3d, the enhancement of the proper power of the aggregated fund, by the percentage of credit which it brings to the bank or banker who administers the fund; which, while it is kept within safe limits, is not an unreal capital, but an anticipation of the product which it will in good time make actual and available,—a process by which nothing but time is borrowed, that it may not be wasted; or, the sum which might be realized is made actual by anticipating the capital required to effect the answering production.

This addition which credit adds to capital, by being well based upon it, is the grand feature of the policy. In it lies the master power, to which the growth of the general wealth is due, and especially is it the beneficent element in the business life of men, which mitigates the inequalities of individual wealth. Credit acknowledges the worth of character. The man who has no other property, is made capital in himself, for his own benefit, and talents and industry are thus lifted out of the disabilities of poverty into their utmost serviceableness to society. Credit is the motor force that raises indigence into wealth, and so cônverts selfishness into beneficence in its effects, and greatly tends to conform the sentiment to the excellence of the providential results. This excellent thing, however, is much abused. Used in bad faith, it is at the bottom of all the pecuniary mishaps of business life. But this is just because it is so essential in the economy of business that it must be active for good, and is therefore always present and liable to be perverted.

As much may be said, and said no less foolishly, against liberty—moral, political, and social. The means of advancement must be capable of mischief, if they have anything of good in them for use. Steam power is just as liable to do mischief, and in the very proportion of its capability for good service. Is there any endowment of mind or morals; any instrument subject to human discretion, which is not exactly as mischievous as beneficial in its possibilities? The sins of the credit system are the best indications of its capabilities of good. A big evil cannot be made out of a little thing. Evils are strictly nothing but abuses.

A society without a credit system is simply savage. A business economy, whose capital should be limited to material property, would be a despotism of property, as inflexible as Hindu caste, and as dead as the insensate earth, where all that is precious is in the fixity of crystals, and all that is common, is as incapable as the rocks in which the gold and silver are coffined.

All of which leads us the further step in the question of currency that embraces the bank note; which in itself differs nothing intrinsically from the check, draft, or certificate of deposit used in transferring the property in money on deposit. But it does differ in form, convenience, availability, and range of circulation, materially. These are very important differences; for, as money itself has its chief serviceableness in its convenience, whatever affects this property is no less important than anything intrinsic belonging to, or wanting in it, as a medium of exchange.

It is obvious that a certificate of deposit, which, like a circulating note, is a promise to pay money, must necessarily be for some specific sum, and nine times in ten must be unadapted for use except by men engaged in considerable business. It is not the thing to carry to the market-house, to a railroad office, or a grocery store, nor will it meet the little current expenses of every day; and worst of all, it would not suit for the payment of wages. If broken up into convenient portions for current use, it would be bank notes to all intents and purposes; and only because a credit or deposit in bank needs to be so used, is the evidence of the claim, shaped into notes of such denominations as will serve the more general and most needed purposes of such credits. The draft of the depositor follows and conforms to every variety of transfers desired, and usually is sent to the bank to be there changed into notes for common use.

The transfer of determinate sums, especially of sums larger than those most commonly required in every day affairs, or among people having no mutuality of dealings, or those who cannot, or do not, meet in any sort of clearing-house operations, can be very well managed by drafts upon deposit banks. These facts help us to see more accurately the office of the bank note. It is plainly limited to the smaller businesses, to daily expenses, and is, therefore, peculiarly the money of the people who live from day to day upon their daily or weekly receipts. Banks do not use them among themselves, except for redemption. Merchants use them only for change, and manufacturers, only for payment of wages in their business. Like specie they come into service only in the odds and ends of affairs, and so, differ from coins only by being so much more convenient for use.

Bank notes are credit money; but they are substantially limited to credit in retail. The wholesale credit money has no such uses and needs no such forms. They are, therefore, the money of people of limited means, and of others for limited expenses. They make the payments of every day and hour, and are ever on the wing. They have not time to earn interest for any owner except the issuing bank, and for it only when they are loaned upon time. The travels and adventures of a bank note would be such a history of society as never yet was written, and never will be. If it were as nearly omniscient as it is ubiquitous, government, philanthropy, political economy—whatever of thought and endeavor, concerned with human affairs, would find in its journal an encyclopedia of facts, which they all need more than they need anything

CREDIT MONEY. 145

else. The freest play of fancy, in following its wanderings, will help somewhat in the estimate of its utility.

By the *bank note*, when spoken of in general terms as an instrument of exchange, is not intended a distinctive designation of paper money issued by money institutions, whether corporate or incorporate. The term means, in this general sense, the circulating note, and as the paper currency of most countries, and at almost all times, consists of the paper of such institutions, exclusively, the term is sufficiently accurate. But in the experience of the United States since the beginning of the late civil war, a supply of circulating notes rising at one time (April, 1864) to the sum of four hundred and sixty millions of dollars, and standing on the first of January, 1871, at three hundred and ninety millions, issued by the Federal Government, served the same uses to the public as the bank notes of ordinary times. These notes, along with a great mass of other evidences of national debt, in other forms and for greatly larger amounts, were issued and circulated on no other basis or pledge for redemption than the faith of the Government. They were not even made convertible on demand into gold and silver. The only form of redemption on demand specifically promised was the engagement to receive them at the Treasury and Sub-Treasuries for all public dues, except import duties. Some additional value was given them by making them a legal tender in all the business transactions of the people, among themselves and with the government, except in the matter of import duties and interest upon the public debt. This money was issued as evidence of indebtedness when the expenditures of the nation greatly exceeded its receipts, and it must necessarily be continued in circulation until it can be either redeemed in specie, or vested in a more permanent form of indebtedness, absorbed in taxes, or withdrawn by all these means combined. Its quantity, in use for four years running, was more than double the amount of paper money in circulation at any time before the war; and after ten years its amount is still (1871) one hundred and seventy-six millions, or eighty-two per cent greater. Beside this great amount of paper, irredeemable on demand, we have had an additional three hundred millions of national bank notes in use, which, as to basis of redemption and convertibility, may be described as in the same predicament; for those national banks, thus responsible to the public for three hundred millions of currency, have held nothing besides United States bonds and notes, real estate, and a little over twenty-three millions of specie, to meet their liabilities to the note holders and to their depositors, which last indebtedness aggregates above five hundred millions.

During nine years specie has been demonetized. It has stood as a commodity of the market, ranging in price, through almost the whole period, from one hundred and twenty-five to two hundred and eighty-five dollars in currency for one hundred in gold. If this difference is taken to be depreciation of the currency, then, it was passing at a discount of from twenty to sixty-five per cent, through the range of fluctuation, which covers quite seven of the last years since the suspension of specie payments in December, 1861.

Here we have the vast business of a nation of over thirty-five millions of people, worth twenty thousand millions in capital, during a war period involving an expenditure of five thousand millions beyond the ordinary business of times of peace, and carrying on, besides, a system of internal improvement of unparalleled outlay, and all effected through the agency of a paper circulation usually styled irredeemable, and, at any rate, for the time inconvertible at the par of gold. That war period has been passed quite six years, and as yet we have had no revulsion; no general or remarkable loss of individual prosperity; no catastrophe to the general industry; and so far from a failure, a positive and constant improvement of the public credit. This picture, if complete, would show to the full the service there is in the circulating note, as a medium for effecting the exchanges of commodities and services, among a people who, in this time of trial, have lived through the ordinary experiences of fifty years in the space of ten, every day indeed may be counted a week of the ordinary business life of a people, and every day of this history will tell as a week in the future of the nation.

Is there anything in all this story, or, is there anything yet to come of it, to keep in countenance the financial disesteem of theorists for the circulating note? Is there enough, in all the frauds and follies incident to paper money, to balance its services in all times, whether they be of war or peace?

Surely there is nothing in the nicknames, depreciated currency, irredeemable rag money, paper promises, unreal, or the like terms, that can settle the policy of commerce and finance as it is concerned in them. Paper money is the resort of all nations under severe trials—let this fact have its due force. There is no such opprobium attached to National, State, or Corporate stocks, though they are all debts resting upon the present and prospective solvency of the issuing party, as much as are national and bank circulating notes, and in no case, a whit more secure, or less liable to abuse, or followed by any other or lesser mischief; but differing from such stocks in one grand particular for the better, in that they are not exportable to foreign countries, nor do they carry with them, as stocks do, a profit to foreigners, who bear none of the burdens of the country which must pay them and their current interest.

We have already claimed for the circulating note the character of being specially the money of the common people, upon whose industry the general welfare so largely depends; and here we think it worth adding to its claims, the fact that it has been to us the only form of money which in our greatest exigency did not desert our service, by going into that of any foreign people. Intelligent patriotism will find in this specialty of the greenbacks and the national bank notes, a title to the name of American money, while philanthropy accords to them besides, the distinctive designation of the money of the common people.

We have seen that a bank of deposit and discount, without issuing a circulating currency, can well maintain itself upon its profits over and above all expenses, and even with an allowance of interest equal to one-half or two-thirds of the rate at which it lends its funds and credit; and that, even while thus limited in its banking functions, it serves excellent, even indispensable, uses to the community, to the depositors, to the borrowers, and to all the dependent industries. We have noticed, also, that it is indifferent to the operations of a bank whether it issues its obligations in the form of certificates for the varied amounts of the credits it gives, or in the form of circulating notes of such denominations as best answer the common purposes of small money dealings among the people. Whatever it promises to pay on demand may take any form which does not by contract alter the liability of the issuers. In practice, however, the circulating notes expose the bank to a run when any reason arises for converting them into specie, whether it be on account of a rise in the value of, or increase in the demand for, the precious metals, or apprehensions for the solvency of the bank, or doubt of its ability to redeem them on the instant of demand. For such reasons, certain banks in the great centres of trade, which can command a sufficient deposit business, prefer to use no circulation for whose redemption they are responsible.

The profit of a circulation is all in addition to the earnings upon capital and deposits, because this profit is made not upon funds held, but upon credit loaned, for which the reserve for redemption need not be any greater in proportion than upon the deposits. The national banks are not required by law to keep inactive more than twenty-five per cent of their total demand liabilities, in order to meet them.

The aggregate loans of twenty-eight city banks (in November, 1869) yielded, at the average minimum rate of six per cent per annum upon their loans, twenty per cent upon the par of the capital, and their aggregate of circulation and deposits amounted to $43,269,000 for the payment of which they held but $13,713,000, so that these city banks were able, under existing circumstances, to lend twice the amount of their capital by the aid of their surplus funds, and thirty-three per cent of their deposits.

Bank deposits, so called, consist to a large amount of mere credits on the books of the banks, being their loans to borrowers. It is safe, perhaps, to estimate their sixteen millions of capital as serving for thirty-two millions of money, another eleven millions of deposits (one-third of the total) consisting simply of bank credits, and ten millions more of bank debts in the form of circulating notes, based upon eleven millions of national debt; and we have in effect a sum of actual money consisting of sixteen millions of capital and six millions of surplus funds, amounting together to twenty-two millions, made to serve as fifty-three millions, or within a fraction of two and a half times the amount represented.

The preceding calculations were made from the bank reports of November, 1869. On the 22d of May, 1871, the same banks report their capital at sixteen millions, four hundred thousand, their loans at fifty-five millions, and deposits at thirty-seven millions four hundred thousand. If their aggregate surplus funds stood at six millions, they were able to lend their effective capital twice, and twenty-seven per cent of their deposits.

So much for the mere credit element of the existing money system, and of its capability, in favoring circumstances, of enhancing the service of the actual money of the country in its industrial and commercial affairs.

To resume. The agencies by which the service of money is utilized by accumulation, multiplied in rapidity of movement, and distributed effectively through its focal centres, are in serial order of adoption and in rank of service: 1st. The simple depository in which money is held for safe keeping, and returned, as it was deposited, to the owner; the property in it being transferable only by actual delivery. 2d. The deposit bank, holding the money and issuing negotiable certificates, or answering drafts, payable to drawee, assignee, or bearer; by which method not only such drafts or certificates become a circulation within a limited range, but the depositary may safely issue his notes or certificates to an amount considerably exceeding the sum in his vaults, either by discounts or by accommodation loans; thus not only increasing the rapidity of the actual money employed, but enlarging its force to the extent of the margin taken. 3d. A depositary for the spare money of the community, making loans upon it, by accommodation, and by discount of assigned debts not matured, and by issuance of the circulating notes which constitute the paper money currency of modern business policy.

All these businesses distinctively, and the whole of them combined, in the functions of the banks of the last two or three centuries, and at the present time almost universally in use, being based—in the simplest and earliest form—upon the reputation of the depositary; and, in the more complicated and completer form, upon actual capital pledged to about one-third of the active amount, and for the other two-thirds, upon credit only.

This being substantially the monetary policy of leading nations, and approximately the proportion of capital to credit in the basis of the banking system in its most general forms, we are not left at a loss to see its advantages, on the one hand, and its risks on the other; nor can there be any doubt of its necessity to the economy of productive and commercial industry.

Business must be done upon trust. It is impossible to conduct, or to forward, the affairs of civilized men, without such trust or confidence as expands itself from the simple confidence involved in all exchanges of commodities and services, into the most artificial and aggregative range of the credit system that has yet been adopted. A hand-to-hand exchange system of direct barter is possible or suitable only to such a state of savage society as subsists in a hand-to-hand battle order of the parties.

There is no resting place between the absolute distrust of the unorganized business of barbarous states, and the most unreserved commitment to credit, as the condition of all economic transactions. Nothing can be done to any purpose by narrowing the system. Everything of improvement is wholly that of providing such securities as it admits of. England has employed to exhaustion all the sagacity and experience of two hundred years, in contriving avoidance of the abuses of her banking system; yet it is safe to say that it is now as liable to objections, and as frequently mischievous as in the first year of its institution. Nevertheless, it has never been for a moment in danger of being abandoned on account of its evils. It has never been admitted that the evils experienced and feared were necessary attendants of the monetary system. It has always been clearly known that some form of credit-money is indispensable, and it is acknowledged, also, that the balance of good and evil has ever been in its favor; for it is seen that immense private and national prosperity has, nevertheless, resulted from it. Still there hangs over the whole matter a mystery which embarrasses the management. Every jar in the working of the machinery provokes the best and brightest of the business, and of the thinking, world to the most strenuous endeavors at amendment, which are never for any long period relaxed; but as yet without any tolerable approach to complete correction. The trouble at the bottom of the whole business seems to be this: the money that everybody believes in —the money that needs no redemption—the money that has a value in itself—is liable to at least two grave complaints: first, it is not, and cannot be made, adequate to the work required of it by those who would dispense with its substitutes, to escape their insecurity; and, second, it is so inconvenient and expensive that the exclusive use of it, could it be increased to tolerable adequacy, would be wholly unendurable. An exclusive metallic currency in the money market would block the wheels of the commodity market, and throw the world back to the economic conditions of barbarism. There remains, therefore, no choice, but to hold by the credit system, and the only hope left is in its amendment in the wisest and most practicable way.

Men must make up their minds to employ unreal money, and

they must in some way make it as capable and reliable as they can. The students of the credit system of business cannot fail to see how a banking system of some kind or kinds is indispensable to the organization, the force, and convenience of industry and commerce, and how the general exchange of services is promoted by its agency.

There follows as obviously these necessary consequences: that every locality requires such a money institution—a centre for every district where spare money may be deposited for safe keeping; where a moderate interest may be made upon such deposits; where mutual debts may be set-off against each other; where the actual amount of money gathered may be enhanced in its operation by such supplemented credit as the banking institutions can safely command; where adepts in business may distribute the activity of such gathered capital and incident credit, through the channels of productive industry, wisely and conveniently, by loans or discounts, to the general benefit of the community, and the profit of the bank; and, where the use of coin may be spared by the substitution of representative circulating notes, of assured soundness, and of denominations required in the smaller transactions of every-day business.

We cannot too frequently recur to the leading idea of money— that its most essential and central quality of service is in its convenience, as an exchanger of services and commodities. This is clear in the abstract, and it rules the policy of the money system through all its actual details. Banks being the agencies or machinery of the money system, it is clear that as depositories, as clearing houses, as reservoirs for the distribution of currency into the channels of its proper work, and, as necessary administrators of all these offices, they are required to be made of and for vicinages of such areas and activities as will bring them home for all their uses. Their number should be limited by no other considerations than necessary convenience of location, and conformity of expense to the service they are to perform.

The organization of banks best approved by thorough experience is that of Scotland, where there are forty banks with three hundred and forty branches, or bank offices, distributed over an area equal to only two-thirds of that of the State of New York, and with a population thirty per cent less. Here there is a banking office for every eight thousand three hundred of the people of the Kingdom. Suppose these banking houses to be each allotted to equal areas, it would make the radius of each banking district but four and a half miles; or, if the half of them are located in the cities and principal towns, the distribution in the villages and rural districts would bring the most distant individual within nine miles of the money centre. These offices, however, are doubtless distributed with regard to necessity for their service, governed by the conditions of business which regard the interests of the banks.*

The striking points in the history of the Scotch banks are their freedom from disturbing fluctuations in the amount of the currency which they circulate, the immense amount of their deposits when compared with those under different policies in other countries, and the exemption they have enjoyed from those general failures which have visited England so frequently.

They allow interest on deposits only about one per cent below the current rates, and they lend money freely on bonded securities: a plan by which the parties accommodated get their operating capital in advance, instead of having to wait until they have the proceeds of their enterprise in notes, which they must discount; that is, it is not on values produced or earned, but on those to be earned by aid of credit, that the borrower receives his accommodation from the banks. Besides all these conveniences provided for the business and industrious public, they issue notes as low as one pound; for, in the whole constitution of the system, and in all its working provisions, it looks to the convenience and aid of the common people. It is not surprising, therefore, that in Scotland there is no horror of banks; no distrust, and none of that perpetual endeavor after change in policy which agitates England and the United States.

It is not at all within the scope of our work to treat the banking

---

* Scotland has 1 bank to every 84 square miles of territory.
  Pennsylvania 1 "   " 232 " " "
  New York   1 "   " 150 " " "
  Massachusetts 1 "   " 38 " " "
  Rhode Island 1 "   " 21 " " "
  Ohio   1 "   " 296 " " "

The territories divided into equal squares would give a radius or half diameter to:—

Scotland of four and a half miles; to Pennsylvania, seven and a half miles; to New York, six and one-eighth miles (but the rural banks would have a radius of seven miles); Massachusetts, three miles; Rhode Island, two and three-tenths miles; Ohio, eight and a half miles.

system. We notice these institutions only as they are, or might be, instruments of the money function in its bearings upon the general welfare. Any wider view of the subject involving them, would overtask our powers, and only exhaust the patience of those to whom this work is specially addressed.

One other specialty may properly be noticed here: the popularity of the "greenback" circulation, for many reasons which need not be mentioned, inclines large numbers of those who are concerned, or, who concern themselves, with the supposed advantages of national banks, to recommend some modification of our present currency system, in such manner as would make the government the source of the supply of our circulating notes. This proposition, if we are right in our apprehension of the machinery and uses of banks, is every way objectionable. There was no fault, under the circumstances which required the issue of the government notes, and their continuance in circulation, or in putting the debt of the nation into the form of a circulating medium; but the government cannot make of its exchequer, or sub-offices, depositories for the inactive money of the people; it cannot lend, as business everywhere requires, upon individual securities, or discount the business paper afloat. Two thousand or three thousand banking houses would be required for the purpose of accommodating the localities with convenient places of deposit and loans. The government could not appoint and supervise the administrators of such a trust. It cannot, and will not, be trusted or burdened with this business in all its required breadth and action. Corporations of the vicinage alone are competent. Their circulating paper can be secured to the holders, absolutely, as is proved by experience of the national banking *system*, now some years under trial;* and for all other matters of complaint the pub-

---

* The national banking law, for which we are indebted to Mr. Secretary Chase, secures the redemption of the circulating notes absolutely, but leaves their conversion into coin dependent upon the general resumption of specie payments. The government supplies the notes to the sixteen hundred banks, organized under the law, in a certain proportion to their several capitals, and upon the security of national bonds, deposited in the federal treasury in the ratio of one hundred dollars to every ninety dollars worth of such notes emitted. Thus the circulation of each bank is limited to ninety per cent of the securities pledged for its redemption. On failure of the bank, the United States Treasury redeems them, if demanded, and sells the pledged securities to reimburse itself. The note holder is made in every event safe against any loss, for the notes of a broken bank are just as good

lic and the authorities must find either complete relief, or such mitigation as the subject admits of. A government might indeed provide paper circulation, but it cannot distribute it directly among the people. It cannot be a bank of deposit, discount, and issue. If it has the wisdom to devise, and the authority to establish, the required instrumentalities, its powers and capabilities can go no further; and, as there is nothing in the proper offices of banks which can be dispensed with, they must be conformed as nearly as may be to this necessity, and the risks and injuries attending them must be borne till removed or abated as evils accompanying an indispensable service to society, which withal, leave behind a vast balance of benefits.

The inference from all these views seems both easy and inevitable, that banking cannot rightly be made a monopoly, as it is by law in the United States, and by contract in England and France; and in effect, by limitation of the circulation and its arbitrary distribution, as under the national banking system of the United States, without inducing many of the abuses complained of, and, at the same time, disappointing the intention, perverting the action, and crippling the agency of the great money function, upon which all business prosperity and stability depend.

It is to be hoped that the experience of generations will soon cure the public of the notion that the instant convertibility of the circulating note is the one thing to be secured, at the expense of whatever uses the banking system serves—cured, if not by a sound view of the general uses of banks, at least by the uniform failure of all attempts, contrivances, and safety-guards employed to

---

as those of a sound one, and the notes of all the banks, wherever situated, are of uniform value throughout the United States.

The grand fault of the system is in its restriction of the amount of the circulation allowed. As this provision at first stood, the amount being taken, the benefits of the law are monopolized. The amount should be limited only by the amount of the securities pledged for the redemption of the notes, and so be practically limited only by the requirements of business. In other words, banking should be as free as other businesses and, especially, free to all localities. With respect to the security of depositors; that is left, as it should be, to the care of the depositors themselves, and they are not permitted to affect the solvency of the circulating notes, as under the old state banking system they so frequently did. Depositors have no just claim for security from the government. Theirs is a private business with the banks. For the authorized circulating money, the Government is every way responsible, and it is also eminently capable of fulfilling its trust.

accomplish that one thing, endeavored in so many ways, at so great losses and catastrophies, as have always awaited the occasion for discrediting the attempt.

The charter of the Bank of England means nothing, and intends nothing specially, except a desperate effort, by desperate means, to prevent a suspension of specie payments. It went into this service in the year 1844, and, behold, the anti-suspension provision has been already three times suspended by the violent intervention of the privy counsel of Her Majesty, under the compulsion of the very exigencies which it was designed to prevent or overrule. Sir Robert Peel, by and with the advice of the "sound currency" savans of the realm, believed he was constructing a safety valve for the paper-money medium of the nation; yet, in the first and every subsequent exigency that put it into operation, it turned out to be a trap, that had to be let up and set again, to serve again only so long as it should be useless, and, therefore, harmless. The fact that the Scotch banks had gone safely and steadily through the crisis of 1793, and that of 1825, when so many of the provincial banks of England were swept off, and not a single Scotch bank gave way, and the failure of all devices everywhere, and at all times, to maintain the redemption on demand of bank paper, when that is made the master idea of the machinery, might induce theorists and financiers to look somewhat more deeply and broadly into the general question. Convertibility is a convenience, but it is not the essence of the circulating note. Solvency is quite another thing, and this secured, there is no people under the sun who will not require the note, even at the depreciation which it suffers during the suspension of specie payments, in preference to doing without it. It is probable that if everything else in the banking system were well cared for, the ultimate solvency of the notes secured, and the whole system set free from the restraints that are imposed solely with the view to keep the paper at the par of gold and silver, the convertibility would take care of itself, or, at worst, prove a matter of trivial importance.

The evils of a depreciated currency, when admitted to the full, are as nothing to the lack of a money supply that keeps productive industry active to the full. Creditors paid in it lose in proportion to its diminished purchasing power, but the mischief stops there; and, what is the difference between the normal and the nominal value of debts, to the losses suffered by the interruption, diminution, or suspension of a nation's industry? If half a year's labor is lost in the United States for want of active capital to keep it employed, and this is valued at but half a dollar a day, there is a loss to those who can bear no loss without suffering, of three hundred and ninety millions by five millions of people, and a corresponding loss to twenty or thirty other millions of people. Will a ten, twenty, or thirty per cent decline in the value of debts, to those who may be presumed able to bear it, be a greater evil? The danger of the arrest of production and of trade, in England, has three times in twenty years driven merchant, manufacturer, and artisan to pray government to give them irredeemable bank notes instead. And the greenback, that does not even promise to pay its face value on demand in gold or silver, or in anything else but taxes and old debts, has won for itself, in the loyal States of America, an everlasting remembrance in praise and blessings.

There is mystery in money, there is magic in it. Abstractly everybody admits this, but in specialties, touching its movements and effects, hardly one man in a thousand will refrain from repairing the machine, though he knows that the regulator and the motor force is to him inscrutable.

If any one doubts this, so broadly stated, we would suggest that he tries his divining power upon tight and easy money markets, alternating every week; on the premium on gold without alteration in the volume of the currency—highest when the national debt was less than half its maximum amount, and declining in an inverse proportion to the measure of the public burdens. Or why, without any perceptible change in the securities, it sells at 135, 165, and 125 within two months? Perhaps all these questions could be disposed of without being answered, if this other question were answered—why should gold gamblers be allowed to fix the standard for measuring the value of national notes at will?

CHAPTER XII.

COMMERCE.

Commerce: Faulty definitions of the term.—Whately, McCulloch.—Territorial division of labor.—Production subordinated to trade.—Benefit of division of labor exaggerated.—Glorification of trade.—Fundamental errors of English Economists; practical and theoretical mischiefs resulting.—Idols of the Den.—Bias of nationality in the philosophy of business affairs.—*Commerce* is direct exchange, Trade is exchange through intermediates.—Trade disintegrates, Commerce develops the man and the community.—Monstrous results of the Trade theory.—The Trader's policy of production.—Rule of climatic law.—Trade law.—Trader's definition of political economy—Its true meaning and scope.—False claims of foreign trade; spoliation its aim, in conformity with the spirit of the times; effected formerly by force, now by fraud.—The motive borrows the credit of the good in the results.—Association without freedom is domination, not commerce.—Commerce is immediateness of intercourse and exchange.—Impediment of space.—Home commerce might suffice in the United States.—The policy of commerce is a national, not a cosmopolitan concern.—Value of imports before the Rebellion; value of domestic exports.—Commerce of the East and West loyal States in 1862.—Estimate of total domestic exchanges.—Consumption of domestic, ten to one of foreign, products.—Difference between economic and market, value.—Foreign goods displace home labor.—Statistics of trade imperfect—official figures unsafe.—Data and differences of European authorities.—United States census reports—their defects—they afford only a basis for approximate estimates.—Proportional market value of foreign and domestic products.—Difference of economic value in transportation and trade profits.—More than half our imports give no employment to domestic labor and capital in further production.—Economic value of foreign imports; they give no employment to domestic labor and capital in further production.—Economic value of foreign imports as only one to twenty-three of domestic products.—Kinds of foreign imports which exclude home industry, enumerated.—Their cost, fifty-seven per cent of our total imports.—Balance of international trade—unfavorable balance, not in the market value, but in the *kinds* of commodities exchanged—the mischiefs.—Difference in kinds and values of labor resulting from different kinds of imports.—Educating and enriching labor.—Money values not the guide in international trade.—Characteristics of legitimate trade.—Sound international trade is supplementary, not competitive.—Unrestricted trade in natural products, only *across* climates.—Cosmopolitan and national economists.—Political economy not a science, but a system of expediencies—it has no universal or permanent principles—its scientific pretensions everywhere at fault.—Competition the regulator of disorders in the trader's school of economists—Bastiat.—Trade in manufactures and works of art.—All foreign trade compulsory—there is no such thing as free foreign trade.

WE have exact and exhaustive definitions of the term commerce in dictionaries—verbal definitions; and, in the authors concerned with the subject in its practical relations, moral, political, and economical, much of effort at logical exposition and elucidation, but withal, less certainty of meaning and availableness in use than ought to be secured. It is among the terms of art, in the system or systems of political economy of which Archbishop Whately says: "hardly one of them has any settled and invariable meaning, and their ambiguities are perpetually overlooked." (Elements of Logic, p. 354.) That the subject is not as clear in the minds of the authorities as one would naturally expect, is plainly intimated by the care that J. Stuart Mill takes to settle the respective claims of Ricardo and Torrens to the authorship or discovery of one of the causes which determine international exchanges. The authorities have, therefore, been very lately illuminated upon that particular point; and their high appreciation of a very small matter shows how little command of the question they had previously obtained, and suggests, besides, that it may not yet be thoroughly mastered.

J. R. McCulloch speaks of commercial intercourse as beginning to grow among men as soon as individuals cease to supply themselves with all the products of labor required for ther own consumption. He adds—"it is only by exchanging that portion of the produce raised by ourselves that exceeds our own consumption for portions of the surplus raised by others, that the division of employments can be introduced, or that different individuals can apply themselves in preference to different pursuits." From this point of *departure*— from which he departs never to return again—he passes instantly to the consideration of *foreign* trade, either distant geographically or internationally, and is thenceforth occupied exclusively with what he terms the *territorial* division of labor, which he says has contributed more than anything else to increase the wealth and accelerate the civilization of mankind. In the division of the topics treated under the general title, he gives the first place in order and rank to the agents of trade—the mercantile classes; and the necessity for the wholesale and the retail dealer, is pushed to its last consequence, in which trade is the substance, and production is only its accessory or minister in civilized life and human progress. Treating of Trade, he is so occupied with the advantages of *distance* in commerce that he thinks "the territorial division of labor, if possible, even more advantageous than its division among individuals," and of the blessings of the latter he is so well assured, that he assigns to it no limits beyond which it may be injurious; simply because the more labor is divided the more production is increased and cheapened, and the more subjects are supplied for trade, and the larger space spread for its extension. Unconsciously, it may be, and all the more irreflectively, the writer's imagination takes wing and prose poetry is pressed into the service of admiration of trade; and roads, canals, steam carriages, all navigable streams, coast and open ocean highways, are glorified; and even such centralization of industries as conduces most to the infinitesimal division of handicraft occupations, is cited as elements of this most beneficent of all human functions—commerce wholesale and retail! Everything is cheapened, everything distributed, everything is first carried away from everybody, everything is afterwards brought back to everybody, and trade grows prodigiously. Besides, trade gives competition all possible influence. Everybody is put to working with and against everybody else, and the author is right in concluding an enthusiastic outburst, "all is mutual, reciprocal, and dependant," if he will only allow us to remember that the same may be said of a chain-gang or of a bench of galley-slaves, and to reflect a little before we join in his exultation. For we cannot help interjecting the question: is man made for products and trade, or are products and trade made for man? Rightly answered, it may appear that the most important element has here been left out of the question, or considered only as subsidiary to things which are properly subordinate. If wealth were understood to be weal, well-being, welfare, instead of finding in the term nothing but vastness of capital accumulated, the political economy of Great Britain would take another character than it bears, and would lose that bias for trade, especially foreign trade, which poisons every spring of thought in all its favorite authors, politicians, and statesmen. But it would seem that there is a mental infatuation which, like that of alcoholic intoxication, believes in the benefit or necessity of that stimulation which enervates the body politic. The directly resulting pauperism, expatriation, rebellion, and all forms of discontent and resistance, teach nothing corrective to a philosophy which holds that "man is a drug and population a nuisance," and makes them so by addressing all its working influences to the promotion of trade at the expense of the human instruments which supply its stores for the aggrandisement of traffic.

England, judged by the workings of her economic policy, is of all countries in the world, least capable of furnishing a theory of political economy for the guidance of any people who would escape the wretched practical results of her system. Men are everywhere so prone to worship the idols of the den in which they are bred that nationality clings to doctrine in all spheres of practical affairs, and the flavor of nativity hangs persistently over every dish they cook for the guests at their feasts of philosophy. The economic doctrines of an island that depends for its prosperity upon the industrial colonization of all the rest of the world, must needs tend to the required subservience of its tributaries; and no moral or mental integrity of individuals, under such influences, will save the propagandists from the vices of thought bred into them by the business system in which they live and move and have their being.

If these free thoughts suggest to the reader the names of Torrens, Ricardo, McCulloch, Cobden, Bright, and Mill, we can only ask that the process of separating the good from the evil be dispassionately performed, and the presumptions of fair reasoning be allowed due weight, until a careful scrutiny shows the truth or error of this exception to the nationality of a cluster of honored names, which it must be admitted, are at least remarkably national in matters of commercial policy.

It would be well if distinctive terms could be employed for the exchanges of services and commodities effected by men immediately and directly, and that other manner of exchange, made through intermediates, middle men, agents, or merchants. Mr. Carey uses the word commerce for the exchanges of services, products and ideas by men *with* their fellow men, in exclusion of all intermediate agents; and employs the word Trade to distinguish exchanges made by intermediates *for* the principals—*commerce*, describing the most direct interchanges, *trade*, the more or less indirect. The two terms have hitherto been so constantly used interchangeably that a difference of application and force cannot be easily made familiar. And the further difficulty arises from the customary use of the word *commerce*, in application to the more indirect trade, and the greater distance between the parties, while the better use would be exactly the reverse.

The difference in the respective consequences of the more, and the less direct exchanges ought to be kept clearly in view, and must be, if we would understand the subject advantageously. The mutuality, reciprocity, and interdependency of exchange, limited in its aims to products and trade, as its central object, and driven to its utmosts, in the confidence that the governing principle leads only to perfection, and cannot, therefore, be mischievous, even in its extremes—that is, when its results are piled up in forms of material wealth—will work very differently from the leading idea that all discipline and development should be directed to the growth of individuality, as well as to association, in the societies of men. Association could be effected in the trader's meaning of the term, and up to the entire scope of his purpose, by the process of disintegrating the individuals concerned in its operations, so far as to suppress all that is common and general in men, for the purpose of enhancing the special in each. The division-of-labor doctrine, while it does provide for the most effective employment of the varied aptitudes of the mass of laborers, may be pushed, under the governing idea of productiveness, to an excess which would change men into a distortion of their physical powers, not unlike to monomania in mind. For an example: a noble-looking old man, employed in one of the cutlery factories of Sheffield, has been for forty years employed exclusively in counting twelve, during twelve hours of every day. Doubtless, the knives and forks were the more accurately and expeditiously assorted in dozens, by this sort of automatic life of the man; but what was the reflex effect upon the man himself? Trade was promoted, but do heaven and earth depend upon trade? The man that spends his life in pointing brass pins, will never learn, because he need not, and had better not learn, even how the head is made or put on. Such division of labor drives him back into the single element of the work which is arbitrarily apportional to each among a dozen or twenty hands, and lo, a pin is produced; and all men wonder at the miracle. Every second of time is pin-pricked into infinitesimals, and the multiplication table breaks down under the prodigious results!

This process may be pushed to the disintegration of the proper human nature, so as to throw in turn every faculty out of gear, and so, out of use, until a man is decomposed, and a pin-pointer is produced! This is the trader's policy of production; but he does not stop here in the work of mincing the mutualities of men, dissolving them into their ultimate atoms, and classifying and organizing them by the affinity of their fractions or fragments. He carries the segregations forward from the division of labor among individuals into a territorial division corresponding to it. He finds a hill-side that is better for pasturage then for corn-growing, and he provides for its exclusive appropriation and employment according to this one of its adaptations; the people of that hill-side must make beef and mutton, and nothing else, because these are its best spontaneous products; and the men of that division must limit themselves in their pursuits and their studies to that one art, else they might diminish the traffic arising from the scientific division of labor, according to territory. Other men, elsewhere, can make blankets cheaper, because they have no territory at all to work, and everybody else must abstain from their alloted specialty of labor. Men are nowhere to be the masters, but everywhere the slaves, of circumstances, and in these unvaried and unvariable conditions are found the natural laws of commerce!

If these theorists would but limit the necessary territorial exchanges of men to the unavoidable; if they would but say that the north temperate zone must get its spices and ivory from the tropics, and the hot climates must draw their ice from the colder, and always use the word *must*, and say they should, only because they *must*, they would have a clean strong grip of a natural law; but when they bring upon us a trade law which looks ever to cheapness of commodities, and pays no regard whatever to the conditions of human welfare, we must insist upon some other meaning and purpose of legitimate commerce.

Abundant provision for trade as a civilizer, wealth-producer, educator, and organizer of the world, exists in the naturally necessary interchanges of products, without arbitrarily dividing all the like regions of the earth into totally unlike pursuits, and leaving it to transportation to unite them only in the market places, while it severs them into distinct and different factors or multipliers everywhere else. But the very definition of Political Economy by the authorities who write in the dominant interest of trade, amounts to nothing more in substance than that given by Archbishop Whately, catallactics, or a science of exchanges, which is very far from the idea that it is concerned with man in his efforts for the maintenance and improvement of his condition, or as technically defined, "a system of the laws which govern man in his efforts to attain the highest individuality, and the greatest association with his fellow men" (Carey, Social Science, vol. i., p. 63). It is claimed for foreign trade that it is a peacemaker among the nations. This is not its history in the past. Maritime trade, until within the period of two centuries last past, was simply what we now call piracy. Its occupation was pillage of chattels, enslavement of men, and extension of dominion in the interest, and for the extension of trade. The nobility and gentry of civilized Europe held any form of industry degrading which was not carried on by murder and robbery. Sir Walter Raliegh went abroad upon the high seas with Elizabeth's commission as a privateer, and John Newton served as chaplain in a fleet of slave-traders. The morals of maritime trade were the last to be reformed in the means it employed and the policy it pursued in international relations. When the age of violence had passed, trade long stuck to its purpose, aim, and end. Pillage took the name of international commerce, and made its predatory invasions of the feebler nations without force of arms, by the force of traffic. The superior arms of the strongest are now only occasionally employed to make way for the superior skill of hands; and invasion of foreign labor markets is effected by pacific means in lieu of the older and ruder warlike invasions, breaking down the defenses of industry by other acts not less effectual than those which use powder and bayonets in the negotiation.

Changing the method with the changes of the times, and so avoiding conflicts with the spirit of the age and the common law of nations, the leading commercial nation of the world is getting rid of her colonial dependencies, and rapidly changing her foreign political subjects into profitable customers. After the suppression of Napoleon, for the first time in her history, she maintained a peace of thirty years. An episode in the Crimea, and an occasional insurrection in India, have merely thrown a few ripples into the pacific current of her foreign affairs; for it is settled that she no longer aims at the rank of a first-rate power, having seen that the policy of peace is the true line of conduct for the maintenance and promotion of her commercial prosperity. The London *Times* struck the key-note when it declared that England lives in a glass house, and explained the figure of speech by admonishing her that she cannot pull a trigger without risking the loss of a customer. Peace with her, means plenty; and trade, she calls commerce, for the happier allusions which the terms can be made to convey, and thereupon claims credit for all the possible beneficence that may associate itself with a world-wide trade intended primarily to make her the "workshop of the world."

Voyages of discovery in the fourteenth and fifteenth centuries, as well as the crusades of the twelfth and thirteenth, claimed as their purpose, and are still credited with, all the incidental advantages to the pagan world which Providence has educed from the evil of their motives and of the means employed with very different aims.

Foreign commerce is thoughtlessly taken to mean association; and such association to imply reciprocity, mutuality, aggregate helpfulness, organization, unity, brotherhood, and all excellent things in the charities of art and life. But association does not of itself secure any such commerce or interchange of helpfulness. An army is an association most effectively organized; but, at what expense to the individuals is the effect of combination secured! Military authorities hold that the nearer men in arms can be reduced to machines, the better for discipline and for battle. Individuality is here utterly sacrificed for unity; combination is not the free play of the natural relations and dependencies; the mutuality is nothing but cohesion, and accordingly, the bread of bondage is rations, bloodshedding is bravery, and the degradation of manhood must be baptized glory. Let us not be deceived by words. Slavery may lurk in human relations which do not obtrude the auction block; and combinations may be crushed masses, though made of living men. Aggregation is not association. A sand stone is only a hardened mass of granulated deposits, not a vitalized organism. No union or communion or interchange of men meets or fulfills the purpose of human existence, or provides for its well-being, that does not give free play to all the faculties of each individual, and promote their growth. In the light of this truth, commerce has its true intent and meaning.

Now let us look at our subject with eyes wide open to all its essential aspects.

Its central and supreme meaning is in its directness and immediateness, which must rule all our thoughts and all our endeavors concerning it. Correspondence by letters is an abridgment of time, but the gain is offset by the difference in favor of personal intercourse. Quickened by the electric telegraph, it becomes instantaneous, but still not personal, or in the true sense, immediate. The tone and the touch, and the sympathetic adaptation of the parties, are lost, and a message may be an offense or a failure, which a look or a gesture would relieve or remove. Distance in place is in the way, though that of time be annihilated. The communication is still indirect. Mineral magnetism is not the equivalent of that which is mental or personal. Steam and electricity are only good against time, they are powerless upon space. If time were annihilated space would still be as great an impediment in itself as ever. For all the purposes of commerce it is *space* that must be overcome. Neighborhood in place is its only avoidance; and, in whatsoever relative locality is important, whether in the commerce of ideas, feelings, or the exchanges of services and their products, nearness is the grand desideratum. In economic affairs therefore we must give the first place to the

COMMERCE OF HOME.

And first of its magnitude, its value, and its necessity:

In such a country as ours, or any other as favorably situated and as well provided with materials, labor, and art, it would not be too much to say that, for life and its chief necessities, we have all that we need, and could, without much detriment or diminution of progress, dispense with foreign trade altogether.

National or political boundaries do not correspond to geographical or climatic divisions, but commerce is, in one aspect, a national concern, and must be so considered.

Taking the time before the war of the Rebellion for the sake of seeing the relative value of home and foreign trade, undisturbed, we find the appraised value of all our foreign imports and exports of merchandise, specie exports excluded, at the highest, fall short of $652,000,000. The consumption of foreign imports in the highest year (1860) per head was $10.80. The value of the domestic exports were very exactly $10 per head. What are these amounts to the value of the domestic exchanges of the year?

We have no official reports of the domestic trade of the several portions of the Union which usually interchange products with each other. The nearest approach to a very partial estimate is that published by the Treasury Department in 1863, in which the transit trade of the Allegheny Mountains and a line corresponding to the central ridge extending northward to the Canada border, and southward no farther than the Potomac River, or the northern boundary of Virginia, puts the value of merchandise transported in the trade between the Eastern and Western States in 1862 at eleven hundred and thirty-eight millions. In this calculation nothing is embraced but merchandise carried eastward and westward at least three hundred miles, or only such goods as were carried from and between the Atlantic seaboard and the Mississippi Valley. Nothing that was carried north and south, between the Atlantic States— nothing exchanged among themselves by the Western and Northwestern States. The usual inter-state trade of the Confederate States, south and southwest, and between them and the north, east, and west of the loyal States, were, of course, omitted; those Southern States being at the time at war with the loyal Union States. This eleven hundred millions worth of through transit in a single direction (East and West) is but as the drop of a bucket to the total domestic exchanges in a time of peace and active business.

We may approach the total value of the commodities exchanged at home by the fact that the products of industry in the Union for the year 1860 were worth four thousand millions.

The imports for consumption of that year were three hundred and thirty-five millions, or equal only to one-twelfth of the domestic products. Not all these domestic products, however, went into market. The producers may be taken to have consumed one-fifth, yet most of the goods thus consumed, though not sold for money, were in fact exchanged for services of families and employees, especially in agriculture, which now employs nearly half the laborers of the nation.

We are warranted in our calculation that the domestic commerce is, in money price, as ten to one of the foreign articles consumed in the country. We do not, however, measure the *economic* value by the market prices of the products of industry and traffic. Far from it. In the United States but little raw material is imported— but little that affords the further profits of converting skill, or employs labor and capital in reproduction. Nine-tenths of the merchandise imported goes directly into consumption. The wines and liquors, the sugar, coffee, tea, jewelry, fancy dry goods, like the toys and trinkets, never take the character of manufacturing stock or materials. And such goods as iron, woolens, and cottons rather displace home labor than furnish it with any form of employment.

The adepts in statistics, who occupy themselves especially with the production and consumption of nations, and with their accumulations of wealth, labor and belabor their subject in all possible ways, and failing of such agreement in results among themselves as might commend their conclusions to the inexpert among their readers and students, usually leave no confident or definite convictions upon the common understanding. The difficulty lies in the want of reliable data for their calculations. In the matter of foreign trade custom-house reports approach the truth, when quantities are given, nearly enough for the statistician's use; but where only values are given, besides the fluctuations in prices, which make wide departures from stable measurements or standards, frauds also greatly increase the errors of fact. So that even among the items of official authorization there is a damaging insecurity—a tickly-bender support for the footsteps of inquiry.

But in the investigation of home production and trade they are all afloat. The European authorities who have, or ought to have, the best means of information, are accustomed to make up their estimates from their tax registers, such as excise duties, incomes, probates of decedents' estates, insurances, export values, investments in stocks, and the like evidences or indications of business affairs. The distances and difficulties which lie between such data as these, and the results aimed at, it will be perceived are very great, and the worth of the results, like the processes by which they are obtained, is a matter of estimation. That they lack assurance is evident from the fact that the highest authorities are very far apart. One set, following Mr. Gladstone in English wealth statistics, takes the income tax as the best basis; another, after McCulloch, relies upon the value of the exports to foreign countries; and a confused crowd of writers, such as Colquhoun, Porter, and Levi, attach themselves to such other indiciæ as they can find among the various signs of business activities. A moment's reflection will show how inadequate and unsafe all these means of calculation must be. The income tax, for instance, is always, and in all countries, infamous for its falsehoods and frauds; besides, if it were faithful and true, according to the intent of the law, it never goes beyond the minimum subject to assessments; as in England, nothing below £100 per annum, and in the United States below $1,000, is embraced, which in both cases leaves out the mass of the earnings of the people, or at least the earnings of the mass of the people. Then again, such a basis as the value of the exports to foreign countries, on account of the vast variations of actual prices, the indifference of customs officers to the declared value of goods not charged with any export duty, the customary under valuations of such as are subject to *ad valorem* duties in the ports to which they are consigned, and the multitude of other caprices and tricks incident to trade, only affords at best comparative estimates of such *foreign* trade, and has nothing further to do with domestic production, and nothing at all with the home consumption. Like thermometers, they might give, if they would, the relative degrees of movement, but they can show nothing as to the alsolute quantities or forces on which they rest. They have their arbitrary zero, freezing, temperate, and boiling or bubble points marked upon the mercurical indicator, and so, some guess may be had at the changes, but no knowledge is afforded of the absolute condition of the thing that is changed.

In the United States, we have another method which has the absolute for its object. Once in ten years we have an official valuation or appraisement of the accumulations of property, and of the products of the next preceding year; but these assessments are made in the first instance by a thousand different officials, who fix prices and quantities upon such an immense variety of grounds that the census bureau must revise the returns by the lights which its chief officers can command. The estimates, averages, and guesses of all these agents afford us results which we are not innocent enough to believe in.

For a statement, in detail, of the sources of error in the decennial census reports, and an estimate of their amount, the reader is referred to our fifth chapter, (*ante*, p. 50).

Notwithstanding all these errors, which are all errors of defect, and of large proportion to the true values, we get a fragment of fact, a point or fraction of basis, from which we can restore the

COMMERCE.   169

parts that are wanting sufficiently well for some purposes; and among the rest, for the inquiry now in hand, a safe estimate may be made by taking care to keep within clearly reasonable limits.

Under these cautionary guides, we take four thousand millions of dollars to be the value, in first hands, of our present annual production of commodities. About the half of these are agricultural and mining products. The half of these last are raw material for our manufactures. The whole may be analyzed thus: one thousand millions worth of agricultural products go without much further change of form into consumption. Upon the other thousand millions worth of agricultural and mining materials, labor and capital are employed which double their ultimate value. (The average value of the raw material of manufactures is given by the census of 1860 at 53.26 per cent of the value of the products.) This gives us a rough start of three thousand millions—to which we may fairly add a third for the values of products excluded by the minimum rule of the census takers, and labor otherwise employed in production and not embraced in any census schedules.

This surely is safely within the limits of our actual production of commodities in the year 1860, which is twelve times the value of our foreign imports for consumption ($4000 \div 335 = 12$), and by a sufficient deduction for products which were consumed by the producers, and which did not go into exchange in any way, the account stands of domestic trade as ten to one in market price.

But be it remembered, by no means the same in economic value, this market price in first hands, taken for comparison of the respective values of foreign and domestic products in our exchanges, leaves out of consideration, or as proportionably equal, the transportation of both,* and the occupation of merchants and profits of

---

* The exports of the United States to manufacturing countries in the fiscal year 1868-9, gold and silver excepted, were of the value of $250,000,000. At $125 per ton, this would give two millions of tons, but not the half of this quantity ever touched a railroad or canal on the way to the sea ports. The return merchandise did not reach the amount of seven hundred thousand tons, and of this amount not more than four or five hundred thousand tons came from the looms, workshops, and iron mills of Europe—thus one and a half millions of tons weight of transportation upon our canals and railroads is enough to allow for the year's foreign trade. But their total traffic amounted to sixty five million tons, and of this the foreign was certainly not more than two per cent.

trade, all of which are manifestly unjust to the trade in domestic commodities, for in the number of removals and of sales, and in the amount of employment afforded by the primitive forms of things, before they reach their ultimate marketable state, or are ready for consumption, there is a vast difference. All these changes and exchanges, with all their accompanying profits, have passed upon the foreign goods before they enter our market, and they here go through none of the stages of conversion for use prior to the point at which they become the sole subject of the trader in finished commodities.

Recollecting this difference against the economic value of foreign imports generally, as they appear in the markets of the United States, let us approximately ascertain their status in this respect.

An examination of the imports of 1860 shows that fifty-seven and one-half per cent of their value was in manufactured goods, ready for distribution to consumers, and only forty-two and one-half per cent in commodities of the kinds which are not native to our own climate, such as spices, dye-stuffs, tropical fruits, coffee, tea, tropical woods, medicines, gums, grasses, and wool coarser than we grow at home. These were either materials for further conversion, or supplementary to our own natural supplies, and thus indispensable and legitimate subjects of international trade.

Our foreign import trade, therefore, which was clearly legitimate and every way unexceptionable, amounted in value to only one hundred and forty-two millions, exclusive of specie, which was as one to twenty-three and one-half of the value of our domestic products exchanged ($3,350$ m. $\div 142\frac{1}{2} = 23\frac{1}{2}$). This latter amount is all that we can logically set to the credit of our foreign import trade, considered in its *economic* value to us. These goods came to us from countries differing in climate, soil, and industrial products from our own. They came not manufactured further than their preservation and transportation required. They supplemented our resources and ministered to our industries.

But the British and French dominions in Europe, with Germany, Holland, Belgium, Hamburg, and Bremen, sent us goods on which the last touches of converting skill had already been ap-

---

Three hundred thousand immigrants were worth more to the transportation lines. So much more valuable to the internal improvement interests of the country are live men, than foreign commodities.

plied. They were ready, not for reproduction, but finished for consumption, and entered into our account, not as stock, but as expenses, to the amount of $193,000,000. They consisted of such articles as these: acids, bleaching powders, clocks and watches, clothing, coal, dolls and toys, dressed furs, hats and bonnets, iron, steel, laces and embroideries, lead, gloves, tanned and dressed skins, sole and upper leather, linseed, essential oils, paints, paper, printed books, salt, silk piece-goods and hosiery, soda, brandy, spirits, wines, chinaware, and manufactures of cotton, wool, worsted, flax, glass, gold, silver, hemp, iron and steel, lead, leather, paper, wood, and zinc. In this list there are no articles which were not of the value of a quarter of a million of dollars. The omitted articles of less annual value are like those that are given—all alike of that character which were luxuries or fancy goods, or such as, while actually of prime necessity, were yet of a kind which home labor and native materials would have afforded us, and which, as imports, could have been dispensed with; and they were liable to the further and chief objection that, in the forms imported, they displaced an equivalent value of our labor and capital, and actually to such extent enforced an idleness of industry and enterprise injurious far beyond the cost or the cash disbursed in their purchase.

People talk of balances in international trade, which they find in the footings of import and export values; and they express the difference in dollars, or francs, or pounds sterling. This is a sheer misunderstanding of the subject. There is and can be no such balances in money values between the exports and imports of a nation's trade, further than the temporary differences in the trading merchants' accounts, which is nothing to the purpose for which it is usually cited. But there is a balance of trade not seen in importing merchants accounts current, no matter how they stand with their foreign correspondents—a balance of vast importance to the parties respectively—a balance which nothing in book credits or debits can settle—a balance that tells long after the book accounts are all evenly closed. It is a balance in the *kind* of trade, the kind of exchanges, which is not in its nature measurable by money values. A trade which inflicts a difference in the productive power of a people—which takes from them their self-supporting labor, and aggravates the mischief of industrial dependency by all the moral and social evil of feebleness, ignorance, and paralysis in the industrial interests of the community—this is a balance to be deeply considered and vigilantly avoided.

There is a kind of labor that requires and employs but little skill; which employs and educates none but the lowest physical powers of the laborer, and repays nothing beyond the means of a mere animal subsistence—a labor of slaves, and sure, to enslave whoever is doomed to it. There are other styles and kinds of labor whose products are the necessities and enjoyments of the proper human life, which, in their several grades, rising to the highest known in the most advanced societies, employ and educate the better and best and noblest of the human faculties, and repay, in their rewards, a duly-proportioned wealth to those who command and secure them.

There is evidently in the progress of things—in the order of Providence, working for the deliverance of men from the bondage of animalism, and from its limitations in resources and enjoyments—a constant endeavor to substitute the insensate forces of nature for the drudgery of human beings, and to remit them by the route, and through the regenerating power of education, from one degree of skilled industry to another and a higher, until emancipation shall be complete—till toil shall no longer fail of its best ends, or absorb any more of the life than is consistent with, and promotive of, the highest style of life of which man is capable on earth.

Money values are not the guides or governors in *this* policy of industry, and the loss or gain of trade measured by the footings of mercantile accounts, decides nothing of any moment in the question of welfare which tests the real loss or gain in all labor and trade.

The world cannot afford more than an ox's wages for an ox's work, or more than a slave's subsistence for his toil, which has no higher aim for him than his mere subsistence; but the world can afford to pay for, and finds its highest interest in employing and rewarding, the nobler ingredients in the work of production, which the mind and morals of the laborer offer in the market.

All this difference lies between skilled and unskilled industry. And in all the difference between the highest and lowest styles of men, and between every degree in the long scale that divides them, there is a choice that concerns all forms and degrees of prosperity to an individual and to a people.

An international trade that favors the development of a nation in power, rank, and knowledge, takes for itself the character of a natural exchange, and brings along with it all the blessings that philosophers demonstrate, statesmen strive for, and orators and poets glorify, in what they call commerce.

But foreign trade has another side or aspect, and that is the one chiefly insisted upon by the cosmopolitans of Political Economy: it opens markets for domestic production, widens and enlarges it, they say, and besides, in effect, makes a universal fair of exchanges for all varieties of commodities; barters surpluses in supply of deficiencies; levels the hills and lifts the valleys of industrial facilities; interchanges the superiorities of all parties, and gives each the advantage of his own, and participation in that of every other; serving the aggregate man of all nations as the hand helps the foot, and the eye supplements the ear, in the individual organism.

Very well: so far as international trade does this, and does no mischief besides, it is just the legitimate commerce which reason and policy commend and necessity itself commands. But is it not plain that all these beneficent reciprocities absolutely imply at once needful and helpful *differences* between the parties engaged in such commerce? The very terms of the proposition confine its claims to exchanges of differences. Reduced to its directest logical form, trade between distant regions means supplementary supplies, not competitive traffic. It means the harmony of varieties, not the domination of advantages. It means, if not equal, at least, common benefits, in which each party finds his own interests promoted, with no kind of loss or damage incurred.

Such trade is conditioned, not unconditional. It must be held in keeping with its proper object. The broadest and most unvarying condition is the necessity of importing whatever cannot be produced on the spot; in other words, with respect to natural products the temperate zones must bring the exclusive products of the torrid and frigid zones from the climates and soils which yield them, if they would have them. We must get our finer furs from the north and our spices from the south; therefore, international trade, in the first place must be *across* climates, as to the natural products of the earth. Under this limitation, and to this extent, trade is supplementary, indispensable, unchangeable, and always free from intrusive competition.

Here there is no dispute about its propriety, or its benefits.

But there are artificial products of labor and skill, which are not marked by this distinction of character, under natural law. And here lies the debatable ground, in which the theorists who set no limit to trade, under their system of cosmopolitanism, differ worldwide from those who hold the very different doctrine that Political Economy is a theory of productive power, and that its dogmas are not universal and unconditional, but subject to conditions and necessary adaptations to the exigencies of nations; or, in other words, that, a true practical economy is national as opposed to universal. These latter of course hold, or, consistently, should hold that Political Economy is not properly a science, but a remedial and directory system of policy, or expediency, variable with the varieties of the cases and conditions to which it applies.

That it is not a science, as chemistry, music, physics, or astronomy, are sciences, is obvious enough, when we call upon its professors for first principles that would command universal assent—when we consult them for details of doctrine; when we try their dogmas by history, or by prophesy, or, when we ask them for a demonstrated doctrine of civil government in respect to their department of inquiry; for a system of currency; of taxation; of education; for a law distributing the products of industry between capital, skill, and labor; for a philosophy of public benevolences, or, for any principles in any way or degree regulative of industrial relations, or of rent, interest, profits, pauperism, internal improvements, distribution of productive functions, regulation of commodity exchanges, or for any practical workings of the world's necessary business.

Would anything surprise or disgust the adepts of this so-called science more than to ask them for a formula for the distribution of the products of industry between the capitalist who supplies the money, the skilled artisan who invents or directs the machinery, and the drudge who supplies the muscular power of their joint enterprise? His system of words and disputes leaves all such matters to settle themselves. The favorite avoidance of such a test is to parade the impracticableness of his principles, as a first principle of his *science!* He tells you that the law of competition (as if competition were not in itself the veriest lawlessness) will take care of the rewards of capital, skill and labor—that, in effect, strife, to the exhaustion of the strivers, is the way to harmony and happiness, or that chaos, without the creative word of control, must ferment itself into orderly form.

Thomas Jefferson said that a pure and simple democracy is the devil's own government. To this pure democracy in government, without constitutional law, without order, rank, or distribution and limitation of functions, pure and free competition, in industry and trade, exactly corresponds; and, accordingly, the last best authority among the French economists of the trader's school, declares that, "if we consider the great object of all labor, the universal good, in a word, *consumption*, we cannot fail to find that Competition is to the moral world what the law of equilibrium is to the material one."—*Frederick Bastiat, Sophisms of Protection, chap. iv.*

Setting aside, then, those natural and necessary exchanges which the laws of soil and sunshine compel, let us examine the principles and policy which should rule in the trade which has artificial objects for its subjects. These, under certain modifications, may be produced anywhere and everywhere; and the practical question arises as to them, under what circumstances should their production be limited to any one region in preference to another, and where, when, and why should the peculiar advantage of their manufacture be neglected by one people and enjoyed by another?

The best general answer to these questions is, that such division should obtain just where it must, and only when it must, and so long as it must, of necessity, be so; which brings us to the still broader declaration that foreign trade is rightfully a matter of compulsion, and never of absolutely free choice.

This is the law of interchange under climatic necessities. Why not also the law under circumstances which equally allow and enforce it? Rightly speaking, there is no such thing as free foreign trade, except as lawlessness gets the name of freedom, or as men are free to violate law.

CHAPTER XIII.

TRADE BETWEEN NATIONS IN DIVERSE GEOGRAPHIC AND ECONOMIC CONDITIONS.

Systems merely remedial must vary with all changes of their subjects.—Political Economy limited to national interests.—A logic-built system suited only to conditions in which no system at all is needed.—The let-alone theory in place there.—Where there is anything at risk, or any choice of policy, self-defense and self-direction are demanded.—" Free Trade" allowed while it favors growth, but forbidden when it restricts home industry.—Exchange values may rule consumption, but may not ruin productive industry.—Prosperity, not prices, rightfully governs policy.—Conditions which require foreign trade.—A warring trade requires a philosophy of conquest.—The British system in history.—Our exports in 1860—kinds—one-eighth of manufactures, seven-eighths raw commodities.—Two classes of American agriculturists broadly distinguished.—Our farmers export but two per cent of their products—our planters, seventy-five per cent of theirs.—Cotton looks to foreign trade, and not to the interest of the laborers or of any other national industry.—Cotton has no patriotism—always a rebel.—Husbandry loyal to all other industries.—An additional half million of people at home would consume all our foreign exports.—These exports always of the coarsest and least profitable kinds of our products.—Superiority of the home market.—Consuming cost of transportation.—The cry for immigrants means the want of a near and constant market.—Rivalry in our foreign market for breadstuffs.—British islands our only European market for breadstuffs and provisions.—Great and rapid changes in the European demand.—Our share in England's supplies.—Ruinous fluctuations in prices.—Home consumption of wheat.—England takes one peck per head; we consume five bushels.—Aggregate of exports to all Europe.—Exports of tobacco.—Only thirty-six per cent of our farmers' exports go to Europe; sixty-four per cent to non-manufacturing countries.—Importance of the *whither* and the *what* we export.—The natural drift plainly indicated.—Uncertainty, insignificance, and unprofitableness of the market commended to us by the trader theory.—The larger quantities are always at the lower prices.—Reflex effect of foreign upon home prices.—General Jackson on diversification of American industries and on foreign markets for our products.—General Grant's concurrence after a lapse of forty years.—Extended domestic manufactures would dispense with the worthless foreign demand.

TAKING the ground that, a system of economy for the direction of a nation's business cannot be uniform or universal in its provisions—that, it is only remedial and directory in its nature, like medicine and civil government, or anything else that has disorder to deal with, and changefulness in the character of its subjects and objects—that, it must be guided by expediency—that, its most general principles must be accommodated to exigences, and that, therefore, it must necessarily accept the presently practicable, as it staggers on through expediencies toward the far-off absolute; and, that, its very best and wisest rules wear out in the work which they direct; we, of course, expect that in every difference of conditions among different peoples, and, at every step of progress in the onward march of the same people, a different measure and movement must be taken; changing with all changes of economic and social conditions, and constant only in the effort of adaptation.

Surely, it is not too much to say that, a system of national economy is properly concerned with its own concerns; and that it must take care of itself, if for no other reason, because no other nation will or can. Accordingly, there can be no universal system for the government of the economic concerns of all the vast varieties of nations.

There are now existing in the world tribes of men in the savage state; others in the pastoral; others purely agricultural; others mixed agricultural and manufacturing; and others who are agricultural, manufacturing, and commercial; and all these are yet further varied by their respective degrees of advancement in each of these classes. Moreover, some of them occupy the frigid, some the torrid, and some the temperate zones; with their capabilities and their destinies, either inflexibly fixed, or greatly influenced, by climatic laws. Nor are national differences of character to be overlooked. They are not all equally capable of everything, nor of the same things. The races of men cannot be treated as homogeneous and equal in all things with which economic systems are concerned. Nay, the very same people, if favorably situated, in a temperate climate, with a sufficient extent of country, and variety of industrial agencies and resources, must, in the progress of growth, pass through all the stages, from the simplest agriculture up to the most perfect and complete diversification of productive industry and international trade.

Now, no code of doctrinal or practical economy can be true for all differences of condition in which communities of men are actually found; and no system will apply to the same people in circumstances materially changed.

Within the Arctic circle and between the Tropics, there is such constancy of conditions imposed by climate and soil; such fixed and narrow limits of industrial enterprise, and, withal, their inhabitants are so far removed from the class of progressive nations—they have so little possibility of growth and its incident changes in themselves under the present rule of the world's affairs—that *they* can have a logical law of industrial life—a permanent political economy, simply, because they need no theoretical system at all. A people that cannot diversify their industry, or increase its effectiveness, depend upon, and are confined to, a natural monopoly of their special products; and that condition of things takes the government of their affairs out of their hands. They are helpless; and the system of political economy which prescribes nothing but competition, and denies and refuses all helpfulness, is exactly the doctrine for them. Their fate and fortunes are at the disposal of the governing nations around them; their dependence upon foreign trade and foreign influence is absolute, for all that is possible above the savage for them. This, by the way, is the sum and substance of the let-alone philosophy. But nations occupying the temperate regions, well provided for progress, and with a future before them, have their fate and fortunes to make or mar by their own management. They are in necessary rivalry with the whole historic belt of the earth's surface. They are exposed to military conquest, to political domination, and to industrial vassalage to their competitors, of equal powers and similar ambitions and aspirations as their own; and it is their right, as it is their duty, sanctioned by every principle of natural morality and international law, to regulate their domestic concerns, and manage them in their own way, for their own benefit.

An agricultural people, at a very early stage, will profit greatly by unrestricted trade with a manufacturing people. But this rule holds not a moment longer, nor a step farther, than such trade ministers best to their own growth in all things that make the well-being of a people; which may be stated, to our purpose, thus: Commerce with superiors is a benefit, even a necessity, up to that point where it begins to repress advancement of the inferiors, and then it must be restricted or ended.

Legitimate trade is reciprocity, not dependence and domination.

In nature and reason it is only supplementary to domestic production. Its broad highway is north and south, across climates, not along them east and west. For the rest—the accidental, the temporary, and circumstantially unavoidable—it is the mutual supply of the things in which the respective parties are *necessarily* deficient, or of which they are at the time incapable. So long only as they are incapable, any people may properly and profitably exchange their coarser labor in the form of raw materials and provisions with foreign manufacturers, or, until their own labor and capital can produce them; that is, exchange values may rule a nation's policy of trade while such trade promotes productive power and general prosperity. When trade begins to cripple production in kinds, qualities, or value, it must be subordinated. All of which means that man, not prices, is the proper object and ruling consideration in commerce. Being compelled to dispose of theoretical dogmas which confront us with an authority that is held to be respectable, and is known to be influential, we return from an enforced digression to examine that aspect of foreign trade which lays its claim to the advantages which it affords to domestic industry by giving it an extension of its markets. There can be no question of its claims in this respect in a country like England—a country which depends in an important degree for its food upon others having more abundant and cheaper agricultural products. Such trade is a necessity of their industrial system. An island that may be covered with a thimble on any good-sized map of the world, determined to make itself mistress of the seas, supreme in the maritime carrying trade, and at the same time "the workshop of the world," must have a philosophy to fit its ambition; and needs to have its system accepted by its tributaries. It needs a foreign system of cheap labor to sustain its own of higher rewards; and it needs to have a supporting and conforming policy to keep up the required drainage of the pauperism which results from its struggle to underwork its customer nations. To these ends its civil government has, for two centuries, bent all its energies; and now, for about a hundred years, it has been indoctrinating the outside world of barbarians with a philosophy exactly corresponding to its own governing policy. Favorably situated for merchandising, it pushes trade one while by force of arms, at another by colonization, and always, by the rivalries of production, pressed to their utmost possibilities, regardless of consequences at home and abroad; and along with these forms of force, carries on an effective system of proselytism which intends submission of opinion to their policy of industrial domination—an instance of political economy being in fact national, in purpose and service, and not a whit the less so for its disguise of universality. But how does this British system suit its industrial tributaries? How has it suited, in time past, its colonies in America—how has it suited Portugal, Turkey, Ireland, and the East Indies?

We cannot and need not enter into this history. Let us see how it stands in relation to the United States in existing circumstances. We take the fiscal year 1860 (ending June 30th), as in our previous data, for the reasons, that it was the year of our greatest foreign trade up to that date—exceeding the average of the previous five years by twenty per cent; the prices were fair; the valuations were at the standard of gold; and, for the additional reason that, it was the year to which the census returns closely apply, embracing, as they did, the latter half of 1869 and the first half of 1860.

In that year our domestic exports, exclusive of the precious metals, amounted to three hundred and sixteen millions of dollars, at custom house valuation.

These exports consisted of agricultural products, animal and vegetable, no further altered from their primitive forms than is necessary for their preservation and transportation beyond seas, to the amount of fifty millions; (of these $45,250,000 in breadstuffs and provisions); the products of the sea and the forests in like condition, to the value of eighteen millions; of raw cotton, one hundred and ninety-two millions; raw tobacco, sixteen millions—an aggregate of two hundred and seventy-six millions; and of manufactures of all kinds, a fraction less than forty millions; which figures give us twelve and one-half per cent, or one-eighth, of the value of our total domestic exports in manufactures, and seven-eighths in such goods as were parted with, as nearly as possible, in their primitive forms. Of these manufactures, it is to be noted, moreover, that there were less than six millions in all forms of iron and steel; just two millions of copper, brass and lead; and of cotton fabrics, less than eleven millions; of leather, and of hemp manufactures, less than two millions; of tallow candles, soap, and spirits from grain, and of lard and linseed oil, a million and a half; of woolens nothing worth a place among the enumerated articles, and of bread and biscuit, half a million; and, nothing else that concerns the farming interests of the country except three and a third millions worth of segars and snuff—eighteen millions, all told, of manufactures from materials furnished by our farmers and planters; or, the foreign trade in these articles made an additional market at home for one-half this value in raw materials.

Our planters and farmers found markets abroad that year for raw cotton, rice, and raw tobacco, and for breadstuffs and provisions to the value of two hundred and fifty-eight millions.

The products of farming and planting that year amounted in value to full twenty-five hundred millions. They had a foreign market for ten and five-eighths per cent of their products in money value.

But there are distinct interests involved in the form of the statement: the agriculturists, other than those who cultivated cotton, as miners dig for gold, for the products which exhaust the sources of supply, and who had no policy beyond the current profit of their pursuit, must be distinguished from those whose business links them into the closest connection with the industries around them—who must secure a steady and sufficient market against competition everywhere confronting them, and must, at the same time, husband and improve the source of their supplies as gold-diggers cannot do, and cotton-planters will not. Our farmers proper had a product worth twenty-three hundred millions of dollars, of which the foreign market took from them but fifty-nine millions worth, or two and one-half per cent, or one in forty dollars worth.

The cotton growers' crop amounted to 5,198,077 bales, of which foreign nations purchased 3,812,345, or nearly seventy-five per cent. They found a' home market for $61,000,000, and a foreign market for $192,000,000 worth. Here we have a vast difference in the respective interests of the planter and farmer in our foreign trade—showing, again, the necessity of attending to the specialties of the many and dissimilar subjects of commercial exchanges. These differences are so great and so important that we can but suggest and submit them for reflection. Cotton, for instance, held foreign relations threefold stronger than its interests at home. Its rule favored neither the laborers employed by it, nor the prosperity of any other national industry. It produced upon the planter none of the distinguishing influences which are expressed in the good old name of husbandman, as applied to the tiller of the soil who depends upon it for exhaustless support. It made the cultivator nomadic by its exhaustiveness. It compelled him to be an annexationist of new territory. Cotton had no patriotism. It was cosmopolitan in all its instincts and interests, for it was a monopolist. It looked to its markets, and knew nothing but money values. It had no impulses that could make its system one that can be governed by the leading idea of productive power. It was exhaustive of its soil, of its labor, and, eventually, of itself. It had, as a special and exclusive industry, all the qualities and characters that made it look to foreign trade for its sales, and for all its purchasers. It was the very ideal of a system of exports and imports, and, therefore, so far was it from embracing the harmonies of all industrial interests that it warred upon them all. It was, from the day it achieved its supremacy in commerce and crowned itself king, in a constant commercial rebellion against the republicanism of diversified labor. Such, indeed, is the character of every isolated pursuit; such is the history of all mining countries that ever obtained the mastery of the world's trade. They would not consider the interests of any industry unless it could be made a tributary. Men are nothing to them but instruments of production, and, the Providence, which we call the world's policy of business, naturally destroys them.

It is not so with husbandry. In its simplest forms it cannot even maintain its own rights and liberties; and it never can grow into strength and maturity but in harmony and interdependence with all the other forms of diversified production. It prospers in a fair copartnership of interests, and has no tendencies against fairly distributed and mutually beneficial industries.

But, let us return to the value of foreign trade as affording a market to the people of the United States. The foreign consumption of our agricultural products, as we have seen, at the highest figure which they ever reached before the time of our civil war, amounted to about two per cent of the annual product. They were taken by the foreign consumers to the value of barely such an amount as would have been consumed by an additional number of people at home equal to one forty-eighth of our population, or about 646,000 people. The exports so taken were necessarily of the cheapest, coarsest, and least profitable of the products of our soil. They were such as grow upon land worth from five to thirty dollars per acre, and which cannot be produced in surplus abundance on land worth more. They are bulky, and are of kinds that, after bearing all the cost of transportation, are sure to meet the rival products of every semi-barbarous country in the great markets of the world which they seek. The other products of land which will not bear distant carriage, in a home market bring prices which makes all the difference in the value of lands near a great city as contrasted with that of the prairies of the remote West.

One more carpenter, blacksmith, shoemaker, or other artisan, in every township in the United States, would give a larger, surer, better market to its farmers than all the foreign world ever did, or ever can afford them. Distance at home of two or three hundred miles, eats up half the value of their produce though they have the entire market of the country to themselves. It costs the price of one bushel of wheat, when it is at seventy-five cents per bushel, to send another from central Illinois to Liverpool; and sometimes, corn in the ear is used in the more distant localities for fuel, because it will pay nothing, beyond the cost of carriage, in the eastern cities of the Union. Shall a foreign market be sought for, in the face of all its uncertainties and expensiveness, to the neglect of a system which will provide a home consumption steady, and certainly remunerative?

The effort to promote immigration from Europe, now stirring the people of every region at the shortest distances from our sea-board cities, is testimony to the truth and force of the views here presented. The cry is for labor, indeed, but the no less important want is, for home consumers. A working man is all the more welcome if he brings with him a family of four or five persons to feed and clothe.

In the President's message of December 6, 1869, we find, involved in a few sentences of the plainest practical recommendation to Congress upon the subject of the nation's industrial interests, a complete exposition of, and directory for, the conduct of our foreign trade. He says "the extension of railroads in Europe and the East is bringing into competition with our agricultural products like products of other countries."

Let us look for a moment at the character and value of the European market for our breadstuffs in a past period, long enough to take in its usual fluctuations. Inasmuch as we have no sale for our breadstuffs in Europe except in the British Islands—all the other European countries needing foreign supplies, receiving them from near neighbors, Russia, Prussia, France, and the Turkish dominions—we have the data for our purpose unusually compact and accurate in matters of this kind: we have the British official reports, and from them we give the facts. We quote the British "Statistical Abstract" of the year 1866, page forty-two, which gives the total imports into the United Kingdom for fifteen years—from 1851 to 1865, inclusive; a period that covers the ordinary range of good and bad British harvests, commercial troubles, and includes, besides, the two years' Crimean War (March 1854 to April 1856). The quantities are given in hundred weights, gross; the flour being reduced to its equivalent in wheat, and thus included in the aggregates. We shall use the more familiar measure expressed in bushels, in rendering the statement.

In the first place, we see the unsteadiness of demand in the wide range of the total imports from all countries; twenty-six millions of bushels being the amount in the lowest year and ninety-three millions in the highest. In only four of these fifteen years did the import rise above fifty-six millions; the average of the other eleven years, selected for their nearer agreement, being forty-one millions; and even these fluctuated from twenty-six to forty-five and one-half millions.

Not only the great range of fluctuation in the demand, which in one of these years was three and a half times greater than in the lowest of seven years before, but the suddenness of the changes are specially noteworthy: in a single year varying from twenty-three millions to forty-two millions; in another year, from ninety-three to fifty-seven and, to add, if anything can add, to the uncertainties of such a market, by far the lowest average imports of any two consecutive years in this period, were those of the Crimean War. These points exhibit the fearful unreliableness of a market for a product that must be sown and prepared for it, a year before it must meet its fate.

But *our* share of the risk runs even tenfold wilder than that of the general demand. In 1855 the United Kingdom took from us 800,000, in 1860, 17,221,546, and in 1865, 2,629,347 bushels of wheat and its equivalent in flour; and in respect to our distributive share of the supply; in 1851 we furnished seventeen per cent of the

THE FARMERS' QUESTION. 185

total import; in 1860, twenty nine per cent, and in 1865, five and three-quarters per cent. While, as if to expose still more surprisingly the capriciousness of this trade, in 1864, the worst year of our Rebellion, for such a calculation, we sent them thirty-five per cent of their total foreign receipts.

The only other grain to be considered is our maize or Indian corn. The British import account stands thus: in 1865, total imports, seven millions cwts.—of this, from the Turkish dominions, over three millions; from the United States, one and three-quarter millions. In 1864, from Turkish dominions, three and two-third millions; from the United States, 294,263. In 1859, 14,417 cwts. from United States, and from European countries, 5,618,727. In 1861 we sent them 7,385,718 cwts., or 512 times more than in 1859, and in 1864 they took from us twenty-five times less than in 1861, and twenty times more than in 1859!

Now look at the variance of prices for our breadstuffs in London: our wheat brought 83s. 9d. per quarter of eight imperial (equal to something over eight and one-quarter of our bushels) in 1855; in 1864, 40s. 5d. per quarter, and in the intermediate years various rates between these prices; at the former price taking 3,609,583 bushels, at the latter 18,811,204, being about $2.44 per American bushel at the highest, and $1.18 at the lower rate, put down in Liverpool or London; cost of freight, commissions, insurance and profits of all intermediate dealers included. The average of this wide range of prices for our wheat was $1.45 per American bushel in the English markets. The average quantity per annum, eighteen and one-eighth millions of bushels, and the variance of quantity was, in the lowest year, 803,607 bushels, and in the highest, 9,100,707—the former in 1859, the latter in 1862, which latter extraordinary quantity brought but $1.47 per bushel, as against the average of British wheat in the same year, $1.63.

Our own population consumes five bushels of wheat per head per annum, 31,000,000 of persons, our number in 1860, giving a market for 155,000,000 bushels.

The British official reports of imports from the United States for the four years 1865-8 show the effects of the railroad system in Europe in lessening our market there for wheat and flour in most remarkable figures. In the four years 1861-4 they imported from us 59,322,160 cwt.—forty-four and one-third per cent of their total import; from all other countries, 74,555,294. But in the four years 1865-8 they took from us but 16,522,509 cwt.—only twelve and three-quarters per cent, and from other countries 113,297,549 cwt., which was eighty-seven and one-quarter per cent of the total. Here, then, we have our average cut down from 18,500,000 bushels per annum in the eight years preceding 1865, to 7,727,837 in the four years since; or, the population of the British islands are now consuming one peck of our wheat per head per annum.

The home consumption of five bushels per head, with a protection of twenty cents per bushel against the wheat of Canada, and an immigration now able to consume our whole surplus, is surely a market better worth striving for, and securing by a policy of domestic industry, which is now increasing this home market at an unprecedented rate.

We have made our arithmetical demonstration of the insecurity and insignificance of our only European market for breadstuffs on wheat and flour alone. In respect to provisions of all other kinds, which are among the transportable products of agriculture, the same story may be told.

To illustrate and prove this we need only refer to our own report of Commerce and Navigation for the fiscal year 1859-60—the greatly largest year of our foreign trade previous to the commencement of our civil war. In that year we exported to British Europe, of farm products proper, to the value of only $18,100,762, and imported from them articles identical with, or corresponding to these exports of the value of $3,902,535, leaving, when deducted, a market for no more than $14,198,227. The commodities here embraced were breadstuffs and provisions of all kinds, hides, tallow, leather, oils, lard, wool, ashes, oil-cake, wax, seeds, hops, oats, spirits, and other raw materials. If we add lumber in all forms ($709,312) we have in round numbers agricultural exports for the year amounting to $15,000,000.

France, which is herself a large exporter of agricultural products, of course did still less. The aggregate value of all similar articles which she took from us that year amounted to barely $1,568,295, and to all Europe beside less than another million and a half—all told, about $18,000,000 worth of farm products proper.

Cotton and tobacco are not included in these amounts, and if the latter claims a place on account of the growing culture by our farmers, as part of their varied crops, then $16,000,000 covers the total export in leaf, and $3,375,000, manufactured.

To get another view of our foreign markets, and of their value to our own agriculture, it is worth while to note that in the fiscal year 1859–60, our total exports of breadstuffs and provisions were $38,858,086, and of these there went to all manufacturing countries in Europe—(Great Britain, France, Germany, Holland, Belgium, and the Free cities) just $13,952,988, or thirty-six per cent of the total; the balance being taken by non-manufacturing countries in the Eastern hemisphere, and in America. Seventy-seven per cent of our leaf tobacco also went to agricultural countries, making together $31,750,000 to those with whom we have no rival industries, while $31,500,000 went to the peoples whom we designate as manufacturing, because our imports from them are such as displace our own products of the like kinds.

Is it not well, as a farmer's question, to analyze our foreign trade in exports, that we may the better understand how far and where our interests lie in the direction of raising raw materials for foreign trade? Leaving out tobacco and cotton we had in our best year of foreign trade a market for agricultural raw materials of all kinds of less than twenty millions, among all the nations to which the trade theorists resign us for our supply of the things which employ skilled labor; and if we add tobacco, the sum is but $31,500,000. The non-manufacturing countries took from us thirty-two millions worth of our manufactures, while the rest of the world took a little less than eight millions worth. Leaving cotton out of the account, the non-manufacturing nations took from us $63,750,000 of our total exports of commodities, other than gold and silver, and the manufacturing peoples took $53,750,000. Which way lies our trade as indicated by our exchanges of farming products with the rest of the world?

Again: our imports for that year from non-manufacturing countries amounted to forty-two and four-tenths per cent, or seven-sixteenths of the whole. Legitimate trade thus far asserted itself in spite of the unfavorable policy which invited our industrial rivals to disturb it.

The farming interest,—so persistently appealed to for the support of a system that assigns to us the function of supplying food and raw material for the higher styles of production in other countries,—

we need only point to the fact that the policy never gave them customers abroad for more than twenty millions worth of their special products—never gave them a promise reliable for even that much, or half that much, in time to provide for it—and always, the quantity so far influenced the price, that the actual profit is exceedingly questionable. The trade in this respect has this complexion: in the four years, 1854–7, when our wheat averaged two dollars per bushel, in London they took 38,764,581 bushels, but when they took in the four years, 1861–4, 110,734,715 bushels, the price averaged one dollar and forty cents. See the difference: at the higher price, 9,500,000, and at the lower, 27,500,000 bushels, per annum.

We cannot settle the profits of this trade, as they fall into the hands of the merchant exporters, factors and other middlemen; but we are clear that wherever the farmer gets the foreign market for the larger quantity, it is at the cost of the lower price; and, whenever the higher prices rule in England, he is reduced in his sales to about one-third of the quantity, as in the instances last cited.

But some one will say—it is the surplus of production only that is so transported, and at any price, it is so much gain or escape of loss. Not so. If $1.40 in London means seventy cents to the farmer in the West, the reaction of the London price cuts down that of all that is retained or sold in the home market, and the foreign sales take off never so much as thirty millions from the annual crop which ordinarily rises to at least one hundred and seventy-five millions. So, if they get at this rate for the whole crop $122,500,000, and the reflected effect of the foreign sales cuts down the price of all but fifteen cents per bushel, the total exportation is a dead loss; it might as well be cast into the sea, or far better, fed to horses and hogs at home; for one hundred and seventy-five million bushels at seventy cents, is worth no more than one hundred and forty-five millions at eighty-five cents.

From all which it appears now, as it did in 1824 when General Jackson wrote his Coleman letter, where he asks: "What is the real situation of the American agriculturist? Where has the American farmer a market for his surplus products? Except for cotton he has neither a home nor a foreign market. Take, [he continues,] from agriculture in the United States six hundred thousand men, women and children, and you will at once give a home market for more breadstuffs than all Europe now furnishes us."

THE FARMERS' QUESTION. 189

The condition of the country is so far changed now, that General Grant points to the home market as the only reliable one, and indicates the causes at work which will speedily destroy even the insignificant outlet which has heretofore been found in the only country in Europe where we ever sold any breadstuffs and provisions at all. Jackson wrote his letter in 1824. Forty-five years have, in a good measure, taken away one limb of Jackson's complaint, by setting in operation, to a great extent, the remedy he prescribed. The home market is tolerably well built up; and it remained only for President Grant to warn us that the foreign reliance is rapidly getting worse, and to urge the maintenance and extension of the system of domestic manufactures which will enable us to dispense with it, without any detriment by deprivation.

CHAPTER XIV.

FREE TRADE AND PROTECTION.

Political Economy not a science; opinions of Daniel Webster and Napoleon Bonaparte.—J. B. Say's work prohibited by Napoleon.—The labor interests of the continent of Europe defended against Great Britain.—" Industry a *property*." Lord Brougham and Joseph Hume would strangle foreign manufactures in their cradle.—British capital the instrument of warfare against foreign competition. HISTORY of protection and free trade in the experience of the United States. Variety and extent of our territory, composition of our population.—British restrictions of colonial industry.—Manufactures freed and fostered by the war of the Revolution; their great progress; Hamilton's Report in 1791; they perish for want of protection between 1783 and 1789.—Testimony of Dr. Williamson, John Marshall, Ramsey, Belknap and Madison.—Protection avowed in the first tariff act of the first Federal Congress.—Washington on the results of protection. —The continental wars, from 1793 to 1815, with our embargo, non-importation act, and our own war of 1812 effectually defended our manufactures.—Congressional report of 1815 proves their prosperity.—Slight advance in the ensuing thirty years.—The free trade period, 1816 to 1824, ending in universal distress.—The evils all remedied by protection from 1824 to 1832.—Character of these tariff acts.—Tariff for protection proved to be most productive of revenue.—Faults, and resulting mischief of the protection theory at this period.— Act of 1832 gave us the first well-principled free list; discharge of the national debt; surplus in the treasury; reduction of income attended by reduction of customs rates—the free trade theory of that day.—The directly contrary doctrine of the free traders in 1846 and 1856.—The same party now again returns to the doctrine of 1832, which is once more refuted by the high rates of 1861-71 as it was in 1824-32; the nullification era, and the surrender of protection.—Capital and labor driven from the Eastern to the Western States.—Enormous increase of the sales of the public lands.—Great reduction of the customs, bankruptcy of the people and of the Treasury.—Increase of imports and inflation of bank credits and currency.—Inflation of the currency due to excess of imports; never did or could happen under adequate protection.—" Periodic " financial and business revulsions due to free trade.— Consequences of the Compromise Act bring about another change of commercial policy, and give us the protective tariff of 1842.—Change from specific to *ad valorem* duties in 1846.—Consequent unsteadiness of its protective provisions. Temporary reliefs from the European famine of 1848; the Crimean War of 1854; discoveries of gold in 1850 and the excessive production and export of Southern staples.—A sufficient success of the protective rates, thus corroborated, once more invites the overthrow of the protective policy.—The reduced rates of the act of 1857 precipitate the issue, and the revulsion and specie suspension of 1857 follow.—A greater and a worse revulsion prevented by the great Rebellion of 1861—grounds of this opinion.—The Morrill tariff and amendments.—The national industry defended and sustained; the expenditures of the war provided; the public debt greatly reduced; the threatened collapse of the country postponed six years; the Treasury overflowing, and, another *pretext* provided for the ruinous policy of free trade.

The reader of these papers will have noticed, perhaps, with some surprise, and it may be with even some less favorable feeling, my reiterated denials of the pretensions of "Political Economy" to the name and rank of a science. It is just here, in the foreground of the great debate, that I join issue with the free trade theorists. Let me shelter my audacity under the authority of two statesmen, one of whom had large opportunity, and as large capacity, for testing its theoretical pretensions, and the other the most pressing necessity for judging its doctrines in their practical application. The first whom I cite is Daniel Webster. In a letter to Mr. Dutton, dated May 9th, 1830, he says: "Though I like the investigation of particular questions, I give up what is called the 'Science of Political Economy.' There is no such science. There are no rules on these subjects so fixed and invariable as that their aggregate constitutes a science. I believe that I have recently run over twenty volumes, from Adam Smith to Professor Dew, of Virginia, and from the whole, if I were to pick out with one hand all the mere truisms, and, with the other, all the doubtful propositions, little would be left."*

My other protector is Napoleon Bonaparte. Adam Smith's "Wealth of Nations" was fairly afloat in 1784. In 1803 J. B. Say published his "Treatise on the Production, Distribution, and Consumption of Wealth," in which he methodized the irregular mass of curious and original speculations of Smith, and gave to the new-born *science* the form and order which has ever since governed the method of cultivating its themes. When Napoleon subjected it to his practical style of criticism, he said, "If an empire were made

* In this sweeping sentence it is to be observed that Adam Smith is expressly named, and among the twenty volumes must have been included Malthus, Ricardo, J. B. Say, and J. R. McCulloch, for all these were in the libraries then, and these authors are still regarded by their followers as *the* founders and the authorities of their school. Our American authors, Carey, List, and Colwell, could not have been included in the verdict of the great "expounder," for neither of these published his works until after the year 1836.

of adamant, political economy would grind it to powder." He prohibited its further publication in France for a dozen years. He saw that the logic of the work was specious, and he knew that it was pernicious; and, being too busy with the government of a nation to enter the lists as a disputant, he interdicted the book.

Under the circumstances he did exactly right. The short answer of a blockade all around the coasts of continental Europe, declared by the Berlin and Milan decrees, was the practical solution of the questions involved. Then, again, the sword cut the gordian knot, and France and Germany were thereby released from industrial dependence upon Great Britain forever. A professor of political economy could not have done as much with any quantity of foolscap.

Napoleon had another idea worthy of him. "Formerly," he said, "there was only one kind of property, *land;* another has since arisen, *industry;*" and he held it as wise and as necessary to defend the one as the other from foreign invasion. He knew that a nation's welfare is not measured by its foreign trade, but by its productive power—that the policy of a huckster is not a directory for the conduct of national affairs; and he freely sacrificed prices, while he fostered the power that produces values. He would not stand haggling over the market cost of commodities, but addressed his policy to the real issue: how shall a nation increase its power to command and consume them? Such minds as his are prophetic. He needed not to wait till 1815, when Lord Brougham, in Parliament, said, "England can afford to incur some loss on the export of English goods, for the purpose of destroying manufactures in their cradle;" or for the avowal made by the renowned Joseph Hume, in 1828, that he desired "to see the manufactures of the Continent strangled in the cradle;" nor needed he to wait for the Parliament report of its commissioner appointed in 1854 to inquire into the state of the population in the mining districts, in which the following argument is addressed to the strikers for higher wages: "Authentic instances are well known of [English] employers having in such times [times of depressed prices] carried on their works at a loss amounting to three or four hundred thousand pounds in the course of three or four years. If the efforts of those who encourage the combination to restrict the amount of labor, and to produce strikes, were to be successful for any length of time, the great accumulations could be no longer made which enable a few of the most wealthy capitalists *to overwhelm all foreign competition in times of great depression.* The large capitals of this country are the great instruments of warfare (if the expression may be allowed) against the competing capitals of foreign countries, and are the most essential instruments now remaining, by which our manufacturing supremacy can be maintained." Napoleon foresaw all these threats of free foreign trade reduced to practice, and fortified the industry of France against them as vigorously as he defended the soil itself against the invasion and domination of foreign foes, and for the same and even better reasons.

These preliminaries are intended to apprise the students of our subject that we take ground, first, against the logic and the method of the theory of commerce relied upon by the free traders, as wholly fallacious and inapplicable; and, secondly, against its practical consequences, as directly and totally opposed to the requirements of our national welfare.

The caption of this chapter intimates our intention to discuss protection and free trade as they interlock and antagonize each other in our national policy. A more abstract and more formal treatment would not so well comport with our design and our limits. With this view we submit a very brief history of the experience of the country in its varied experiments of the respective systems.

Almost within the memory of living men, the United States have risen from the complete subjection of colonial dependence, and from the condition of separate provinces, united by no political bond, to that of a compact, rich, and independent nation; outranking the empires of the old world in territorial extent, and varied capabilities of production; equaling the strongest of them in population; composed of representatives of all the progressive races of mankind; embracing the soils and climates of the whole habitable globe; shaped into a continent convenient for internal commerce, with a sea-coast so deeply indented, and a lake and river system dissecting the mass so thoroughly, that a domain only one-sixth less than the area of the fifty-nine or sixty empires, states and republics, of Europe, and of equal extent with the Roman Empire at its largest, is cut, for the purposes of internal and external commerce, into twenty islands of the size of Great Britain. Here are all the conditions, in ample proportion and suitable combination for the rehearsal of the world's history, and nothing lacking to work out a world's destiny; and here we have precipitated upon us every social, political and economic problem of the past and future of human history, with the people of every kindred and clime for the subjects and agents.

The history of such a country's commerce and industry, so far advanced as ours already is, cannot fail to be more instructive than that of any other. The development has been so rapid; the successive periods of protection and free-trade have been so frequent and sudden; and the results so plainly marked, that the varied experiences must be conclusively demonstrative of the doctrines and policies so well and so thoroughly tried.

The colonies were held under restraint so absolute that, beyond the common domestic industries, and the most ordinary mechanical employments, no kind of manufactures were permitted. In 1750, a hatter shop in Massachusetts, was declared a nuisance by the British Parliament. In the same year an act was passed permitting the importation of pig iron from the colonies, because charcoal, then exclusively employed in smelting the ore, was well-nigh exhausted in England; but forbidding the erection of tilt-hammers, slitting or rolling mills, or any establishment for the manufacture of steel. In the same year the great Earl of Chatham, alarmed at our enterprise, declared that the colonies ought not to be allowed to manufacture so much as a hob-nail. This was protection, after the manner of that day, for England, and open ports and free-trade in all its bearings, for the colonies.

The British navigation laws were enacted in the same spirit and to the same intent—to hold the colonies in commercial and industrial vassalage to the mother country. Then, we were restrained by force of law from diversifying our industry freely; now we are persuaded to accept the like dependency upon superior ability to monopolize our market, by leaving the choice of our industries undefended against an equally aggressive and an equally potent supremacy.

A protective period followed. The interruption of commerce with Great Britain during the war of the Revolution awakened, per force, the manufactures of the States that had the materials and the labor power, so that at its close they found themselves considerably advanced in those skilled industries which make a nation self-supplying. From the success attained, Alexander Hamilton, in his celebrated Report upon Manufactures, in 1791, argues the practicability and the duty of encouraging our manufactures. He enumerates, in detail, seventeen grand departments which were then well established. They prevailed as well in the Southern as in the Middle and Northern States; and he is particular to embrace "a vast scene of household manufacturing," which not being yet displaced by steam and machinery, as it has been since, he says, supplied, in different districts, two-thirds, three-fourths, and even four-fifths of all the clothing of the inhabitants. Of textile fabrics he reports, that in several kinds, the domestic fabrication was not only sufficient for the families themselves, but for sale, and to such extent in some cases that they were exported to foreign countries.

These household industries were, soon after the peace of Paris, (1783), effectually suppressed, so far as they had before been productive in excess of the home supply, by an inundation of foreign goods; for after the date of the treaty of peace, and previous to the organization of the Federal Government—a period of seven years—there was no protective power in the old confederation, and no concurrence of policy among the several States. In the first Federal Congress, a member speaking of this period of free trade, said, "We bought according to the doctrine of modern theorists, where we could purchase cheapest, and were soon inundated with foreign commodities: English goods were sold at lower rates in our maritime cities than at Liverpool or London. Our manufactures were ruined; our merchants, even those who had hoped to enrich themselves by importation, became bankrupt, and all these causes united had such an influence upon agriculture that a general depreciation of real estate followed, and failure became general among the proprietors."

Dr. Hugh Williamson, describing the distresses and disorders of the year 1786, says, "The scarcity of money is so great, and the difficulty of paying debts has been so common, that riots and combinations have been formed in many places, and the operations of civil government have been suspended."

Chief Justice Marshall, in his "Life of Washington," speaking of this crisis generally, and particularly of the causes which led to Shay's Rebellion, says, "On opening their ports, an immense quantity of foreign merchandise was introduced into the country, and they were tempted by the sudden cheapness of imported goods, and by their own wants, to purchase beyond their capacity for payment." The consequences, as soon as they had time to work themselves out, he thus describes: "The bonds of men, whose competency to pay their debts was unquestionable, could not be negotiated but at a discount of thirty, forty, and fifty per centum; real property was scarcely vendible; and sales of any article for ready money could be made only at a ruinous loss." Ramsey's History of South Carolina, and Belknap's History of New Hampshire, show that the distress was as general as intense, and that it displayed itself in "a disposition everywhere to resist the laws."

This state of things, more than any other, impelled the States to draw closer the bonds of political union, and to grant the needful powers to Congress to establish an effective system of commercial regulations for the nation. Mr. Madison, in a letter to Joseph C. Cabell, dated September 18th, 1828, fully and conclusively demonstrates this point. No one can read this letter without being convinced that, above all other causes, the sufferings of the country from the evils of its unprotected industries literally drove the loosely confederated states into a "more perfect union" empowered to provide more effectually for the "general welfare." Protection of the home industries against foreign rivalry was not only the sentiment, but, under pressure of a terrible experience of absolute free trade, had become the sensation of the day. In the heartiest sympathy with this general feeling, Washington wore a coat of domestic cloth on the day of his inauguration, "giving," as a New York journal of the day said, "to his successors, and to legislatures of after time, an indelible lesson as to the means of promoting national prosperity." The preamble to the first tariff act of the first Federal Congress, passed on the 4th of July, 1789, echoes the urgency of the public feeling, in answer to petitions poured in from every State, not excepting commercial New York, or planting South Carolina. It reads thus: "Whereas it is necessary for the support of the Government, for the discharge of the debts of the United States, and *the encouragement and protection of manufactures*, that duties be laid on goods, wares, and merchandise imported," etc. This first protective act was followed by another of the 10th of August, 1790, largely increasing the duties already imposed.

The happy results of this policy became immediately apparent—instantly, indeed—as soon as the languishing industries felt the reviving touch of the nation's fostering hand, because the confidence of security has the power of credit to anticipate time. As early as October, 1791, Washington, writing to La Luzerne, holds this language: "In my tour I confirmed by observation the accounts which we had all along received of the happy effects of the General Government upon our agriculture, commerce, and industry. The same effects pervade the Middle and Eastern States, with the addition of vast progress in the most useful manufactures."

The protective rates of the several tariffs passed before the year 1804 were quite too low to answer the intention by their unaided force, but in 1793 the opening war of the continent of Europe, which was to last, with slight remissions, until 1815, operated upon both our productive and commercial interests in the happiest way. The destructive war of England and her allies with the French Republic and Empire, the consequent disturbance of all transatlantic labor, and the suspension of specie payments by the Bank of England, which lasted from 1797 for full twenty years, raised prices abroad, and thus afforded an ample defence of our domestic markets. These again were helped by our embargo of 1807, the non-intercourse act of 1809, and finally by our war of 1812; all these causes together afforded such a shelter, and gave such an impulse to our infant manufactures, that we not only met the home demand, but were able to furnish a surplus for exportation. A Congressional report of 1815 puts our cotton and woolen manufactures at more than sixty millions per annum, with above one hundred thousand workmen employed. Thirty years afterwards Secretary Walker estimated the products of these two branches of manufacture in the United States at no more than eighty-nine millions, or less than fifty per cent increase.

England in that thirty years increased the exports of her products from forty-two millions of pounds sterling to one hundred and thirty-five millions, official valuation, or two hundred and twenty per cent.

As in the case of the war of Independence, that of 1812 had the effect to extend our manufacturing industry by excluding foreign competition, and to increase rapidly and greatly all values, as well of raw materials as of manufactured goods, labor, and real estate; thus giving a well-distributed prosperity to workmen, to land-holders, and to international commerce.

But after the battle of Waterloo, and the general pacification of Europe, England, France, and Germany went to work; the duties of the tariff of 1816, unsupported by the previous diversion of the European embroilment, were wholly inadequate. Our prosperity went down under a flood of foreign importations, and from 1819 to 1824 the country presented a picture of general distress, with shadings nearly as deep and dark as the corresponding crisis, which followed the war of the Revolution. Seven years of peace at both periods, with the country's labor undefended, inflicted a hundredfold more injury upon the people than any such periods of war for the defence of national rights ever did or could do. The intolerable mischiefs of the free trade policy in the last, as in the former instance, brought reflection to the nation. A Democratic Congress ordered the republication of Hamilton's Report of 1791 on Manufactures, which was now felt to be far better entitled to be called "An Inquiry into the Nature and Causes of the Wealth of Nations" than Adam Smith's treatise bearing that title; the agricultural Middle, Northern, and Western States joined with those more occupied with manufactures, as in a common interest, to impose higher duties upon imports, and the tariff of 1824 was passed. There was, however, something too much of the spirit of countervailing duties in this act, and something too little of the sound expediency which should have ruled its provisions. These faults were, in a good degree, avoided by the tariff of 1828. Its average rates upon the dutiable, and upon the total imports, ran something higher, as in the circumstances they should do, than those of any tariff enacted since. The success of all its aims was absolutely perfect. One of the results which most surprised the Opposition party at home and abroad was the fact that it proved just as favorable to the national finances as if that had been the exclusive object of the policy. It accomplished all the aims of the men who devised it; but the impulse which prompted its enactment transcended the principle which should have ruled its special provisions. Its supporters did not venture upon a free list so large and so necessary as the policy of protection demands. Protection is simply *defense;* nothing more, nothing less, and nothing else. Every deviation from this ruling object is, sooner or later, mischievous. The framers, perhaps, feared a failure of revenue. The statesmen of the time had not had a sufficiently large experience of a true protective policy to comprehend fully its working forces in every direction. They had a lurking fear that adequate protective duties must necessarily diminish the revenue from customs. They did not, and they could not, understand the matter as a still more varied and complete experience has instructed us, after forty years of additional observation and trial.

In 1832 the duties of 1828 were modified; tea, coffee, and a large amount, in variety and value, of foreign imports, which in no way interfered with domestic production, but rather ministered to it, were exempted from taxation. But, the whole national debt had been too quickly reduced, the mass of individual and general prosperity had been realized too suddenly, and the most fortunate people under the sun were seized with the belief that the accumulations in the national treasury would soon become unmanageable, unless they took early measures to provide against its overflow. The economic sciolists were as sure as they could be of anything, that a reduction of the rates of duty to a given percentage would reduce the revenue exactly as much. The same party—embracing the theorists who learn all they know by thinking, and those who theorize without the help of thought—afterwards made up their minds that the lower duties yield the larger revenue. Secretary Walker, in 1846, built this doctrine into a free trade axiom. Secretary Guthrie in 1856 acted upon it as an unquestionable truth, and now their lineally descended disciples are quite as sure that the higher the rate the larger the revenue! We have had enough of this.

In 1832, six or seven years of adequate protection had passed, and the time had come for a change. The terrible experiences of the periods of free trade which followed our first and second war with Great Britain were forgotten. Statesmen had arisen who knew not George the Third. The country had waxed fat as Jeshurun, and it was time to kick the policy that had "covered it with fatness." South Carolina went into nullification, Virginia sanctioned the doctrine; Alabama and Georgia took the same ground; Calhoun resigned the Vice Presidency; Hayne and Webster made immortal speeches; the foreground candidates for the next presidency foresaw their danger; and "the Father of the American system," the "great compromiser, and pacificator" postponed the Rebellion, by giving it all that it asked then, with a fairly implied promise of all that it might ask thereafter, and so, we took another turn of the free trade screw, in the shape of the compromise act of 1833.

Under this act, which abandoned the protection of domestic

labor, the imports, in the first three years of its operation, averaged one hundred and twenty-two millions, against an average of seventy millions for the last five years of the act of 1828. At the end of 1836 there was a surplus in the treasury of forty-six and a half millions. Was not this ample proof that lower duties yield the larger revenue? Not a word of it. Forty-four and a half millions of this amount came from the sales of the public lands. They never before yielded more than three millions in any one year. In 1834, the first year of the compromise, they yielded five millions, in 1835 nearly fifteen, and in 1836 nearly twenty-five millions. The revenue from customs was less in every one of these three years than it had been since 1826.

A movement, collateral and concurrent, ran along with these changes in the industrial policy of the first three years of reduced duties upon imports. At the beginning of the year 1834 there were in circulation in the United States ninety-five millions of bank notes; the loans and discounts of the banks amounted to three hundred and twenty-four millions; at the close of 1836 the bank circulation had swollen to one hundred and forty-nine millions; and the loans and discounts to above five hundred millions; an increase, in each of these particulars, of above fifty per cent in three years! In May, 1837, the banks suspended specie payments all over the country.

This is the order of the facts: a sudden increase of imports, amounting to seventy-five per cent; a sudden increase in the bank circulation and discounts, amounting to above fifty per cent; a sudden increase of the sale of public lands, equal to four hundred per cent, or, as forty-five millions to nine.

These facts mean this, and nothing else: an increase of the imports called for the increase of bank issues and credits, and the labor and capital previously employed in manufactures in the Eastern and Middle States, crowded out by the influx of foreign goods, were driven to the West to seek investment and support. The whole history of the United States, without an exceptional instance, shows that whenever the treasury was gorged by receipts from customs and the proceeds of the public lands, a money crisis was in full pressure, and, that a general bankruptcy of Government, banks, and people inevitably followed. No excessive bank issues and credits ever once occurred, or could occur, (previous to the date of the great Rebellion), under a protective tariff. And we add that, no overdealing in anything except foreign commodities can greatly or even considerably, shake the finances of the Nation and of the people, simply because no other sort of speculation or overtrading, be they ever so wild, throws out of employment the industry of the country and the capital associated with it in production.

This proposition is commended, by the facts involved, to the consideration of those who are accustomed to blame our periodic revulsions upon an extravagant credit inflation, or upon a depreciated currency. Such revulsions are neither inevitable nor inexplicable. Our history exposes the causes plainly, and suggests the remedy; and what is better, the means of prevention. Just give our labor and capital their well secured opportunity for maintaining the industrial independence of the country, and we will have no more of them—under a protective tariff the people can sustain another war of four years with any foe, domestic or foreign, and another five thousand millions of expenditure, as they have sustained the last, without one of these "inevitable and inexplicable revulsions."

Well, the seven years of unprotected American industry, stretching from 1833 to 1840, drove the people once more to reflection, and a general revolt of the country once more branded the alien policy, turned its advocates out of power, and replaced free trade by the protective tariff of 1842; which was by far the best one we have had to this day. In four years it had fully demonstrated its wisdom by extricating the country from all its difficulties, except the theories of the Revenue Reformers of that day, and the resistance of that portion of the Nation whose system of production never intended the labor of the country for the benefit of its laborers, or looked to the prosperity of the Union for the sake of the Union. Among them, they modified the tariff of 1842 in 1846, chiefly by substituting *ad valorem* for specific duties, for, this mode of assessing imposts opens the door for all sorts of frauds, especially those of undervaluation in the invoices, and the equally dangerous device of temporary underselling, even at a loss, for the sake of crushing out the competing home industry which the imports must meet in the invaded market. Still, the tariff of 1846 was discriminative in its schedules, and protective in its rates, in spite of the vices incident to its administration; and the Nation's boundless energy and resources fought the good fight under it with an average of advantages. A succession of lucky chances fell in to corroborate it—the general scarcity in Western Europe, followed by the famine of 1848; the discovery of gold in California, in 1848-9; the Crimean war in 1854-56; a tripled export of domestic productions, occasioned, in part, by an accidental foreign demand, but mainly by an exhaustive enterprise in the product of cotton and tobacco for exportation, which in ten years advanced from fifty to one hundred and forty millions per annum; and above all, the indomitable enterprise of the people—*all these* together brought about such a measure of general prosperity, that the old enemy found its opportunity in a full treasury for another assault, and a successful one, upon the policy which always exposes itself by its very successes to the charge of having accomplished its object and fulfilled its mission. Accordingly, a twenty-five per cent reduction of the duties was effected in 1857, and was followed, necessarily, by another sudden increase of imports, with another suspension of specie payments at its heels. The imports for consumption now went up to $11.82 per head of the population from $5.42, or to more than double the average at which they stood in 1846; and the bank circulation and loans, following, naturally, were also something more than doubled —the loans rising from three hundred and twelve to six hundred and thirty-four millions, and the circulation from one hundred and five to two hundred and fourteen millions, which was not only a doubling of aggregate amounts but left a margin that nearly doubled the *per capita* average of the increased numbers of the population —another instance for the deception of the bullionists, but another proof that credit and currency inflation *always* follows excessive importations. The public debt in the mean time had gone up from sixteen and three-quarters to twenty-nine millions, and rose, still further, to sixty-four millions in 1860 under the tariff of 1857.

Judging by all the experience of the past, the short suspension of September 1857, would have been followed in 1861 by a general explosion, if that other grand result of free trade, the great civil war, had not come down upon us and broken up the rule of all financial precedents. The imports *per capita* in 1836, the year preceding the great revulsion of 1837, were $10.93; in the year preceding that of 1857 they were $10.88; and now, in 1860, they had risen to $10.80, an amount which, under non-protective tariffs, always insured the return of the "inevitable and inexplicable" plague within a twelvemonth.

In 1861, and as yet, for the last time, another turn of the tide concurred with the outbreak of the Rebellion, as the like return of the redeeming and corrective policy of protection always came, to meet and repair the ravages of the free trade system. It gave us the Morrill tariff, and that, with its amendments, raising the rates upon duty-paying imports to nearly the average of the tariff of 1828, put us through the civil war, and for six years of peace has averted a collapse of our credit, and sustained our labor enterprise, to the extent and with the fullness of effect, that has in all past times aroused the resistance which never misses its opportunity. With a debt of twenty-three hundred millions upon us, the Treasury is overflowing. From customs more than equal in amount to all other sources of public revenue during the last two years, the Treasury has paid of the principal of the public debt above two hundred millions, besides bearing all other charges, and, accordingly, free trade is again rampant and resolute and armed, as of yore, with all its favorite arguments for such a reduction of duties on imports as they think the Treasury can spare. Again, the goose that lays the golden eggs has grown so fat that she is just ready for the spit!

Under the conviction that history rightly rendered is philosophy teaching by experience, this brief sketch of the effective and instructive points in our frequent and violent contrasts of policy is submitted as a study for candid inquirers. Its details would greatly strengthen our argument, but we have been compelled to confine the narrative to the facts and figures which are the summaries and the interpreters of the particulars.

CHAPTER XV.

DOCTRINE AND POLICY OF PROTECTION.

What Protection is and what it intends.—In its exactest sense it is Defense.—Domestic industries encouraged by other means than protection strictly implies and employs.—Bonuses, market monopolies, and countervailing duties not of its essence, nor embraced in its policy.—Bonuses employed by Colbert—their difficulties and dangers.—Government subsidies not of its system nor embraced in the principle.—The protective principle vitiated by the spirit of countervailing duties, and practically weakened or destroyed.—The British system, repudiating protective, adopts countervailing, duties—a change of terms to cover an unchanged policy.—Henry Clay and his compeers led astray by accepting and substituting them for the substantive, self-supporting, and unconditional doctrine of protection proper.—Principles and aims of protection defined, and its subjects and operations ascertained and limited.—It is not *taxation*.—It recognizes no distinction between luxuries and common necessaries of life.—Its spirit refuses invidious classifications of society.—Duties that are not defensive are taxes under another name—they are foreign to protection.—The rule of taxation is by *ad valorem* assessments.—Protection has no regard to values, and refuses the *ad valorem* rule.—*Ad valorems*, in customs duties, infamous for their frauds, perjuries, inequality of operation, and treachery to the interests of home labor—everywhere avoided, except when employed to defeat protection.—The Prussian Zollverein in striking illustration.—Protection is not adverse to foreign trade in principle or operation—it allows and favors supplementary commerce, and restricts only injuriously competitive trade.—It does not look to revenue, but it does, incidentally, secure it.—The system in our history entitles it to be described, a tariff for protection with incidental, but always abundant, revenue.—The finance tables of the Treasury Department show that "revenue tariffs" always, before the Rebellion, failed to supply revenue, and that protective tariffs always met the expenditures of the Government.—Our highest rates of duty have given us the largest foreign trade—in 1860, under an average of nineteen per cent upon the dutiable imports, only two hundred and eighty millions worth imported; under a forty-six per cent duty, in 1870, the imports rose to four hundred and fifteen millions.—English superiority excludes manufactured goods, yet her imports have swollen from seven hundred and forty to thirteen hundred and thirty-three million of dollars in ten years.—The tariff rates of France almost prohibited foreign manufactures, yet commerce rose two and a half times in twenty years.—The adage, "if you don't buy you cannot sell," a plausible sophistry as applied to American trade.—Protection intends the utmost possi-

THEORY AND POLICY OF PROTECTION. 205

ble diversification of the Nation's industries.—Argument of the free trade authorities for confining the United States to the production of provisions and raw materials.—Different educational and pecuniary value of different kinds of labor.—Changed condition of laborers in modern production.—The necessity of preserving the whole range of choice among the varied industries, in order to give employment to every variety of powers and faculties.—Special interest of women in the reserve of labor suitable to the sex.—Extent to which they were found capable of the manufacturing arts in 1860.—The concessions of social and political power in expectation, demand a special care in securing for them the largest range of industrial employments.—They must be either in the self-supporting, the dependent, or the dangerous class of the community.—The freedmen of the South must have opportunity to enter the occupations of skilled labor, or go back to the drudgeries to which slavery formerly confined them. Already their labor has gorged the cotton market, its price has nearly touched the lowest which it ever reached, and wages must go down with it.— A diversified, which must be a protected, range of industries equally necessary to our women and negroes.

It is in place now to state what Protection is, and what it intends. The treatment of this topic, however brief, will necessarily embrace a notice of the policy, as it has been tried in other countries, under modification of their varied conditions.

The force and value of Protection in its essential, its operative sense, is fully covered by the word *defense*. This is more and better than a mere synonym—it measures the meaning of the word, and it restricts the principle exactly to the province of its rightful rule. Protection does encourage and foster the industries to which it is applied, but, encouragement sometimes embraces bonuses, extended by the government, or exclusive privileges of the market secured to industrial enterprise, or other exceptional forms of favor; which are not simply *defensive* against foreign competition. Sometimes protection takes the shape of countervailing duties, imposed to retaliate foreign legislation adverse to the domestic exports of the country adopting them. The first of these forms of encouragement is liable to serious objections, in most of the instances in which it is employed, and, at best, requires extraordinary skill and discrimination in its use. Colbert, the great finance minister of Louis XIV., gave, from the national treasury, two thousand livres to each loom put to work, for the purpose of establishing the system of textile manufactures, which took its origin, and owed its great and enduring success, to that and other effective forms of support. The like policy has been, in a multitude of instances, followed by the governments of Europe; and, liable as the measure was in its nature to abuse, and abused as it generally was, it has since fallen into general reprobation. It often was "class legislation" in an offensive form, and is only allowed now under cover of some other pretext which gives it protection: such as subsidies, under the guise of contracts for carrying the mails at sea; or gifts of public lands and the loan of the national credit, to railroad corporations for the construction of highways for the carriage of the mails, and military transportation in the deserts, and over the Rocky Mountains of the United States. Of this system of government aids to private enterprises, we have nothing now to say, except that it is not that protection of the common interests of the community which is strictly defensive in its essence; and, while we take no present exceptions to it, we also abstain from making any defense for it; it is not Protection, in our sense of the term, or our meaning of the thing. It is broadly distinguished by the circumstance that it means money paid out of the treasury to the benefit of specific enterprises, and is not general, uniform, and equitable, in its operation, unless made so indirectly by the wisdom, impartiality, and diffusive beneficence of the grant; of which, by the way, it is very hard to be sufficiently assured.

The principle of countervailing duties is indeed defensive and protective, but in a narrowly limited range. While England legislated in an unfriendly spirit upon the interests of our domestic exports and maritime trade, the spirit of resistance to aggression swallowed up the true principle of protection. The popular argument, then most effective, turned upon this retaliatory aspect of the policy; and, when the evil was tolerably well abated, protection, proper, had lost its support by the loss of its accidental and non-essential provocation. England, about forty years ago, finding her policy of foreign trade endangered by the existence of the protection system of other countries, whom she needed as customers, and requiring no further protection of her own home markets against foreign competition in them, gave up the name and opposed the policy, but retained so much of it, nevertheless, as her interests demanded, under the name of countervailing duties. Thus she now protects her manufactures of tobacco, spirits, and sugar, by a system of duties upon their import, equivalent to a barrier of fifty millions of dollars a year, against their introduction from abroad. These duties are not adopted to counteract or punish any foreign nation's tariffs upon any of her exports, but to equalize the excise duties which the government lays upon the domestic production of the kinds of articles so charged.

If British free-traders will not allow us to call a fifty-million charge, upon these manufactures, over and above the imposts laid upon the raw materials, protective, because they are only intended to countervail her own internal taxes upon the like articles, we may be allowed to exclude the term from our definition of protective duties, proper. Our principal and sufficient reason, however, is that protection, passing under this name, confuses our reasonings, and, besides, falls mischievously short of the true principle and purpose of defensive duties upon imported goods. We might, indeed, effectually retort the English dodge by employing the phrase to cover the difference between us, in the cost of labor, the interest of capital, and the heavy burden of our domestic taxes upon production, and call the import duties, not protective, but countervailing to the great advantages our rivals hold over us in our home markets under an untaxed trade in their competing commodities; but we prefer the downright and direct avowal of the principle, and the frank maintenance of the policy essentially belonging to it. Moreover, we remember how unwisely the very ablest advocates of "The American System," in the earlier days of Clay and Webster, and before England had adopted free trade, threw their force upon the merely counteractive feature of the policy, and we are sure that, turning the argument for protection upon the pivot of countervailing duties, damaged the principle greatly when their particular provocation was removed. Countervailing legislation could find its reasons only in the practice of foreign countries, and however well justified, still made the true principle depend upon an accident, or a caprice, or a mistake of governments over which we had no control. It was a resting of our separate and independent rights upon the aggressive wrongs of our enemies, while they kept that injurious attitude towards us; but did nothing for the maintenance of those rights, when the injury took a different form. They need defense, by their intrinsic necessities, let foreigners infringe them in whatever manner they may choose.

By protection we mean needed defense of industrial enterprises whose success is the common interest of the community. We do not mean " class legislation," or the establishment of monopolies in production or trade, but the development of the productive power of the Nation, with a due distribution of its benefits to every industrial interest of the whole people. Protection means, first, freedom of industry and trade at home, and eventually, free foreign trade. It must have nothing in it of the spirit of war, either between classes of interest at home, or with the nations abroad. It is a law of national welfare, and as a law it intends liberty, and cannot employ any form of compulsion, except for its defense and maintenance. The spirit of justice and peace which pervades and rules it, requires that in the selection of enterprises to be fostered, the legislature shall be guided by the same prudence that governs a man in giving credit, or other aid, to his neighbor entering upon a new business, or embarrassed in an old one—the fair probability that he will in due time be able to make himself independent of such assistance, and fully repay to the helper all his advances—that is, the enterprise must be practicable, promising, timely, and generally beneficial; else it is not a case to be so assisted, and is not entitled to the favor.

As no favoritism to classes must be indulged, so, no hostility to any class can be allowed. For this reason, the notion that luxuries should bear higher duties than articles of common necessity, has nothing of the proper policy of protection to industry in it, nor, indeed, has it anything else to recommend it to the acceptance of the masses, but the contrary.

Protection is totally misunderstood, and fatally abused, when it is reasoned upon, or employed, as identical with *taxation*. It means and intends the protection of domestic labor, skill and enterprise, and of the capital which they employ. These are not benefited by a tax, under the name of an import duty, upon such luxuries of manufacture or of agriculture as the country cannot produce for its consumption. Invidious distinctions in a tariff of customs between the consumption of the rich and of the poor, have no help in them for the labor of the poor. Moreover, those things are usually classed as luxuries which the poor cannot well afford to purchase. To burden them distinctively is simply to put them still further out of the reach of the poor; and like all other prejudices of classes, it only operates to the injury of the weaker party, and under the guise of a preference for the common people, really keeps up the worst of aristocratic distinctions —those which touch the most general interests of social life. Tea and coffee were treated by our revenue laws as luxuries until the protective principle set them free of duty in 1832. So soon as they went into the free list, they became the common fare of every cottage in the country. Coffee for the twenty previous years was taxed five cents per pound; and teas, from fourteen to sixty-eight cents, according to quality. These duties were *taxes*, pure and simple, for they did not protect any American industry. Since then we have imported for consumption as much as seven pounds of coffee per head of the total population, or nearly twice as much for the actual consumers. What would the laboring people have gained by paying about three-fourths of the annual ten millions of duties, under the old rule, upon the article, in order to tax it as a luxury? Or what would they have gained by confining themselves to inferior teas, at fourteen cents a pound duty, in order to make wealthy people pay sixty-eight cents on theirs? If we apply this doctrine of luxury to silks or furs or any other article of dress which we do not produce, its effect would be that the wife and daughters of the man of moderate means, when they go into the street or to church, must betray the economy which his circumstances compel. Protection, ruled by equity and tending to equality, is guilty of no such misdemeanors as this. When *taxing* is the object for the uses of revenue, lay it on wherever it should be borne, and in reference to the ability to bear it, but never allow the idea to enter a tariff for protection; and this for other reasons which will hereafter appear.

While upon this point, the essential distinction between taxes and protective duties, we must be indulged with a word upon the manner and rule of assessing protective duties.

In levying internal taxes, or taxes upon imports for the support of Government, the *ad valorem* rule of assessment distributes the burden equitably upon all the various species of taxable property. A fixed percentage, according to valuation, covers fairly and uniformly all its subjects, the intention being, that every property holder shall contribute to the support of the Government in proportion to his means, and every consumer in proportion to his consumption, when unhappily the public exigencies require such an extension of its demand. The *ad valorem* rule with its universality of range, has no place in the policy of protection. To admit it in the assessment of duties is to sweep away the whole doctrine of protection. Free traders are its consistent advocates. To give it any influence whatever in our reasonings upon protection is to confound and vitiate the whole process. The enemy has sown these tares in our field while we slept, and must not be allowed to reproach us with the faults of the harvest. Previous to 1846, *ad valorems* were not tolerated in our tariffs, wherever they could be avoided; and when protection true and earnest was restored, in 1861, specific duties were restored, not extensively enough, indeed, but with a resolute purpose to avoid the departures from principle in fixing the rates, and the never-absent frauds, of the *ad valorem* system—frauds by which the industry of the country is cheated of its defenses, and the treasury of its revenues, and all honest importers are discounted disastrously by their unscrupulous rivals in trade. They offer a premium to dishonesty; they falsify invoices; they pay for perjury in the custom house; they make semi-smugglery a policy of trade, and demoralize the whole merchant class by discouraging and fining truth and integrity heavily. They are everyway fitted, in purpose and practice, for defeating protection, and are, accordingly, a prime principle of free trade. England, having respect only to her revenue, and fair play among her own importers, scouts *ad valorems* from her lists of impost duties. When she was deriving twenty millions of pounds from customs, she took but one quarter of a million in *ad valorems*, and such were their inherent and inseparable frauds, that parliament appointed a committee to rid the customs schedules of every possible vestige of them. This committee indicated its object and intention, by charging artificial flowers by the cubic feet in the box containing them, overlooking all differences of value, to escape the frauds of undervaluation. Not a government on earth that knows what it is about, gives them any toleration; and especially those which intend protection repudiate them just as they do free trade in any other disguise.

One of these disguises, and the most insidious of them, takes the shape of what is called among us, "a tariff for revenue with incidental protection," assessed upon imports by the *ad valorem* rule. In this form, even when stripped of their other inherent frauds, their malignant hostility to the protection which is intended or pretended, is conspicuously manifest. Their workings are after this fashion: when the prices of foreign goods are so high that little or no protection against them is required, the duty per cent upon such value carries up the prices to an absurd extent, and protection is mocked with the aid it does not need, and charged with an exorbitance which it did not intend; and, when prices go down the duties go down with them, and protection altogether fails just where it is needed. Another feature of their mischievous principle is, that they make the government a party and an accomplice when by underselling, the foreigner aims at crushing out a domestic industry. Then the price is put ruinously low and the *ad valorem* duty goes down in the like proportion, thus making the tariff itself a full partner in the trick. The steel rail manufacture newly introduced in the United States, affords a clear example of the vice of which the foreign enemy so easily avails himself.

Protection aims at and addresses all its measures and methods to the defense of the industry employed in the production of a commodity, and has nothing to do with its market value. It confronts the importer with the purpose to secure the right of domestic labor in the production of the article against all its disadvantages, and lays on any amount of duty that will do that.

The Prussian Zollverein is, and ever has been, purely protective. In the earlier years of its operation it charged cotton goods, without any respect to quality or value, thirty-two dollars and twenty-five cents upon every hundred pounds weight imported. The effect of this specific duty was that *coarse* shirting paid the equivalent of ninety per cent upon its invoice value; *superior* shirting paid only thirty-two and a half per cent, and fine printed cottons were admitted at eight and three-fourths per cent. The Zollverein intended protection and not revenue. It took care of its infant manufactures effectually, by the heaviest duties, and properly abstained from *taxing* those goods which its laborers were not yet able to produce. It did not exclude those finer goods from its markets, nor its common people from their use. On the same principle, and with the same purpose, it charged all kinds of cutlery at a uniform rate, by the pound, letting in razors, penknives, and the like fine wares at a merely nominal rate, and laying the protective stress upon hatchets, axes, and a great variety of hardware, which the Germans were able, under sufficient defense against Great Britain, to manufacture for themselves. This was protection pure and simple, and the result was, as the Germans advanced in skill from one stage to another they found the specific rates of each successive stage sufficiently protective, though constantly declining in *ad valorem* rates, until in the end, which was steadily and persistently guarded, German cutlery attained superiority in quality and greater cheapness in price than the foreign articles, which if admitted under inadequate protective duties, or, under a *revenue* tariff system, would have crushed the enterprise of the people in the bud. Germany, to day, shows what her fifty years of fostered and defended industry could do for a people so low in the scale of European powers, that her fortresses were garrisoned with French troops and her territory under French dominion, till England, that had been subsidizing her through the Continental wars, finally overthrew Napoleon the First at Waterloo, as Germany has just now overthrew his nephew at Sedan. But we are running again into history, in the development of a theoretic principle, because truths that have working force in them always tend to the facts which vindicate them.

The system of protection employs, exclusively, duties upon imports to effect its objects; and, intending only to defend domestic industry, it properly selects for its operation only those foreign products which compete with the freedom and extension of such domestic industries as the country is prepared to undertake with the view of self supply. It is not arrayed against foreign trade and exchanges in anything else than those commodities whose admission injures the labor and prevents the enjoyment of the home market. Wisely devised and worked, it never does in any respect, nor to any degree, repress or diminish any healthful foreign commerce. Its legitimate object is to preserve for the people an unlimited choice of occupations fitted to their economic conditions. It will not forbid or burden the importation of wheat into territories incapable of producing such grain, nor will it tax any amount of importation of such grain or any of its substitutes, which supply its own deficiencies, unless where such an import represses its own production. The rule of the principle is to freely allow and favor all really supplementary trade, and to oppose none but such as is injuriously competitive. Looking steadily to the fullest employment of its own labor, and the greatest practicable development of its native resources, including raw materials, available capital, skill and enterprise, and their most judicious enhancement, it turns away from all other aims and avoids all their embarrassments; and it has nothing to do with market prices except as these affect productive power and act upon consumption.

If, owing to the circumstances of the country, a tariff of protective duties can also be made to secure an adequate, or any considerable, amount of revenue to the government, the principle and policy of the system freely allows such an excellent accompaniment as a consequence of its own necessary operation; and it is a striking characteristic of the system that it always does do so. As long as the circumstances of any nation require the imposition of duties upon foreign merchandise for the defense of its own immature or otherwise embarrassed productive forces, and just so long, it also pays its proceeds into the national exchequer. Only when, as in England, protection is no longer necessary, and its levies, therefore, fail, does protection fail to replenish the public treasury. In proof, so far as our own experience is concerned, it is a striking fact that, every period of sound protection which we have enjoyed, has amply provided for the national expenditure, and only the tariffs constructed with the sole or principal view to securing revenue have utterly failed to accomplish that intention. Any expert in statistics acquainted with the concurrent events, need but to glance over the column headed "Customs" in the general table of treasury receipts from the year 1791 to 1860, to see the clearest proof of this fact. He will invariably find that the first and second years of every free trade tariff are marked by a sudden increase of the amount of these duties, with a rapid decline thereafter, till the end of the period, at which the deficit of receipts marks the utter failure of all such tariffs to provide a sufficient revenue for the ordinary expenses of the government; and he will see, also, a regular rise and steady sufficiency of customs for the uses of the government from the second year and through each succeeding year of the protective tariffs, until such amplitude of exchequer supplies is again destroyed by its wretchedly delusive successor, designed to provide revenue only, or, in some cases, "revenue with incidental protection."

I ask no man to accept my statement of this instructive history gratuitously; let him study the subject for himself; and, it is not too much to ask him to do so, before he ever again talks of a "revenue tariff" as something different in rates and subjects from a truly and permanently protective one, as concerns the finances of our own country in its past history or its present condition.*

* Under the unprotective tariff of 1816 the customs went down from thirty-six millions in that year to thirteen millions in 1821; under the protective tariff

Some of the propositions here so briefly presented for the purpose of describing the principles and aims of the system, demand something further in their exposition.

We have said that protection is not restrictive of foreign trade—and we mean to say this both with respect to the money and the economic value of such international commerce as a true policy provides for.

On this point it is in itself conclusive of all debate to refer to the fact that in 1860 the highest value of foreign imports was reached. The dutiable goods imported in that year amounted to two hundred and eighty millions, under an average rate of nineteen per cent. This was commerce under free trade. In the year 1870 the dutiable imports had risen to four hundred and fifteen and three-quarters millions, at an average rate of forty-six and three-eighths per cent. Here we have a system of duties two and a half times higher, allowing or inducing an importation within a fraction of one and a half times greater than under the lower rates!

This is a sufficient refutation of the charge that protective duties are restrictive of foreign trade, so far as the United States in their economic conditions are concerned. But the same thing is just as true of all nations, in all possible differences of conditions. We will take an extreme case: The English authorities, led by J. R.

---

of 1824 and 1828 they rose to twenty-nine millions in 1833, rising steadily and gradually with the growth of the general prosperity. Under the compromise act of 1833 they declined to eleven millions in 1837, and under the protective tariff of 1842 they rose again to twenty-six millions in 1846. Under the act of that year they fluctuated, going down eleven millions in a year, at two periods, and up again eleven millions in a single year, and stood at sixty-three millions in 1857, showing through the whole course of the act of 1846 the *unsteadiness* of its protective provisions and the mischiefs of its *ad valorem* rates—it was then, at one of those inflation stages which belong to the character of revenue tariffs, and which invariably indicate their explosion. The act of 1857 came just in time to precipitate the result, and accordingly the receipts from customs fell in one year twenty-two millions, which was a million less than they had been seven years before. Next comes the crowning demonstration under the several protective tariffs or amendments of that of 1861. The revenue from customs has risen in nine years from forty-nine to one hundred and ninety-four millions. Which of these were the true revenue tariffs? Not one of them except the strictly protective tariffs, and they exactly in the degree that they were protective. Every so-called revenue tariff was a failure of its avowed purpose, and a catastrophe to the Treasury and the business of the country besides. I appeal to the record—there the facts stand in overwhelming force.

McCulloch, and followed in England and America by all the lazy thinkers of his school, put their point thus: "Those who will not buy need not expect to sell; and conversely; it is impossible to export without making a corresponding importation." Now how does this plausible platitude sustain itself in its application to our system of protection of manufactures—the very thing against which it is leveled?

England does not buy foreign manufactures, yet she expects to sell and does sell her commodities. Her superiority in production amounts to an almost total exclusion of manufactures from her ports; they amount to only a fraction less than six per cent of the total value of her imports, yet those totals amounted in 1854 to seven hundred and forty millions of dollars, and in 1864 to thirteen hundred and thirty-three millions.

Again, take France, with her protective rates and restrictions almost prohibitive of competition in her own markets. During the ten years, 1827 to 1836, her aggregate imports and exports amounted to thirteen thousand three hundred and sixty-one millions of francs. After an interval of twenty years, in the ten years from 1847 to 1856, with her prohibitive system in full operation all the while, they had risen to the value of thirty-one thousand three hundred and sixty-one millions.

These immensely varied results utterly demolish the wretchedly unmeaning aphorism that is employed to array the protective system against the interests of foreign trade, even when measured by its money value. It would be too stupid to propose it against the *economic* value of the trade which it guards, selects, and secures; and we may dismiss it without further remark on this head, having already in our chapters on "Commerce" amply exposed its mischief to the labor and enterprise which it touches only to destroy.

If there is any one of the intentions of the protective system worthier than another of the heartiest approbation, it is its design and its power to diversify the industries of the people who adopt it. As the elucidation of this topic involves some of the vicious generalizations of the let-alone-theory of foreign trade, they may be appropriately noticed here.

The jumble of truisms and generalities of this school of economists owe their origin to a curious class of college professors, professional *litterateurs*, metaphysicians, and professional world-menders. Such is their description in England, Germany, and France, and among them may be found, here and there, a few theologians who have taken leading positions among the authorities, covering with their "pale cast of thought the native hue of practical affairs, and turning awry their currents till they lose the name of action;" while here and everywhere their antagonists are, in the main, men of practical acquaintance with, and interest in, the affairs of individual and national concern.

Taking for example the case of a country like our own; comparatively young, exceedingly fertile, capable of every variety of agricultural production—from the cereals that affect the cooler climates of the North, to the sugar and cotton that demand a semi-tropical temperature—with its improved lands very cheap, and millions of unappropriated acres that may be had for little more than the cost of preparing them for the plough, and in all respects eminently fitted for furnishing provisions and raw materials. The inference drawn by these theorists is that, nature, by these circumstances, makes farming, planting, and lumbering our distinctive occupations, and invites our energies into these special fields of industry. Now, there is nothing in a statement so general as this that anybody need dispute. But there are some other things just as true, which must be considered before we draw from it a practical policy of national conduct.

In the first place : if labor is really the source of wealth, and the various forms or kinds of labor are not equally remunerative to the individual, or beneficial to the community, it behooves us, as soon as we are in a condition to choose among them, to ascertain whether exclusive agricultural labor is the most advantageous that we can adopt. We know, very certainly, that the wages of labor are not in all things equal; that its products are of unequal value in the market; and, that all varieties of work are not equally educating, because they do not all alike employ and develop the same moral, intellectual, and physical faculties ; and we know that wages and profits of employment grow with the education and training required for the men thus variously engaged. The difference between skilled and unskilled labor is apparent enough, and the difference between their respective products and other results ought not to be forgotten when a people are in condition to make an election among them. Nature has no more determined that any particular country, capable of anything else, shall confine itself to agriculture, than that Washington should spend his life as a land surveyor, because there was a wilderness full of that work for him in Virginia, and he was an expert in the business. The matter for that young man to decide, in choosing his occupation, was how he could best promote his own growth in worth and power, and best serve the general welfare; and this is the very question for a community to solve in deciding upon its industrial policy. Nature has nothing to do with it, except in providing the means. Man is her master, on condition that he will be his own. Industry is no longer drudgery, mere muscle-work; it is the art of making nature work in man's service obediently. It is not a matter of indifference to an individual or a community what sort of labor he or they shall adopt, when a choice presents itself. Unmixed agriculture cannot develop the skill and enterprise of a people, for the reason that it cannot accomplish that division of labor which brings into use every variety of ability, and associates a community by distributing its functions helpfully in accumulating wealth. The perfection of any organism, its rank and its worth, and the possibilities of its progress and growth, depend upon the number of its elementary differences, and, on their duly balanced activities. It is in the multitude of his parts and powers, and in the due exercise of all of them, that man takes rank of fish; and a community, which is, in respect to interests and development, an aggregate man, a larger humanity, is put under the same law as to the component individualities, and depends upon the same conditions, for its worth and welfare.

Without a very large diversification of productive businesses, one-half of its population—its women—must be put into the supported class or driven to unsuited drudgery. The modern system of manufacture has taken from the household the spinning-wheel and the hand-loom. Four-fifths of the productive force employed upon textile fabrics is now the province of capital, in machinery, factories, and raw material. The domestic industry which a century ago was in the hands of women, is now taken from them; and if they are not admitted to a participation in the employment and profit of such products, they are turned idle, or remitted to useless work that pays nothing to them. In the degree that they are, or may hereafter be, admitted into the government of the social and civil state, they will go into the dangerous class, for the very reason that they will be pecuniarily dependent upon the community.

In 1850 women were twenty-three and a half in the hundred hands employed in the mining, mechanic, and manufacturing arts in the United States. Under the less favoring tariff of 1860 they had declined to twenty and a half per cent of the total employees; but still their contributions to, and interest in, the manufactures of the country at that time, show the importance to the sex of reserving to the home industry of the people the supply of such commodities as are fitted to their capabilities, which is, in some degree, indicated by the fact that in 1860 the women employed in such works were in number fully fifty-four per cent of all the hands engaged in them. Eighty-five millions of dollars were the wages paid to the aggregate of the employees, and the product was valued at four hundred and six millions. The whole number of women so employed were 212,383; together their wages in the year amounted to $33,500,000.

Are not women greatly concerned, and is not the whole people as much interested in saving for the sex such a mass and such a value of suitable labor? Nay, would not a complete system of protection throw out many thousand males who now preoccupy the places fitted for women, and give them that much more of independence and of the advantages of every kind attendant upon self-supporting employments?

The signs of the times fairly promise the concession of all that is substantial, and all that is due to women, from the sex now governing them and controlling their welfare. This growing enfranchisement and responsibility of the subjects imperatively demand that all the necessary accompaniments should be provided.

Men have *worked* themselves into civilization and the sovereignty of the elements, so far as they have gone, by skilled labor in diversified branches of industry. The same thing, and all approaches to it, however attained, can be maintained only by the same means and processes. Women, no more than men, can get possession and enjoyment of their abstract rights but by conforming to the law of progress, and the mere investiture of any kind, or any number of franchises, cannot secure their benefits to any class, sex, or race of mankind, but by compliance with the conditions on which such rights and liberties depend.

Before leaving the special dependence of our women upon the policy which alone can secure them the independence and the development which self-supporting industry affords, it is proper to turn their attention to the kinds of remunerative labor for which they have proved their fitness. The aggregate of wages and the numbers of the sex engaged, above stated, were employed in the manufacture of the following among the occupations reported by the census of 1860: Paper boxes were made by 1,090; carpets, 2,771; clothing, 77,871; cotton goods employed, 76,110; hats and caps, 4,243; hosiery, 6,323; millinery and dress making, 5,537; paper, 4,392; straw goods, 6,803; umbrellas and parasols, 1,410; woolen goods, 17,796; boots and shoes, 28,574; cigars, snuff, and tobacco, 3,721. Now these goods, and an endless variety, and a very great value, of other articles not enumerated, are the very commodities for the production of which foreign manufactures are in active competition with us. Let down the bars, and our women will be driven out of this immense field of employment, and excluded besides from at least an equally extensive additional territory of production for which they are well prepared, and ought to enjoy. Those among them who are agitating for the right of suffrage ought to be careful at the same time to qualify their constituents for a wise administration of the political power which they expect to wield. The ballot and idleness go badly together; they demoralize each other badly. Better for the disfranchised and for the public weal, if both sexes of idlers were debarred from the exercise of the law-making power, than confer it upon either, if the franchise only tends to throw the holders into the demagogue market. The masculine voter can make nothing out of his ballot but the corruption of office seeking and the opportunity of selling his soul at the polls, unless he be really independent of politics as a trade.

The freedmen are in a somewhat different predicament. The ballot is to them protection from the persecution of the ruffianism of the country, and the means of security from the general prejudice of color. In this respect it is to them the greatest of social benefits. Women do not need it for these purposes; they are not exposed to the evils of an inferior caste in society. But the lately enfranchised negro, is in exactly the same position as our women in respect to the labor question. If the opportunity for entering the field of the skilled industries is destroyed through the preoccupation of our markets for their products, by the cheap labor of foreigners, they will be driven back to the very kinds of labor which occupied them in slavery, and they must accept the low wages which the world allows to such drudgeries.

Without property, without education in the arts, they are as yet confined to the old-time kind of plantation work. Their labor has already restored the cotton product to the stage it had attained before the Rebellion, and the price of the staple in its gorged markets is already nearly down to the figure it reached when it was at the lowest. American cotton sold at seven and three-quarters pence at Liverpool in 1860. It is now quoted at seven and a half pence there, and is steadily declining toward the price it held in its worst days, when no wages were paid to the cultivators, and the masters made no profit in its cultivation. How long will this system continue before the former slaves will be upon as short an allowance as ever they were. A diversified industry is the only thing that can save them from that bondage of poverty which differs only in name from chattel slavery. Our white women and our slave men, until lately, were always classified together, in respect to their political status. They are now, and must for long, be in the same economical category. The law of the industrial life of the one, is the law of the other; and nothing is more astonishing to one who sees their equal position in relation to real personal liberty and independence, than to find philanthropists arguing and voting for a system of international trade that must hold them both alike in dependence, and whatever of disability and degradation, they are respectively exposed to.

CHAPTER XVI.

THE MOST PROMINENT AND PLAUSIBLE OBJECTIONS TO PROTECTION.

Protection of national labor unfairly classed among the obsolete restrictions of industry and trade.—Protection, the reciprocal of allegiance, embraces the interests of labor, and commands its defense.—Countervailing legislation in defense of foreign trade unquestionably right, but still more imperatively demanded against injuries of domestic commerce.—The natural differences of national conditions, enough for all beneficial foreign commerce; the accidental differences are not to be perpetuated.—Production precedes exchange, and productive power takes precedence of trade in national policy.—Protection, so far from interfering with the individual's choice of occupation or market, aims solely at securing their liberty by providing their opportunity.—Liberty without its defenses is a mockery.—Free trade, a modified form of rebellion—the spirit of insurrection against the law of order.—Not that government which governs least, but that which best promotes the public welfare, is best.—Who pays the duty?—When non-protective duties are imposed the consumer must pay them. Domestic competition in the home market throws a part or the whole of the duty upon the foreign producer.—How prices are affected by domestic competition.—If a protective duty, in any case, raises the prices above a given rate, it also holds it from ever rising higher—it permanently defends consumers against monopoly prices.—If it affords profits unduly large, domestic competition immediately reduces them to the ordinary standard, and secures a constant reduction of prices in keeping with all improvements in production.—No rise of prices can go above the point which equalizes the protected industry with all others in the community.—To forbid this, is simply to forbid native enterprise to enter upon any industry which foreigners have preoccupied, until wages are reduced to the lowest known in the world; till capital is as cheap, because as abundant, and skill, with its education denied, is as great—conclusions alike preposterous and atrocious.—Nine-tenths of the consumers are also producers, and have the largest interests in all the results of protection.—The benefits of the policy distributed among all classes, and all are immediately repaid and refunded any temporary increase of prices.—Fallacy of the assumed fixity of price upon which the increased cost of a protective duty is calculated.—Cost of iron as affected by various rates of duty—of lead—of steel rails.—Prices of foreign commodities always fall under protective duties.—The testimony of consumers of an important foreign product.—Effect of duties upon foreign imports reflected upon competing domestic products: statement of the free trade argument by their accepted exponent of the doctrine.—His cypherings and their impossible results.—The equally monstrous consequences of the

"Revenue" duties which the party proposes and advocates.—Their revenue duties shown to cost consumers, on their own principles, an average of ten times the amount of revenue which they yield.—The "Revenue Reformers" inextricably entangled by the *reductio ad absurdum* of their system.—Following their doctrine, the customs from which they are required to raise one hundred and fifty, cannot be made to yield more than twenty-five, millions.—The consequences to the tax payers.—Absurd workings of the assumed principle—the larger the domestic production the greater the burden of the revenue duty, and the only escape is the abandonment of any industry that any other people adopt.—Our taxes now fifteen per cent of our annual products. Must we bear this ourselves and give an untaxed market to our foreign rivals?—Effects of protective duties summarized.

THE discussion of the subject now in hand is embarrassed by the thousand and one special relations which protection holds to the social and industrial interests of the people, and resultingly to the financial health of the Government. I have endeavored to present the principle in its nature, its adaptations, and intentions, as it interlocks and conflicts with the antagonist theory of trade, for I could not advantageously, within the limits of this treatise, give it a more formal and systematic array. Following the same plan of treatment I propose to consider in this chapter the most prominent and plausible objections urged by free traders; and, in their appropriate places, to discuss the doctrines of free trade, or the foundation upon which it is made to rest.

The free trade logicians overload their argument with an insufferable tediousness of instances in which the governments of times past interfered with the business affairs of their people. They enjoy themselves beyond limits on "the limitation of the powers of government." They put themselves among the foreground advocates of civil and political progress, in clamoring for the greatest possible extension of the let-alone principle of governmental policy; all for the purpose of carrying over to the doctrine of protection the odium of the old-time usury laws; the arbitrary regulation of wages and prices; the grants of monopolies; the laws in restraint of working-men's combinations; the restraints despotically imposed upon the freedom of opinion and publication, with all the other abuses of authority which can be pressed into service. These oppressive and repressive exercises of the civil power are justly under condemnation now, and it is much to the purpose of the party of professed progressives to put protection of home industry into the class of obsolete usages, which are discredited by the spirit of modern progress. It can then be overwhelmed with an epithet, and all argument of its special merits is escaped.

That protection, however, which is the reciprocal of allegiance in the philosophy of law, must, nevertheless, be allowed as a duty of government, however much the power may have been abused. The range of the duty and the mode of exercising the just power conferred, must be coextensive with the nation's necessities, especially when it is limited, as in the case of regulating international trade, to such measures of defense as are required against foreign interference, whatever form it may take, with the freedom of the people in their choice of the ways and means of self-support, and of employing their own labor in the pursuit of wealth. Government is bound to adopt countervailing and defensive measures against the mischiefs and injuries threatened or inflicted by foreign governments or people, by their commercial or maritime action upon domestic rights and interests; and, it may do this by whatever means the case requires and warrants. This will not be disputed, or at least, needs no further vindication than its mere statement.

Laissez-faire can scarcely require the sovereign power to let its own people alone, and permit all other people to do what they please against the national interests. Should a foreign government exclude our ships, or our products from its ports, or injuriously burden our commerce, is our own legislature to be refused the power, or denied the capacity, to protect the national interests so oppressed? Yet such measures would only affect that exceedingly small portion of our productive industry which is involved in our *foreign* trade; and surely it cannot be admitted that there is no corresponding protective and defensive power which may be rightfully addressed to the support and safety of that tenfold larger commerce which we have at home, and the thousandfold larger interest which belongs to the freedom of domestic labor.

A foreign people, with larger and cheaper capital; longer experience and its greater skill; cheaper and more abundant labor, and many another decided advantage in a competitive struggle, find their interest in making us their customers for their own benefit at the expense of our own labor system; and yet we are forbidden by the spirit of progress to employ the self-preservation power of nationality in abatement or avoidance of the mischief! Free trade in its basis principle allows the individuality of the nations, and all their economic differences of conditions, but this only as a ground for their cosmopolitanism of trade. The more unlike the communities of men are, the better they are fitted for trade exchanges, and the more permanent these differences can be made, and the more the resulting dependency of each upon the others can be increased, the better for trade! Our answer to this is, that the *natural* differences are enough for the commercial relations of the various societies of men; but the accidental abnormal, and injurious conditions by which they are differenced are not to be accepted, but to be amended, for the sake of due progress of all the parties. In natural sequence production precedes exchange, and the answering principle in logic requires that productive power should have precedence of trade interests in the direction of national policy.

From such freedom of international exchange as utterly ignores all national distinctions, necessities, and means of economic progress, these people carry over a cluster of abstractions to their theory of individual freedom. They insist upon " the *right* of the laborer to choose his own occupation ;" that " every man has the *right* to dispose of his own labor, wherever and whenever he thinks it most advantageous to himself," and that " every one is better able to choose his own industrial pursuit than the government can be." Such mere truisms as these no protectionist disputes, nor is he otherwise bound to notice, than to expose their impertinence in the argument. All such platitudes are answered in a word: Protection does not interfere in the choice of men's occupations; with their choice of markets; nor, with any other thing, right, or business engagement that anybody ever claimed. So far from this, its whole end and aim, and its only possible operation, are to secure the *opportunity* for such freedom of choice—for such freedom in industrial production, and such freedom of exchange, as the people who adopt it require for the defense and advancement of their individual and national prosperity.

Abstract freedom conceded, with its necessary defenses withheld, is a mockery. Letting everybody loose to prey upon everybody else, if they can or will, is not liberty, but lawlessness. To expose the weak to the strong; to make the markets of the country a melee of the nations; is just such a privilege as the rough-shod donkey offered to the chickens in the barn-yard when he proposed a free dance, with its unrestricted liberties to the partners, upon the *Laissez-faire* principle of *sauve qui peut*.

Free traders make an utterly unfair use of the maxim, "that government is best which governs least." They push it to the length of saying that, in trade, no government is best of all. They avail themselves of the indignation which the obsolete restrictions upon industrial and commercial liberty of the by-gone despotisms provoked. They are full of that revolutionary spirit which, to resist abuses, runs into the diametrically opposite error, as the most effective rallying cry of resistance. Wise moderation has not that full commitment, that squareness of issue joined, that plump oppositeness, which most strongly enlists and incites parties in warfare. This is the spirit of insurrection with its battle-cry of "Liberty against the Government." But people must govern themselves even in freedom, and they must defend themselves until millennium comes, and there is some point at which lawlessness must be checked and authority be introduced; and it is best to get rid of the overstrained maxims of rebellion when authorized and organized government is required. Disorderly principles serve very well for pulling down Babylon; but when Jerusalem is to be built and established, order, degree, and direction are demanded, and it is then time to adopt and respect the doctrine that the principles and policy of that government are best which best promote the welfare of the people—which best execute themselves by their reasonableness, practicability, and utility, and are least liable to abuse; or, the most expedient is best.

The great point which free traders make and most persistently press against protective duties is, that, as they are imposed for the purpose of equalizing the prices of domestic with foreign products in the home market, they must necessarily increase the cost of such commodities to the consumer. This is not clear, nor is it in general true of the foreign article so charged; for a part, or the whole, of the duty may be thrown upon the foreigner, either in abatement of his profits, or in reduction of the wages and price of the raw material, or, of all together. This depends entirely upon the competition offered in the domestic market. If the foreigner has a monopoly of the product, he can charge the whole of the duty upon it to the consumer. There is nothing to hinder him. This is obviously true in the matter of tropical commodities sold in the United States.

Five cents import duty upon coffee, and twenty-five cents upon tea, are nothing else than a domestic tax collected at the custom house. Such tax protects nothing native, and nothing native checks its charge upon the consumer; he must pay the whole duty, and the importer has possession of our market as free as if no duty at all were imposed. The same thing is true of *all* commodities imported which meet no competition, or no effective rivalry in the market other than that offered by other foreign traders.

Suppose the price at which the foreign article can be profitably offered, to be fixed, which it is not and cannot be, but, for the purpose of trying the case, let this point be assumed. Domestic labor and capital cannot yield it at that price, but would be enabled to do so by charging it, if worth one dollar, with a twenty-five per cent duty, and such a charge is accordingly levied. At the beginning of the contest, it might seem that, both the domestic and foreign article would be raised to that price. But, we now have a condition of things in which the foreigner, to hold the market, must reduce his profits, or lose the trade, or much of it, and the home-made can well be supplied at one-dollar and twenty-five cents. The results are of two kinds, the foreign article cannot go *above* a dollar and a quarter, because it will be driven out by the native. This is a great point attained. It is now no longer at the option of the foreigner to raise the price as occasions would otherwise tempt him. And if the protective duty has increased the cost to the consumer, it holds it down to that point thereafter.

Protective duties are imposed to encourage home industry. The cost of production, during the process of improvement in the business, will decline regularly, and may do so very largely—sufficiently to afford the article at one dollar, or the supposed remunerative price of the foreign commodity at the commencement of the contest for the home market. This is not assuming a shade of probability too much. And then who pays the duty, if the importer still contends for the market? Plainly he must pay, or lose, the whole of it; he must suffer it in abatement of profit, or in reduction of wages, and as long as he does so, the consumer has the product at the former price, and the duty goes into the national treasury, as so much tax paid by the foreigner for the privilege of our market. These two things are then secured: first, the market price is held down to the figure at which native production can afford it; and second, it is reduced progressively to the extent which native skill and experience acquired can effect. The maximum cost is fixed for the benefit of the consumer, and an assured decline of that maximum is certainly provided for. If the dollar and a quarter yields a large profit, home competition will immediately pull it down, and never cease reducing it until the profit falls to the average of all other investments and enterprises.

But, at first, the duty does raise the price, or means to raise it, above the point at which the foreign article is then sold; but not above that at which it may be held in the absence of all competition. Granting this, let us see how high such price may go under protection. Manifestly no higher than will raise the wages of labor and the profits of capital in that to the level of other businesses : which means this, and nothing else or more, that wages and profits in such a business were previously below the general level. This is the limit of the rise, absolutely and permanently fixed. Now, what is the objection of the consumer to such equalization? Will he answer that this particular industry, so to be fostered, requires protection because it is not so favorably conditioned as others which ask no assistance, and ought, therefore, to be abandoned? Abandoned, till when? Will he answer? What other reply can he give than "to the time when wages shall be as low as in the country of the rival, which monopolizes the trade by underpaying its laborers! or till capital shall be as cheap and skill and experience as great!" And will he tell us when these things shall be, and how they shall be brought about? Shall wages be driven down with us, by the hungry strife for work that has lowered them to the starving point abroad? Can skill be acquired while its education is denied? And will capital be accumulated by the process of limiting its employment to the least remunerative investments?

A general answer to this general objection is sufficient. Education must be paid for, and it always repays its cost if it be sound, practical and serviceable.

Who are the consumers that free trade pleads for so importunately? Are not quite nine-tenths of them in the United States also producers? Opening up new avenues of occupation for them and enlarging old ones, has the effect first of diminishing competition for the sale of labor. It also withdraws from some industries a portion of producers and makes them consumers for the remainder. It gives and secures for all a home market that can be defended against all injurious invasions from abroad. It enlarges the diversification of labor, and adapts it to the capabilities of thousands and even millions of such persons as would otherwise be unproductive, and fall into the supported or dangerous class of the community; and thus, by distributing the benefits of the policy upon all classes and conditions of society, it immediately repays all the earlier enhancement of prices, and forthwith commences to lower them permanently and securely.

But we have gone too far, in allowing prices to be fixed or restrained by anything else than the force of home competition. It is a curious assumption of the free traders that always makes any given price of a foreign product the standard or basis from which they count the increased cost to the consumer of the duty imposed upon it.

It does seem like a waste of words to expose this fallacy, but an instance or two out of hundreds will at least give the facts to be explained for the help of those who do not or will not see the principle that rules the subject:

In the year 1844 the duty on English common bar iron was $25 per ton. The price in the New York market (average of the year) was $61.83. The cost less the duty, it is assumed, would have been $36.83, and the *ad valorem* duty was, therefore, sixty-eight per cent. The price, with the duty off, we will call the prime cost for the purpose of our demonstration. The rate of duty was twice lowered between 1844 and 1860: in 1846 it was reduced to thirty per cent, and again, in 1857, to twenty-four per cent upon the prime cost.

Now look at the effect of these varied rates upon the price:

```
1844, duty......$25 00 per ton.........Prime cost......$36 83 per ton.
1854   "    ......  16 42    "       .........      "    ......  54 70    "
1858   "    ......  10 04    "       .........      "    ......  41 85    "
1860   "    ......   8 22    "       .........      "    ......  34 23    "
```

Here we see that in the first stage of diminished rates, when the duty fell $8.57, the cost rose $17.87. At the second stage, when the duty had fallen $14.96, the price was still $5.02 higher than in 1844, and when the duty had been reduced $16.78, the cost had fallen but $2.60.

Take another instance: in 1845, under the protective tariff of

1842, the duty upon pig lead was $3 per hundred pounds; the price in the New York market (average for the year) was $3.37½. The duty being eight hundred per cent upon the prime cost, or as the free traders argue, the lead might have been had for thirty-seven and a half cents, duty off. From 1847 to 1857, under an *ad valorem* duty of twenty per cent, the price rose at a pretty even pace, beginning in 1847 at $4.31, and ending in 1857, at $7.03— the duty reduced to one-fortieth and the price considerably more than doubled! Who paid the duty in 1844, when the domestic production was protected; and who paid the twenty per cent duty in 1857, when the domestic rivalry was driven out of the market?

One more instance, because a much more recent one, must be added:

In 1864 the importation of steel rails began in the United States. They were sold that year to our railroad companies at $162 to $135 per ton, in gold. In 1867 American manufacturers began to supply the market, the foreign rails went down to $115 to $110 per ton. In April 1870 they were lowered to $72, in New York and Philadelphia; now in 1864 the duty being levied in *ad valorems*, was equivalent to $46.60, in gold, and was paid by the American consumer, which would leave to the rail makers one hundred and one dollars and ninety cents as the prime cost of the rails; in April 1870, the duty, being an *ad valorem*, fell to $18, and left the producers in England but $54 per ton, gold.

Here American competition reduced the price in our Atlantic cities to $4.80 less than one-half it had been at, six years before. Such, in these instances, has been the effects of protective duties upon prices of foreign products in the domestic market. The railroad companies in great numbers, including the most important of them, petitioned Congress in 1870 to raise the duty upon these rails, and, to make them certainly protective, asked that they be changed to specifics, and fixed at $44.80 per gross ton, for which they gave the reason that they "as users of steel rails and transporters of the food and material for American manufacturers and their numerous employees and skilled laborers, do not desire to be dependent exclusively upon the foreign supply." They would rather have the rails they require at eighty or even a hundred dollars per ton, than pay, as they did in 1864, an average of one hundred and forty-eight for them. They wish to have the rates held down to such a figure as Americans can make them for, and therefore, would have the domestic make sustained by a sufficiently protective duty. Do they undertsand their business? And are not all consumers thus protected by the policy that home production secures to them from the unlimited demands of the foreign monopolists?

There is nothing which the free traders make so much of, or press so urgently upon the inexpert and uninformed of their audiences, as the reflected effect of protective duties upon the prices of the domestic products. Their whole doctrine turns upon prices, and they are bound to make the most of them. This party in the United States accepts the late special Commissioner of the Revenue as the expositor of this point in their appeal to the populace, and rely upon his statistical arguments as the most effective of their weapons. I quote him only to authenticate my statement of the propositions on which they throw their force. In his official report to the Secretary of the Treasury dated December, 1869, will be found in detail the data and the inferences which I must condense in a brief but sufficiently forcible array. He says, in so many words, that a reduction in the duty upon foreign salt would be followed by a corresponding reduction in the price of the domestic article. In a dozen other instances, in other words, he says the same thing. He makes a law of prices out of this position, and bases all his calculations of the amount of relief the people must obtain in the cost of home-made commodities, by any given percentage of reduction in the duties imposed upon the competing commodities of foreign origin brought to our markets.

On this ground and for this purpose he proposes the remission of $750,000 in the duties collected from foreign pig-iron in the fiscal year 1867–8, and says that such a reduction would relieve the consumers of domestic pig iron of no less than $10,800,000, thus reducing the cost of the total foreign and domestic consumption by fifteen and four-tenths times the amount of the duty if retained. A reduction of $600,000 upon the duties charged upon foreign salt, he says, "would relieve the community of a tax, in the first instance, of $3,900,000 per annum;" a reduction of $3,500,000 upon the duties charged on hides, leather, all the manufactures of leather, tanning barks, lastings and serge, would have the effect of "relieving the people from a burden of taxation, as already demonstrated, approximating the sum of $18,000,000;" and $1,262,020 of duties upon imported timber and lumber, in all forms, wholly remitted, would, by the same principles of calculation, reduce the cost of all such articles produced at home for consumption no less than $16,000,000. In the aggregate of these four classes of goods alone, the import duties upon similar products are made, by the commissioner's logic and computation, to enhance the cost of the domestic product $48,700,000, while their foreign correspondents yield only $6,112,000 of revenue.

This doctrine applies to all other duty-paying imports, and to the reflected effect upon the prices of the domestic commodities which divide the home market with them. Let us try it through the entire range of its supposed operation:

The official value of all such foreign goods, so charged with import duties, which met the competition of American goods in the year 1867–8, was $178,000,000; the aggregate duties amounted to $85,400,000—an average of a small fraction less than forty-eight per cent. We have no authoritative estimate of the value of such goods manufactured in the United States in that year, but we can guess. The increase of the year 1860 upon 1850 was eighty-five per cent; the product of 1860 was $1,885,000,000; eighty-five per cent will be little enough under all the circumstances to add to the value of 1860 for that of 1868. This gives us 3,487 millions as the value of the products of the year. On which sum, according to this theory, a forty-eight per cent increase of cost to the consumers must have fallen, and therefore the duties charged upon the foreign import surcharged the prices of their domestic rivals the total sum of $1,673,760,000, or nine and a half times the amount of the duties secured to the treasury by the system of raising revenue at the custom houses!

This is frightful, atrocious, horrible, and—ridiculous. But it is agony and oratory for the stump, and a "big thing" in statistics for the tongues and pens of the Innocents whose philosophy is bounded by the multiplication table.

But do the experts among the propagandists of free trade themselves believe it?

This same Commissioner, in full possession of his economic logic and unmeasurable arithmetic, in this same report, proposes to put an aggregate duty of $38,000,000 upon imported sugar, molasses, and melado. This is just fifty-two and one half per cent upon their invoice value in the year 1867–8, which being reflected upon $23,750,000 worth usually produced at home, must enhance their market price a fraction over $12,000,000. Add to this the duty itself and we have a round $50,000,000 put upon the cost of these sweets to the consumers. This is enormous taxation indeed; for by the rule of the Commissioner, if the duties were wholly remitted we might have had the entirety of our supply, foreign and domestic, for $83,600,000, but under its malign operation, they must necessarily cost us just $50,000,000 more, that is thirty-eight millions in duties upon the foreign, and twelve in enhanced price upon the domestic.

He treats woolens and worsteds and cotton goods in the same way. Taking his own data for the calculation he proposes to raise $30,000,000 upon cottons, woolens, iron, steel and lead, at an expense of $94,500,000 of increased cost to the consumers of these foreign and domestic goods. But his schedules provide for a revenue of $150,000,000 a year from imports. Without an unnecessarily tedious calculation, I cannot give the precise figures for the total tax that his proposal would inflict upon the consumers, but a safe average would put it at ten times as much. We confront the Revenue Reformers with this result of their financial system. Some of them having felt the force of this *reductio ad absurdum*, bluntly propose to set every foreign article free of import duty which meets in our markets any quantity of the like kind of domestic production. The doctrine which they all profess, and the arguments they all use, drive them, whether or no, into this trap. They are compelled to be absolute free traders in respect to all goods, wares and merchandise which compete with our own products, but merciless in the burdens that they must throw upon all commodities which our own soil and labor cannot produce. To see how this principle would work upon the federal revenue, we need but look at the several classes of our usual imports, their respective values, and yield of duties. Taking Mr. Wells' schedules, which will be found on the one-hundred and twenty-eighth page of his report, I see not how more than twenty-five millions of the hundred and fifty of revenue which he expects, can possibly be derived from imports which do not compete with our domestic supplies. And it follows, if this doctrine of reflected prices is true, or if its advocates believe it to be true, that they are bound to release our total importation from all but about twenty-five millions of taxes, and throw something like two-hundred and twenty-millions of the necessary revenue of the government upon domestic property and industry. They must do this, and they must abandon their duties for revenue, or, they are bound in reason and conscience, to withdraw their assaults upon protective duties as a cause of a tenfold cost forced upon home-made goods.

One curious effect of the doctrine which we have been pressing to its consequences is, that the more productive our industries may be, the worse is the effect of any duty laid upon the rival products of foreign origin. For instance, if we import ten millions worth of a class of goods under a twenty-five per cent duty, and manufacture a hundred millions worth of the same kind, the consumers must bear twenty-five millions of increased price upon the domestic goods; but if we import a hundred millions and manufacture only ten, the consumers of the domestic article suffer only to the extent of two and a half millions; which is followed by this unavoidable consequence—it is ruinously oppressive to the consumers, to tax any article of foreign make which we can make at home; which must have the further consequence of a surrender of our markets to anything and everything that anybody abroad may choose to send us, unless we can undersell them, with the whole burden of our national debt, and federal, state, and municipal taxes for a makeweight in their favor. Our taxes are now not less than fifteen per cent of our annual products; must we bear these ourselves, abandon the industries which foreigners may choose to monopolize, and give a free market to everybody except ourselves? The doctrine of duties reflected upon home prices requires this. What is the answer of common sense?

When considering the effect of home competition upon the prices of foreign imports, the facts presented seemed entirely sufficient to explode the notion we have now been confronting with its preposterous, absurd, and every way monstrous results.

It would be as tedious as unnecessary to give the instances, either in particulars or summaries, which prove that protective duties, levied in the strictness of the principle, always secure the consumers from arbitrary prices; always in good time reduce prices to the level of general rewards of labor and capital; always throw their burden upon the foreign producer, when judiciously adjusted to the conditions and capabilities of the people; often, indeed, even going further and trenching upon the usual profits of the producer, and always repaying an hundredfold, any nominal increase of prices, by putting every variety of capability to profitable employment; and increasing the wages and profits as much to the consumers, who are all immediately or indirectly interested in the general benefits secured.

A very brief notice of the experience of other nations, which we promised at the outset of our treatment of the complex questions involved, will sustain all that is here claimed for the policy of protective duties directed to the support and development of that labor on which all wealth depends.

CHAPTER XVII.

PROTECTION IN THE HISTORIC NATIONS.

Protection in England—her struggle for supremacy in industry and trade; her rise from the lowest to the highest rank in Europe.—Measures taken to make her "the workshop of the world."—How she built up her woolen manufactures by five centuries of protective duties—prohibitions, bonuses, and penalties—and her iron industry by similar means during a period of over one hundred and twenty years.—In wool, iron, and coal she possessed *natural* advantages, and free traders credit her success in these industries to this cause; but by protection she naturalized her cotton manufactures, and enlarged them till their products outmeasure the value of all her other exports.—Beginning the business in 1740 by prohibiting the oriental fabrics which sold at three times less price than the domestic product, and maintaining the defense of the home industry until all successful competition was impossible.—In 1846 free trade was proclaimed by statute, but England never remitted or abated a protective duty till her own supremacy defied all rivalry in her home markets.—By countervailing duties she still defends her burdened industries, and her present policy is just as protective as her interests require.—The new Empire of GERMANY owes its existence and its eminence to the protection measures of the Zollverein.—History of protection in BELGIUM.—The natural resources of the Kingdom, the policy of trade employed, and the provision made for the prosperity of her manufactures, agriculture, and commerce.—Her population the densest in the world, and its growth double that of Great Britain, and her emigrants nineteen times less.—Protection in FRANCE maintained the most wasteful of governments, educated the artisans which initiated the skilled industries of all Europe, and has sustained her finances through the revolutions of a century.—The protective and prohibitive policy of RUSSIA has raised the kingdom from barbarism to the rank of a first-rate power in Europe, and emancipated twenty millions of serfs. The opponents challenged to find in all history a nation that has risen to the front rank, or any one that has maintained a high position, except such as have steadily maintained a protective policy adapted to their national conditions and international relations.—Free trade in the history of nations—TURKEY.—Free trade proclaimed by the Sultan three centuries ago.—Then Turkish superiority defied competition in production.—Modern agencies have so cheapened products, that Turkey, unable to command them, has lost not only her foreign markets but is compelled to surrender her home commerce to foreigners.—The "sick man's" complaint explained.—His dissolution waiting only for agreement among the dissectors.—Helpless herself, and no help from her free trade protector.—How her trade has declined.—How she supplies her exchequer, and debases her current coin.—Ireland, effects of the Act of Union; driven by its free trade provisions from the workshop to the potato field; famine, pestilence and emigration the consequences, and England hopeful of the extinction of the nation.—INDIA another victim of English free trade; half a million starved in a few months in the granary of the world—multitudes, who formerly produced the finest cotton tissues, driven from skilled industries to the lowest drudgery of agriculture, and famines increased in frequency and extent for more than half a century under British rule.—PORTUGAL under a free trade treaty with England precipitated from her pride of place among the nations to the condition of a burden upon the hands that ruined her. Differences of race, religion, and geographic position will not explain the fortunes and misfortunes of the nations here reviewed.—Only by one rule can they be classified—the one class having all protected their domestic industries; the other, surrendered them to the domination of foreigners.

WE open this section of our argument upon the vantage ground of the wide world's experience. The testimony of all history proves this broad proposition: not a single nation on the earth has attained a leading position; not a nation in the past or present has maintained the rank that entitles it to be called a "power," except those who have firmly maintained an adapted policy of protection in the direction of their international relations. England, being one of the very best of the examples in proof, is entitled to our first consideration.

Every one who knows anything of her history, knows that through a long struggle she raised her commerce and manufactures from the lowest to the very highest rank among the nations, not of Europe only, but of the world. Her chances for attaining and maintaining supremacy in production and trade in an even-handed struggle, under a let-alone policy, were simply hopeless. Great Britain occupies a territory not more than one-fourteenth of the extent, and has, even now, a population equal to only one-eighth of the natural labor force of her European rivals—Russia, in Europe, being excluded from the computation. The one-half of these peoples were far in advance of her at the beginning of the strife. Such were the odds against her, and such the proved capabilities of her opponents. How did she address herself to the great work of self-development, and achieve her grand success? By following the policy which she now urges upon the nations still in the conditions from which she herself has risen, and in her progress passing through such a series of stages as represent all the varied conditions of her contemporaries in the present? Did she entertain such hallucinations as we get now from free trade theorists, poets, transcendentalists, factors, brokers, and smugglers? Did she aim at universal mastery through cosmopolitanism in trade? On the contrary, she went resolutely to work under such a system of protective measures as challenges comparison, and by them achieved her grand successes. These measures may be arrayed under the following heads: prohibition of competing imports; prohibition of the export of raw materials; bounties upon production and exportation; restraints upon colonial manufactures; differential duties in favor of her own commerce; sumptuary laws encouraging such kinds of production as seemed to need help in that form; active and substantial aid to the immigration of artisans from the continent; prohibition of the immigration of her own skilled workmen, and of the export of machinery; wars undertaken with the sole object of opening up and monopolizing foreign markets, and, every other species of regulations and interferences which promised in any way to make her "the workshop of the world." All this is known in a *general* way. The particulars would astonish any one to whom they are unfamiliar. From the year 1331 down to 1834 the woolen manufactures were steadily protected; beginning with fines, maimings, imprisonment, and death as the penalties for exporting native wool or importing foreign cloth, and maintaining such penalties in force for quite four centuries. In 1746 these were softened down to transportation for seven years. [See Blackstone's Commentaries, title, Owling.] The latest of these penalties was not repealed till 1825. Here we have an "infant manufacture," nursed through a period of five hundred years, coming to a confident maturity which now mocks at a rival in its cradle which has never yet had ten consecutive years of fostering care!

Iron imported in foreign vessels was charged, as early as the year 1710, with a duty of £2, 10s. per ton, which was raised at successive periods, till in 1819 it stood at £6, 10s. in English, and £7, 18s. 6d. in foreign vessels. This was adequate as well as earnest protection of the domestic manufacture, for as early as seven years after the last-mentioned date England was actually producing her own iron at £3, 13s. cheaper than the cheapest of her competitors in all Europe. Being thus secure against all rivalry in the home market the duty was reduced in 1834 to £1 per ton.

England's command of the finest wool at an early day, and her possession of iron ore and mineral coal, have been offered as the sufficient cause of her great proficiency in their manufacture. These were her *natural* advantages, and the justification of her great endeavor to improve them. We have shown the means employed to secure success. That the mere possession of the raw material is not the whole explanation is shown by a still greater triumph in another department of her established supremacy: England grows not a pound of cotton, yet in 1860 the real value of her exports of cotton goods amounted to fifty-two millions of pounds sterling, while those of iron, steel, wool, machinery, and silk amounted to no more in the aggregate than forty-one millions.

Here then, we have a case in which nature did nothing for England, but in which she managed to naturalize an utterly foreign manufacture, so as to make its products exceed the half of her total manufactures and products exported to foreign countries. Her earliest supply of the material was from Cyprus and Smyrna, afterwards from India and China. Until 1790 America had sent her none. When she commenced the manufacture of cottons, say about the year 1740, the East India article could be afforded at less than one-third of the price of the domestic, and, had its importation been permitted, the British manufacture could not have fought its way into the home market. But notwithstanding the inequality of the contending parties, in the natural order of things, the exotic character of the raw material, the freight upon the import, which was then enormously high, and the unparalleled perfection of the foreign art, the people found a way of meeting the exigency. It was done by an act of Parliament, which reads thus: "Calicoes, painted, stained, or dyed in Persia, China, or the East Indies, shall not be worn or used in this kingdom;" and further, "all such goods, whether mixed, sewed, or made up together for sale with any other goods, shall be forfeited; and the person in whose custody, knowing thereof, the same shall be found, or that shall dispose thereof, shall forfeit £200." The British tariff act, passed in 1819, still prohibited the manufactures of all countries east of the Cape of Good Hope, and charged those of Europe fifty to sixty-seven per cent.

About the year 1818, the application of steam power, and the employment of the machinery which has so immensely increased and cheapened production, was fairly established in England. For full twenty years afterwards she maintained her protective system, and then, when it was rendered unnecessary by the superiority which it had produced, it was abandoned, and the English authorities began to propagate those doctrines of free trade which her matured industries could well bear. In 1846, the new policy suited to the new aspect of the nation's business was installed in the statutes of the British Parliament; that is, all that is intended and actual in the policy became the public law of the land; but the operative provisions amount to nothing more than the opening of the British ports and markets freely *to all commerce which her own supremacy in production* EXCLUDES! As we have already shown, the existing system of countervailing duties is still preserved to protect such of her manufacturing interests as require them; and we are justified by the facts in saying that, her whole system of commercial regulations have been for five centuries, and remain to this day, the most complete, adequate, and successful instance of the employment of the protective policy that can be found in history. With one other word we conclude this brief review—England never once, and never in any instance, repealed, or remitted, or abated a protective duty on any foreign goods until after, and generally long after, it had accomplished all its objects, and left her safe from all competition.

PROTECTION IN OTHER COUNTRIES OF EUROPE.

For the wonderful results that have crowned the policy in the German States now included in the customs union of Prussia, commonly called the Zollverein, we must content ourselves with what we have said in our strictures upon the system of *ad valorem* duties, in a preceding chapter, and elsewhere when the history of the German industrial system and its achievements were in point.

Our whole case might be safely rested upon the facts of the industrial and commercial history of the little kingdom of Belgium alone. In territory she is only a trifle larger than the State of Maryland, and has not quite one-fourth of the area of New York or Pennsylvania. In these limits she has a population of four millions nine hundred thousand, which gives four hundred and thirty-three to the square mile, which is full twenty-five per cent more dense than that of England and Wales, and nearly thrice the density of Massachusetts. The productive industry required to support such a population is presumptively very great. She is well supplied with raw material, and obviously is not stinted in labor power. The success of the Belgians in the manufacture of silk, glass, linen, and woolens, has given them a world wide reputation; and her carpets and laces are known as the finest in foreign markets, and are found there in amazing abundance. Small as the territory is, it combines in a remarkable degree, and in remarkable balance, capabilities for agricultural, manufacturing, and commercial industry. Her customs system shows how wisely she has guarded all these interests. She secures a home market for her raw materials by defending her manufactures adequately. She finds a home market for her breadstuffs and provisions by employing all her hands busily in every form of converting industry; she fosters her skilled industries by barring out all competition with their products; she favors a very large transit trade by offering every inducement to the bordering nations, and to foreigners trading with them, making her roads a general thoroughfare; her lands are cultivated like garden grounds; her factories are alive with industry, and are carrying away the iron trade of northern and eastern Europe from England; her foreign commerce grew, after it was liberated from the dominion of Holland and Spain by the French in 1830, till it stood, in 1860, at double the proportion of the United States; and Belgium is now about ready for free trade: she has put herself, through wise and persistent protection, into the list of the nations that no longer need any defenses against her industrial and commercial rivals.

I must not detain the reader with a statement of the tariff rates which have secured all these results. A specimen or two will give the spirit of the whole. Raw tobacco is admitted at nine-tenths of one cent per pound—the manufactured is charged three cents; raw sugar at two cents per ton—the manufactured or refined must carry $185.68 per ton; raw wool, free—woolen manufactures, charged ten, twelve, twenty-one, twenty-six, and thirty-two cents per pound. There is not an item in all the schedules of the Belgian tariff that gives any more countenance to free trade or any of its maxims than those which are here quoted.

The differential duties charged upon imports in *foreign* vessels, in favor of her own, are, in the average, quite one hundred per cent, which have had the effect of preserving for her own mercantile navy her whole trade in domestic exports and foreign imports for consumption.

It is worth noting here that Belgium increased her population sixteen per cent between the years 1840 and 1850, while the United Kingdom of Great Britain grew but a scant eight per cent in the same time. Protection against free trade in the matter of population, with all the odds of density against Belgium under the trial.

Again: the immigrants to the United States during the period of 1840–60 from Belgium were equal to only two-tenths of one per cent of her population in 1860; while those from the United Kingdom amounted to three and eight-tenths per cent of hers; so, the chance of living at home was just nineteen times better in protective Belgium than in free trade England.

For the growth of wealth in France we beg leave to refer the reader to our fifth chapter, where its rate and amount in the first half of the present century are given in sufficient detail to exhibit the effect of her system of international commerce, which J. B. Say thus correctly describes, " for thirty years nearly every law passed on custom house matters has been intended either to establish or to consolidate the system of protection and prohibition." Writing in 1826, this high authority among free traders, says, " France at present contains the most beautiful manufactures of silk and wool in the world, and is probably indebted for them to the wise encouragement of Colbert's administration. He advanced to the manufactures two thousand francs for every loom at work, and, by the way, this species of encouragement has a particular advantage—the bounty enters into reproduction." It will be recollected that Colbert was Intendant of Finance and Minister of State under Louis XIV. His policy supported the most expensive and wasteful of French monarchs in the seventeenth century; and it did more, it educated more than half a million of those artisans who in 1685, upon the revocation of the Edict of Nantes, fled from France, and settling in Switzerland, Germany, Holland and England, created there the industries which enriched the countries of their adoption.

The prosperity of manufactures in France is too well known to require any description here; the results concerning the national welfare are unhappily too much confused by the political despotisms and popular revolutions which make up the history of the nation for now above three-quarters of a century, to allow of any very clear examination within our limits. But this much must be admitted—under the most absolutely restrictive system, maintained from the earliest days of the first Bonaparte to the fall of the third, France has advanced greatly in natural and individual wealth, and has grown through the whole career of her crazy political disturbances to be the leading manufacturing nation of Europe. Her terrible history would have been passed unnoticed but for the fact that her industrial system has revived her fortunes after every revolution, and kept her public credit quite as high as that of any other European State except that of England. The French three per cents were up to seventy on the hundred immediately before the outbreak of the late War with Prussia, when our own sixes were not above ninety, and our fives were but eighty-six. In nothing has she had either wise or stable government except in the defense of her industries, and this has kept her from utter destruction, and will restore her again when the present riot is quelled.

The Russian policy, like that of France, has long been sternly and guardedly defensive of the labor of the Empire against the invasion of products from Western Europe. Under this system, it is enough to say, she has emancipated twenty millions of her serfs, and has risen, within the memory of living men, from barbarism and contempt to the rank of a "power" which has no equal in the Eastern hemisphere except the new empire of Germany.

A volume would be required for a full array of the evidence which could be adduced in proof of the proposition advanced at the beginning of this section—that, not a nation on the earth has attained a leading position except those who have firmly maintained a policy of protection adapted to their national conditions and international relations. Will the disputants try to find one?

FREE TRADE IN THE HISTORIC NATIONS.

Free trade has had a fair trial in the old world. Its history is indelibly recorded in its results. We propose now to show from free-trade authorities the effects of their favorite policy in those countries of Europe and Asia in which it has had its most complete demonstration.

Three centuries ago, the Sultan of Turkey proclaimed unlimited freedom of foreign trade, retaining a bare five per cent duty or port charge upon imports, which it seems has long since been reduced to three per cent. Turkish superiority of skill and experience was more than a match for the rude industries of western Europe in the old-time manufacturing methods and agencies; but upon the introduction of the modern improvements, which almost miraculously multiply commodities by means of steam and machinery, the oriental races were exposed to a destructive competition in all their markets, foreign and domestic, and Turkey fell from its preëminence, and became the "sick man" of the nations. The countries which have availed themselves of the modern appliances in production, and protected their labor interests from foreign invasion, have nothing to do now but divide the apocalyptic dragon's dominions among themselves when they can agree upon the distribution. Free-trade England will make no resistance; her occupation of the protectorate, like Othello's, is gone, and she will get none of the spoils, nor even save her plighted honor.

Even so lately as fifty years ago we were wearing Turkish goods in the backwoods of America, but now the subjects of the Sultan cannot hold their own markets against foreigners. J. R. McCulloch says: "The Turkish manufacturers of muslins, ginghams, handkerchiefs, etc., have suffered severely from the extraordinary importation of British goods, so much so, that of six hundred looms for muslins in Scutari, in 1812, only forty remained in 1831; and of two thousand weaving establishments in Tournovo, in 1812, there were only two hundred in 1831." Again, he says: "Though our [British] muslins and chintzes be inferior in fineness to those of the East, and our red dye (a color in great esteem in Turkey, Persia, etc.,) be inferior in brilliancy, these defects are more than balanced by the greater cheapness of our goods; and from Smyrna to Canton, from Madras to Samarcand, we are everywhere supplanting the native fabrics." Of Turkey's foreign trade he says, "the exports are very trifling—ships carrying goods to Constantinople either return in ballast or get return cargoes at Smyrna, Odessa, etc.;" and of the interior traffic he says: "the trade is in the hands of Jew brokers, some of whom are rich." Duties upon imports, three per cent, and twelve per cent upon domestic exports, explain the condition of the revenue, and its pinching necessities; but the stronger proof is in the desperate resort to a rapid debasement of the government coinage. For this again we have McCulloch's authority—"The Turkish coin has been much degraded. The piastre, which a few years ago was worth two shillings sterling, is now (in 1838) worth little more than four pence." The Turk's sickness is explained. He has caught the Irish disease, imported in manufactured goods from Liverpool.

Ireland was, not very long ago, as it had been for ages, the seat of learning and of the useful arts, in an eminent degree. In the last quarter of the last century, the books printed in Dublin, and the woolens, linens, and cottons, of the Irish looms, were common in all the markets of christendom; but the union with Great Britain was effected in 1801, and in 1821 the last traces of national defense against the overpowering competition of the kingdom that had swallowed her up were effaced. By the terms of the union her almost prohibitory duties upon English calicoes and muslins were to expire in 1808, and those upon woolens in 1821. Look at the results: in 1800 there were in Dublin five thousand hands employed in woolen manufactures; in 1840, only six hundred and two. In making carpets, seven hundred hands at work in 1800; in 1840, none. These are the average proportions of the respective dates for the silk-weavers, calico-weavers, and cotton-spinners. England wanted cheap labor and cheap food, and free trade with Ireland answered the intention. But how did they answer Ireland? Thrown out of mechanical employment, the Irish laborer was driven to spade-husbandry and potato-raising, until the potatoes sickened under the forcing system which necessity compelled, and the soil got sick of the spade-men; and famine, pestilence, and emigration, *quartered* the population between the years 1841 and 1851! The London *Times* rather likes this situation of things; it says, "The tribe of Celts will soon fulfill the great law of Providence, which seems to enjoin and reward the union of races. It will mix with the Anglo-Americans, and *be known no more as a jealous and separate people*. Its present place will be occupied by the more mixed, more docile, and more serviceable race which has long borne the yoke of sturdy industry in this island, *which can submit to a master and obey the law*." The same paper at another time, said: "For a whole generation man has been a drug in Ireland, and population a nuisance." Mark the date—a whole generation, that is, since the free trade provisions of the Act of Union came fully into play. And mark the avowed intention: Irish extinction to be accomplished by starvation and expatriation.

George Thompson, in a speech delivered in the House of Commons fifteen years ago, describing the results of British rule in INDIA, said: "At the close of the last century, cotton abounded, and to so great an extent was the labor of men, women, and children applied to its conversion into cloth, that even with their imperfect machinery they not only supported the home demand for the beautiful tissues of Dacca, and the coarser products of Western India, but they exported to other parts of the world no less than two hundred millions of pieces per annum."

In 1813 the trade of India was thrown open and the native industries were exposed to unlimited competition. At the end of twenty years after, the men, women, and children had been driven from the workshops to the fields, and all demand for labor was at an end except in raising rice, cotton, indigo, and opium. Mr. Thompson's picture of India under free-trade rule has such free dashes of the pencil as these: "Some of the finest tracts of land have been forsaken and given up to the untamed beasts of the jungle. The motives to industry have been destroyed. Go with me to the northwest provinces of the Bengal Presidency and I will show you the bleaching skeletons of five hundred thousand human beings who perished from hunger in the space of a few short months; yes, and of hunger in what has been called the granary of the world. Famines have continued to increase in frequency and extent under our sway for more than half a century."

PORTUGAL is another witness to the character and influence of the policy urged upon us by the people aspiring to the mastery of commerce and the monopoly of all the skilled industries of the wide world. In 1703, Portugal, so lately the leading commercial nation of Europe, concluded a treaty with England, by which she bound herself to admit English wares into her ports at a fifteen per cent duty, for the favor of an English tax upon her wines one-third less than that imposed upon the wines of France. Mr. McCulloch reports the inevitable results thus: "Formerly Lisbon had about four hundred ships of from five to six hundred tons burthen employed in the trade with South America, but at present there are not above fifty ships engaged in foreign trade, and of these the burthen does not exceed 150 tons. The produce of Portugal sent to foreign countries is almost entirely conveyed in foreign ships." Mr. Cobden, another free trade oracle, summed up the whole story, about fifteen years ago, when he said that "Turkey and Portugal had become a burden and a curse to England." She had made them her dependencies, not by force of arms, but by force of trade, and now they were upon her hands like the worn-out slaves of a Southern plantation under the old regime.

The ready answer to this indictment of the policy, and of the nation which has employed it in the destruction of so many other nations, is that the Turks are Mahometans, the Indians are Pagans, the Irish are Celts, and the Portuguese are, if nothing else, Catholics; but the French are at once Celts, Catholics, and infidels; the Russians are not Catholics; the Belgians are almost exclusively Catholic, and the Germans are both Catholics and Protestants. Differences of faith and of race, differences of national conditions and habits, will not serve for the causes of the different economic fortunes of all these peoples. The fortunate among them are not distinguished from the unfortunates by any likeness among themselves of national character, or of geographic conditions. The victims are, like those of the small pox, of every variety of constitution, undefended or unprotected by vaccination.

And how does it happen that peoples unchanged in faith, or place, or character, who were once first in the ranks of industry and commerce, are now last and lowest? and how does it happen, also, that each and all of them are in the one category of peoples who have lost the command of their home markets by surrendering them to the control of cheaper producers?

There is nothing clearer or truer in human reasoning than that labor is the source of wealth, and that its freedom and diversification are the measure of its productiveness; and an infraction of this law of national life, must be followed by its natural and necessary penalties. The suggestion of faith or race or any other specialty in explanation of results, is utterly unphilosophical, and foolishly impertinent. Universal history testifies that not a single nation on the globe, in the whole range of history, has reached independence and wealth; not a nation even holds the rank attained, but such as have firmly maintained a protective policy in the regulation of their international trade.

CHAPTER XVIII.

GUARANTYISM.

GUARANTYISM: Civilization, not differentially defined.—The present age a transition phase of society requiring a distinctive name.—Precedent conditions of civilization.—Societary movements, their characteristics—Patriarchism, Barbarism, Greek Democracies; growth in bondage; Feudalism, uprising of the masses —rights demanded, not duties conceded, in the revolt.—Support of the poor and education by the State, questioned.—Natural rights grounded in selfhood.— Reign of individualism relaxing; at war with association.—Rights and duties reconciled in guarantyism, corresponding movements in religion, in civil government, and the military system.—Achievements in arts and sciences, not the distinction of the last hundred years.—Societary reformation, the glory of the present age—in politics—in organized diffusion of Christian knowledge by protestants—temperance reform—anti-slavery—public schools—statistics of education—public libraries, periodicals.—Charities.—Diminution of capital crimes; corporal punishments; imprisonment for debts.—*Insurances;* history of; recent increase of.—SAVINGS BANKS in England; happy influences; in the United States; vast aggregate of deposits; statistics; indicate the associative impulse.—*Corporations* the type of coöperative unions; material and spiritual springs of coöperative association.—Coöperation in bondage—in freedom.— Labor's difficulties.—Selfhood becomes social—the gain leads to the good of the principle.—*Beneficial Societies,* vast accumulation of the fund in England.— No reports of beneficial societies in the United States.—Provisions and management—easy rates and liberal reliefs—moral influence.—They grow rich.

CIVILIZATION has no logical or distinctive definition. Writers, concerned with it as their special subject, have not even attempted to determine what it is, and what it is not. It is vaguely recognized as a phase of human society, and it is ranked as the last and highest form yet developed; but it is not differenced by any of its exactest descriptions. There is moreover, a lack of philosophic accuracy in treating it as a phase, or a different form, or appearance, of the same substantial thing. It is not a thing defined, nor can it be held within the fixed limits of either description or apprehension. It is a thing of progress, of degrees, and, therefore, a complex of phenomena. We all know what we mean by it in special applications, but these are so numerous, and so various, that our conceptions or notions of it do not serve in scientific classification. Treated or taken as a particular *form* of societary organization, the idea of some constancy and fixity of character intrudes, which is an error of essence, for its essence is changeful progressiveness; and its changes are so great in degree, that they take on real changes in kind. If the Jews, Greeks, and Romans, were all civilized peoples at the commencement of the Christian era, what shall we say of the Chinese now; and what of Western Europe any time in ·the last five centuries; and, especially, in the year 1870? If the Moors were barbaric when they held the dominion of Southern Spain, how were the Greeks civilized under Alexander the Great? One descriptive name for all these is not more exact or discriminative than calling the North American Indians and the Negroes of Central Africa, both alike, savages. We have not, because we cannot have, logical definitions of these phases of human society. The races and nationalities are not in any of their conditions, differenced as insects, fishes, birds, and beasts are in zoological characters. Yet there are differences between their various states; and that which we call civilization, is not only unlike the others, but it actually shows as great and striking unlikeness to itself in its epochal transitions.

Apprehending that we are now, and have been, for about a century, in a distinctly marked period of civilized progress, we want a name, which, though it must necessarily be vague, may yet be serviceable, because required to mark a change and a difference as great as any that have put men upon the use of the generally accepted terms for all the other marked unlikenesses in human societies. It was for the purpose of emphasizing with its due force this era in the progress of civilization that we postponed its further description by its characteristics at the close of our third chapter, until we should have first examined such of its features as seem now to be leading the more advanced nations to an order of their economic affairs that will some day be looked upon as another era in the ever progressive development of the race. Certain of its societies or families have now, as we think, fairly entered upon a new stage of progress, which demands, for distinctness of theoretic treatment, a new descriptive name. For this purpose we borrow and adopt the term *Guarantyism*, without intending to insist upon it as definitely descriptive of a change realized and completed, but as applicable to a border, or mixed, condition and drift, not well defined, yet apparent; marked, but not clearly distinguished; recognizable, but not clearly separated from the stage in which it is arising for a new departure; as so many other changes have begun in unnoticed movements, and afterwards revolutionized, by slowly reforming, human institutions; as waves that are clearly distinct at their crests, but less and less in their slope toward the trough where they are inseparable and indistinguishable.

To get this apprehension clearly let us look at the aspects of civilization before the changes began which characterize the evolution that we are about to consider:

In the patriarchal system the family rule was protracted beyond the proper maturity of its subjects; repressing their growth and abridging the liberties necessary to such growth. Barbarism loosened what was left of the ties proper to the family in the patriarchal order, and allowed a little more of liberty and responsibility; or, in terms which we prefer for their directer allusion to the things necessary to progress, a little more of individuality with its incident capability of freer association. It, too, was slavery, but it was political and personal slavery, in longer and weaker chains than those of the despotic power of the head of the tribal family. It began to recognize the individual's right to life and property, and to some modicum of right to self-service and self-government. It abdicated by degrees the absolutism of the priestly office, allowed some system of municipal law, and administered distributive justice by the rule of custom, privilege, and tradition—the will of the ruler was bounded by the law of the realm; and customs and institutions were at least fixed, and the community was organized and established, with some degree of stability of rights and security of interests. But individualism was still greatly repressed. In things most material to growth and development, the masses were still crushed into a crippled uniformity. Even the miscalled democracies of Greece had this grievous and repressive character. Men were banded and led, as the buffaloes of our prairies are, by the strongest and boldest of the herd. The track of the leader limited the adventures and the enterprise of the whole body. Great efficiency was secured in the execution of every common purpose; but national independence was mistaken for civil freedom, and, consent was not choice. Individualism, in all that the commonwealth commanded, was suppressed; and only in those movements of mind and feeling which were indifferent to the commonwealth was liberty allowed.

But men grew under the barbarism of Greece and Rome as they did under that of Egypt and Asia; and as they grew still faster and greater under the feudal rule in Western Europe; where first and most was felt the revolt of individualism against depotism, ever strengthened by its cumulative ameliorations—rising from tribal bondage, through monarchy more and more limited, until rebellion and revolution became possible and irresistible.

This whole process in Europe, rightly understood, was simply a revolt against the one-man power that overruled every other man's distinctive rights. The consummation aimed at through all the struggles of the last five centuries of modern progress, more or less clearly intended, was the right of self-government, by the most appropriate and best answering political machinery. Along with this effort for securing civil liberty and for the redress of injuries suffered by its denial, grew the doctrine of reserved rights, which no government—not even governments by the people themselves—may now in anywise invade, either for good or bad; such as the rights of conscience in religious faith and worship—the right to regulate one's own family—the right to do anything, and to leave anything undone, which does not immediately and directly infringe upon the like rights of others.

If we look closely into this sentiment as it grew from tacit obedience up to full-fledged self-government, we will find that it rather took care of rights than provided for duties. The farthest that it at last conceded to the national authority was military service and necessary revenue. All else of public or social duty must be left to individual free will. Of the social charities none must be exacted, except the scanty support of the poor, which a common humanity consented to extort from the reluctant and inhuman, and this, not so much as a corporate debt as from the greater convenience of organized almsgiving. The common education of the people by the state was resisted on the ground that it is an infringement of the voluntary principle—nay more, we have in vogue at this day a philosophical or logical system of political economy, popular all over Europe and America, founded and built upon the basis of natural rights, and grounded solely upon the self-hood of individual freedom. But individualism, severed from association, has run its race, as it has served its purpose. It has dethroned the tyrannies of all preceding systems of opinion and government, and now, at the end of its absolutism, is merging into association in the form of Guarantyism.

Thus, Civilization, in the proposed distinctive sense of the term, is best understood as the assertion and vindication of the rights of the individual, and the reformation of church and state politics, with this intent and to this end. Guarantyism may be described and distinguished as an effort for the promotion of association, reconstructed and amended, upon the basis of that large development of individualism acquired by its struggles against the earlier forms of unityism, which held the spirit of free association in abeyance.

We have a parallel history in the long, and at last successful, struggle of materalism in science against the earlier rule of its antagonist, spiritualism; and in the returning movement of the rapidly growing sentiment of spiritualism, reformed, liberalized and regulated, displacing the undue preponderance and consequent abuses which it held during the dark ages and still maintained in great force to the end of the eighteenth century.

We have another correspondence, in another necessarily associated movement, with a similar revolt and a similar returning tendency toward a rectified system of association: political revolution in the violence of its struggles went into Anarchy in its War with Despotism in the seventeenth and eighteenth centuries, in England and France; until revolution had so far done its work that Order became a necessity, and its establishment worked a reaction which eliminated the abuses of authority and began the reëstablishment of political and civil authority, guarded and abated by so much of the popular liberty won in the long contest, as the subjects were capable of using beneficially.

These correspondences in religious opinion and political institutions are analogous to the renascence of the associative movement of the present epoch, so long held in check by the revulsion of individualism against the repressive unityism of the patriarchal, barbaric, and earlier civilized forms of society.

In the military system, introduced by the monarchies of the fifteenth and sixteenth centuries we have another analogy: it comported with the spirit of feudalism, but it was sternly resisted afterwards by the growing spirit of liberty among our English ancestors; and the governing powers were forced to rely upon enlistments for the occasion, and volunteer recruitments for domestic defense—Individualism asserting itself, and the associative impulse emerging to supply, while it supplants, the former public policy.

Treating civilization as a growth, and regarding its successive phases as an evolution of its own inherent forces, it might, perhaps, be expected that we should give the chief prominence and value to its achievements in the arts and sciences which have marked its progress, and especially, those triumphs of mind over material forces which illustrate the history of the last hundred years. These, indeed, are signs, and they are wonders as well; but it may be questioned whether in all the varied forms of enterprise, discovery and achievement, the present century is a much further advance upon the last, than the thirteenth was upon the twelfth, or either of the intervening ones upon its immediate predecessor. The eighteenth and nineteenth differ in glory from the sixteenth and seventeenth, but these compare as grandly with the respective ages preceding them, and they contributed, besides, as nobly to that which has followed, and now overshadows them.

Material progress is necessarily an enhancement, at the rate of compound interest, and the last accumulation of every successive period owes its surpassing attainments to the enlarged capital which it inherits. Neither in kind nor in degree, do the latest achievements of science and art exceed in their *rate* of advancement, those from which they sprang.

The magnetic telegraph, the relative circumstances considered, has its rival in the discovery of the mariner's compass; and the printing press was as great a step in advance of the earlier mode of multiplying copies, as steam power applied to service in production, travel, and transportation, over the machinery which it excels and supercedes. The magnitude of the results in the later period is greatest; but so much as this can scarcely be said of the *rate* of advancement. Distinguishing the efficiencies involved in societary development into three classes—those which are employed in the mastery and amendment of material conditions; those devoted to mental endeavor distinctively; and those which concern moral and spiritual life—it is apparent that we, of this age, have scarcely advanced intellectual vigor more rapidly than the generation of two hundred years ago; that our grandest conquests in the realm of physics are but the normal outgrowth of the seed sown in good soil by our fathers, to whom the enhanced fertility, as well as the greater product, is justly due; and, that we must look to what the present time has done, and is doing, in the work of social amelioration, for its distinguishing glory.

Political regeneration in the service, and for the sake of all classes and races, began its great career in 1776, and crowned itself with its last promise fulfilled before the first centennial anniversary of its birthday. The movement begun in the youngest of the nations, with capacities ripened in the oldest, has kept the lead, indeed, but it has been followed at greater or less distance, but still followed, by the kindred peoples of the same common stock. Suffrage and representation in government have grown, by sympathy, in all the nations of which ours was born. All the offshoot peoples from the European stock are responsive to the grand example of the greatest republic of colonial origin.

The last hundred years has distinguished itself by the spread of Christian knowledge in heathen lands, and by labor for the extension of the religion and morality of the Scriptures, more than any of its predecessors—the British, American, French, and German Bible, Tract, and Missionary Societies are of this period—all of them except the Moravian, which antedates the era of the Protestant enterprises of this kind by but a few years.

The first movement of organized effort in the temperance reform was begun in the United States in 1825. Father Matthew began his great work in Ireland in 1830, and numbered above two millions of his countrymen among his converts before he finished his labors.

It is quite impossible to esitmate the benefits conferred upon the world by these systematic benevolences, addressed to the moral and social amelioration of society, by the associative agencies of the era which are thus so decidedly characteristic of the present times.

In 1786 England had one hundred and thirty ships engaged in the slave trade, and the traffic was not abolished by statute there until 1807. In the United States its suppression had been provided for by a clause in the Federal Constitution adopted in 1789, and negro slavery itself had been abolished by several of the States nine or ten years before. As early as 1754 the Quakers had forbidden it among themselves; but it was not more than forty years ago that voluntary organizations were formed in the United States and Great Britain for the suppression of the system of negro slavery, which, beginning in the British colonies in 1833, was finally consummated in the United States by authority of the Constitution in 1865, and the whole colored race was enfranchised by another amendment proclaimed on the 30th March, 1869.

Charity schools date as early as 1687 in England, but common schools opened for the children of the whole people, and maintained at the public expense, and generally diffused throughout the principal nations of Europe and the United States, had their earliest date quite within the transition age which we now are concerned with, and their great extension has happened within the last fifty years.

As late as 1839 after a grant of £30,000 for national education, proposed by Lord John Russell, had passed in the Commons by a majority of two votes (on a vote of five hundred and forty-eight members), the House of Lords went in a body two days after to ask the Queen to rescind the grant.

The vast proportion to which the common school system, as a state institution, has grown, scarcely admits of statistical statement. In all the States of the United States, north of the boundaries of the slave region, it has long been in successful operation.

It appears from the census of 1860 that five million persons were then receiving instruction in the various educational institutions of the country. This number is equal to sixty-six per cent of all the white population between the ages of seven and eighteen, and to seventy-five per cent between the ages of eight and sixteen. For a better apprehension of these numbers, it may be noticed that in Prussia,—where education is compulsory upon all children between the ages of seven and fourteen, and where the result was found in the fact that in 1845 there were only two young men between the ages of twenty and twenty-two, in the hundred, who could not read, write, and cipher,—the number of scholars at schools were but one to every six and two-tenths persons, while, at the same time, of the total white population of the United States there were as many as one to every four and nine-tenths persons;—the State of Maine, exceeding in her proportion of scholars at school all other States in the Union, and the United States exceeding all other countries whatsoever, except Denmark, which had one to every four and six-tenths persons.

In New England only one person over twenty years of age in every four hundred of the native whites is incapable of reading and writing, and in the non-slaveholding States, taken together, but one in forty inhabitants, or two and five-tenths per cent; and this rate is very materially increased by the immigration of illiterate persons from Europe, for it is in these States that they nearly all settle. Besides, these embrace the new and sparse settlements of the west and northwest, where the institution of schools, and attendance at them, is greatly embarassed by the natural impediments of pioneer life. This must account for the fact that, twenty years ago, the illiterate of Indiana were seven and one-quarter per cent of the white inhabitants; while in New York and Pennsylvania they were less than three per cent. Arkansas and Tennessee, both affected alike by the system of slavery and sparseness of population, had above ten per cent, and North Carolina, in the same conditions, above thirteen in the hundred of her white population who could not read and write at the age of twenty.

As an accompaniment, and in some good degree, an index to the work of popular education as administered by State authorities, the libraries, other than private, in 1850, held four and one-half millions of volumes, and the number of political and periodical papers, literary, scientific, religious and secular, had an annual circulation then of four hundred and forty-six millions of copies. Ten years afterwards, when the population had increased but thirty-five per cent, the number rose to nine hundred and twenty-eight millions—an increase of one hundred and seventeen and one-half per cent; or, in 1850, the annual circulation afforded an average of a fraction less than twenty-two copies to each white person in the Union, but in 1860 was equivalent to a supply of thirty-four and one-third copies per person; and, in keeping with these signs of an extending and improving education of the people, it may be noted that the value of the books published in the latter year increased in the decade from three and four-tenths millions to eleven and eight-tenths millions of dollars, or two hundred and forty-seven per cent; and that of the job and newspaper printing at the same rate.

In the social virtue of almsgiving the present age is not distinguished from, at least not above, the preceding centuries of Christianity, but we can claim, for the time, the better and kindlier administration, as a characteristic of the passing centenary—a better provision for the wants of pauperism, and an extended sphere of the beneficence which it expresses. All such improvement as the spirit of the times has impressed upon the legal system of relief, belongs to the period which has diminished the number of capital offences from fifty or sixty, a hundred years ago, to three or four in the present day in England,* and along with this, has abolished the torture of corporal punishment inflicted in the days of the early Georges. The abolition of imprisonment for debt, the reformation of prison treatment, and the exemption of more or less of insolvents' property from attachment, belong in like manner to the nineteenth Christian century.

In the United States, in all these charities and benevolences, we are grandly in advance of the mother countries of Europe. Scarcely a State in the Union punishes any offence with death except murder in the first or highest degree. Treason, Europe's highest crime of old time, with us is reduced almost to the rank of a misdemeanor; not a single individual of all the millions engaged in the late Rebellion was capitally, or otherwise punished as for crime against the sovereignty of the Federal Union, whose criminal code, nevertheless, still retains the punishment of death for the crime of slave-trading on the high seas; and, we may safely add that the tenderness for life, growing out of the higher appreciation of liberty, and along with it, which makes conviction for capital offences almost impossible, and has abolished the penalty of death in one of our States, bids fair, ere long, to substitute some form of correction combined with restraint, for the ultimate and remediless infliction of the death penalty.

Thus much in illustration of what we have assumed to be the distinguishing characteristic of the last hundred years of the history of civilization, as it is shown in amendment of the political and legal institutions of the most advanced of the nations.

* Blackstone, Commentaries, Book iv., chap. 1, says: "It is a melancholy truth that among the variety of actions which men are daily liable to commit, no less than a hundred and sixty have been declared by act of Parliament to be worthy of instant death." This book was first published in 1770. His annotator, writing in 1840, says: "many of these rigorous acts have lately been repealed, and milder punishments have been substituted."

Along with these social ameliorations, effected through the forms and forces of municipal law, we may claim for the age a vast extension of the various systems of insurance—life, property, and maritime—with their indemnities against loss, and assurance under risk, which associates the parties in mutual and participated protection against the consequences of unavoidable injuries, to which the parties are exposed. Maritime assurance had a very early origin; as early, it is said, as the first century of the Christian era, and the policy was recognized and enforced by law in Italy as early as the year 1194. In the year 1667, the first after the great fire, insurance of houses and goods began in London.

The superintendent of the insurance department of the State of New York reports, on March 1, 1865, one hundred and sixty-two joint stock and mutual fire insurance companies in the State, fourteen marine, thirty-one life, and one casualty company, with gross assets amounting to one hundred and fifty-one millions of dollars, and adds that, " several of these companies now receive an annual income exceeding the annual revenue of some of our State governments and many European principalities and Kingdoms. Some idea of the rate of increase in this business may be formed from a comparison instituted between them in the years 1860–4. The aggregate premiums of one hundred and fifty-seven companies—of fire, marine, and life insurance—chartered by the State, rose from twenty-four to thirty-nine millions; the assets from sixty-seven to one hundred and four millions; the fire risks in force, from nine hundred and sixteen, to sixteen hundred and fifteen, millions. Here we have an increase in the values insured of seventy-six per cent in a period of only four years, beginning the year before the Rebellion and ending before its conclusion, notwithstanding the large deduction of insurances of every kind, usually taken by the Southern States, which must have happened.

Akin to insurance institutions is the savings bank system, of which the earliest instances fall within the centenary now elapsing. These banks may be said, indeed, to have taken their effective form, and acquired all their importance within the present century. The earliest traces of them are in Hamburg, in 1778, and in Berne (Switzerland), in 1787. Their general adoption in France, Prussia, and England, occurred between the years 1816 and 1820. One of the first attempts, of which we find any notice, to realize such an institution in England, was made by Mrs. Priscilla Wakefield, at Tottenham, near London, in 1803; and the earliest on a large scale at Edinburgh, in 1814. Soon after they were fairly started in England (in 1816), they were brought under parliamentary regulation. Their progress was very rapid. From 1817 to 1828, inclusive, the commissioners for the reduction of the public debt received from the directors of savings banks the sum of £13,746,546, for which government paid four per cent interest. In 1861, the aggregate capital of these banks, in the United Kingdom, was £41,—546,475. In England and Wales, £36,855,508, when the total securities held by the Bank of England were, at the highest, a little under £30,000,000. Quite the half of the depositors in England usually have less than £20 apiece in these banks; one-third of the whole number, less than £50; and, only one-sixth of the whole number held more than £50. These facts show them to be the institutions of the provident poor people of the realm; and it is this feature, so conspicuously prominent, that entitles them to a place among the associative movements of the present times. Mr. McCulloch describes them as "banks established for the receipt of small sums, deposited by the poorer class of persons, and for their accumulation at compound interest. Under the Act of Parliament of 1844, the interest payable to depositors is not to exceed three per cent per annum. No depositor can contribute more than £30, exclusive of compound interest, to a savings bank in any one year; and the total deposits to be received from any individual are not to exceed £150." He gives, for the year 1850, the number of depositors in these banks, in the United Kingdom, at one million, ninety-two thousand, five hundred and eighty-one; and the average amount to each at £25; more than five-eighths of them, however, averaging only £6; and one-fourth of them at £31 apiece, only. He says well, that "the principle and object of the savings banks cannot be too highly commended. Until they were established, the poorer classes were everywhere without the means of securely and profitably investing those small sums which they are not unfrequently in a condition to save, and were consequently led, from the difficulty of disposing of them, to *neglect opportunities of making savings*, and nothing could be more important, in view of diffusing habits of forethought and economy amongst the laboring classes, than the establishment of savings banks, where the smallest sums are placed in perfect safety, are accumulated at compound interest, and are paid, with their accumulations, the moment they are demanded by the depositors."

The first savings bank in America was opened in Philadelphia, in 1816. The spread and growth of these institutions in the United States, and their present condition, cannot be ascertained with such completeness as would make it worth while to attempt a statistical statement. But in general terms we are warranted, by the data at hand, in putting their whole number at above five hundred, with an aggregate of deposits exceeding two hundred and fifty millions of dollars. Some notion of the relative magnitude of this grand sum, thus accumulated and employed in the business of the country, while it is at the same time paying good interest to the depositors, may be had from the corresponding money movement in the national banking system which embraces almost the entirety of the banks of issue in the country. The controller of the national currency reports their aggregate capital at four hundred and twenty millions, and the aggregate individual deposits at five hundred and fifty millions. Put these sums together and we find that the savings banks of the nation are the depositories of an amount equal to one-fourth of all money collected and distributed by all the other banks in operation, other than those of private bankers.

In the year 1862 there were two hundred and fifteen savings banks in the six New England States; 452,637 depositors, averaging $204 each, and aggregating $94,325,066; in New York and Pennsylvania there were one hundred and twelve banks; 360,693 depositors; averaging $206 each and aggregating $77,450,397. In 1864, the New England States reported an increase of ten banks, 79,694 depositors, and an increase of $25,104,347 to the aggregate of their deposits, averaging $224 to each depositor. The State of New York had made a still greater increase in three years, rising from 310,693 depositors and $67,450,397 in amount, with an average of $214 to the credit of each in 1862, to 456,721 depositors, $111,793,425 in bank, and the average of $244 each, in 1865.

We have not quoted the activity and extension of insurance and savings institutions as instances of the associative movement which we regard as characterizing and distinguishing the hundred years past, which we have called the age of guarantyism. They are not of the essence, but they cannot be overlooked, among the evidences of the times in which the stage of individualism is merging into association, and selfhood is growing into coöperation. They are incidental and collateral, but they are symptomatic and inseparable. They are the earliest strivings and the outward accompaniments of an impulse that is translating the brotherhood of men into coöperation in industrial pursuits, and copartnership in risks and profits. The principle of legal corporation is the very earliest form of the perception of the benefit of mutuality—the first indistinct realization of its serviceableness; for it is true that, every societary movement in the progress of the race has a material, answering to its spiritual, spring, and always its harbinger. Harmony of interests in business affairs, naturally enough, precedes the harmony prompted by social sentiments, among the masses of mankind. Material interest is as the bud of brotherhood, its material profit is the plainest and strongest persuasive, but the social germ grows with its growth and ripens in its fruit. A legal corporation is the simplest type, as well as the earliest form of coöperation. In it we have the unity and identity of interests which convert numbers into one artificial person, with perpetual succession and joint and equitable participation of all its beneficial products, at the expense of its joint maintenance and a fair division of its risks and losses.

Capital, as distinct from the labor of which it is the secured fruit, very early in civilization went into association, and this tendency measures the growth and grade of societary progress. All the great works of modern times are the results, and the evidences of its force in its free movement. The pyramids of Egypt, and the cities, roads, and canals of the barbaric ages were produced by associated labor in bondage. The greater works of the latest times have come from capital associated in freedom. Labor in liberty is now learning the force of union, and beginning to provide the conditions for securing its advantages. Money is the dried and preserved fruit of work—it will keep and will bear the attrition of the necessary fellowship which gives it multiplied efficiency. Labor is a live thing, with susceptibilities, and incapacities, which make the conditions of perfect association hard to secure, but which are indispensable to the fusion of identity, and the required harmonies of coöperation. Men must be better before they can grow nearer, and a very high grade of excellency is necessary to general coalescence. They must coincide before they can thoroughly correspond.

In the infancy of civilization men begin to club their cash; a little later they unite to divide risks upon realized property most exposed to loss; a little later still, they venture, in the first strengthenings of faith, to joint management by its necessary agents, in order to provide for profits—they invent partnerships, securing them as well as they can against the treacheries that are incident to trust; and a little later still, the associative movement recognizes the social charities which they can serve. Marine, fire, life, health insurance, legal corporations, which exempt the corporators from all loss beyond the definite value in the venture, are so entirely material in their motives, that corporations have been long described as things without souls. That they have powerful bodies is the reason that they get leave to live and work for their owners. Yet evil as their reputation is, they have some of the virtue of principle, as well as that of efficiency, and they are found convenient forms for exerting more and more of the social force, as they are extended to other and finer uses. The office of almsgiving is by all improving societies devolved upon the corporate authorities; and benevolence, which is in its nature voluntary, takes upon itself the compulsory character of a societary obligation. A donation comes to be a tax, that the duty may be equitably apportioned and thoroughly performed. Instead of the pyramids that barbarism compelled, arise the poor-houses built by consent, with a grain of the involuntary built into them out of the constrained contributions of the reluctant. Here the material and the spiritual springs of movement begin to work together, somewhat to the damage and deterioration of each, yet to eventual advantage in the compromise; and men learn the ways and means of " looking not alone upon their own things, but also upon the things of others," and, whether they expect " to receive a hundredfold for all they give here, in the world to come," or not; or, whether they are induced to make so long a loan of goods and chattels, or not, they discover that the charities, as investments which make such large returns to the giver, can be administered on business principles to the very highest rate of profit. By this time they have gone through and graduated in the social branches of insurance, dividends, and profits, which begin and *end* in property interests, and are ready for other movements that pay risks, dividends, and profits as they go, and do not end in immediate individual benefits; movements that secure self better than any that refuse association, and whose expenses and losses are the lightest of all that beleaguer them, and are at the same time not *dead* losses even when they happen, because they are vital to the highest ends, and in the effects intended.

Having banked profitably upon property and credit, and even made capital of their mortality for the use of their survivors, they proceed to extend the investment of their possible casualties of health and fortune, and thus convert them into a fund provided for the redress of their evils and injuries. After saving funds come beneficial societies, under a hundred forms of organization, in which provision for relief in sickness and misfortune are the special objects of associated contributions.

Beneficial societies having no need for a central government, and not being required to report their statistics to the civil governments in England or America, their numbers, growth and work cannot be estimated. That they are very extensive in England and Ireland, where they are known as "friendly societies," is indicated by the amount of their aggregate deposits standing to their credit in the year 1850, which was $5,000,000, averaging $688 to each contributor. This sum is nearly six times the average amount standing to the credit of each depositor in the savings banks of England at the same time; which is explained by the difference of the management of their funds in the two institutions. In the savings banks the deposit is liable to be withdrawn at will, but in the friendly societies the capital and interest must be held in reserve for the relief of the members as the casualties occur for which it is provided. The total fund remaining at any time is just the surplus of the provision for the purposes for which it was raised, and so large a surplus as this shows the amplitude of the provision raised from the very trivial contributions of the members. They are described as "associations, chiefly among the most industrious of the lower and middling classes of tradesmen and mechanics, for the purpose of affording each other relief in sickness, and their widows and children some assistance at their death."

Corresponding associations in the United States are called "beneficial societies," having the same objects and controlled in the same way. Not specially recognized here, as in England, nor put under direction by the law, nor having any responsibility, or needing any protection, they make no public reports, and we have no official statistics of their number, funds, or work. They are, however, very numerous, and proportionately useful. Each association determines for itself the conditions of membership, the weekly or monthly contributions, the weekly allowance to the sick, the amount of funeral expenses allowed to members and their families, and the cash and care promised to widows and orphans. The allowances in sickness are usually quite equal to the ordinary earnings of the beneficiary, if they are not even greater than those of the skilled laborer; and, generally, the tax upon the members is not larger per year than the relief granted for a week's illness; besides, the funeral donation is always sufficient to cover its expense. At such easy rates is insurance provided for sickness and such casualties as disqualify the members for self-support.

As a matter of policy, as well as principle, these societies guard the general moral conduct of their members by expulsion for crimes and misconduct discreditable to the association; and they refuse relief for sickness and accidents plainly traceable to intemperance or to practices contrary to public morals.

It is true of them generally that the societies grow rich, even to the extent of requiring, in some of the oldest and largest of them, an occasional distribution of the manifest excess of their common funds among the members, by whose contributions they have accumulated beyond the charitable requirements for which they were intended.

The like provision made by the rapidly-multiplying secret societies of the time, checks the growth of the primitive associations, and they are, accordingly, found to prevail chiefly among the Roman Catholics, to whom membership in secret societies is forbidden by their Church; and, among such Protestants as are unwilling to encumber themselves with the additional requirements and expenses of the secret orders.

CHAPTER XIX.

GUARANTYISM—SECRET SOCIETIES.

GUARANTYISM—SECRET SOCIETIES: Free Masons.—Growth of Secret Orders.—*Odd Fellows*—origin, success—Colored and British Odd Fellows—Negroes and women excluded—Rebekah degree—Statistics—Ratio of reliefs to revenue—Expenses of membership—Suspensions and expulsions—Geographic distribution of the Order—Law of climate—Political possibilities.—*Knights of Pythias*—Rate of increase—Statistics—Abundant resources—Geographic distribution of the Order—Revenue and reliefs—Charities—Expense of membership—Penal provisions—German lodges—Exclusion of women and negroes.—*Temperance Societies*—History—Propagandism.—*Temperance Orders.*—*Sons of Temperance*—Organization—Numbers and revenue—Benefits—Death rate—Expulsions—Beneficial provisions dropped—Female members—Causes of declension of the Order.—*Beneficial Orders*—Multiplex membership—Ample provision in sickness—These Orders prevail just where they are most needed—Growing liberality to women—Prejudice of color.—*Colored Orders.*—*Order of United American Mechanics*—Abundant resources—Trivial expense of membership—Junior Order—Order of foreigners.

WITH secret societies our inquiries are concerned only so far as they are involved with, and indicate the associative movements of the times, and, as they provide for the risks and casualties of life, or, to the extent that these societies make their members partners in common misfortunes, and mutual insurers of each other's temporal welfare, with the incident help that there is in the moral discipline, and careful surveillance of the membership exercised by the association.*

Free Masonry, for several reasons, should be first noticed and disposed of. It claims precedence by its rank and antiquity. It is, however, exceptional in this inquiry, being much older than the age of guarantyism proper, independent of the great popular movement which specially characterizes the last hundred years of societary history, and comparatively but little more adjusted to the new, than to the olden time. Free Masonry is, as it must be, affected by the

---

* The reader, perhaps, ought to be apprised that the author is not now, and never has been, a member of any secret Order or Association.

changes that, in the progress of things, impress upon all institutions of men; but it has not arisen from the exigencies of the present phase of civilized society, is not one of its fruits, nor a specially good index of its character. Its civil, social, and charitable work may be, and probably is, all that its advocates claim for it; and it may be liable to all the objections made against it, or it may be wholly free from them. In either case, neither its members, its funds, nor the amount of its reliefs, are necessarily involved in that order of things which gives its special character to the new age, however it may conform or contribute to its movements.

But, within the present century, there have arisen an immense variety of secret orders and associations that are rolling on with cumulative force, and bid fairly now to aggregate the entire mass of the advancing communities of christendom. Some of them are purely benevolent in their avowed objects; their paraphernalia, degrees of honor, and other attractions, being only designed to increase their fascinations, and promote their progress; others, and indeed, in some degree, all, may minister to ends less worthy, and less important; and they may be just subjects of exception, too, in matters more or less important to their members and to the community; for all human institutions are liable to the imperfections and abuses of human frailty. But we are not now concerned with anything in them, intended, incidental, or possible, except their tendency to promote, and their service in displaying, the characteristic impulses of that advanced, and still advancing, phase of civilization, in which we see repellant and discordant individualism giving way to the emergent spirit of coöperation, and effecting the organization of benevolence in all the forms of which the age has become capable.

Among these societies, working for and towards reunion and limited guarantyism, ODD FELLOWSHIP, by its age and numbers, its wealth and rate in growth, takes precedence.

The Order, in America, was founded in the year 1819, by five members. Its sentiment—" The Fatherhood of God over all, and the universal brotherhood of man;" its motto—" Friendship, Love, and Truth." The Order claims to have enrolled over half a million of votaries within its first half century. Its lodges have spread into every State in the Union, some of the islands of the Pacific, and into the British American Provinces, and Australia, where it has recently absorbed a somewhat older but much weaker order, originally founded in Great Britain; with which the Colored Odd Fellows of the United States, excluded from fellowship by their white brethren, under the long prevailing prejudice of color, are in full fellowship. In common with other associations of whites in the United States, whose general profession of philanthropy, humanity, and benevolence in the past, had a like limitation in principle and practice, the Odd Fellows excluded negroes and women from its membership; and the former from all forms and operations of its charities. The prejudice of color is the reason, and the whole reason, of the severance of the American from the English brotherhood; and this difference had to be overcome in Australia by its surrender there, before a unity of jurisdiction could be effected.

Very recently, by the creation of what in the Order is called the *Rebekah Degree*, women are admitted into a collateral branch, without acquiring all the privileges and immunities of full membership, but are made capable of its charitable offices, and, to some extent, of its dignities and authorities within their own degree, in which they participate with male members: the Rebekah Degree being constituted of both sexes. This sentiment is progressive, and evidently tends to the concession of larger and larger participation to the long-excluded sex. It is not necessary here to trace the influences that are gradually widening the humanitary spirit of the Order for the admission of a sisterhood into the brotherhood, and it is, also, unnecessary to look for the probability of the new order of things amongst us in its necessary tendency to break through the prejudice that has hitherto barred out the colored race from its universality of brotherhood and benevolence. But we may expect that all changes in the general sentiment of society will reflect their effects, sooner or later, upon those whose assumed position is in the advance, and who are specially pledged to advance the "universal brotherhood of man."

The progress of this American Order is a sign of the times, and so significant as to give interest to some of its general details. From the report of the Grand Lodge of the United States, held at San Francisco, in September, 1869, we take the materials of the following tabular statement, exhibiting the growth of the membership and revenue, and of the relief afforded during the three last decades.

Decade.	Revenue.	Reliefs.	Initiates.	Proportion of reliefs to revenue.
1830-9	$ 327,935	no record.	18,060	....
1840-9	4,933,492	$1,864,115	179,754	37.78 per cent.
1850-9	12,951,453	6,064,397	234,252	46.82 "
1860-9	13,111,133	4,846,518	228,193	36.96 "
Totals	$31,324,013	$12,775,030	660,259	41.21 "

These totals need some explanation. The excess of eighteen and a half millions of revenue over expenditures in relief of brothers, their widows, and orphans, is due to cost of conducting the lodges; such as regalia, rent, fuel, light, salaries, and other expenses, with probably an aggregate fund of nine millions in the treasuries of the lodges, available for all uses. The initiates sum up 660,259 within forty years, but the reported membership in June, 1869, was only 268,608. The difference of 400,000, nearly, must be accounted for by deaths, suspensions, and expulsions. The number of brothers relieved during the last year and the year before does not amount to quite nine per cent of the total membership of either year, and the deaths of the year ending June, 1869, were but eight-tenths of one per cent of the membership at the beginning of the year. The average reliefs, in proportion to the revenue of the forty years, was forty-one and twenty-one one-hundredths per cent, but the proportion of the last two years was but thirty-two per cent. The total revenue of the year 1867-8, ending June 30, 1868, of the lodges and encampments, amounted to $2,364,295, and of the year 1868-9 to $2,630,316. The tax per head to the total membership would thus appear to be nine dollars per annum; but the invested funds must have yielded nearly half a million to the revenue, which, being deducted, would reduce the average taxation per member to about eight dollars per annum. This is, indeed, a cheap rate of assurance for the health, and provision for the burial expenses of the members, with relief of widows and orphans added. The increase of the membership has been about ten per cent per annum during the last five years. This is double the rate of increase in the membership of the Methodist Episcopal Church in Pennsylvania during the same time. The death rate in the Odd Fellow societies is also apparently in their favor, but, perhaps, not really so. The deaths in the Church are as twelve to eight in the Order; but the Order selects its candidates, excluding the unhealthy among men, all women, and all of both sexes under twenty-one years of age.

The suspensions of the last two years number 25,721, and were equal to thirty-one per cent of the initiations; most of these, however, were for non-payment of dues. In the Grand Sire's address, delivered in 1868, he says that "in the last twenty years there have been 214,990 members suspended from membership, and, with few exceptions, for non-payment of dues." About one-third of the members suspended are usually reinstated; so that about twenty per cent of the initiations are lost to the Order from causes which do not involve any other unfitness or unworthiness than "suspension" implies.

The expulsions are annually something less than one per cent of the total membership. Their names and offenses are published, and besides those that are made "for conduct unbecoming an Odd Fellow," nearly every crime against society, and every form of moral depravity known among men, are in the list of offenses. Among these, drunkenness, with its attendant crimes, figures first in the number of its subjects. It is curious to see how far the severest discipline of the lodges reaches in rebuke of private vices—a great many cases are given of expulsion for lying, slander, neglect and abuse of family, gambling and keeping gambling houses, violation of the laws of the State in restraint of liquor selling, selling liquor to drunkards against the remonstrances of their wives, refusing aid to sick brothers, and, in one case, diluting the liquor administered to a sick brother. Rioting and assault and battery frequently occur in the list, divulging secrets of the Order in a few instances, and in one case "general meanness" is the charge. It is safe to say that the offenses here named are probably rather flagrant degrees, and publicly offensive; for, it cannot be assumed that the members in good standing are wholly free from any and all of them. In the last report of the Grand Lodge the expulsions for the State of Pennsylvania are given at 121 "for conduct unbecoming Odd Fellows." Names and offenses not given; but, for all the other States, the offenders and their specific misdemeanors are published without reserve. The aggregate for the year is summed up at 1,081.

The geographic distribution of the Order in the United States is something curious. The whole membership in June, 1869, was

268,608; of these Pennsylvania had 69,770, or twenty-five per cent, while New York with a much larger population had but 17,950 members, or only six and two-thirds per cent of the total membership in North America. More curious still, climate or race seems to have its influence here as in other societary facts and movements. Between latitude 39° and 42,° north, seventy-one and eight-tenths per cent of the total membership is found; that is, in the District of Columbia, Maryland, Delaware, Pennsylvania, New Jersey, West-Virginia, Ohio, Indiana, Illinois, Missouri, Iowa, Kansas, Colorado, Nevada, and California—fifteen States and Territories, there are 192,954 of the Order. The six New England States, New York, Michigan, Wisconsin, Minnesota, Oregon, Nebraska, Montana, and the British provinces—all lying above latitude 42° north, had but 54,111 members, or twenty and one-tenth per cent of the total; and all south of 38°—fourteen States and Territories—had 21,536, or a fraction over eight per cent.

The Rebellion, of course, had some effect upon the membership in the southern belt of States, from which they have not yet recovered, but the law of climate and its effects upon the inhabitants, rules here, forcibly and conspicuously. Else, how shall we account for the phenomena in the northern belt, in which a population of nine millions of the inhabitants of the Union, in 1860, with three millions and a half in the British provinces, to be added, should show but twenty per cent of the total membership; while the middle belt with no more than twelve millions of people (12,359,870 free people in 1860) has seventy-two per cent. Or, if a comparison of communities in the nearest equality of conditions, and located most nearly to each other be chosen, we have this result: in 1868 the six New England States and the State of New York cast 1,402,612 votes at the Presidential election, and together, in 1869, had 37,137 Odd Fellows, which are equal to two and two-thirds per cent of their voters. Pennsylvania cast 655,662 votes at the same election, and had, in 1869, 69,770 Odd Fellows, or eleven and one-half per cent of her voters. The proportion of Odd Fellows to the Presidential votes, in 1868, of Pennsylvania, New Jersey, and Ohio was eight per cent, or a little more than three to one against New England and New York.

As we shall have other occasions for noticing sectionality or locality in other instances of social coöperation, we will just now note the fact that the New England States, with a population of 3,135,283 in 1860, had together 19,187 Odd Fellows in 1869, and Pennsylvania numbering 2,906,115 in 1860, had in 1869, 69,770 Odd Fellows.

Here we have a society which has been growing in membership for several years at the rate of ten per cent per annum, with its revenues increasing at the rate of above eleven per cent, and a surplus, over and above its real estate, of about nine millions of dollars, while increasing its charities at the rate of eight and one-half per cent per annum. Power doubling about once in seven years, if it shall have the gift and grace of continuance. It embraces indeed less than four per cent of the total voting population of the Union, but it measures from eight to eleven per cent of the voters of the Middle States, and is therefore of great political importance; or, it is at least capable of great political influence if it could be so employed. But, I apprehend that its future will not answer to its present attainment, and its progress in the immediate past. Other associations, availing themselves of its special advantages and attractions, and relieving themselves of whatever is less favorably addressed to the public demand, will more and more abate its rate of progress; or so amend the institution itself, as to answer the same purpose—they will better, or they will supplant it.

We have another Order, generally like that of Odd Fellowship, which is making very rapid progress; it may be in virtue of a better adjustment to a different class of the community. It is not yet seven years old, and, lacking the complete sectional organization of time and experience, its statistics are not attainable with satisfactory precision.

The order of the KNIGHTS OF PYTHIAS was founded on the 19th of February, 1864. In April, 1870, it had about seventy-five thousand members in the United States. At the annual session of the Supreme Lodge, held at Richmond, Virginia, in March, 1869, the subordinate lodges were—thirteen in the District of Columbia; one hundred and forty-six in Pennsylvania; twenty in New Jersey; thirty-two in Maryland; ten in Delaware; eight in New York; seven in Virginia; five in Connecticut; two in Louisiana; two in Nebraska; two in California; one in West Virginia; and one in Ohio. The rate of growth is indicated by an increase of fifteen lodges in Maryland in the next ensuing nine months, and of eighty-eight in Pennsylvania in the same time. The number of members in Pennsylvania, on the 31st of December, 1869, was thirty-six thousand and ninety-three, or one-half of the Order in the United States. The revenue of the Pennsylvania Lodges during the year was $277,627; the reliefs paid, $60,734—a trifle less than twenty-two per cent of the total receipts, thus falling below the proportion of the reliefs of the Odd Fellow Order to their total revenue, about eleven per cent. But this may very well be accounted for by the recency of the organization of the Knights, and their probable less liberal allowance to sick members; and the proportionally less number of widows and orphans requiring support. The funds on hand and invested by the Order in Pennsylvania, at the last-mentioned date, were $183,664; so that they may be regarded as amply provided for the contingencies which call for their charities.

The locality of these beginnings of the Order are found, like those of the Odd Fellows after fifty years of progress, nearly confined to the middle belt of States, or, climatically stated, between the 38° and 42° of north latitude.

The qualifications required in candidates for initiation are: they must be white males, over twenty-one and under fifty years of age, of good moral character, with all their parts, healthy, sound, and free from any mental or bodily infirmity, able and competent to earn the means necessary for the support of themselves and families, and a belief in the Supreme Creator and Preserver of the Universe. The initiation fee, not less than $5.00; weekly dues not less than ten cents per week, with an assessment for the funeral fund; the amounts of each, subject to the decision of the several subordinate lodges, at any rates above these minimums prescribed by the Grand Lodge of the State. A probationary period previous to vesting the right to claim benefits, is imposed, and benefits are refused to members disabled by infirmities previous to admission, and for any disability originating from intemperance, and vicious or immoral conduct. The minimum fixed for funeral expenses of members is $30. The support of widows and orphans is obligatory upon the subordinate lodges, but the amount of appropriation is left, as it must be, to the discretion of the particular lodge to which the deceased member, through whom they claim, belonged. The average cost of all the benefits provided and secured to the members seems, from the data afforded by the statistics of the Order in Pennsylvania, to fall under the sum of eight dollars per annum, exclusive of the initiation fee, which is paid but once, with a trifling addition for two or three degrees afterwards conferred. The whole of these degree expenses being less than ten dollars. Suspension is inflicted for failure to pay dues, and for minor offenses against the rules and requirements of the Order. Fine, suspension, or expulsion, is the penalty for offenses against the corporate laws, for frauds, drunkenness, and immoral or criminal conduct of any kind, but the Order is more chary of its penal records than the Odd Fellows. They make no report of their expulsions, either of the number, names of offenders, or of their misdemeanors. In the report of the Grand Lodge of Pennsylvania for the term ending June 30, 1869, the initiations reported are 6,779; the suspensions 1,507; and the deaths 96; together, 1,603.

Nearly twenty of these lodges use the *German language* in their "work" or in the conduct of their lodge business. Almost all of these are situated in Philadelphia, and are, probably, natives of Germany.

The actual condition and the prospects of this Order cannot be confidently inferred from the statistics given to the public; but if not among the forces they are certainly one of the signs of the times. They utterly exclude women and colored men from their association, and they are remarkable among their class of associations for embracing immigrant residents, who yet use a foreign language in their proceedings. Their rules do not require citizenship.

The Temperance Reform had its beginnings in the United States— it has had several revivals and beginnings in various organized forms. Its history may be thus briefly stated: New York organized the first temperance society in 1808. The first in Great Britain was started in 1829. In 1831 the first Congressional society was formed in Washington City. Before this date a great number of local societies were formed throughout the country. A very general movement in all our communities prevailed about the year 1830, and all the auxiliaries of propagandism were vigorously employed with apparently great success. In 1840–1–2 the Reformed Drunkards', originating in Baltimore, awakened a general revival; signers to the total abstinence pledge were added until of both sexes and of all ages they numbered millions. The multitudes, however, had no common bond of union, except that of their voluntary obligation to practice abstinence from the use of all inebriating drinks, and the common effort of the discipleship to propagate reform by oral and printed appeals, and with very great unanimity, an endeavor to check, or prevent, the use of intoxicating liquors, by legislation in restraint or prevention of the retail trade in intoxicating drinks. Of weekly and monthly periodicals, in newspaper and pamphlet forms, there have been as many as thirty-five or forty in existence at a time, and nearly all the time, within the last thirty-five or forty years. The tracts and handbooks devoted to the same service have, perhaps, not been exceeded in quantity by the like publications of any one religious denomination in the country; and, out of the general movement has grown a general advocacy of the cause in all the pulpits, and a constant support by the secular press. As an advance step in the same direction there are more than half a dozen, perhaps twice as many, inebriate asylums in the nation, established for the cure of the *disease* of drunkenness, and all of them reasonably successful in effecting their intention.

Simply as a voluntary endeavor by a host of earnest men and women, in every rank of life, for the promotion of a great, and greatly needed, social reform, the general movement is a grand indication of the distinguishing character of the century in helpfulness of associated benevolence. About thirty years ago, the felt necessity for a closer tie among the subjects and agents of this reformatory work, and a greater efficiency, and better direction, of its agencies, put vast numbers upon the formation of "Orders" after the type of Masonry and Odd Fellowship, in the hope of strengthening the bonds and securing, as well as extending, the success of the cause.

The Order styled the SONS OF TEMPERANCE was, I believe, a little the earliest of these. It was instituted in the year 1842, and as early as 1845 availed itself of degrees, honors, paraphernalia, secret signs, and whatever of such fascinations as could be commanded for propagation and permanency. They added to it the protective and remedial features of the common type of "Beneficial Societies," by which an allowance was provided for sickness of the members, for their burial expenses, and for the charities required by widows and orphans.

From their official reports we gather these prominent points in the history of the Order: after the model of the United States

Government the jurisdiction of the Order—with organizations conforming—is divided into subordinate, grand, and national divisions. A grand division in general, embraces the territory of a State. As early as 1847 they had twenty-two grand divisions in the United States and Canada, and thirteen hundred subordinate divisions, embracing one hundred thousand members. In the twelve years 1848–59 they initiated an average of sixty-three thousand per annum, and had a revenue of about $428,000; out of which they paid $118,000 yearly in benefits to members and their families. This amount is twenty-eight per cent of the total receipts; in this respect falling very little short of the charities of the Odd Fellows. The total receipts of all the subordinate divisions in these twelve years amounted to $5,084,477, which exceeds the total receipts of the American Bible Society, in the same time, a full million of dollars.

The reliefs paid by the Order, as by other societies of kindred character, were determined by the members of the particular divisions to which they belonged, but may be stated, accurately enough, at about as much for a week's sickness as the annual tax upon the members, along with whatever might result to the family at death. The average mortality in years quite recent has been one-half of one per cent of the membership. The violations of the pledge have been a little over ten per cent of the total members per annum, and the members annually expelled were nearly twenty-four per cent of the number admitted.

The prosperity of the earlier half of the Order's past lifetime, seems to have greatly declined in the last twelve years. The receipts which in the former period were about $425,000 per annum, have fallen off to $182,000. The benefits paid have declined from $118,000 to $17,000; and the membership does not now exceed ninety-seven thousand. This is all that is left of quite a million of initiates, claimed by the Order since its first establishment. The reduction of the annual benefits to one-tenth of their former amount, with a nearly equal number of members, is accounted for by the fact that the beneficial provision has been dropped from the constitutions of perhaps nine-tenths of the subordinate divisions; and the actual diminution of their numbers, is accounted for, by themselves, by a great absorption of the material of recruitment by other societies and Orders that have arisen in the mean time. In the beginning of the year 1870, their activity was somewhat revived, and they seem to be partaking of the general progress which the principle of total abstinence is again experiencing in the country.

As an organization it has, in a great measure, lost the associate principle of health insurance, and has fallen that far out of harmony with the spirit of the times. The Order is, indeed, little else than a temperance society, held together by the attractions of their ceremonial. *Women* have, within the last four or five years, been admitted to equal privileges in the Order. In 1868 they reported nearly ten thousand ladies admitted, and forty thousand lady visitors to their social assemblies. The Grand Secretary speaks of the initiation of women as not only a feasible project, but of great advantage to the Order. This feature of their policy had a sort of beginning fifteen years ago; but has become an integral part of the movement only within two or three of the last years.

In 1859, when the Order was at the height of its success, its officials believed they had put themselves at the head of the temperance movement, and expected a future of stability and progress corresponding to that which they had enjoyed in the past.

I know not what were all the causes which have disappointed this confidence, but I think that a misapprehension of the force of the coöperative impulse, at work in the mass of society, is a sufficient explanation, without any other. There may, there must, have been many untoward influences besides; but without provision for this demand, no excellence of aim or of organization would have availed; and with it, all other imperfections would have been greatly lessened in effect, and amended in fact. The mutual insurance principle, in decided force, would have taken care of all the concomitants of the associations. Mere Temperance Societies have again and again failed to perpetuate themselves. They have not the religious bond of unity, and, without the ties of material interest, they die out as organizations as soon as the revival fervor abates. Besides, the "sons" were too slow in securing the corrective and inspiring aid of the "daughters" of temperance.

The jurisdiction of the National Division embraces the British American Provinces. A National Division was established in 1868 in Australia; and the United Kingdom of Great Britain has one of its own.

This society has a propagation fund, and keeps a lecturer in the field. It has its own newspaper organs, also, and seems determined to work its machinery vigorously; but it needs reconstruction, or, what will answer just as well, the absorption of its active elements in other Orders which have grown out of it, and, for that reason, outgrown it.

The societies, based upon the Temperance pledge, or embracing it as a condition and a duty of membership, are so numerous that their statistics are not attainable with tolerable precision. Nearly all of them which are offshoots of the Order of the "sons" have the beneficial provision in their constitutions. The names of a few of these several "Orders" which, I believe, are the most numerous in membership and prosperous in their achievements and prospects, will give a hint of their spread and prevalence. There are of this class such as: The Temple of Honor; The Temple of Honor and Temperance; Good Templars; Ancient Order of Good Fellows, and Good Samaritans.

There are, besides these, many other "Orders" whose principal aim is provision for ill health, and burial benefits. A few of their names will serve to indicate the prevailing spirit of association: The Social Friends; Sons and Daughters of Arcanum Ark; Independent Daughters of the Union; Anglo-American Beneficial Society; Ancient Order of Female Druids; Mount Moriah Temple of the Masonic Tie; Annunciation Female Beneficial Society, and a host, besides, of the like general character.* Of their numbers,

* I am indebted to Mr. Thomas M. Coleman, of the *Ledger*, for the following list of Secret Orders in Philadelphia, whose existence is known to him, and in a large majority of which he is himself a member: Improved Order of Free Sons of Israel, *Beneficial*—Knights of Helcium Arma—Knights of Friendship—Knights of Honor—Knights Templar—Ancient York Masons—Ancient Order of Good Fellows —Order of Heptasophs, or Seven Wise Men—Sons and Daughters of Arcanum Ark—Sons and Daughters of America—Order of Masonic Ladies—Daughters of Temperance—Daughters of Samaria—Independent Order of Good Samaritans, *both sexes and colors*—Order of Progress, *both sexes*—United Order of American Mechanics—American Protestant Association—Brotherhood of the Union—Improved Order of Red Men—Independent Order of Red Men.—Sons of Temperance, *both sexes*—Temple of Honor and Temperance—Cadets of Temperance—Independent Order of Cadets of Honor and Temperance, *both sexes*—United Order of Sacred Temple of Liberty, *both sexes*—Knights of Pythias—Independent Order of Odd Fellows—Encampment of Independent Order of Odd Fellows—Order of Female Druids—Association of Independent Order of P—, *female*—Temperance Beneficial Association—Independent Order of Good Tem-

resources, and differences of constitutional provisions and administration, it is impossible to obtain complete reports. Like the forty or fifty religious sects of a great city, they have shades of difference in doctrine and ritual, with no common centre of registration, and the most active in the membership of either are not able to give a census of all.

Some peculiarities of one of the societies of very recent origin, and unusually rapid growth, deserve special notice—the Order of *United American Mechanics*. The constitution declares the purpose of the Order to be protection against "foreign competition and foreign combination;" to promote the interests, elevate the character, and secure the happiness of the working men and mechanics of *this* country. In particulars, the objects of the Order are declared to be—" 1st. To assist each other in obtaining employment; 2d. To encourage each other in business; 3d. To establish a sick and funeral fund; 4th. To establish a fund for the relief of widows and orphans of deceased members; 5th. To aid members who, through Providence, may have become incapacitated from following their usual avocation, by obtaining situations suitable to their afflictions." The members must be natives of the United States. Relief in sickness is refused when it results from intemperance, or other immorality. Suspension or expulsion is the penalty for intemperance, and for gambling. In 1869 the number of members in Pennsylvania, New Jersey, Delaware, Maryland, and Ohio, was twenty-one thousand, of which Pennsylvania had eighty-four and one-half per cent. The total increase of the year was twenty-five per cent upon the membership of 1868; and the increase of 1870 was very greatly more rapid. With respect to its financial condition, the same facts hold that we have observed in all other societies which provide for the relief of sickness of the members, funeral expenses, and allowances to widows and children.

The O. U. A. M. in 1869 were taxed in benevolences of this kind with no more than twenty-eight per cent of their receipts in the year. The receipts of the widow and orphan fund were above

---

plars—Junior Order of United American Mechanics—True Temple of Honor—The Mystic Band of Brothers—Patriotic Order of Liberty.

That this list, made by the most competent Reporter of the Secret Societies in Philadelphia, does not embrace the whole of them, is certain, which shows how numerous and various they really are.

$6,000—the expenditure less than $3,000. The balance in this fund was then $23,000. The councils of Pennsylvania in the year paid out, total reliefs, $33,622, about two dollars, average, per head of the membership,—the average receipts from the members being $7.76 for the year. At so slight an expense the society is able, and more than able, to meet the assurances it gives. The death rate of the year was only seven-tenths of one per cent.

The Order has a *junior* branch, temperance being a prominent feature of their constitution. In 1869 they had seventy councils in Pennsylvania. They meet weekly; attendance reported to be good. Their exercises are educational in the conduct of meetings and of debates. The juniors must not be under sixteen years of age. The head of the Order says these junior societies are to the parent Order what Sunday-schools are to the churches.

The Order excludes negroes, foreigners, and women from membership. As a counterbalance, in part, there are quite a number of Mechanic Councils in the country to which none but Germans, or sons of Germans, are admitted.

These secret societies differ from the churches in this, that they are wonderfully interlocked, and generally hold to each other the most harmonious relations. Many persons belong to several of them at the same time, and are entitled to reliefs from all that they belong to. It is not an unusual thing to see obituary notices in our cheapest daily papers, in which two, three, four, or even six or eight secret orders are notified of the funeral. These notices always indicate very plainly that the subjects belong to the class in the community which specially needs the reliefs which they have so providently secured; such persons, as for the most part must, under the disabilities of sickness and the bereavements of death, fall into the "supported class" if they have not wisely put themselves into the provident class by fair purchase of an insurance against the casualties of life. One man assured the writer that he belonged to twenty-three societies, and carried all their passwords in his memory. He must have been paying seventy-five to one hundred dollars *a year* for the chance of an equal allowance for every *week* of sickness with a funeral allowance to his family from each of the Orders of which he was a member. It is probable that, as a rule, the people, in very moderate circumstances, who adopt this kind of insurance provision, fortify themselves with the rights and claims of two or three societies, so that for a premium of say fifteen dollars a year, paid in monthly installments, they are entitled to draw three reliefs, amounting to as much per week, and three funeral benefits to the use of their families, which may amount to a hundred or a hundred and fifty dollars.

The most significant feature of this great movement among the populace is, that it prevails just in the right regions and grades of pecuniary condition—most general just where it is most needed. For example, upon inquiry, I have had the one answer from housekeepers, that in their opinion all the better class of colored female domestics of the city belong to one, two, or three beneficial societies.

One of the most observant and best informed among the leaders of this popular movement expressed this drift of the common people of the time, by saying, as a summary of his own observations: "Orders are the Order of the day." "Indeed," he remarked, "if you will worm your way through the popular promenade of a holiday, when crowds are taking their exercise and airing you may be assured that a great majority of the mass hold membership in relief societies."

A number of the "Orders," here spoken of, admit women to full membership; and this seems to be the tendency of the most prosperous among them. Many others have established branch or side degrees, to which women are admitted; some have gone no further than establishing *social* degrees, which carry no "benefits" with them, but allow women to contribute to and enjoy the open festivals and convivialities of the Order. A few organizations, with very fair prospects, make women eligible to membership and to the offices of the Order, even to that of the chaplaincy. The greater and older, and as yet, more powerful of the secret societies, have done little for women, except by their charities proper. But even with them the beginning of the end is getting a footing, and the assured promise is, that on the great common ground of mutual assurance, the long rejected sex will promptly be admitted to an equality of right, coextensive with its equality of need. The prejudice of color is another embarrassment to the practice of that universal benevolence which all the "Orders" profess. This feeling deprives the people of African descent, in the United States, of the great assistance which a broader liberality would afford them, but it has the effect of driving them upon self-help, and, to their credit, it must be said, that among them there are very fair imitations of their white exemplars in every sort of associative organizations. They, too, have their "Orders" of the upper class, and of all grades from the aristocratic brotherhoods down to the simplest and least pretentious. Of the humbler grades they are, in proportion to ways and means, actually in advance of the corresponding classes of white people. They are organizing in the ratio of their need, and relatively, this is generally greater, for all reasons, than in the parallel ranks of the dominant race.

Of one Temperance Beneficial Order we have this report: The *Good Samaritans*, organized in the year 1847, had a year or two since twenty-two thousand members. It claims to be the first of all the Temperance Orders to admit women and colored people to full membership. How will these things be in the millennial "Order?" That is, how are they in the Divine Order? In the mean time, the progressives must wait, and the conservatives may console themselves with the certainty that no change will come until society is ready for it, and then, it will hurt nobody.

The attention of the writer was first drawn to the astonishing number and activity of the secret societies of the day, by noticing as often as two or three times a week, in one of our morning papers having a circulation of above fifty thousand copies, from ten to twenty calls for their meetings. Whoever will any day examine these notices of society meetings, and the reference to society membership in the obituary column of the most popular papers, will be convinced that "Orders are the Order of the day," and will see abundant reason for concluding such an examination with the conviction that, indeed, the present is the age of guarantyism, and that the associative movement is *the* distinguishing feature of the time.

CHAPTER XX.

COÖPERATION—SURVEY OF THE FIELD.

Coöperation—*Survey of the field:* Three classes of guaranty associations—those which organize the social charities—those which economize the expenses of subsistence—those which equitably divide the profits of production.—Selfhood made social by expansion of its aims.—A nation, a loose political association.—Organization vitalizes its constituents.—Difference between money lending, at interest, and profits of capital invested in production.—Slavery and wages.—Labor at wages and money at interest, both hirelings.—Interest of money.—Notions need correction.—Stages in history of business development.—Coöperative stores.—Elimination of middle-men.—Merchant service, uses and abuses.—Merchants of old.—The merchant a "producer."—Monopoly of common carriers.—Monopoly of large capital.—Domination of wealth.—Any remedy?—Political power grew in the past as wealth does now, and worked its own cure.—Resistance to domination of wealth, commenced.—Revolt of philanthropy.—Historic parallel.—The remedy grows with and outgrows the evil.—Current products of industry immensely greater than accumulated capital.—Labor's dependence upon capital in modern production.—Freedom arises in bondage.—Education by labor, and of the laborer.—The baby giant not yet weaned or named.—Trade unions and strikes correspond to the insurrections from Wat Tyler till the French Revolution.—Laws of order working in disorder.—Coöperation, the lawful marriage of capital and labor.

HAVING now done what we could in the presentment and discussion of that class of voluntary associations which make provision for relief of the casualties which affect health and life, with the necessarily incident discipline exercised over the public morals of the membership, the drift of our inquiries leads us, next, to consider the associative enterprises which look specially to the *business* interests of the people engaged in them. A general classification of the associations which we include under the term guarantyism, may help to a clearer apprehension of their characters and differences. They may be distinguished sufficiently well as of three kinds; 1st, those which organize the social charities; 2d, those which secure economy in the expenses of subsistence; 3d, those which intend an equitable division of the profits of productive industry: all these have a community of risks and benefits as their conditions of association. The first class we have treated in the preceding chapter. They are all, in the points with which we are here concerned, characterized by their tendency to convert the charities of social life into equitable claims, held by right of proportionate contributions by the beneficiaries, and by giving a new nature to the acquisitiveness of individualism; changing it substantially into benevolence when trained into the service of corporate aims and ends.

We have spoken of the two springs of societary action, the material and the spiritual. In the class of relief societies, both these motor forces are active in the results, no matter which prevails in the purpose of the agents, or which is wholly wanting in the impulse. In all cases the pecuniary benefit is secured, and may be enjoyed even by the man whose social affections are not at all engaged. The providence which his selfhood prompted is, by the corporate direction given to its accumulations, transubstantiated into charity in action, and a private vice is thus transformed into a social virtue. Association, we have seen, vindicates its material policy by ample success in every well-managed organization. They all grow rich relatively to their required expenditures. The invested property and reserved funds grow always more rapidly than the numbers and wants of the claimants. Just as the accumulated wealth of every advancing nation in the world grows much more rapidly than its population; and the latter for the like reason as the former: a nation is a society loosely combined in its methods of accumulation, but closely united in the general and ultimate dividends of the common industry.

The consideration of those two classes of associations which have the savings and profits of business for their respective objects, and which intend and endeavor a change in the economic order of trade and production, requires such a preliminary examination of the existing order of the business system as may discover the promise of their coming, and the prophecy of their success, in the signs of the times, as the shadows of the dawn herald the coming of day.

Money, the ripened fruit, and embodiment of the energies of industry, is naturally earliest in availing itself of the productive force of association. All institutions designed for the investment of savings, for safe-keeping and accumulation, are of this class. Conspicuous examples are banks of deposit, discount, and circulation, so far as their capital is held in partnership. All money-making corporations belong to it, whether they be concerned with public improvements, such as railroads, canals, telegraph lines, or manufactories, worked by partners, who participate in the expenses, losses, and profits; Savings banks are in the same category, and so are all kinds of insurance companies. They are all marked by one common character—association of capital; and they all have the force of the material and moral spring combined in their results. It may sound oddly to ascribe anything of moral or social to money-making corporations, that are proverbially destitute of soul—that in law are only artificial persons—that cannot die or go to judgment, in the sense that natural persons do and must; but, under that government which "from seeming evil still educes good," and makes the evil of the world answer the ends of a wise purpose that must ultimately triumph, and will not be baffled for want of either wisdom or power, in the administration of disorder—that makes martyrdom a means of fresh vitality, and death and hell efficient servants of life and order—why may not money banks, as well as parsimony, avarice, and all the forms of a blind acquisitiveness, in all other shapes and apparatus of their activity, by the simple conversion of their selfishness of motive into social operation in their effects, be made beneficent, and so, moral and spiritual, too, in their service? Association, with the aim of accumulation, is the regenerating instinct of capital; and equitable divisions of the product, are the good works of these incorporated bodies, into which a spirit enters in lieu of the lacking human soul, just as the lightning of heaven informs and vitalizes a rubbish of zinc and copper scraps in orderly organization. Organism springs to life, whatever be the material in the structure, provided only the material be capable of the vitalizing influx. The business brotherhood of men, takes form earliest in capital, for the "dried fruits" of labor have none of the repugnances, the incompatibilities, the incapacities of the live laborer; to whom the benefits of a corresponding coöperation cannot come till he is fit, and to whom it will come in the degree of his fitness. Labor in its savage, its barbarous, and, even in its early civilized phases, either consumes all its produce, or hands over the surplus to organized capital—dead to its producer, but with a germ of growth in it to the cultivator, who makes it yield some thirty, some sixty, some an hundredfold.

Savings banks and similar institutions, under other names; and life, fire, and marine insurances, having either accumulation of profits to the stockholders, division of profits among all the contributors or insured persons, or only indemnity against losses, ought to be separated in classification by this rule: are the investors only money-lenders in effect, as all those are who make their deposits at a stipulated rate of interest; or, are they partners in the losses, expenses and profits? The distinction is a broad one. The lender of savings parts with the great agent of production. The borrower has its use and service to the utmost of its capacity. He is working his credit as capital; he puts credit into stock, and makes other people's capital work for him at lower rent, wages, or interest than it earns for him. The mere lender of savings works for other people's capital, and with it, for them, at a loss of some of the profit, and a greater loss of development and power in himself. The wages system is certainly a grand advance upon the slave system, for it is free in its spirit, and may be free in action under favoring circumstances. It differs from the state of being property, sold and bought, by the circumstance that wages means the sale of whatever is salable of the man *by himself*, and the buyer is another party with interests that may be either adverse or favorable.

The self-employed man, like money employed by the owner, is never on sale, either for wages or interest. Interest is the wages of money which is not in the active service of its owner. His money is a hireling. The laborer, with his little deposit in a moneyed institution, is a hireling in person, and his property is a hireling in use, just as he himself is.

Just here lies the difference between a savings bank and a building and loan association: the deposits in the latter work to their utmost for the depositor, who is both lender and borrower. In the former he is only a lender, and that necessarily, at a rate of interest less by the expenses of the institution, and the difference of interest rate which makes up the profits of the institution. These profits are really very large—so large that they actually do refund the entire investment in building associations in about eleven years, or in about the time that money at six per cent doubles itself at compound interest, with the solid practical effect of making a man the owner of the building he occupies after paying only the equivalent of its rent for about a dozen years.

The same principle rules all business engagements in which the man is his own employer, either jointly or severally—either in association or with a sufficient capital of his own to carry on his business and hire others to do its work.

The science of labor has not been so devised as to command a general understanding and acceptance, but its theory is clearly capable of logical statement.

Many of the prevalent opinions and partial judgments concerning the questions involved need correction for the vindication of fundamental principles.

In the matter of interest, for instance, it is commonly felt to eat like a canker into the means of the borrower. It is known to be, according to its rates, one of the most potent forces ruling production. Its low rate in Europe against double or treble its rate in the United States employed in like productions, and which compete in the same markets, is enough of itself to settle the fortunes of the rival enterprises. It is known, moreover, that money-lenders, upon a large capital of money and credit, make larger accumulations than any other industry can command; and it may be hastily inferred that money, by force of its rent or interest, makes larger gains than labor and skill employed in the production of commodities. There is confusion in the conclusions thus drawn from premises individually true enough in themselves, but not in their relations and mixed results.

The lender of large sums at short intervals has compound interest upon them, and the current yield is large in amount. The lender of very small sums may have his interest compounded, indeed, and, like the greater capitalist, has all his time on his hands for making other gains. But the one has commanding means for opportune operations in the markets; the other may sink all his in a month's sickness. The one reserves them for opportune employment; the other lays them up idle for the very reason that they must not be used.

Whoever has wealth enough to maintain him for twenty years may do nothing but receive his interest at five per cent per annum, and he is provided for his lifetime, and at the end of it has his capital intact and undiminished. The difference between a considerable and sufficient surplus, and the small savings that will not more than cover contingencies, is world-wide. To the one it is an implement, a machinery of large production, substantially without risk; to the other, it is a crutch, to be used only when he breaks a leg; or a reserve, to be consumed when his daily bread fails with his working strength.

In the matter of the support afforded by interest, it is true that only *too much capital is plenty*, and, that too little puts the owner upon looking for the best way of making his little useful in active service, rather than in waiting for accidental need.

The policy of business, like other things, has its growth and successive stages of development. First, the capital consisting of surplus gets organized; afterwards, the social charities, beginning with public almsgiving; then to insurance of property against risks; next, provision for "rainy days," with a slowly growing mutual fund for relief against sickness and the privations that follow death—all these are a sort of insurances; but they all take, in their earlier stage, the shapes that give their profit over and above the provision required, to the capitalists, as distinct from the contributors; they all have, indeed, the germinal power of association in them, gradually unfolding; some of them yielding their proper fruits to the cultivator; some of them, reserving largely of those fruits from his grasp, and leaving little of the residuary for the equitable owner. At a still later stage the advance is from the blade of promise toward the corn, with the assurance of the full corn in the ear to the use of the husbandman, who having sown his own seed in his own ground, reaps the whole harvest that his labor yields.

This brings us, in the growth of guarantyism, to coöperative stores, as that system of provision for current consumption is called, which is not yet self-employing, but is so far self-helping that it is self-supplying, so far, at least, as the elimination of middle-men, merchants, hucksters, and mere exchangers, can be dispensed with, and with relief, in proportion, from their support, from their frauds and their gains.

These intermediate exchangers are interested to put as great a distance and difference of place and of price between production and consumption as they can. This is their inherent vice. They, as a distinct order of industrials, are necessary and serviceable in the degree that they are indispensable, and, no further. In all beyond this, they are mischievous. How they have thriven in their department of the work that life demands! Twenty-five hundred years ago, the merchants of Tyre were described as " Princes, and her traffickers as the honorable of the earth." Later, upon equally sacred authority, those of a prophetic Babylon are said to be "the great men of the earth ;" and, again, the people of that symbolic city are doomed to destruction, for this reason, among others, that, " the merchants of the earth are waxed rich through the abundance of her delicacies." And yet again they figure in the threatened catastrophe as deeply involved in the ruin which their agency wrought: " The merchants which were made rich by her, shall stand afar off, for the fear of her torment, weeping and wailing, and saying, alas, alas ! that great city, that was clothed in fine linen, and purple, and scarlet, and decked with gold, and precious stones, and pearls ! For in one hour so great riches is come to naught. And every ship-master, and all the company in ships, and sailors, and as many as trade by sea, stood afar off, and cried, when they saw the smoke of her burning." It seems, however, that these princes and great men of the earth were, by professional instinct, very free traders, indeed, for, besides the stuffs of the artisan, and the products of the agriculturist, crowding the list of their goods like a ship's manifest of our own day, they also traded " in slaves, and the souls of men," whatever the last item may mean that can have any application to the business of our modern sea-ports, which, however, the whole invoice seems to have in its purview.

That the merchant is a necessary intermediate—a producer in fact—and as much so, in his way as the miner, the transporter, or any other agent or invention that saves time and overcomes space, is clear enough. By his service the perfection of all production is made attainable, for by the division of labor its products are improved and multiplied. This makes the exchanger a necessity to all the ends of useful industry ; and, while conformed to his function, and restrained to his proper use in the world's business, it is idle and unmeaning to class him as a non-producer, or in any sense an impediment or a parasite. But he is intermediate between the producer and consumer, and by perversion of his office he becomes an obstacle in commerce, and a burden upon the parties which he should serve. It is to the necessity for intervention that he owes his place in the world's required exchanges; and he finds his interest and his temptations of interest, in increasing the distance and cost that can be put between the parties to the commerce which he conducts. Roads, carriages, ships, which economize time and abridge the inconvenience of space, can be used to counteract their true intention. They are instruments of association in themselves, but they are capable of multiplying the intermediate agencies of commerce, and increasing the dependency of the parties which they should liberate. The better these instruments are the more they take the conditions of monopolies. The larger the number of persons they are made capable of serving, and the greater the commerce they can move, the further they are removed by their value from the control, and by their management, from the best service of the community. It is essential to the railroad that its owners shall have the exclusive right of way. No one but its managers can put a carriage upon it. No outside traveler or trafficker can compete with its facilities of transportation. It has exclusive privileges. Even the natural highways and the common roads and rivers may be monopolized by capitalists, and the servants of the public, within certain limits, become its masters in the matter of travel and transportation. Competition, in most other branches of industry, the regulator of charges, is easily defeated of its power in transportation, and, accordingly, as we know, rivalry here always fails. Opposition omnibuses on our city streets cannot hold out in their struggles half a year. They are either underworked to exhaustion, or, bought up, if that proves the cheaper way to the monopolist lines. Railroads, like city water-works, forbid all attempts at limitation of their prices by exclusive occupation of the route, and of the agents of transit. A gas company once in possession of the ground is in position to defy all resistance. It can and does regulate its prices by the balance of its own interests. The rivers are free in their course. They are not private property; but their use is easily monopolized by commanding capital. Common carriers upon their waters are run off the track, as omnibuses are in our streets. The heaviest capital soon starves out its competitors or buys them up; and steamboats settle into *lines*, and have the privilege without charters, by virtue of the wealth that needs no odds in the struggles of competition. Passenger lines in ocean navigation fall within the same influences, and are controlled in the same way. Common carriers everywhere soon get sole possession, and the occupancy of the world's highways, by land and water alike, may be treated practically as private property. Neither the breadth of mountain or prairie, of river or ocean, with all the room they give, can secure the free practicable use of their capabilities to any, against companies which have the means of occupying and commanding their passage ways. Tracks over land, and routes over seas, are free, indeed, to private carriages and to vessels of every kind for whomsoever can bear the cost of their own conveyance and commerce in them; but no one can become a common carrier, or take any part in that branch of the mercantile function, in the face of a heavier capital that would monopolize it.

Doubtless, such monopolies must address the interest of the community in securing its custom, but they need go no further in accommodating the public then cheapening their service in the smallest degree that will secure their own ends. Even while carrying goods and passengers for nothing, they are only aiming at the monopoly of the route, and intending to replace the losses of the strife when they shall be in condition to make their own terms. Roads that divide business often reduce fares and freights for the purpose of selling out on their own terms to their rivals. Charters for roads that threaten competition are obtained to be sold with the same view, and the protection of competition is thus constantly defeated. In a word, transportation companies and corporations are fast becoming the masters of commerce, under the system of modern improvement in its methods; just as wars are decided by the power of wealth in providing their instruments and engines. The dominion has passed from the lords of blood to the lords of gold, as the aristocracy is dominated by the millocracy of England. Is there no remedy for the inevitable tendency of the age in this direction? Was there no remedy for the civil despotism that grew step by step with all civilized progress, a few centuries ago? The common people's strength only enhanced the disparity of power in their masters—while it was growing, but had not yet grown to self-assertion and self-defense. Governments that did not consult or regard the public interests, nevertheless, did depend upon the very power which they trained into their service. The basis forces had some room left to grow; not much, but still enough for their own enhancement. Tyranny was deluded into increased oppression by increased aggrandisement through the growing worth and wealth of its subjects; but, at last the embryo life burst into independence by force of just those powers which had before aggravated its bondage.

Is there any parallel of promise in the struggle now going on between accumulated wealth and its sources and subjects? Let us see—every civilized country in the world is now growing in wealth twice or thrice faster than in population. The distributive shares of all peoples have greatly increased in the century which we have named as the age of guarrantyism. All the means of production have been multiplied incalculably, through the aid of machinery or the substitution of artificial for natural labor. The people of France have thrice the food that they had a hundred years ago, the people of England have thirty times the cotton cloth; and capital in the hands of the wealthy class of both countries is increased by tale of coin and credit money tenfold, with an efficiency in production multiplied ten times again, as against the mass without property other than labor-power and skill. The power of wealth in the world's work now is as a hundred against one in the times when the plough, the loom, and the anvil were driven solely by hand-power—a hundred to one in an array of antagonism, and growing, as all societary forces are growing now, with accelerated rapidity. Considered only in their past and present potencies, it is not at all to be wondered that philanthropy has been for a century or two devising radical revolutions in the policy of distributing the wealth which labor and capital jointly produce.

Communism, St. Simonism, Fourierism, Shakerism, and many other forms of reorganization, or social reconstruction, sometimes with, sometimes without, the religious sentiment of brotherhood incorporated, have arisen and gone into abortive endeavor, from no other conviction and impulse than the demonstration of the ever-growing disparity of power between wealth and labor. These reconstructive efforts are exactly the counterparts of those other blind struggles of the levelers of political and civil power, which began with Wat Tyler and ended in the primal days of the French Revolution. Absolute democracy in civil and social polity, and communism of property, are cousins-german in reform, and each is grounded in the correlative maxims—" power is always stealing from the many to the few." " Policy is ever making the rich richer and the poor poorer."

Neither of these proverbs of the people is true, nor ever was true. The few, indeed, grew, and are yet growing, more powerful; but the many are growing more rapidly, only they have not yet got a commanding hold of the machinery of civil government. The rich are being made richer, vastly richer. It is no longer a figure of speech to call a merchant, in goods or money, a millionaire. We have them in hundreds; men in England and America, of whom a dozen or two could pay off those vast national debts, which nobody, fifty years ago, believed the whole nation could ever pay. David Hume said, in 1776, that the national debt of England, then not one-third of its present amount, was a mortgage on half the wealth of the whole nation. Yet there is wealth enough in London or Liverpool, or New York, now, to redeem the national debts to the last dollar, without spoiling a holiday in either. Yes, the wealth of the wealthy has grown fabulously; yet it is as nothing to the increase of the aggregate wealth of the millions of men who are now doing the world's daily work. Our civil war cost us more than five thousand millions; it was all actually contributed day by day as it was expended. If all the assets of all the banks of the Union, in 1860, had been confiscated; if their capital, real estate, coin, and other resources over their liabilities, had been tumbled into the Treasury, the sum would not have reached $900,000,000; yet the two-thirds of the Union paid up six times that amount in four years, and were richer than when the first loan was raised. I say, all the expenses of the war were actually paid during the war; for the national bonds, which we call the national debt, are the receipts for it. In the aspect of debt, these bonds are only claims for distribution of the expenses borne unequally by individuals while the unsettled balances were accumulating. The amount of the bonds held abroad, which, in 1865, were as nothing to the total expenditure, is the only deduction to be made in estimating the current contributions of our own people. A little reflection will show how erroneously the wealth of the wealthy is commonly contrasted with the accumulations of the people. At any county fair now held, there is more money's worth in the equipments, the "turn outs," and the apparel and jewelry of the visitors, than the whole real and personal property of that county would have been rated at seventy, or even fifty, years ago. There is more money spent by the industrial populace in travel, amusements, furniture, and dress, than the whole country was worth in the very recent time when there was not a daily paper published outside of the Atlantic cities. What are the fortunes of the thousand millionaires of the nation to the massed wealth of the millions of the people!

We are constantly forgetting this, and so we are foolishly fearing the issue; and the best men are prone to turn to the devices of despair for the remedy of the apparently ever-growing evil; not perceiving that the corrective is growing potentially with still greater rapidity: just as men's hearts failed within them in that other strife of the many against the few, in the age of civil revolutions, forgetting that the many were the *many*, and that every failure of open resistance showed the growing strength of the resistance which failed—not knowing that success is the outgrowth of failures oft repeated, and that men blunder into success as a child toddles into pedestrianism, strengthening its limbs and steadying its steps by every stumble it makes, and gathering new strength like Antæus, every time it touches its mother earth.

What have we now at work upon the popular welfare? On the one side, productive industry, so welded to machinery that every workman is the hireling of capital, so that to make a pin, which will pay cost in the market, you must begin with an outlay of fifty thousand dollars; and no man will buy a cotton shirt unless a hundred thousand dollars were employed in producing it. All forms of industry, which the times permit, require an aggregate of capital that no workman of merely ordinary means can at all command, either in cash or credit. On the other hand we have, in the possession of the unpropertied mass, an amount of skill, without which the millionaire's mill cannot turn a wheel, or run a spindle, or head a pin. They have, also, an education, acquired in service at wages without profits, by which capital has grasped the wonderful wealth which the modern methods of production have yielded; and along with this grandest element of all—this new-made force of skill—an education of brain in literature and available science, or science applied, which we still call skill. For want of knowing what it is in essence and force we have not yet invented a descriptive name, or descriptive names, for distinguishing between the art that builds a bridge, runs a locomotive engine, manages a stationary one, constructs a railroad, or levels a canal. They are all engineers, forsooth, though they must understand mineralogy, hydrostatics, architecture, geometry, mathematics, mechanics, and half-a-dozen other sciences, for either construction, reparation, or superintendence: very respectable portions of Michael Angelo, Archimedes, Sir Christopher Wren, Sir Humphrey Davy, Benjamin Franklin, and Robert Fulton, must be rolled into one man, in various assortments, to make what we call an engineer, or foreman of a factory, or of a machine shop; and all such men, with their multifarious adaptations of their great exemplars, we class together under our meagre phrase, " skilled artisans."

Do we apprehend the wealth-producing force there is in these hirelings of capital? Do we understand how much they have grown into their several arts, and how much they are able to grow out of them, for their own service? What is the meaning of trade unions and trade strikes, that act now throughout all advancing communities like free masonry, issuing their orders from the grand lodges that are the foci of their mind and muscle? Are they only a declaration of helplessness under wrongs? Are their frequent failures only a proof of their feebleness? Are they not, on the contrary, the riots, insurrections, and revolts, that ripen into revolutions, and, at last, establish governments, and administer them? And what will come of them when they shall have blundered, and sinned, and suffered enough to grow wise and good by their purgatorial development? Slaves, emancipated by powers not their own, by mere docility get into positions of harmony; but rebels, that work out their own freedom from actual bondage, have their own follies and crimes to struggle with; but nothing that they do or leave undone affects the final result, however that result may be postponed or hastened. The laws of order are ever working through their disorders, and from seeming evil are still educing good.

The working men of the time see colossal fortunes growing out of their toil, which, however better and better requited, as it grows more and more efficient in producing its joint results with capital and machinery, are still not evenly divided to them. Their wants grow with their wages, and they want, above all other wants, some share of the profits, because they think that products are the joint issue of the agents which are their parents; and they are beginning to see that lawful marriage of the generators of wealth must establish the legitimacy of the issue, and the lawful claims of each party to its production. Coöperation is the marriage of labor and capital, and they are beginning to perceive that bone and muscle must be able to say to capital "bone of *my* bone and flesh of *my* flesh," and let no man put them asunder or keep them asunder, that the lawful fruits of the union may be jointly and justly enjoyed.

CHAPTER XXI.

COÖPERATION—STORES, MANUFACTORIES, BANKS.

Coöperation—stores, manufactories, banks—embrace all the branches of business economy.—" Disjunctive conjunction" of "Political Economy."—A science of labor promises a true political economy.—Lawless competition against orderly emulation.—Coöperative stores or economy in expenditure.—Burdens of the retail trade.—Force of aggregated capital.—Every dozen of families support one of traffickers.—Conditions of reform.—*Rochdale Pioneers.*—Self-help and self-supply—success.—Profits rise with increase of capital from four and one-half to twelve and one-half per cent, in twenty years.—Benefits and safety of cash sales.—Avoidance of the vice of "buying cheap and selling dear."—Coöperation differs from ordinary partnership.—Spread of the system in England.—Statistics.—Central organization of coöperative societies.—Coöperation in *Germany.*—Herman Schultze.—One thousand associations in Germany in 1869—business of sixty millions a year.—Rise in connection with popular education—obstructed by French radical agitation.—Popularity among all classes.—German differ from English, societies.—*Credit* banks—principles governing their management.—Capital.—Reserve fund.—Rate of interest indifferent to the borrower.—Money value of credit—extent of the business.—A Jacob's ladder of credit.—Profit and loss.—Statistics.—Statistics of all branches of coöperation in Germany.—Interaction of banks and stores.—Coöperation in *Spain.*—Education and association.—Indoctrination after the manner of the Roman Rostrum.—*Russia.*—Communes.—Emancipation of the serfs.—Rural population, nine to one of the total.—Russian fairs.—Coöperation indigenous.—Insurrectionary spirit of Western Europe unfriendly to coöperation.—Radicalism in Prussia.—Agrarianism.—Labor unions of Prussia.—Wages of colliers—a strike and its results.—Hostility of the insurgent spirit to property rights.

In common use this term is restricted to such organized combinations of individuals as are designed to relieve them, as far as practicable, of intermediates in productive industry and commercial exchange. Coöperation is partnership in profits, equitably distributed in proportion to the severalties of contribution of capital, labor, skill, and management. This is more exactly the description of those associations which are properly called "Coöperative Labor Societies," or partnerships of industrial producers.

Another, and in natural order, an earlier form of coöperative business associations, are partnerships of consumers, who purchase in gross such commodities as they require for ordinary use, and distribute them according to their respective needs, at the least possible cost of distribution; being jointly the owners and venders, and severally, the final purchasers of the goods provided; thus eliminating the merchant, at least in the last stage of distribution. The company are the purchasers at wholesale; and the agents of the retail have no interest in the business, other than that of employees, or servants, of the company. This form of the movement is known as " coöperative stores."

There is a third form—the natural outgrowth of the two stages just noticed, which in Germany is styled " The Credit Banking System." The emphasis of the descriptive name falls properly upon the word credit, in the title. They differ from the ordinary money banks mainly in this, that they lend only to the members, or depositors, of whom each for all, and all for each, are virtually the indorsers. By this provision of the organization credit is given to borrowers who can command credit nowhere else, nor on any other possible conditions.

Here, in these three modifications of coöperation, we have provision made—1st, by coöperative stores, for economy in the necessary expenses of subsistence; 2d, retention and equitable apportionment of *all* profits to the active partners in the production of commodities; and, 3d, a provision of credit, and distribution of the profits of money as a money-maker, among those who furnish the capital stock.

There are no more, and no other, branches of the economy of the individual, and of the household, than these. Men in business are either consumers, industrial producers, or bankers in effect. All the interests and functions of material wealth and well-being are these, and these only, when reduced to their substantive forms. The transporters and traffickers in unorganized business are but the adjectives or ministers of consumption. The capitalist, the manager, the employer, and the hireling, in productive work, merge into one in coöperative industry; and the Credit bank depositor is in like manner lender, borrower, and banker, in one, as far as credit and interest on capital are concerned. Put these three forms and aims of coöperation together, and the entirety of wealth-producing and wealth-preserving agencies are embraced. They mean that subsistence shall cost no more than actual labor deserves—that the entire profits of production shall be secured to the actual producers, and, that money shall yield all its earnings to its true owners; and, still further, that credit, or the benefits of anticipated earnings, shall be provided and accorded in equitable proportion to investment and proved character.

Having passed, in our review of societary progress, the partial and incomplete, in its varied methods and means, and arrived at the stage which is logically symmetrical, self-sustaining, and having a circumference defined, and supported upon its centre; our study begins to take the proportions and relations of a science.

Political Economy, as it is, has too many incongruities, too many inconsequences, too many *disjecta membra*, too many refractory, and too many accidental forces, to offer anything but a diversity of topics for logical inquiry. It lacks relation, dependency, and corroboration of points; but coöperation, which, in its inmost meaning is harmony, looks as if destined to work itself into a system that, with organized labor as a basis, firmament and continent, may be constructed into a science in the true sense; having only the incident of exchange, in its present disorder, as an exceptional appendage—an exception not subject to law but ruled by expediency. The great function of exchange, within the sphere of organized labor, is controlled by its own harmonic principles; but outside exchange, reacting upon that within, is necessarily abnormal, intrusive, and discordant.

The deadly action of Competition, which is the dominant force in trade, as trade now exists, is in constant hostility to the correlative and corrective principle of coöperation. As an associative stimulus it should take the name, as it has the character of Emulation. So long as cut-throat competition is the reigning spirit in the world's business affairs, it will beleaguer, invade, and disturb the better order, and compel more or less departure, for necessary accommodation.

Coöperative stores are the earliest embodiment of the grand harmonies which progress must achieve. Their characteristic features, their working forces, and their general results, will suffice for the presentment of their qualities and promises. They are but a step, and, therefore, the first step, in advance of the common partnerships in business affairs, with which the world has long been familiar. The principles involved are not novel, but the parties and the special aim of their adoption is decidedly new. The opulent class have never had any difficulty in combining capital with a view to the profit of its operations in large amounts; but coöperative stores are the invention of the needy, the economical, whose policy is not accumulation directly, but economy of expenditure, pressed upon them by their necessities. Unable, as individuals, to buy at wholesale, they have been heretofore obliged to bear the burden of many intermediate profits, before the necessaries of daily life reached them. The support and the gains of a host of intermediaries are always charged upon those who must buy at retail. The whole merchant class, with their dependencies, rests upon the ultimate consumer, in the old mode of distribution; and the supporters of this great burden, aware that their evils lie in the interruptions of the route between the producer and consumer, begin their removal by clubbing their little means into a mass that will advance them nearer to the earliest grade or stage of purchasers. For this end they require only so much of concurrence and combination as jointness of their aggregate contributions affords. This is far short of such agreement of action as jointness of industrial production demands; and is just so much the more easy and practicable. A clear perception of their simplest interest is motive enough, and some wisdom in the selection of the necessary agents, and trust in their capacity and honesty, are all the moral qualifications required for the effectual working of the enterprise. The resources of the company are not the greatest difficulty, by any means; because the individuals have, and must have, the funds to buy the prime necessaries of life; and all that is necessary is to combine the little rills of outlay, which are wasting in their separate routes to absorption, into a river of the several affluents, and then they have all the massive strength of union. If a hundred men must, and do, find five dollars a week each, to be expended upon food for themselves and families, purchased at retail prices greatly enhanced by the intermediate charges, then they have, by uniting their funds, five hundred dollars in a lump, with all the power the larger sum gives them to avoid the burden of the middlemen's support; and, whatever this amounts to in percentage of increase upon the wholesale costs is saved, less the trivial expense of purchasing and distributing by their own agent, who works in their employ and for wages, without profit, and without the temptation of the trafficker to deteriorate the quality, or reduce the quantity passing through his hands. The possible savings of this policy are not easily calculated, but a safe basis for estimation may be founded upon the report of the mercantile agencies of New York, which gives one store and storekeeper for every one hundred and twenty-three persons of all ages in the United States. This would give one family to be supported by every twenty-four. This statement, however, does not embrace any but such of these agencies as rank as merchants who purchase their goods in the principal cities; leaving out of view the mass of small traders, peddlers, transporters, and other middlemen, all of whom live better and more expensively upon the profits of their trade than do the laboring class which contributes so large a proportion of their gains. It seems not extravagant to say that every ten or twelve families who live on wages must support one other family in far better style than they can live themselves, under the prevalent hand-to-mouth system of supplies through the multitudinous machinery of the retail trade. To get the idea sufficiently impressed, one need only walk the business streets of our cities, towns, and villages, and observe the unbroken blocks of retail stores, held at high rents, employing hosts of dealers, and supporting their families and their lawyers, doctors, and clergymen, with their luxurious indulgence of leisure and of dissipation added, to form some idea, or, at least, feel some of the force of the burden that the last and poorest purchaser of their goods and wares must bear. To get rid of this prodigious tax coöperative stores offer themselves, in theory at least, as a remedy more or less coextensive with the evil.

But there is a wide distance between a principle and the facts in which it takes effect. A thousand contingencies intervene; and the worst of all the dangers in the route to realization, is the incapacity, the unfitness, of those who most need the working benefits. The thing in itself is practicable, surely. But has it ever yet gone into practice successfully? Are the necessary conditions at the command of those who would make the experiment? There is one grand model instance, which, however familiar to those who have been students of the coöperative question and attentive to its history, is, nevertheless, such an exemplification of the principle that it is worthy of rehearsal here.

THE ROCHDALE PIONEERS.

In November, 1843, twelve of the laborers of Rochdale, North Lancashire, one of the great wool manufacturing counties of England, met to talk over the one great subject of their life struggle—their subsistence; and to devise some way of making the two ends of the year meet somewhere else than in the parish work-house. All the usual resorts and devices of despair were discussed and dismissed; for they had all been tried, abundantly, and had as abundantly failed. The discussion ended in the conclusion, "there is no help for us but self-help; and, as we cannot get higher wages, there is nothing left for us but to make what we do get *go further.*" Out of that wondrously wise word there has grown not only a fabulously abundant fruit, but an exemplar of the redemption of labor from its hopeless pauperism in Western Europe, and its more hopeless *strife* with capital, yet to be realized, all the civilized world over. These twelve men made their beginning, and thirteen months of persistent effort gave them a membership of twenty-eight flannel weavers, and a capital of £28 ($135). They rented a store-room, paying the rent in advance, which, with other expenses, left them at the time with only £15 to enter upon business. This sum they invested in flour, butter and sugar. * * * In 1865, twenty-two years after their first meeting, the Pioneer Society had five thousand three hundred and twenty-six members. In the first quarter of 1866 their sales amounted to £52,870 (equal to $1,025,678 for a year), of which the profit was £6,516, or twelve and one-quarter per cent. The stock of the members amounted to about £15 each, in the aggregate, £78,610.

In Blackwood's Magazine, of March 1867, we have the following general statement of results up to the 18th December, 1866, being taken from the eighty-eighth Quarterly Report of the "Equitable Pioneers." "The affairs of the society are in a prosperous condition; the number of members steadily increases; the amount of cash received for goods sold during the quarter was £68,216, being an increase upon the corresponding quarter of the year 1865 of £13,042; the profits of the quarter, £9,281. The gross profits of the year were £31,934." The gross profits for the year appear to be about fourteen per cent. Their goods being sold at about the same prices charged by other retail dealers, the average gains of the trade are fairly indicated by this percentage of advance upon wholesale cost.

The success of the store operations is established. The figures given show the extent. Its prosperity led to an extension from the mere business of vending commodities to enterprises successively adopted for producing the supplies most demanded by the customers. In 1850 a butcher shop was set up. In 1861, from five such shops, belonging to the society, they sold nearly six hundred thousand pounds of beef, mutton, pork, and veal. In 1852, shoemaking and tailoring; a little later, coal dealing, and in 1867, a bakery were added. In 1865 these pioneers of the coöperative store, under a different name and organization, had a flouring mill running that was doing a business of £148,533 with a yearly profit of £12,511, or nearly ten per cent. In 1855 the same persons established a cotton factory, employing three hundred hands and two hundred and fifty looms. Since 1863 a building association has arisen, employing a capital of £52,500, which furnishes its members with good houses at a reasonable cost; and, to all this, a life insurance and burial society has been added, with a capital of over £15,000. So, the working capital which stood at one hundred and thirty-five dollars in 1843, in twenty-four years grew to over one million.

These facts and figures must be accepted as a demonstration, on a large scale, and on a sufficient experience, of the practicability and the utility of the coöperative plan of self-help and self-supply. By this policy the Rochdale weavers broke through the thicket of their distress, and fairly earned the title that they prophetically gave themselves—equitable Pioneers. They have shown how the poorest laborers, on the scantiest wages, may escape the wretched quality, and beggaring cost, of such retail purchases as their class generally are exposed to.

Beside the economy in expenditure, and the accumulation of capital and credit secured, they have been able to do some other things for themselves, quite as worthy of note. They have a library of nine thousand volumes. Not less than two and a half per cent of the profits are annually devoted to educational purposes. In 1866, the sum of $1,450 was expended for newspapers, microscopes, globes, maps, and other educational apparatus, and increase of the library. The news and reading rooms are provided with English reviews and magazines, and metropolitan and local newspapers.

Does this statement seem extravagant, and such results, achieved from such resources in one-quarter of a century, impossible? The product is astonishing—but not incapable of convincing proof. Every one knows that single individuals have built up fortunes as great, from means as small, and in time as short. But the answer is—these individuals have done it by lucky speculations. The thing, however, is demonstrable by the simple rules of arithmetic. Let an expert take one shilling as capital, treat it as invested in merchandise paying a profit of but ten per cent per annum, reinvest these profits, and the interest also, four times a year, and he will see that this trivial capital, united with an equal amount, contributed by six or eight thousand other persons, will bear all the incidental expenses, the necessary charities, and collateral donations to educational uses, reported of the Rochdale enterprise, and leave a working capital of at least a million of dollars. This calculation allows nothing for withdrawals of dividends, interest or principal, which, of necessity, must occur, and have, of course, occurred in the business of the Pioneers. In their eigthy-eighth quarterly report, they give the account current of their business for twenty years—from 1845 to 1864. The first of these years stands on their books thus: 1845, No. of members, 74; amount of property, £181 12s. 5d.; amount of sales, £710 6s. 5d.; profits, £32 17s. 6d. 1864, No. of members, 4,580; amount of property, £55,840; amount of sales, £174,206 8s. 4d.; profits, £22,163 9s. 9d. In the twenty years, the total amount of sales was £1,294,830, the profits £130,300—an average of over ten and one-half per cent. Will the reader notice the vast increase of the profits per cent on the larger sales of the last year of this period. The four and one-half per cent on the sales of 1845 could not be made to cover more than the expenses of the store, however economically conducted; but the twelve and one-half per cent upon a total of sales two hundred and forty-five times greater, left a large margin of net gain above expenses. This is a simple and direct demonstration of the benefit of increased amounts produced by aggregating lesser sums, and giving them the momentum, the weight and velocity, of forces massed and united. This is the effect of association in the material elements of power.

The system under which this store and its branches (for it has as many as eight of them in the town) conducted business, needs consideration. The society did not attempt to sell goods below the rates that individual dealers could afford. They attracted business by the assured quality of their goods, and by dividing, quarterly, the net profits among the purchasers, in exact proportion to the amount of their several purchases. They avoided the rivalry and strife of underselling—a game at which greater capital would have bankrupted them so soon as their business had become worth the crushing, and at which their antagonists would have worsted them in one day's struggle. They sold at the fair ordinary prices of the general trade, registered the sales, and induced their customers to invest the dividends, by all that is influential in the policy of ordinary savings banks, and in the feeling of property funded to those who never had any other. A fair trial of the plan, by which nothing was hazarded, had its proper effects. The declared dividends, however small, were bonuses to the customers and were felt to be gratuities in fact—a feeling happily expressed by an old woman, who was advised to draw out her money from the store, which she was told was going to break. "Well, let it break. If it does, it will break with its own. I put in but £1, and I have £50 there now."

The store sold only for cash. All the improvidence on the part of customers, and all the risks to the vender of the retail credit system, were thus wholly escaped. The sales were not only for cash but at the current fair prices, by which the purchaser escaped the temptation to buy and consume so much the more, and so waste the difference, which the store reserved for them, to be divided and credited in due time.

Again, the word "equitable" had even more potential significance than the word "pioneers," in the title. The system left no place for, and gave no encouragement to, the plundering spirit of "buying cheap," which eats out the very heart of honesty. Here there could be none of that higgling over price, which, if not stealing quite, has the tone and purpose of getting something for nothing, and in turn, generates that kindred necessity of selling nothing for something, which is called "selling dear," in the creed of the worshipers of competition. At the pioneers' store price has almost nothing to do in the purchase; the article is good, and the cost at retail, in the end, will be exactly what it costs wholesale with nothing but expenses added.

And again, these expenses are as nothing to those of the traffickers, who must gain custom by extravagance of advertising in all its forms—in handbills, gay fronts, high rents, numerous clerks and solicitors for custom, with the multifarious expenses of the enterprise which rivalship compels. All this mischief and its resulting burdens are escaped by the store, whose attractions are the equitable principles of, only good goods, cash sales, and pro rata division of actual expenses and profits. Clerks, storekeepers, and all assistants alike, do their work for their stipulated wages, and have no temptation to either extend the business by any indirection, or to deal unfairly with any customer. The common inducements to common offenses are all that they are exposed to; the business adds nothing of its own. It will be observed that all the features of this business look solely to the one object of making the same outlay for the necessaries of life, for the things that we consume, *go further* than it can go in the competitive retail trade that prevails in the usual course of business.

It has been objected that the term, coöperative, is not strictly descriptive of the stores which are distinguished by that name—that they differ in nothing essentially, as a business system, from ordinary commercial partnerships—from joint stock companies, or from life assurance companies, that give bonuses to their policy holders; because all these are either commercial associations or dealers in something which allows participation of profits. Reduced to their elements, and stated in verbal definitions, it may be so; but chemists find very different properties in combinations, produced by mere differences in quantities and modes of combination among the same constituents. These stores are associative in impulse and in operation, and are in act and fact coöperative, in many of the best efficiencies of their working forces. There is a difference of degree in the coöperation that runs a mill to grind our corn, a shop to prepare our meat, or make our boots and clothes, saving the profits for the joint operators, and in running a store for the distribution of their products ready to enter into consumption; but there is no difference of kind in the coöperative movement. The difference of degree is in this, that the one requires little more concurrence than paying money and receiving goods over the same counter, while the other demands a personal friendliness, a personal association, at least, and a union of minds in all the processes necessary to production. At Rochdale the one led to the other by mere increase of strength, and enlargement of trust and confidence in the agents of the respective stages. It seems to me sufficient to mark whatever of difference there is in them, by the familiar terms, coöperative store, and, industrial coöperation.

The practicability, and the working method, of the coöperative stores, have had a largely varied trial in other conditions and in other hands than those that belong to the model instance which we have just detailed, so far as an exposition of the system requires, and, as might be expected, the history has the usual diversity of successes and failures.

The example of the Pioneers had the effect of spreading a net-work of similar societies all over England. By an official report, laid before the British Parliament, it appears that in 1863 there were four hundred and sixty associations in England with a membership of one hundred and nine thousand; their sales amounted to over $15,000,000, their property was valued at $3,000,000, and the profits, shared among the members that year, amounted to more than $1,000,000. Most of these were new societies then; not more than one-eighth of them over three years old, and only one in fifteen was seven years old. The inevitable difficulties of beginning were upon the most of them; yet, they were fairly successful and full of promise. Those of the North of England created a central association for the purchase of merchandise at wholesale. This is managed by the Rochdale Pioneers. In 1865 they disposed of goods to the amount of £142,000 to one hundred and sixty-five coöperative stores, which was an increase of £55,000 upon this business in the preceding year. We give these figures with the dates for the purpose of showing the rate of their growth, which is very striking in the four next succeeding years. In 1867 the number of Coöperative-Store Societies in England and Wales, registered under the Industrial and Provident Societies Act, was five-hundred and seventy-seven, comprising one hundred and seventy-one thousand eight hundred and ninety-seven members; having an aggregate share capital of £1,473,199 ($7,144,628); doing business to the amount of more than $30,000,000 annually, and realizing thereon a *net* profit of nearly $2,000,000, or six and two-thirds per cent above expenses. The expenses of some of these stores do not amount to two per cent on the amount of business done; some of the newest and weakest make scarcely any profit at all. The best established, with the largest capital and business, clear as much as ten per cent, and the dividends of these would be much larger to their members, but for the very considerable amounts paid to customers who are not members; to whom, however, a less rate is allowed, with the difference inuring to the depositors. The percentage allowed to members is generally as three to two to non-members. A very equitable proportion, and one that answers well all the interests of both parties.

GERMANY.

The establishment of coöperative stores was later in Germany than in England, and did not, as in the case of the great exemplar, proceed from the laborers, but from men who belonged to the educated class. Herman Schultze, of Delitzsch, formerly a District Judge, and more recently a Prussian deputy, began in 1850 to propagate the doctrine and to organize these institutions. The movement took its rise among small independent tradesmen, formed into societies which aimed by cash advances for the wholesale purchase of raw materials and supplies, to maintain successful competition with the manufactories which, by force of capital, held the monopoly of production.

This movement already extends all over Germany, and throughout all classes of its people. In 1850 the associations numbered only half a dozen; in 1869 they had multiplied to more than one thousand, embracing three hundred and fifty-thousand members, doing a business of sixty millions of dollars in the year, and holding three and a half millions worth of property. It is worthy of note that coöperative store societies, now so generally prevalent, made very little progress for full ten years after their first introduction. The factory employees, who were mainly interested in their formation, had then but little experience of any sort of organization, and but a vague and ineffective consciousness of their jointness of interest, and still less notion of the mechanism required for the advancement of their common welfare. Those most conversant with the history agree that the decisive impulse followed upon the establishment of the system of educational societies, which dates about 1860. Herr Schultze was able to report in 1861 no more than fourteen coöperative-store societies, when there were no less than one hundred and sixteen of small independent tradesmen whose operations were limited to the wholesale purchase of raw materials.

In 1863 the movement was temporarily checked by the radical agitations, led by the great socialist, Ferdinand Lasalle, who pressed upon the people the French doctrine of help from the State, in opposition to the great leading principle of self-help, which is the corner-stone and grand distinctive principle of coöperation. This conflict of policy led to discussion through all the ranks of the laboring population, and the result, besides the education in the principles and measures involved, has been such a general and resistless spread of the policy inaugurated by Schultze Delitzsch, that anything like definite statistics of the progress would be adequate only for the immediate date of their publication.

The plan or plans of these German stores are considerable modifications of the English Pioneer system, without any decided improvement upon it in any particular, and upon the whole, less sound in theory and beneficial in practice. They are, however, not so closely confined to the class of workmen. They have been adopted extensively by societies of civil officers, and military men, and not a few nobles, also, have availed themselves of the felt advantages; even ladies of rank drive in their carriages to these stores in Berlin, Vienna, and Hamburg, showing a general feeling in all classes of the community of a necessity for reforming the retail trade. The Germans resident in St. Petersburg, Russia, have also adopted the policy to a marked extent. The gentry there engross the advantages and participate very largely through all Germany, but on the whole, the laboring people of Berlin, Upper Silesia, and the Lower Rhine, hold the greater share of them, and in them.

The German societies in general differ from the English in three particulars; 1st, they, for the most part, confine their trade to their own members, with the view of providing for their own consumption more advantageously than they can in the ordinary retail trade, and do not seek gain by dealing with outsiders. 2d, the German societies take their dividends out of the store as soon as they are declared; not looking to accumulation of the capital and extension of the business and of its profits. 3d. Many of the societies furnish their members with tickets which serve for purchasing at other stores, doing in this way a commission business, which is every way far removed from the coöperative principle, and forms no such bond of union as belongs to ownership of stock and joint interest in profits.

CREDIT BANKS.

In another branch of economic association Germany has far outstripped the kindred reforms of other countries. They have added to savings in expenditure for necessary consumption, and to joint interest in productive industry, that other crowning achievement which provides the capital of Credit, with all its attendant advantages; thus completing the circle of self-supply in all the elements of material wealth. Much for the amelioration of the condition of the laboring masses is achieved when the profits of the retail trade are secured to the customers who support it; much more is accomplished when the laborer receives the whole value of his contributions to productive industry; and there only remains to be made provision for the use of capital at the easiest possible rate— this the Credit bank system of Mr. Schultze supplies. Theoretically, he "regards capital as surplus produce, the result of abstinence, set apart for production. All that is required for Credit is security and profit in production. The only requisites for production are labor and capital. If labor can borrow capital there is no reason why it should not reap the usual profit of capital. The great want is security for the lender." This he proposes to find by association. A single laborer, having no property, can give no security. He may die, but in association the aggregate members are the security.

The essential features of the plan are: risks reduced to a minimum by granting loans only for *productive* purposes, and limiting their amounts to the average requirements of the borrowers; and, the maximum of responsibility is secured by limiting the borrowers to members of the association. The members being all liable for the debts of the association, and the association for the indebtedness of the members. All members are required to pay an entrance fee of one thaler, (seventy-two and one-half cents) and a monthly contribution toward the price of a share, of not less than twelve and one-half cents. The shares are about forty thalers, each member can hold but one share, but its full price may be paid up at once. The capital of the bank is the total of the subscriptions, and of the money borrowed for its use. The credit of the bank is well based, for there is a capital, a reserved fund, and unlimited liability of all the members. Responsibility continues after a member withdraws, but it may be released after twelve months. The reserve fund is formed of entrance fees and a percentage of dividends with which retiring members are taxed.

The gains are from interest on money lent. The expenditures are interest upon money borrowed by the bank, cost of administration, and losses.

The business is governed by the general rule of lending for no longer period than the bank can borrow. The bank borrows at four and one-half per cent, and lends at from eight to fourteen per cent. The rate of interest charged to its borrowers is of little moment. They are members and receive again their dividend of the surplus earnings of the money so borrowed by the bank, and of whatever of capital is owned by the bank itself. The borrower here is assumed to be one who can give no such security as is required by ordinary bankers or lenders, and, therefore, can borrow nowhere else. If the bank by its great credit can borrow at say four or five per cent, the borrower from the bank gets his supply from it at no greater increase than his share of the expenses of the institution, no matter what rate of interest is charged to him. In other words he pays his fellow members the smallest possible commission for substituting their aggregate and absolute credit for his own individual negative credit in the money market. The money value of this credit is all the profit which he can make out of capital, working for himself, or, all the difference that can be made out of working with capital for its profits, and working for capital at wages.

The success and the rate of growth of the system in Germany are shown by the following report of its business: in 1862 there were two hundred and thirty-three credit banks, with seventy thousand shareholders, doing a business of $16,790,000 in the year. In 1865 Mr. Schultze established a central bank, to give the smaller associations access to the general loan market, thus interposing an establishment of the highest credit, for associations less known and esteemed, just as these interpose their higher credit for the benefit of their individual members—a Jacob's ladder of credit planted on the earth and reaching the zenith of the system. This central bank began with a capital of $150,000, in shares of $150 each. There were in that year, 1865, in business connection with the central, four hundred and ninety-eight associations, having one hundred and sixty-nine thousand five hundred and ninety-five members; doing a business of $67,569,903. There were, besides, about eight hundred other associations, with one hundred and fifty thousand members, who made no report to the central bank. The losses on this business of sixty-seven millions were but $20,000; the net profits were $371,735.

The latest information that I have, shows the workings of the coöperative stores and credit banks upon each other and upon the extension of the principle to productive industries. In April 1870, thirty-seven societies of the Prussian-Rhenish provinces had combined agriculture with coöperation, employing steam engines among their implements. There were sixteen hundred and eleven workingmen's banks and loan associations. Of these six hundred and seventy-five were in Prussia, four hundred and eighteen in Germany and Austria, and two hundred and eighty-nine in Bohemia. In six hundred and sixty-six of these there were two hundred and sixty thousand and seven hundred members, who were working upon a capital of $10,240,499, which was all their own, and on a borrowed auxiliary capital of $32,888,142, from which they make an average clear gain of two per cent a year. Their total business of 1869 shows an average gain of seventeen per cent. Some of the associations do not report, but so far as is known, the entire German coöperative societies number about two thousand six hundred and fifty, with an aggregate of one million members, and a business of not less than $220,000,000, in 1868.

The founder of the German system, in a recent publication, speaks of the process of its growth, in effect, thus: "With the banks have grown up 'coöperative stores,' to enable the members to secure advances on their work, and to find in the store a place of deposit and of sale. The guarantee of the maker enables the store to warrant the goods to the purchaser, and, as the management is in the hands of practical workmen, their examination is an incentive for the manufacturer, and a security for the customer.

The members of the coöperative stores and of the banks are nearly the same, so that they are able to participate in the profits and advantages of both institutions; and the workman, who gets advances from the bank, is enabled to pay them off promptly with the proceeds of his work deposited in the store."

SPAIN.

The formation of industrial societies was fairly commenced in 1862; a few of them have a still earlier date. In 1870 one hundred and ninety-six were reported, with twenty-five thousand members, and doing an aggregate business of twenty-two and a half millions of dollars a year. The movement here is exclusively among the operatives. An independent enterprise, formed by people of wealth and education, for the purpose of giving free evening instruction to workingmen and their children, beside its own excellent objects, is made to subserve the coöperative movement among the industrial populace. Masses of illiterate men, who have absolutely no other means of education, are brought together. The method is by lecturing and questioning the audience on topics of household economy and coöperation, not unfrequently mingled with political discussions, and employing assistants mixed with the crowd to excite interest, and encourage participation by the audience. In this way coöperative stores, bakeries, social kitchens, and the general policy of the labor interests, are familiarly and effectively presented. The English and German laboring people have their popular tuition well supplied by printed books, tracts, and newspapers, but Spanish propagandism, in lack of these, makes its dusty-foot forums answer for the time and circumstances quite as well, or better.

RUSSIA.

Previous to the emancipation of the serfs the working policy of the Communes considerably resembled the coöperative system, as it might be applied to agriculture. The Russian Commune may be generally, and sufficiently well, described for our purposes, thus: A plot of fertile land containing, say one hundred thousand acres; on its border are situated the villa, stables, and offices of the lord of the manor. He owns, by inheritance, ten thousand acres, the remaining ninety thousand are virtually the property of the serfs, which they work for themselves in their hours of leisure. In the centre is the communal village, with the gardens and farms around it. The village has about one hundred and fifty inhabitants. Each of the fifty families is entitled to garden and farm land in equitable proportion to its number in family, with enlargements or diminution of area according to the increase or decrease of the number and need. The partition and appropriation of the lands is under the government of a Board, elected for the purpose by universal suffrage. The lands thus divided are, however, the property of the commune, and not of the individual to whom they are assigned. He cannot convey or sub-let his lot. When the households are diminished by marriage or death the Board alters the lot and apportions the quantity deducted to a newly-formed household or to some family which has increased in number. It is said that no real mischief results from such changes of apportionment, and very little trouble attends them. The commune is a little republican nation, ruling itself comfortably within the limits of its liberty. Emancipation has made the old-time serfs nominally free, but it has not, by any means, removed the grievances of their former condition. They are made owners of their lands, but they are burdened with the heavy obligations that in Russia attach to property holding. When they were slaves they enjoyed almost the entire product of their lands; now, this is taxed to a very large part of its value. There are nearly six thousand of such communes in the country, with as many chief villas or little cities, and these are taxed very heavily to meet the necessities of the government.

More than ninety per cent of the population is rural, and the cities are very few. The internal commerce of the people is mainly through their fairs. But little encouragement is afforded for building towns; and the merchant class is but an insignificant part of the nation. The number of the merchants is but as one to one hundred and eighty of the population. The merchant evil is, therefore, not very great, and the need for coöperative stores is comparatively small; barter at the fairs answering most of the ends of necessary exchanges. The agricultural labor of the country is already nearly all that coöperation in production, in that department, requires; and the communal habit and instinct are ready for such extension of the system as the rising fortunes and expanding business of the people may require. Feudalism is a rude outline of industrial association in political and social bondage. Civil liberty, replacing slavery, will have less of the savage spirit of repellant individualism to combat in establishing the proper relations of men, in Russia, than it finds in the modern democracies.

What we have shown of the industrial coöperative movement in Europe will suffice for its presentment and analysis. It has a foothold in Italy, France, Belgium, Switzerland, as well as in the countries which we have so exhaustively discussed for the purpose of exhibiting its rapid growth, great success, and the many modified forms impressed by the characters of the nations now making the trial.

In Europe the system has encountered a great resistance, both as to principle and policy, from the insurgent spirit of the laboring class among the nations, where the evils of poverty have inspired a revolt against the oppressive dominion of capital, combined with political despotism. The laboring people of Western Europe are now, and have been for a long while, and threaten to continue for a long time to come, in a state of insurrection against the existing rule of capital in production. France holds the lead in the agitations of theory and plans of reform, and is formidable in propagandism among the people of Germany, Italy, and Great Britain. Her philosophy is socialistic, communistic, and radical, in various modifications of the terms; and its doctrines and devices are hostile to those of the coöperative movement. The principles and policy of Herr Schultze Delitzsch's system have been everywhere resisted and embarrassed by the attractive, and zealously urged, theory of the French propagandists. A meeting of the Workingmen's Union of Prussia, held in January, 1870, at Berlin, fully reflects this influence, and exhibits its characteristic features. There were present eighty-nine delegates, representing over twenty thousand contributing members, efficiently organized, and a total constituency of about one hundred thousand. After full discussion, resolutions were unanimously adopted, embodying such doctrines as these : the recently enacted laws of Prussia, regulating industry, are an advance toward its freedom and assurance of its rights, but the unequal strength of labor and capital is only increased by the amendment in principle. This practical aggravation of labor's disadvantages, however, will hasten the crisis, by precipitating a solution of the social question. On the subject of landed property, one speaker said that the sole capital possessed by any one is the capacity to work; the soil which supplies the means is the property of humanity, and it is the will of the Creator that it shall be reconquered for humanity. The laborers, he said, are eighty-six and the proprietors are but fourteen per cent of the population; the laborers are the real owners of the land; all means of production, including the soil, should be common property. With the first productive organization, and the assistance of the State, the disorganization of the present, and the construction of the new order begins. The other speakers concurred, and the convention adopted the sentiments expressed.

The first effect of the law of 1868, conceding the right of the workingmen of North Germany to combine against their employers, was the formation of labor unions. The next, was a strike of the miners in Lower Silesia, where wages are lowest, even in Germany; a coal-digger getting but forty-five cents, and a carrier but thirty-five cents a day. These people struck for higher wages in December 1869. Six thousand were thrown out of employment. In a month their funds were exhausted; $70,000 in wages were lost, and $80,000 were expended in supplies. Then nine hundred married men submitted; three hundred unpracticed hands were added, and the work went on as it best could, with the diminished force. The unmarried men held out. The final result was a sort of triumph for the strikers, at the cost that may be inferred from the submission of those upon whom it pressed hardest, and the actual losses of all the rest.

It is specially unfortunate for the laboring people now everywhere combined in unions for the betterment of their condition and advancement of their rights, that their speculative principles are so largely derived from the French school of agitators, who, while organized as labor unions, are much more largely occupied with socialistic and political objects. They are better understood by the name assumed by their compatriots in Spain where they call themselves "Unions of *Resistance.*" The governing spirit of the French movement is hostility to property rights, to capital in the hands of the present holders, and resultingly, to a practical union of existing capital with labor in productive industry. This is not progressiveness, or reformation, but revolution: a war with, not an amendment of, the present order of things, as impracticable in effort as false in theory.

CHAPTER XXII.

COÖPERATION IN THE UNITED STATES.

Coöperation in the United States: Recent introduction.—Attitude of labor to capital in the United States.—Labor not in despair—saving, not the rule or the means.—New England, harder pressed and more provident.—Coöperative stores of the St. Crispin Order—very few stores in Pennsylvania—none in the West or South.—Very few coöperative industrial unions in the country.—Troy Foundery—immense profits of.—Economy of coöperative production.—Dividend of net profits, as wages for good behavior.—Economy of material and tools estimated at ten per cent of the product.—Somerset Foundery.—Aristocratic Associations.—Advantages of the per cent dividend of profits—and faults of the plan.—Stores ought to be connected with coöperative factories.—Carriage factory in New York.—Building and Loan Associations.—First established in Great Britain.—The earliest in the United States—in New Jersey and other States—Failure of in New York and New England.—Number and capital invested in Philadelphia.—Plan and policy—complete fulfillment of the design in ten years or less.—How a renter becomes owner in a dozen years.—Slaves buy their freedom with profits of extra work.—Custom against conviction.—Capital associated with service in the whaling business.—Possible savings of skilled labor in the United States—accumulation of in three years, equal to forty-three per cent of the capital employed in the nation in 1860.—French popular loan.—Popular loans in the United States during the Rebellion.—*Competitive versus coöperative system.*—Labor Unions *versus* the union of labor.—" Supply and Demand" doctrine.—" Division-of-labor" doctrine.—Prevalent political economy, the apologist and philosophy of disorder—merely a huckstering theory.—Bastiat glorifies the cut-throat competition of individualism.—Professor Perry against Labor Unions.—Free trade labor auction.—International Labor League.—Labor Unions against the union of labor and capital.—Despotism surrenders its own liberties.—Necessity and rightfulness of Labor Unions.—Tacit combination of capitalists.—Labor Unions drifting and tending to a happy issue, but must be directed by a policy of peace, self-help, and harmony with the existing order of industry.

It must be recollected that these papers are *studies* in Political Economy, and that we are no further concerned with the histories and statistics of economic affairs than as they serve to elucidate the particular subjects under consideration. The topics involved in this section of our inquiries, are, for the most part, concerned with the industries and exchanges of the passing time; they are matters of the latest dates. The movements just now considered are affairs of but a dozen or twenty years' experience. They have scarcely settled themselves into permanent forms. They are all subject to the contingencies of time and trial. Their histories are rather promises than accomplished facts. Moreover, it is next to impossible to collect reports of their actual states, and as hard to judge of their working forces from the immature experiments which they have as yet undergone. They are studies still even to the agents engaged in them, as well as to those who are only occupied with their principles of action and their apparent drift towards complete realization. This is more especially true of coöperation in the United States. The country is yet so young, its conditions so full of reliefs and escapes from the evils which press upon the old world, that its people are not driven with the same force into measures of defense against social evils, everywhere else almost unendurable. The demand for labor here is relatively so great, that in respect to all its products, except those which foreign trade supplies, it is able to command quite reasonable and mutually equitable terms from the capital that employs it. At least, labor here, however many and however just its complaints, is not in despair. It is not in the conditions that left the Rochdale Pioneers destitute of all hope except in self-help. For one of our working men that lives in apprehension of the poor house, a hundred are thinking of going to the State Legislature or the Federal Congress, and a thousand entertain very promising expectations of a house and lot in town, or a farm in the West, in good time for the establishment of a family, that shall begin life well advanced in the means of living and of enjoyment. The common school in all its grades, the current instruction of the newspaper, accessible to everybody, with the examples, within every one's own observation, of grand successes among the poorest who aspire to, and industriously work for, the advance of their fortunes, amount to an assurance of hope full of the happiest influences. A system of savings that must run twenty or thirty years to the fulfillment of the intention has not much attractiveness. Very few of our laborers have any thought of living and dying where they are born. Everything among us is on springs, and everybody is locomotive. It is a wonder to find members of three generations of one family in any of our cemeteries, just as it is as likely that one shall find a man wearing his grandfather's coat as owning his grandfather's land. We are very seriously engaged in making money—making fortunes, rather; but we are not so hard pressed yet as to do this by making savings. A penny or two of difference either way in the price of a pound of tea, makes a corresponding difference in its consumption in England. With us a difference of ten times as much in the cost, would never be seen in our importations for consumption. Insurance institutions of every sort that provide for accidents, and in relief of casualties, we embrace freely, but coöperative organizations for saving expenses, or for building up fortunes, are not felt to be pressing necessities by our common people. It is for these reasons, and owing to this general state of mind, as I think, that neither coöperative stores, nor industrial associations, have made much headway among us. In the New England States, which have drawn nearer to the conditions of the old countries than any of the Middle or Western States, these stores are regarded as firmly established; yet even there, only forty-two of them were reported in January, 1870, and the oldest of these, except one, had been in existence but three or four years. Twenty-five years ago, "Protective Unions," somewhat resembling these in aim and principles, had quite a run; but they have all disappeared except one in Worcester, Massachusetts, and it owes its continuance to essential changes in its administration, bringing it more nearly into conformity with present requirements than by the original plan of its organization. For the rest, it is curious to observe that the successful establishment of coöperative stores of supply, which dates no further back than the year 1866, is mainly due to the auxiliary influence of the Order of *The Knights of St. Crispin*, which have in Massachusetts alone one hundred and seventeen lodges, and thirty thousand members. Corroborated by the ties of brotherhood in a secret society, and governed by its organization, coöperation in retail selling and buying is made practicable. This Order, and a dozen or a score of similar orders, embracing other callings and businesses, exist everywhere in the Union, but scarcely anywhere else have they adopted the provident system of supplies in the common necessaries of life—simply, as I suppose, because Yankee thrift and economy are nowhere else so imperatively demanded. So far as these stores have been tried and well managed, they have yielded profits and benefits in kind and degree quite equal to the best of similar establishments in Europe.

Pennsylvania has one successful store of this kind in the anthracite coal region. It was set up in 1856, and in 1869 was able to make a handsome report of its business, its prosperity, and its prospects. There may be others in the Middle States, but if there be, they have gained no notoriety.

It is true that these stores have in every instance fully vindicated their policy when well conducted ; yet it is just as true, that they are only adopted where their need is most imperatively felt.

The history of industrial coöperations among us is still more meagre of instances. There are several examples of marked success, indeed, but even these are not organized on the principles that cover the whole broad ground of the associative policy. At Troy, New York, for instance, thirty-two iron moulders, in the year 1866, associated with a capital of $19,500. They have been abundantly successful. It is said that they divided ninety per cent upon their stock and labor in the third year. Their dividends, however, were not paid out, but were invested in new stock in the firm, enabling it to employ more men and rapidly enlarge its business. But the institution is so far from being an instance of coöperative association, in the sense and service which addresses itself to the relief of the industrious unpropertied poor, that it is, in fact, only a partnership of capitalists, or of workingmen who are their own employers, by virtue of the considerable stock which they were able to bring into the concern at its commencement. They had but eighty-five members in their third year, and they hold it as a condition of their business that there shall not be more than one member in it for every $2500 of stock paid up. A strike in 1866 drove them into the enterprise on a capital of $600 to each member; but the governing policy is a return to the amount first determined upon. Notwithstanding the enormous profit made, they do not undersell their rivals, nor are they tempted to do so. Their profit is principally the result of the economy in the conduct of the business, due to the interest of proprietorship in the workmen. The foundery conducts itself; for every man in it is an interested conductor. The executive chief of the works says that, "out of twelve hundred tons of pig iron, we can make, using the same pattern, one hundred more tons of stoves than any private establishment in Troy." Here association gives a profit of about ten per cent upon the value of the products. This is margin enough for defense against rivalry in the market, and enough to build up the fortunes of the partners. These Troy founderymen do not even profess benevolence to the craft. They seek no extension of their system; but, availing themselves of the benefit of the associative policy, they derive its advantages and demonstrate its benefits to all who would adopt it.

We have met with another mode of inducing and securing economy in the use of materials, the employment of tools, and increase of production, by dividing ten per cent, in one instance, of the net profit of the business to the workmen, on condition of good behavior in all respects which concern the prosperity of the proprietors; and we have seen the case in the newspapers under the caption of "successful coöperation." But the scheme differs in nothing from the common system except in extending wages from work paid by the piece or by time employed, to a wages reward for good behavior. It is worth notice that this ten per cent of profits so offered is about the equivalent of the ten per cent of larger product at the Troy foundery, and thus shows the money worth of the economy secured by giving the workingmen the full value of their care and fidelity to the proprietary interests, and so, is good evidence of the policy of the association of labor and capital in productive industry.

There is a foundery in Somerset, Massachusetts, on the plan of that of Troy, a "close corporation," confining its membership to as many as the capital can employ; keeping its secrets and its results to itself. It was established to make as much money for itself as possible, not to prove that manufacturers make too much. Its basis is fixed at $2,000 capital for each member. They say that no less sum will give a moulder constant and remunerative employment; that smaller subscriptions too greatly enlarge the membership, and that from this cause other similar establishments have failed, as at Pittsburgh and West Troy. This establishment gives support to about fifty families. At Worcester "The Bay State Boot and Shoe Factory" employed five hundred hands in 1867. It divides the net profits, *pro rata*, according to the work done—to males, earning above $100, and above $50 to females. The sum divided in the first year was equal to four and one-half per cent of the wages paid to all the laborers. Casual hands get nothing but their wages. The advantage to the firm is constancy of the workmen and the avoidance of strikes—another instance of a joint interest of capital and labor, and of the available influence of labor upon capital found in its reserve of moral power.

In a currier's shop in Boston a similar policy has resulted in $100 extra to each of five workmen employed during eight months. The good results under such a system to the employer are more work from the same tools and machinery, no strikes, constancy of the workmen; and, to the employees larger reward, or reward for good qualities and good behavior, with all the moral benefits arising to them.

The injurious error in all these plans for inducing the laborers' best services by extra wages in the form of a dividend of the net profits is in distributing, instead of funding, the share of profits. The sums so allowed are never sufficient for, nor are they invited into combination, as capital in the business; nor are they of much account as saving-fund deposits. Their aggregate in large establishments, however, would be large enough for the institution of coöperative stores. In Charleston, for instance, one such store, on a $7,000 capital, does a business of $150,000, furnishing food for three hundred and eighty-five shareholders at first or wholesale cost, less the expense of management, and it repays, besides, to non-stockholding customers a good percentage upon their purchases. Such stores should be connected with all industrial institutions. The small extra dividend of profits, added to the usual wages, impresses no one, but, joint ownership in a store or bank, with thousands in capital, is felt, and it works as a force, over and above all the other advantages which it affords. Such stores induce men to settle down near their place of work. A rise of value in adjoining real estate is a noticeable and important result. The Troy manager says : " We have colonized the neighborhood. Lots of land that cost the first purchasers $123 have already risen to $800." Among all the advantages of a thoroughly coöperative system, this last mentioned is not the least important.

In the city of New York a very extensive carriage manufactory has now for several years been conducted under the policy of allowing the workingmen a dividend in the net profits, as compensation for the greater care and fidelity which a participation in the value of the product induces.

These instances are cited only for the purpose of exhibiting their principles and policy. The prevalence of the plan is so great that I cannot even attempt to enumerate the examples, nor to mark their great variety of modifications. Merchants have, time out of mind, been in the habit of giving their chief clerks a share in the profits of their business, for the purpose of securing and rewarding their best services, and manufacturers often do the same thing. Such an interest held by a non-capitalist employee, however, involves him in the risks and liabilities of the concern as a partner by legal construction, and exposes him to the consequences of the management in which he generally has no potential control. When the extra allowance is held as a mere gift by the proprietors, the liabilities of partnership are escaped, but the interest accorded loses something of the influence of the possessory feeling determinately settled. A marked example is afforded in the case of the great Paris printer, M. Paul Dupont, who carried on a business of five millions of francs a year before the late war in France. He divided ten per cent of the net profits among his workmen, according to their individual merit, and not in regular proportion to their salaries or wages. He has done this for twenty years, and has combined with the system of donatives, saving funds, coöperative stores, libraries, and beneficial institutions.

All this, however, is not coöperation in its true sense. It lacks the essential principle of making the workman his own employer, but it proves the practical advantages to both parties of giving the employee a joint interest in the results to such an extent as will command the best service by equitably rewarding it. The *ten* per cent allowance adopted in the instances cited seems to be the estimated profit of the plan in almost all the many cases which have fallen under the writer's notice, and it is repeated here as a significant fact. Can it be possible that the very best hands at wages are this much less profitable to their employers, than when they are stimulated by an equitable regard for their best care, economy, and skill in the performance of their work? Capitalists, one with another, and one time with another, do not make more than ten per cent of the product as net profits for themselves; yet it seems that they can afford as much to their workmen on the better plan of a modified coöperative system, and still save as much for themselves. We do not give too much emphasis to this practical result of an equitable distribution of the joint product of capital and labor, but, it illustrates the principle which lies at the bottom of the system, and prophesies, while it provides, a remedy for the existing disorders in industrial pursuits.

Besides the forms of associated business organizations already noticed, we have in the United States, an active and considerably extensive system which nearly resembles the Credit banks of Germany in principle, with a difference in objects and operation, but even more immediately and largely capable of the like intention. These are the *Building and Loan Associations.* In Pennsylvania they are incorporated and regulated under a general law of the State. Edmund Wrigley, Esq., of Philadelphia, in 1869, published a very well digested exposition of their history, plan of operation, and general results, to which the reader is referred for the details which are not compatible with the limits and objects of this treatise.

The first institution of the kind, it seems, was established in Scotland in the year 1815, under the supervision of the Earl of Selkirk. They thence gradually extended into the manufacturing districts of England and Wales; were afterwards established in London, and soon became general throughout Great Britain, until they reached the number of two thousand and fifty societies in 1851, with an annual income of four millions of pounds sterling, according to the report of the Registrar. The earliest in the United States, it is believed, was established in Frankford, Philadelphia County, in 1840. In the City of Philadelphia they now hold the first rank in number and amount of invested funds. They prevail very extensively in the State of New Jersey. A few exist in North and South Carolina. There are some in Minnesota, more in Nebraska, and a considerable number in Baltimore. In the City of New York they have failed of success, and they are scarcely known in New England.

In Philadelphia above a thousand of these societies have been chartered; some of them never organized, some failed through mismanagement, a number have closed their business upon a complete fulfillment of their design; and there remain now about seven hundred in active operation, with an aggregate working capital of between five and six millions of dollars.

The value of the shares is limited, by the incorporating law, and is usually fixed at two hundred dollars, payable by the subscribers in installments of one dollar monthly on each share. The society commences its business as soon as a sufficient number of shares are disposed of. The funds of the society are derived from the monthly dues of the subscribers, the premiums upon loans made to the highest bidder among the stockholders, upon mortgage on real estate, the profit retained upon withdrawals of stock before the ultimate result is reached, and very largely, from the interest upon loans which is paid monthly, and reinvested during their continuance. The great accretions of interest compounded monthly are seen in the fact that one thousand dollars, at six per cent simple interest, paid annually, doubles itself in sixteen years and eight months, while the same sum, with its interest compounded monthly, doubles in eleven years and seven months. It is clear, therefore, that in less than twelve years the interest alone would refund their money to the subscribers, and it is, therefore, quite credible that some of these institutions, by the addition of fines and premiums added to the accruing interest, are able, as they have proved actually, to complete their enterprise in ten years. A few very well managed ones have accomplished their intention in even less time. Mr. Wrigley gives the figures to show how a tenant availing himself of the profits of membership in a building and loan association, by adding about twenty dollars a year to the rent of a house, may, in eight or ten years, become the owner of one equally valuable.

By complying with the conditions of membership a man, by so small an advance upon his ordinary rent, gets possession of a lot of land suitable for his use, erects a building upon a loan from the society, secured by mortgage upon the premises, and without much additional effort eventually becomes the owner. The association is to him a credit bank, enabling him to anticipate the savings of a dozen years, and to enjoy their fruits in the mean time, all the while perfectly secure of the result, and ever afterwards the absolute owner in fee of his domicile.*

The argument from successful instances might be greatly extended, without being proportionately strengthened. The advant-

---

* The activity of this movement in Philadelphia is only fairly indicated by the fact, that of thirty-two applications for charters to the Court of Common Pleas, at the April term, 1871, seventeen were for building and loan associations, while seven of the remainder were for beneficial societies.

ages of reformed and improved methods in the conduct of men's business affairs are more frequently demonstrated than adopted. Human nature is not by any means a stupid, but it is a very willful, thing. It may be convinced without being practically conformed. Many years ago, a slaveholder in Louisiana, sold their time to his slaves to be paid for out of the value of their extra work. Two or three successive sets of them, under this stimulus, purchased their freedom. The proprietor made more money out of them by this policy than if he had sold their bodies upon the auction block. No one failed to see the pecuniary advantages of the system, and—no one adopted it. They maintained the slave system till it exploded. Customs obstinately resist convictions and conditions, and usually refuse reform until revolutions compel.

Where business cannot be safely or profitably conducted upon the wages system, partnership of profits, without capital invested, is, of necessity, accorded, as in the whaling business, which has been carried on for a century in the United States under this kind of coöperation, or policy of rewards proportioned to risks and services requiring the higher qualities of the laborer.

Reformers are very confident that the best way of doing things will sooner or later be adopted; but it is well for them to possess their souls in patience, for, usually, it is only when no other way will work at all that the best is accepted. Nothing short of oft-repeated business disasters in the cotton States will drive the planters into a system of self-sustaining and self-supplying diversification of agricultural production. Slavery is abolished there, but the industrial system proper to it must die by inches, and the incidental suffering will be ascribed to anything and everything else than the inherent vice of the obsolete policy. Every season that their crop goes into the market which it gorges, the planters see and acknowledge the mischiefs of their system, and threaten a reform, and accordingly (to custom) never do; but they will, when no choice is left to them, and, probably, not before.

Under correction of these convictions, let us now look at the practicability and necessity of coöperation in productive industry.

The relation of labor to capital in modern production is shown by the census of 1850, 1860, and 1870, to hold the proportion of about twenty per cent of wages to the value of the products. If we deduct ten per cent from that value for the profits of capital, the agency of labor in the business is about twenty-two and one-quarter per cent or two-ninths of the investments concerned in the work or business. Labor's equitable share cannot be claimed to be more than one-quarter of the joint product of capital, machinery, and industry at wages. In other words, the accumulations of past labor are as three to one in the forces currently employed in further production in the manufacturing, mining, and mechanic arts, as they are now carried on in the United States.

This shows the part that capital plays in these branches of business, and labor's dependence upon it, for its effectiveness, that is, the measure of the relations subsisting between them.

There are now about six millions of Americans working for wages. Suppose that their savings could be made to reach, in the average, seventy-five dollars a year; the aggregate would be four hundred and fifty millions—a very pretty capital this if associated in active use. Now let us see how such possible accumulation of savings in other than agricultural pursuits counts up. In 1860 the reported capital invested in such business, consisting of real and personal estate, including cash and credit, amounted to one thousand and ten millions; the raw materials consumed in the year cost one thousand and thirty-one millions, and the wages of labor three hundred and seventy-nine millions. The products were valued at eighteen hundred and eighty-five millions—products to capital, one hundred and eighty-six per cent.

There were one million three hundred and ten thousand hands employed. Their savings, at seventy-five dollars per annum each, would be ninety-eight and a quarter millions. Add to this sum, accumulated in one year, the credit which it would command, and we have a working capital of one hundred and fifty millions, equal to fourteen and one-half per cent of the capital which, in 1860, yielded eighteen hundred and eighty-five millions of products, and which would, at the same ratio, give them one-seventh of the total yield of the mines, mechanic arts, and manufactures of 1860. But their wages that year amounted to one-fifth, or twenty per cent of the product. This loss of current profit is to be set to the account of the real estate and machinery which must be provided to begin with. A larger capital must, therefore, be provided to increase the profits. Take two years savings, and the yield would be twenty-nine per cent of the product of 1860, and three years, by the same rule, would cover forty-three and a half, or seven-sixteenths of the like yield—the usual wages being all the while allowed for current support, less the savings assumed to be practicable.

We conclude that, whatever may be said upon the moral possibility or probability of such coöperation of the laborers as might achieve these grand results, the economic possibility is demonstrable, and its realization is the right drift of reformatory endeavor. The latent capability of the masses has been more than once demonstrated within the last twenty years. The instances show how the account stands between the aggregate of existing and disposable capital, and the possible savings of the industrial masses.

In France, when Louis Napoleon required a large loan for the purpose of carrying on the Crimean War, he turned from the bankers of Europe to the people and asked them for five hundred millions of francs. They subscribed, and were ready to pay into the treasury, fifteen hundred millions! In the United States, in the second year of the great Rebellion, the Secretary of the Treasury appealed to the people of the loyal States (when, if the whole capital of the banks had been emptied bodily into the Treasury, it would not have sufficed), and they responded by furnishing him with one hundred and forty millions of dollars. This vast sum, of which not less than eighty millions were supplied by the working people, was a trifle compared to the contributions from the same source in the following three years of the war.

Our argument thus far assumes or supposes a continued antagonism of capital and labor. But capital is not necessarily, and will not long be, actually excluded from fraternity with industry. As we have seen, in Germany, the people's Credit banks borrow money abundantly, and take all its profits, beyond the interest paid. So everywhere, the accumulated wealth would easily be drawn, upon sufficient securities, into a partnership of harmonized interests. Property is not robbery, as the French Socialists regard it; and communism, as they propose it, is opposed in all its features, alike to individual rights and the general welfare, and is at the same time, the worst enemy of true association. False principles inserted into the machinery of associative organizations, must in the end grind themselves out, by the counter-working of the essential truths which they encounter; but at all the cost of the sufferings and failures of misdirected effort and misapplied power. It is not the strikes, which express hostility to capital, that achieve any of the triumphs casually secured, but it is the power of combination, which they evince, that indirectly furthers their intention.

COMPETITION *versus* COÖPERATION.

"These are contrary the one to the other," as St. Paul says of the "lustings of the flesh against the spirit and of the spirit against the flesh." We have already noticed the conflict between the Delitzsch system and that of the French radical reformers as it occurred in the earlier days of the coöperative movement in Germany, and indicated the obstructive action of the "Labor Unions" upon the *union of* labor in Europe and America. This spirit of antagonism between the two great parties into which the progressives and the revolutionists of the laboring mass are divided, has one of its roots in the common and natural feeling of resistance to wrong and its resulting evils; and another, in the theoretical system of a very large and influential body of political economists, who have for their help the essentially rebellious spirit of modern civilization. The authorities upon which the competitive school stands, justify its spirit, but curiously enough, while they oppose the procedure of the "Labor Unions," supply their doctrinal basis. Adam Smith and after him J. B. Say and John Stuart Mill, teach that the law of "supply and demand" is the sole regulator of the rewards of labor, as well as of the value of all products; and they all alike insist upon the free play of this law of theirs in all circumstances, and in all cases of exhange. No place or force is allowed by this theory for combination of either labor or wealth to regulate prices. The authorities of this school, on the contrary, agree in sustaining the philosophy and policy of free competition between the producers, the consumers, and the venders of all commodities, and between the individuals of each class. They all alike hold that the utmost possible division of labor, both in industrial production and in territorial distribution, is its highest and happiest organization, and the aim and end of all possible improvement of its system, and the thing to be pursued and achieved; which means nothing else, under the present order of things, than the reduction of the industrial classes into a wonderfully complicated form of machinery, with capital for its motor power, director, and employer. Indeed, when closely examined, the system of doctrines which we have accepted from them is simply a logical underpinning of the very order of things, which the "Unions" are organized to resist and which the theory of reform criticises and condemns. It is simply an endeavor to find a philosophy that will justify the reigning disorder in the existing relations of capital and labor. A philosophy which considers the well-being of neither producer nor consumer, but, looking only to the interests of the trader, has all the law and the prophets in this, the greatest of its commandments, "buy where you can buy cheapest and sell where you can sell dearest." The life and soul of this school's teachings is fully expressed by Frederick Bastiat, and accepted by his party everywhere as the latest and best of its oracles, thus: "*Competition* is democratic in its essence; the most progressive, the most equalizing, and the most communistic of all the provisions to which Providence has confided the direction of human progress." If further exposition and application of this fundamental principle were wanting, we have it in the language of Professor Perry, the American champion of the system, explicitly given in these words: "The guilds of the Middle Ages, and the Trades Unions of our own day, are examples of voluntary associations for the purpose of regulating the wages of their members by combined action. * * * *The spirit* of Political Economy, which is the spirit of freedom, *is against such associations for such purposes.* If any man has a service to render, let him offer it freely, and make the best terms he can with whoever wants it." This is free trade carried from the province of international exchange of commodities into the domestic workshop, where not only products, but all that has a market value in the body and brains of the producers, are to be subjected to a chaffering and huckstering of manhood for money.

The *International* Labor League, established, I believe, in 1864, and the Labor Unions which are in sympathy with, and sustain it, drift in the same channel—they are all Unions of resistance, to capital, first and always, and to coöperative industrial associations, next, because these accept and avail themselves of the ruling order in the functions of productive industry, and withdraw themselves from the hostile array of the resistants; their attitude being, in effect, a protest against the doctrines and policy of strife, and their successes a demonstration of the harmony, or rather identity, of interests in the parties now unhappily and unwisely at war.

Labor Unions, by their scales of prices, indeed, prohibit competition between the members of the same craft, but this is done only the more effectually to maintain competition between the buyers and sellers of labor. They do not aim at the abolition of the wages system, but, by all the force which combination can command, to rule its rates,.and compel compliance of the capitalists who employ it. Their constitution is one of unnatural and impracticable independence—independence attempted in an order of things of which the essence and governing spirit is mutual inter-dependence! To assert its own rights and liberties it wars upon the rights and liberties of the party opposed; and in their procedure this universal law follows them and vindicates itself—" Whoever will put a chain on the heels of any man shall have the other end of it fastened around his own neck." The spirit of domination, must to itself be despotism—freedom must be surrendered by any that deny it to others. War cannot be maintained but by implicit obedience to the commanders. The soldier in any field of strife puts his liberty and life under the power of his commanders. The array is coöperation in bondage, just as the association of a poor-house is brotherhood in beggary. Whoever closely watches the situation of Unions, driven to extremes of resistance, will see reason for the saying that "the way to make hell is to turn a heaven upside down."

Trades' Unions are, nevertheless, not only thoroughly well warranted by principle, but they also derive no small authorization from their universal prevalence. Every trade, and every distinct branch of every trade, is, in the cities and principal villages of all free countries, effectively organized. This, so far as it goes, is coöperation, and is capable of its best uses. It is, indeed, a necessity. Without such concurrence as true and rightly directed association secures, workingmen would be helpless in the hands of their employers. They would, in lack of mutual support, invite despotism in the management of their business interests. The very best promise of the very best results to such Unions is in the great fact that they are capable of association. In the multitude of counsellors there is safety, when a common interest brings them into conference. The capitalists who now hold the machinery and materials of production, which in relative value and efficiency are as three to one against the labor employed, are easily combined for their own purposes. They are tacitly and effectively, even where they are not formally, united in action, as in interest. The counterpoise of Unions among workingmen for the like purpose is just as legitimate, but not more or less so. When righteousness and peace meet they may kiss each other, but self-defense at least is a necessity where strife is the rule. The machinery is right in so far as it is mutual and necessary; and the comfort in it is, that, work as widely as it may from the right way in the days of its infancy, the trials and training of experience, leading it forward still, and upward, through defeats and triumphs, through all its sins and sufferings, as well as successes, will be ever tending toward the desired ends. That saying of Gœthe is every way true—"A good man, even in his dark strivings, is ever in the right way." But the sooner workingmen attain to soundness of directory principle, a clear view of the true aim of all their efforts, and an earnest conformity in practice, the sooner they will escape the troubles and sufferings of the educating discipline which they must more or less undergo. They are "endeavoring to keep the unity of the spirit" among themselves, but they must be careful to observe the other limb of the Apostle's injunction—" in the bonds of peace." They must learn that they must adjust themselves to whatever there is in the order of things which cannot be resisted, and, as a first step toward the reform of their circumstances, put themselves right. Do they intend to take the rule of the world's business affairs into their own hands, for their own benefit? Let them begin by ruling their own share of that business, and thus test their fitness, and qualify themselves for the agency they would assume. Until they are generally capable of coöperation within the range of their present possibilities, they will not be ready to administer the whole range of industrial operations; and, when they are so capable, they will not need or desire to usurp a larger authority.

APPENDIX.

THE LAW OF CLIMATE IN PARTY POLITICS.

THE reader, if a *student* of economic and social questions, cannot fail to feel a profound, and at the same time a curious, interest in the climatic law of migration, generally and briefly stated in our fourth chapter. He, perhaps, will have looked for our reasons for dividing North America, including Canada, into three, rather than any other number of, political departments, under the rule of geographic and isothermal laws. It would be tedious to indicate the details of fact and speculation upon which the division adopted seems to me to rest. Mr. Carey, in his first announcement of the law, arranged the States and territories of the United States into four climatic zones or belts, as will be seen in the appended article extracted from *Forney's Press* of the 22d of December, 1859, and in my statistical elucidation I followed the scheme of his proposition. This point resting, as it does, upon speculation (which I trust may never be verified by a corresponding political division of the Union), and liable to such a number and force of counter-balancing influences as promise to effectually prevent its demonstration in the experience of the nation, may be remitted to the consideration of the curious. The isothermal divisions may be fixed at three or four or six, as further and closer examination shall dispose inquirers to determine. The number within this range is, in point of principle, indifferent.

The idea of such natural divisions of the territory of North America, with corresponding political organizations, is not new, though the law upon which they rest has been so lately promulgated. While the adoption of the Federal Constitution was in debate, the writers of the *Federalist* gave the question of the possible number of distinct governments, that would result, on failure of the general union, their most earnest attention; and it is curious to notice that Mr. Jay, in the fourth number of that inspired work, speaks of three or four possible governments, into which the original thirteen States might be divided. Alexander Hamilton in the thirteenth number, devoted almost exclusively to this subject, holds this language:

"The entire separation of the States into thirteen unconnected sovereignties, is a project too extravagant, and too replete with danger, to have many advocates. The ideas of men who speculate upon the dismemberment of the Empire, seem generally turned towards three confederacies: one consisting of the four Northern, another of the four Middle, and a third of the five Southern States. There is little probability that there would be a greater number."

This he gives as the more generally prevailing notion of the disunionists of the time; but, now look at his own management of the premises, and the results which he draws from them:

"If we attend carefully to geographical and commercial considerations, in conjunction with the habits and prejudices of the different States, we shall be led to conclude, that in case of disunion, they will most naturally league themselves under two governments. The four eastern States, from all the causes that form the links of national sympathy and connection, may with certainty be expected to unite. New York, situated as she is, would never be unwise enough to oppose a feeble and unsupported flank to the weight of that confederacy. There are obvious reasons, that would facilitate her accession to it. New Jersey is too small a State to think of being a frontier, in opposition to this still more powerful combination; nor do there appear to be any obstacles to her admission into it. Even Pennsylvania would have strong inducements to join the northern league. * * * The more southern States, from various circumstances, may not think themselves much interested in the encouragement of navigation. They may prefer a system, which would give unlimited scope to all nations, to be the carriers as well as the purchasers, of their commodities. Pennsylvania may not choose to confound her interests in a connection so adverse to her policy. As she must, at all events, be a frontier, she may deem it most consistent with her safety, to have her exposed side turned towards the weaker power of the southern, rather than toward the stronger power of the northern confederacy. * * * Whatever may be the determination of Pennsylvania, if the northern confederacy includes New Jersey, there is no likelihood of more than one confederacy to the south of that State."

The number of the *Federalist* from which this extract is made, is dated November 28, 1787, and Hamilton was then considering the

APPENDIX. 333

divisions into which the old thirteen States must immediately fall, if the adoption of the Federal Constitution should fail.

To understand him exactly the opening words of this last quotation must be attentively noted; he says: "if we attend carefully to geographical AND commercial considerations, *in conjunction with the habits and prejudices* of the different States," that is, of the States then existing, they would most naturally league themselves into two governments, in the event of their *immediate* separation.

'The purpose of these citations is to show that the natural divisions of the Union as held by the observant men and enlightened statesmen of that day corresponded sufficiently well to afford the support of observation and experience to the climatic distinctions of pursuits, populations, and policy which Mr. Carey's law alleges. And just here the late fulfillment of Hamilton's theoretical views, by the great Rebellion, is sufficiently close to give great weight to the climatic principle which, though unknown to him, was the efficient cause of the effects which he clearly understood. The division between the loyal and the secession States in 1861 fell just where Hamilton indicated it, though with a strip of "debatable land," consisting of Delaware, Maryland and Kentucky, between the broadly and decidedly separated States.

We would have it noticed, also, that the lines which are given as the supposed boundaries of the division into three governments, as well as that one which Hamilton fixes between the two political organizations which he thought the more probable, all alike run east and west, and that they correspond accurately to well distinguished belts of temperature.

The phenomenon, like the fall of the apple, was familiarly known, and it only remained for a Newton in social science to reveal the law, and give it exactness of application.

On the 36th page, *ante*, we ventured to assert that if the climatic law of migration and inhabitation of the earth is true, it must be also true that science, literature, and religion must obey it; and in their migrations, follow the same line of march, and this for the obvious reason that the races who modify opinion and speculation, according to their respective mental and moral constitutions, and impress themselves upon all their pursuits, enterprises, and achievements, migrate along their several lines of climate; let me now add that the *politics* of the emigrants carry with them their native hue, of which rather astounding doctrine, the annexed article is submitted as curiously but conclusively in proof. We commend it to examination, especially of those who may meet it with the strongest feeling of incredulity; and we take the liberty besides of recommending our younger readers to take up the census report of 1870, so soon as it shall be published, and for themselves try the doctrine upon the facts which it will afford them. The method and process of the inquiry are plainly indicated in our management of the problem. Moreover, we take the liberty of saying here, to young men, ambitious of distinction in the practical questions of social and economic relations, that without a good ground-work in statistics, they will never attain an available and well-assured proficiency in political economy. This advice seems all the more required after the frequent and emphatic denials that we have given, in the course of this book, to the commonly preferred claims made by statisticians and politicians for their arithmetical data.

(*From* THE PRESS *of Thursday, December* 22, 1859.)*

PENNSYLVANIA'S POSITION IN THE UNION.

A letter written by MR. CAREY, our well-known political economist, to a friend in Massachusetts, and first published in the Boston *Transcript* of the 26th November last, is attracting very general attention among the politicians who are concerned with the forecast of the coming Presidential campaign. The subject of the letter is the proverbial preponderance of Pennsylvania in our national elections. It is a fact that no candidate for the Presidency has yet been elected by the popular vote of the Union against or without the vote of Pennsylvania, except the elder ADAMS. In 1824, she gave her twenty-eight electoral votes to JACKSON, which secured his plurality of fifteen in the electoral college. In the seventeen Presidential elections of the past, her vote has uniformly indicated the choice of the nation, except in the case of JOHN ADAMS. Yet, it is also true that only in one instance has her electoral vote, of itself, determined the result; that is, the majority of the successful candidate has generally been larger, sometimes greatly larger, than the number of her electors in the college.

MR. CAREY, looking for the causes of a fact so steady and regular in its manifestation, traces them to conditions, circumstances

* See note on page 39, *ante.*

and facts, where they have not heretofore been looked for. It is obvious enough that a State which has never held more than one-seventh of the electoral power of the Union could not thus constantly, by her own proper power, determine its Presidential elections. It must, therefore, be ascribed to some constant cause of concurrence with her political action, on the part of other States, whose votes, with hers, make up the constitutional majority which she is observed to lead or carry with her.

For the natural cause of such concurrence and sympathy of political action, MR. CAREY inquires, and finds it as he believes, in the law of emigration, or that tendency which determines men to choose their new residences in climates nearly resembling those which they are accustomed to previously to their removal. The circumstantial, or, in philosophical language, the accidental cause of Pennsylvania's constant supremacy in the politics of the nation, is in the fact that she is one of a number of States which are the balance of power in the Union. The States which lie north of her northern line of latitude are so nearly balanced against those which lie south of her southern line, that her power, combined with that range of central States of which she is the exponent, easily determines the contest in favor of one or the other party. Divided as the North and South are, and have ever been, the middle or central States as they lie geographically, and the moderate and conservative as they always are politically, must have the power to hold the antagonists, on either side of them, at arms-length, and to settle their disputes by the exertion of the balance of power principle, and thus maintain the position of political supremacy in the Union.

To present MR. CAREY's views upon the subject of emigration, and its political results in our history, we extract his own very brief and general statement:

"To begin, let me ask your attention to the simple law which governs the movements of men, who by the process of peaceful emigration are seeking improvement of their condition. Look where you may, you will see that such persons seek the nearest approach to the temperatures to which they have been accustomed—the Highlander going to Canada, and the Irishman coming to our middle States, leaving to the Spaniard and the Portuguese the more sunny lands of the South. So, too, has it been among ourselves—the people of New England having overrun New York north of the highlands, a part of northern Pennsylvania, the northern third of Ohio, Indiana, Illinois, and Iowa, and having settled the three northwestern

States: those of New Jersey, Pennsylvania, Delaware, and Maryland, having meanwhile colonized nearly all the remainder of the four Western States, and being likely soon to occupy the larger portion, if not almost the whole, of the Territories which are now to enter the Union as the States of Kansas and Nebraska.

"To Virginia and North Carolina have fallen the Territories that are now Kentucky, Tennessee, and Missouri, while South Carolina and Georgia have taken possession of Alabama, Mississippi, Louisiana, and most of Arkansas and Texas. As a consequence of this, we find the Union divided into *four great zones*, the white population of which, as ascertained by the last census, may approximately thus be stated:

Northern, say	8,000,000
Northern Central	5,700,000
Southern Central	4,000,000
Southern	2,300,000
	20,000,000

"Nearly three-tenths of the voting population, as here is shown, sympathize much with Pennsylvania, and hence it is, and not merely by reason of her own intrinsic strength, that *as she goes, so goes the Union*. Not only are the tendencies of this portion of our people, as now exhibited, eminently conservative, but, as reference to history shows, they have been more consistently in accordance with the ideas of the men who made the Revolution, than those of any other. Hence it is that they have been so much in harmony with those of North Carolina, Kentucky, and Tennessee, as well as with those of the better days of Virginia, all of these, with Missouri, now passing so rapidly toward freedom, constituting the Southern centre."

The propositions of our author here given are so new, and, in all respects, so important for other purposes, as well as for those of national politics, that we have taken the pains to subject the data on which they are made to rest to a careful examination. Let us state the results in our own way. After examining the facts and figures as thoroughly as our time and resources allowed, we found that *State boundaries*, as they exist between the north and north-central zones, could not be made to conform to the facts of the case, as they turned up under examination. Nor do they serve with mathematical accuracy for the limits of the more southern zones. As lines of latitude and lines of equal temperature were not consulted in the location of State boundaries, it was not to be expected that exact correspondences between isothermal and territorial lines should occur. Adopting the four zones of MR. CAREY, however, on grounds that seem to us entirely conclusive, we locate them thus:

Taking the southernmost point of Connecticut for a starting point, the southern line of the north zone will fall at about 41¼ degrees of north latitude. This line, carried westwardly, will cut Pennsylvania a little south of Wilkesbarre, Williamsport, and Mercer, on the Ohio boundary, and will throw all the Pennsylvania counties north of it into the north zone. The same line, carried through the State of Ohio, will pass by Warren, Norwalk, and Defiance, on the Indiana border, throwing something between one-fourth and one-fifth of Ohio into the north zone. The same line, continued westwardly, will throw about one-seventh of the State of Indiana, one-fourth of the State of Illinois, and three-fourths of Iowa, into the northern zone. For the southern line of the north-central zone we adopt the thirty-ninth degree of north latitude. This line enters at Cape May, passes by Annapolis and Bladensburg, in Maryland, and through Hardy and Barbour counties, in Virginia, and enters Ohio at the mouth of the great Kanawha river. Two or three counties of Ohio, about one-seventh (at the southern end) of Indiana, and one-fifth of southern Illinois (Egypt), will fall south of this line; and entering Missouri above the mouth of the Illinois river, and emerging at the mouth of the Kansas river, throws the northern two-fifths of Missouri, or all north of St. Louis, into the north-central zone.

The south-central zone, bounded on the south by the thirty-fifth degree of latitude, and by the thirty-ninth parallel on the north, will embrace the southern half of Delaware, the southern half of Maryland, nearly all of Virginia, North Carolina, all of Kentucky, Tennessee, the southern corners of Illinois and Indiana, the southern three-fourths of Missouri, and the northern half of Arkansas.

To the south zone will fall South Carolina, Georgia, Florida, Alabama, Mississippi, the southern half of Arkansas, Louisiana, and Texas.

Carrying these lines out to the Pacific coast, the northern one-fourth of California falls into the north-central, the middle half into the south-central, and the southernmost one-fourth into the south zone.

Now, let us look at MR. CAREY's law of emigration as the census of 1850 exhibits the facts involved in it:

In Michigan the whole number of immigrants was 257,006. Of these, there were born in the north zone:

New England, New York, (and British America, 14,008)............... 178,717
Born in north-central zone.. 33,103
Born in the south-central.. 1,564
Born in the south zone............ 401
Born in Europe.. 39,023

Thus, of the inhabitants not born in the State, five-sevenths were from the north zone, including Canada; one-seventh from all the States south of the north zone, and one-seventh Europeans.

In Wisconsin there were 242,376 immigrants. Of these, 202,758, or five-sixths of the whole number, were born in the north zone and in Europe. In the north-central zone 31,066, or a little less than one-sixth of the whole, and in all the more Southern States only 4,413, or about one-fiftieth.

Passing from these two new States, which are high up in the north zone, to two which lie low in the south zone, we have the following facts from the census:

In Alabama, the whole number of immigrants............................ 183,324
Born in the south zone.. 108,720 or $\frac{7}{12}$
Born in the south-central.. 64,143 or $\frac{4}{12}$
Born in New England..:........... 1,861 or $\frac{1}{66}$
Born in all the other States........................... •................... 2,367
Born Foreigners.. 6,538
In Mississippi, the whole number of immigrants........................ 155,793
Born in the south zone.. 83,242
Born in the south-central.. 62,465
Born in New England.. 923
Born in all the other States.. 3,482
Born Europeans.. 5,500

Here only one-thirty-fifth of the whole number of immigrants in Mississippi were born in the States north of 39° north latitude.

From these instances, we think the truth of Mr. CAREY's general proposition is well sustained. Emigration is ruled by climatic laws. We purposed to exhibit the same law as it applies to the Western States which lie in the two middle zones, but must content ourselves now with stating that their statistics bear as closely upon the proposition under consideration as those of the States on the extreme North and South given above.

The emigration from Europe supports the theory well. Of those from England, Ireland, and Scotland only one in fourteen were found in the States lying south of 39 degrees north latitude;

while of the Germans, one in seven are in that zone, as it is determined by the lines of latitude; but one-half of these are in Texas and Missouri, and even here the climatic law most probably prevails, for while the isothermal, or lines of equal temperature, correspond very nearly with the parallels of latitude as far west as the Mississippi river, those which enter the Atlantic coast at the 40th and 35th degrees of north latitude deflect rapidly beyond the Mississippi southward, falling as low in middle Texas as the 35th and 30th. So that while a large portion of Missouri is in the north-central zone, as determined by geographical lines, a very large portion of the north and west of Texas is in the same zone, as determined by its mean annual temperature. If this point holds, as we suppose it must, then the German emigration is no exception. One-half of the number must be subtracted for the States of Texas and Missouri, and this will restore the average to one in fourteen of the foreign immigrants settled in the south zone.

It will be recollected by our readers that the isothermal lines in that part of Europe from which our emigrants come lie about ten degrees farther north in Europe than they do in the Atlantic States of the Union. Great Britain and Prussia lie above the fiftieth degree, and all the rest of Germany above the forty-fifth of north latitude. Their emigrants to this country find their customary temperature above the thirty-fifth and fortieth parallels here, and accordingly the census reports thirteen out of fourteen of them residing in the States above these lines, or, more accurately, within the isothermal lines of their native countries. This fact obtains so accurately that the Danish and Norwegian immigrants, whose native countries are above the sixtieth parallel, are found in this country in our most northern regions. From Sweden there were 2,449 in the north zone; in the south only 436. From Norway there were in the north zone 11,705; in the south zone but 211, and 105 of these were in Texas. And while there were 147,711 from British America, only 1,067 of them were found south of the thirty-ninth parallel.

We are accustomed to speak of man as a cosmopolite, and perhaps too hastily conclude that he is so much less governed by climate than animals and plants are, that he is at once independent and regardless of temperature. But the statement evidently needs correction. The *species* is adapted to all climates, but the families and kindreds are governed by it in their migrations. This to us is a new and surprising result of this investigation. We are helped by it to understand the destination of the African race among us. It is a question of geography much more than of institutions with all the races. In a new country like ours, where immigration has the power to determine the institutions, sentiments and pursuits, avocations and opinions; natural temperament and civil polity, go together, and this may be the reason why the controlling influence of climatic laws has not before exhibited itself to observation.

The next step in the theory we are considering is, that the emigrants from Europe, and especially those from the Eastern States of the Union, carry with them the characteristics of the several regions from which they remove, and so give a similar complexion to their political creeds and industrial policies. We have laboriously examined the votes of the zones, as we have located them, in the last Presidential election, and we obtain the following results:

In those sixteen counties of Pennsylvania which lie, according to our division, above 41¼ degrees of north latitude, and within the north political zone, FREMONT had 39,916 votes, FILLMORE 1,107, and BUCHANAN 24,908. FREMONT's plurality over BUCHANAN, in these counties which belong to the north, and, as we see, voted with it, was 15,008, or as 40 to 25. In the balance of the State, BUCHANAN's vote was 205,802, FREMONT's 107,594, or nearly two to one.

In those sixteen counties of Ohio which lie north of the political line, FREMONT had 39,488 votes, BUCHANAN 22,042—a plurality of 17,446. FREMONT's plurality in the whole State was but 16,623. Again, in the State election of last October, the whole Republican majority was 13,500, while in the Western Reserve—the counties which we give to the north zone—the majority of that party was 15,000, showing that, outside of these counties, the Democrats had 1,500 majority.

In the nineteen counties of Illinois which lie above the line of the north-central zone, FREMONT had 41,847 votes; BUCHANAN had 16,122—plurality over BUCHANAN, 25,725. In the other counties, BUCHANAN's plurality over FREMONT was 34,784. Not a county in Illinois south of 40 degrees gave FREMONT a majority, and some of them, in the extreme south of the State, gave him no more than 2, 5, and 9 votes respectively; but these last lie all below the 39th parallel, and belong, therefore, bodily, to the south-central zone.

In the twelve counties of Indiana which are north of the line assumed, FREMONT had 15,835 votes; BUCHANAN, 12,752; but in the whole State BUCHANAN's plurality over FREMONT was 24,295.

Iowa gave FREMONT a plurality of 7,784 votes, but in the counties lying south of the north zone BUCHANAN's plurality over FREMONT was above 4,000 votes.

Looking at the States and parts of States lying in the north zone, we find the following results: For every forty votes cast in them for FREMONT, BUCHANAN had, in Vermont, 11; in Massachusetts, 15; in northern Illinois, 16; in northern Ohio, 22; in Maine, 23; in northern Pennsylvania, 25; in New York, 28; in Michigan, 29; in northern Indiana, 32. These proportions, it strikes us, indicate the political sympathies of the people among whom they occur to be closely connected with their respective nativities; and we may here state that the rule holds as well of the people of the north-central zone where the institutions are very similar to those of their northern sister States, and yet their political biases are as distinct and different as if they were separated from each other by some cause of quarrel or opposition of interests.

We confess that we are greatly surprised to find geographical and climatic lines running through the politics of our people with so near an approach to mathematical accuracy as our figures have shown us; but we can see no error in the process by which these remarkable results are arrived at. The subject is a study for the curious and capable. Our data are not all given, nor, it may be, are they quite clearly presented, but we submit the statement in the confidence that it is substantially correct. The practical inferences remain to be drawn, which can now be very briefly given:

The popular vote of the north zone in 1856 (making the necessary deductions and additions, to adjust the returns of the States to the lines which cut them) was.. 1,625,913

The popular vote of the south zone.. 404,151
Do   do   south-central.. 715,766

Together.. 1,119,917
Plurality of north over south and south-central........................ 505,996
The popular vote of the north-central zone (making the necessary additions and subtractions)....................................... 1,341,862
Balance of power in popular votes in the north-central, as between the north zone and the south and south-central................... 835,896

In the electoral college these several regions stand thus:

NORTH ZONE—Maine 8, New Hampshire 5, Vermont 5, Connecticut 6, Rhode Island 4, Massachusetts 13, New York 35, Michigan 6, Wisconsin, 5, Iowa 4, Minnesota 4—making 95 electoral votes.

SOUTH ZONE—South Carolina 8, Georgia 10, Alabama 9, Mississippi 7, Arkansas 4, Louisiana 6, Texas 4, Florida 3—51 electors.

SOUTH-CENTRAL ZONE—Delaware 3, Maryland 8, Virginia 15, North Carolina 10, Kentucky 12, Tennessee 12—60 electors.

NORTH-CENTRAL ZONE—New Jersey 7, Pennsylvania 27, Ohio 23, Indiana 13, Illinois 11, Missouri 9, California 4—94 electors.

This geographic division puts the balance thus: The south and south-central against the north zone, 111 electors against 95—or a plurality of 16. But Ohio voting out of geographic order, gives to the north a majority of 7.

The north-central zone has 94 votes when Ohio is in line, 71 without her—leaving a clear majority of 64 to determine the issue between the extremists who lie upon her north and south borders.

Now, if this doctrine of climatic and political sympathy holds good in logic and in experience, Pennsylvania's position in the region that rules the Union is demonstrated and accounted for; and it is presumed that the National Conventions of the coming Presidential campaign will consider the subject, and provide for the struggle with reference to it.

Whoever will look carefully for the reason of dividing the south-central from the more southern slave States, may find it in their past history, and in the clear indications of their future destiny.

This subject invites further observations. It has its range through the whole field of ethnological science and of civil history.

W. E.

P. S. For the geographic and climatic distribution of the secret Orders of the United States, see *ante* pp. 268, 269, 271, 277; and, of the Coöperative Unions in England and Prussia, see pp. 300, 306, and 308; noting the fact that the region in the United States east of the Rocky Mountains, between 39° and 42° of north latitude lies in the same belt of mean annual temperature as Prussia and England—another curious example of the coincidence of climatic conditions with societary movements.

INDEX.

A

Activity of the vital organs, law of distribution of............................ 79
Ad valorems, mischiefs of in tariff of 1846.. 201
Ad valorems, rule of taxation, alien and hostile to the principle of protection.. 209
    vices of.. 210
Affinities result from differences, and in the ratio of their number...... 10
African negroes, not savage... 28
Africa, savage.. 26
Africans, residence of, in the United States explained......................... 35
Agricultural industry, exclusive, exposed to famines............................ 59
Agricultural production, advance of, limited... 57
Agricultural production of France, doubled in thirty years.................. 48
Agriculture combined with coöperative stores...................................... 310
Agriculture in its infancy benefited by trade with manufacturing countries.. 178
Agriculture, unmixed, cannot organize industry................................... 217
Agriculturists, American, two classes, broadly different—farmers and planters; farmers export but two and one-half per cent of their product, planters export seventy-five per cent of theirs................... 181
Almsgiving changed from a charity to a debt....................................... 261
America, European colonization of.. 26
American manufactures sheltered by the War of the Revolution......... 194
Analogies forced upon things not analogous.. 74
Analogy of savage society to individual infancy................................... 18
    of patriarchism to childhood.. 20
    of barbarism to youth.. 23
    of civilization to manhood... 24
Anno Domini 1776.. 253
Annual production in U. S., value of... 169
Anti-slavery, history of 253
A posteriori method, the vice of metaphysics and of political economy... 76

INDEX.

A posteriori reasoning fails, where the focal point of facts falls outside of observation and experiment.. 76
A posteriori, the system of, is capable only of unmixed materialism, and has never had any success in subjects whose life is joined with liberty.. 76
Arts and sciences, not the distinctive glory of the last centenary.......... 252
Asia barbaric.. 46
Association and individuality, their necessity.. 9
  their physical analogues.. 10
  counter-balance and corroborate each other.................................. 10
Association freed and restored... 251
Association in bondage—in freedom.. 260
Association, stages in the growth of... 260
Association without freedom is domination, not commerce.................. 164

B

Balance, broken, of Europe being rectified... 37
"Balance of trade" not in difference of values but of kinds of trade..... 171
Bank circulation exposes the banks to *runs*.. 147
Bank circulation never in excess except under free trade..................... 200
Bank currency, inflation of, due to excess of imports............................ 200
Bank note as a traveler... 144
Bank notes.. 143
  the money of the common people.. 144
Bank notes, their service outweighs their faults 146
Bank of Amsterdam, history and service of 139
Bank of England, charter of, a failure... 150, 155
Banker's certificates of deposit multiply the service of money............. 135
Banks of deposit as early as the Christian era 135
  collect and employ idle money.. 138
  sources of profit and credit.. 141
  instances.. 142
  their service.. 138
Banks distribution of, in Scotland and United States............................ 152
  number and localities of, required... 151
Banks of circulation may lend twice their capital and one-third of their deposits... 148
Banks of deposit, discount and issue... 133
Banks, rule for distribution of... 151
Banking business, elements of... 142
  benefits of 142
  order of development... 149
  transfers the property in coins.. 139
Banking should be as free as any other business................................... 154
Banking system, indispensable.. 151

Bastiat on competition.. 175, 328
Barbarism a great advance upon the previous forms of society; Moors
 and Mahometans of the Middle Ages, superior in all things to the
 contemporaneous civilization of the Caucasian family............... 20
Barbarism and civilization, distinctive characteristics of.................. 22
Barbarism culminates in the youth of manhood................................ 27
Barter, the type of a true commerce.. 109
Belgian tariff, eminently protective.. 240
 protects her shipping... 240
Belgium, growth of population in... 241
Belgium, territory, population, manufactures, agriculture, commerce... 239
Beneficial societies among colored women..................................... 279
Beneficial societies, easy rates of insurance, liberal reliefs, and moral
 influence—they grow rich... 263
Beneficial societies in England, extent of.. 262
Beneficial societies in the United States.. 262
Berlin and Milan decrees.. 192
Bible, tract, and missionary societies of the age............................... 253
Bonaparte, Napoleon, on Political Economy.................................... 191
Bonuses and countervailing duties... 205
Books and newspapers published in 1860....................................... 255
Boot and shoe factory, Bay State... 319
Borders of Asia and Africa, stationary... 27
British demand for our provisions—quantities and prices................. 184
British Economists, fundamental errors of....................................... 159
British navigation laws... 194
British policy of trade and doctrine... 179
Brougham would crush all foreign manufactures in the cradle.......... 192
Building and loan associations, history of....................................... 322
 great progress in Philadelphia, principles, profit of..................... 323
Building associations.. 284
Business functions, three classes of... 296
Business policy, stages in development of....................................... 286

C

Calhoun, Clay, in 1833... 199
Capital and labor, harmony of.. 325
Capital, association of, in various forms... 283
Capital, definition of.. 40
Capital, finds a motive, in its interest, to afford equitable share of joint
 products to labor.. 88
Capital in association... 260
Capital in civilized labor.. 121
Capital, quantity of, and quality of labor, relation of....................... 87

346 INDEX.

Carey and Bastiat	87
Carey's law of distribution of wages and profits	98
Carey, H. C., character of his system	5, 6
Carey, H. C., law of climate	39, 331
Carriage factory in New York	320
Cash sales, policy and principle of	303
Catallactics	163
Census estimates of wealth in U. S., sources of error	50, 168
Census reports, one-third less than annual products in the United States	50
Centuries, the last five, how distinguished	252
Charities converted into equitable claims	282
Chatham, Earl of, would not allow the colonies to make a hobnail	194
Chemistry, a wonder-working adjuvant of human labor	56
Christendom, in the dark ages	30
Christian knowledge, spread of in the last centenary	253
Circulation, effect of rapidity of, not measurable by multipliers	137
Circulation of money and of the blood, in what respects unlike	136
Circulation, rapidity of bears relation to the quantity of represented money	136
Circulating medium, its analogy to circulation of the blood	136
Civilization and liberty rest upon credit	143
Civilization, defined by its history only	32
Civilization, distinctive character of	251
Civilization, elastic and composite	30
Civilization, late development of	30
Civilization, not logically defined	247
difficulty of definition	247
Civilization, the European form of societary life	26
Civilized races of Europe, no decay of	27
Clearing house, payment by set-off	118
Climate, laws of, govern human migrations	34
Climate limits science, literature, and religions	35
Climatic belts, three in North America	38
Climatic law determines the future unions of States	38
Climatic laws, prevent permanent domination of the superior races	36
Climatic law rules settlement in the United States	34, 331
Climatic law in party politics	331
Climatic law in distribution of secret societies, and coöperative unions	268, 269, 271, 277, 300, 306, 308, and *note* 342
Clothing and lodging, equivalents of artificial heat	65
Coal, power evolved	55
Coal, seven tons give the power of seventy thousand women in manufacturing	56
Cobden, on Portugal and Turkey	246

INDEX. 347

Coinage, changes in value of, since the eleventh century	113
Coinage at British and American mints	116
Colbert, fosters home manufactures	205
J. B. Say's account of his policy	241
Colonization, a relief of suffering during ages of disorder	62
Color, prejudice of	279
Colwell, Stephen	5
Commerce	•157
faulty definitions of	158
Commerce and trade, distinctive definition of	160
Commerce is immediateness of intercourse and exchange	165
Commerce, legitimate, insures supplies to the oldest countries	62
Commerce of home	165
might suffice for the United States	165
Commerce of savages	16
Commodities, value of in exchange	124
Communism arises from fear of the ill-distribution of wealth—a mistake and a failure	290
Communism, hostile to coöperation	313
Communistic opposition to coöperative stores in Germany	307
Compensations and substitutions in providential provision	63
Competition, Bastiat on	175, 328
Competition defeated and excluded in transportation	288
Competition of underselling avoided	303
Competition, the enemy of harmony	327
Competition, the soul and centre principle of free trade	328
Competition *versus* coöperation	227
Compromise, act of	199
Comte, on the stages of societary development and their correspondence to those of individual life, *note*	24
Consumers are also producers	227
Consumers, every ten must support one merchant	299
Consumption and production in United States	51
Convertibility, not the essence of the bank note	154
Coöperation, a fully rounded system	297
Coöperation between master and slaves in Louisiana	324
Coöperation in Spain, how propagated	311
Coöperation in the United States	315
Coöperation in the whale fisheries	324
Coöperation, in the United States, less urgent than elsewhere	316
Coöperation, practicability of	324
Coöperation, resisted by insurrectionary spirit of Western Europe	313
Coöperation, stores, manufactories, banks	295
Coöperation supplies credit, and market for products	310
Coöperation, survey of the field	281

INDEX.

Coöperation, the system of agricultural industry in Russia	312
Coöperative associations, what they mean	296
Coöperative foundery at Troy, New York, great success of	318
at Somerset, Massachusetts	319
Coöperative industrial societies in United States	318
Coöperative industry, economy of	318, 321
Coöperative labor societies, definition of	295, 296
Coöperative movement, difference of, in England and Germany	307
Coöperative store in Charleston	320
Coöperative stores, dealings with members and non-members	306
Coöperative stores, definition of	295, 296
Coöperative stores, extension of in England	305
Coöperative stores, inexpensiveness of	304
Coöperative stores in New England	317
Coöperative stores in Pennsylvania	318
Coöperative stores, practicability of	298
Coöperative stores, the first step in guarantyism	297
Coöperative stores, their properties and uses	286
Coördination and subordination in living organisms	11
Corn, burnt for fuel in the West	183
Corporal punishment abolished	256
Corporation, legal, its meaning	260
Corporations, moral character of	283
Cotton always a rebel	182
Cotton crop under slavery policy	324
Cotton crop of 1860, quantity and value	181
Cotton manufacture, how protected in England	238
Cotton, rapid decline in price of	220
Cottons, consumption of, in England	58
Countervailing duties in English policy	239, 206
Countervailing duties, not protective in principle	206
Credit, abuses of	143
Credit, a Jacob's ladder of	309
Credit banks, constitution and policy of	308, 309
statistics of	309
Credit banking system in Germany	296
Credit, how provided for unpropertied men	308
Credit, its functions and power	140
Credit makes capital of character	143
Credit modifies the money demand	117
Credit system must enlarge with all progress in society	150
Credit, the broad basis of civilized business	149
Crimes, capital, one hundred and fifty in England; diminution of	256
Currency, depreciated, evils of, less than of a lack of the money supply	155

Currier's shop in Boston	320
Curse, the primal, has a promise in it	73

D

Death rate, greatest in the least dense populations	72
Death rate in England, France, Prussia, and United States	72
Death rate in London varied in one hundred years	72
Debts and funds, no evil in decrease of value of	130
Definition of value	87
Definition of wealth, the measure of man's power over nature	41
Definition of political economy	9
Democracies of Greece, faults and virtues of	249
Democracy, the polity of savages	17
Deposits, largely consist of bank loans	148
Differences, the natural, enough for foreign commerce	223
Differences, unity and coöperation of	31
Discovery in natural law, followed closely by practical application	57
Disease, a broken balance of excitement	79
Dismal school, conflicting theories of	74
Dispair, theory of, grounded in disorders of society	74
Distributive law of inhabitation of the earth	32
Distribution of wealth, laws of	87
Diversification of industries, the aim of protection	215
Diversification of pursuits essential to the welfare of society	12
Division of labor, benefits of, exaggerated	159, 161
Division of labor doctrine, abuse of	327
Division of labor, territorial, J. R. McCulloch	158
Divisions of the United States—Jay and Hamilton	331
Doctrine, a test of	84
Domestic exchanges in 1862, estimated value of	166
Duty paid by the foreign producer	226
Duties, protective, who pays them?	225
Duties reflected upon domestic prices, absurdity of	230

E

Earth, not one-tenth of the, fully cultivated	59
Economy in expenses, leads to coöperation in production	305
Edenism	14
conditions of society in	15
Education, as a counter-balance, to excessive fertility	81
Education in the arts repays its cost	227
Eighteenth century, achievements of	31
Electricity against time	55
Elements of matter, man's power over	56
England begins to advance in the fourteenth century	30

350   INDEX.

England draws from foreign raw material four-fifths of her exports..... 61
England, history of protection in 236
  woolens 237
  iron 237
  wool, iron and coal, protection of cottons 238
England needs customers and feeders on cheap wages 179
England our only European provision market 184
England, supplements her natural labor power by steam force equal to
 one-fourth the inhabitants of the globe 55
England, the world's debt to 68
England would crush foreign manufactures in the cradle 192, 193
England's foreign policy of trade, change of 163
England's sanguinary protective laws 237, 238
England's war upon foreign manufactures 192, 193
English Colonies, growing independence, and industrial emancipation of 88
English domination in the world's markets, end of 88
English manufactures, foreign materials, wages, and profit of 61
English protective duties never repealed till they were useless 239
Engineers, indefiniteness of the term 292
Equivalence of money to values in exchange, unfounded 115
Era, new, in manufacturing industry, why fixed in 1814 99
Era, the new, in civilization begun a hundred years ago 248
Europe and the United States increase their labor-power six times by
 the aid of coal 55
European people only have passed through all the stages of society,
 and show no signs of declension 27
European races, their work of three or four hundred years 31
Europe, stable goverments organized in, fifteenth and sixteenth centuries 31
Evil is inverted good 143
Excessive activity of one organ at the expense of others 79
Excess of life supplies its waste 42
Exceptions do not prove the rule 83
Exchange the great disturber of coöperation 297
Exchanges, the life of man, a round of 107
Experience, not always directory 29
Extension of average lifetime in the present century 64
Exports, American, coarse and low-priced 183
Exports of England, value of domestic and foreign materials 61
Exports of manufactures to agricultural nations 187
Exports to manufacturing and non-manufacturing nations, relative
 value of 187

F

Faculties, human, do not spring from suffering 16
Faith-force above fact-force 140

INDEX. 351

Faith, like the mechanical powers, multiplies force miraculously	140
Faith sustains hope and charity	60
Famines in Ireland and India explained	59
Famine in Northeast Prussia	59
Famines in the earlier ages, frequent	58
Famines and plagues disappear as population increases	58
Famines, remedy for	59
Famines, their frequency in modern India	245
Farmers' question, the	177
Fasting commanded, the	12
Facts do not always indicate laws	43
Federal Government adapted to differences in union	38
Federal Union of the United States, the model of nationalities	37
"Federalist;" Jay and Hamilton	331
Fertility, human, contradictory theories of	74
Fertility of the soil, not exhausted by right cultivation	60
Feudalism allied to barbarism	30
Feudalism, association in bondage	313
Figures in statistics need rectification by facts	100
First free list in tariff act	199
First pair, the, provision for	15
conditions of Edenic Society	15
Flanders and Toulouse two centuries in advance of England in manufacturing industry	30
Flax and cotton, supplement and displace wool	65
Food and life, *possible* quantities of, unknown and indifferent	75
Food and population disproportioned according to Malthus	58
Food, human, demanded, limited like the product	58
Food, increase of, in France	60
Food of men, vegetable cheaper and more abundant than animal	65
Food of the common people at end of the seventeenth century	92
Food, prices of, remain nearly stationary, why	126
Food of the inferior animals, vegetable against animal	65
Food, provision of, adequate	59
Food, supply of France, increase of	48
Force and speed required in subjugation of nature	54
Foreign imports crush domestic manufactures	195
Foreign trade of United States in 1860 analyzed	180
exports seven-eighths raw and one-eighth manufactures	180
Formation of society	14
Fortunes, private, immense growth of	291
France excludes manufactures, growth of trade in	215
France, density of population in	48
France, growth of production one hundred and thirty-one per cent in twenty years	47

352   INDEX.

France, increase of food in.. 60
France, increase of food production... 48
France outstrips England in rate of increase of wealth..................... 47
France, success of protection in.. 241
Freedmen hanged in the reign of Henry VIII................................... 29
Freedmen, their prospects in the new order of industry.................... 99
Freedom must be surrendered by those who refuse it....................... 329
Free foreign trade, no such thing rightly exists................................ 175
Free Masons... 264
Free-trade abuse of the maxims of liberty.. 225
Free trade, British, its character.. 239
Free trade driven to tax only the goods we cannot produce............... 232
Free trade in the historic nations... 242
Free trade in Turkey, Ireland, India, Portugal............ 243, 244, 245, 246
Free-trade period 1833 to 1841, mischiefs of, repaired by tariff of
   1842.. 205
Free-trade philanthropists.. 220
Free-trade policy, its preposterous consequences.............................. 233
Free trade suited to savages... 177
Free-trade truisms are nothing in the dispute............................ 224, 225
French communism, principles of... 314
Free traders, description of.. 215

G

Galvanism, electricity, electric telegraph, dates of............................ 57
Gas from water in expectation... 68
German lodges of United Mechanics... 278
Germany, coöperative stores in.. 306
   difference of origin, and movement... 306
Godwin, Parke, acknowledgment to.. 6
Gold and silver, differ from paper money.. 115
Gold and silver money does not by its quantity depreciate................ 115
Gold, premium on.. 156
Goldsmiths, the deposit bankers as lately as 1661............................. 135
Golden age.. 15
Good Samaritans, admit women and colored people........................ 280
Government cannot administer a general system of banking............ 153
Governmental changes of the future, to be internal reforms............. 37
Government, best, definition of... 225
Government, limitation of the powers of... 222
Grain and provision market in England, our share of....................... 184
Grant, General, on farmers' foreign market...................................... 189
Grant, President, on our foreign food market................................... 183
Greeley, Horace, acknowledgments to... 6
Greenbacks, popularity of.. 153

Grounds of popular error in respect to relation of man and food......... 43
Growth of wealth in the most recent decades, law of....................... 52
Guaranty associations, three classes of....................................... 281
Guarantyism.. 247
Guarantyism, an effort at free association................................... 251
Gulf States, the Southern zone.. 38

H

Hamilton, Alexander... 6
    report on manufactures.. 195
Handicraft answers to science in effecting uses............................. 57
Hands employed in mining, manufacturing, and mechanic arts in 1860 93
Harmony of interests of laborer and capitalist............................... 98
History, the habit of, broken in the United States........................... 29
Home commerce and foreign trade, relative value of....................... 165
Home markets for agricultural products..................................... 183
Home market, the farmers'.. 186
Horde, formation of the... 16
Horses, price of in 1696... 112
Human progress, in economics, tending ever to better and cheaper
    supplies... 66
Human fertility not a constant quantity....................................... 42
Humboldt's estimate of increase of metallic money.......................... 116
Hume and Mill on effect of increase of money............................... 123
Hume, on stimulus of money... 121
Husbandry always loyal.. 182

I

Imponderables, the latest subjects of human dominion..................... 67
Imports, economic value of.. 170
Imports, kinds of, from Western Europe...................................... 171
    per capita under the free trade and protection tariffs............... 202
    proportion of, legitimate subjects of trade............................ 170
    proportion of, ready for consumption.................................. 170
    small value of, to domestic transporters.............................. 169
Imprisonment for debt abolished.. 256
Improvements in changes of form and place.................................. 108
Improvements in travel, transportation, and production................... 64
India, British residents in... 34
    British rule in, history of her trade and decadence.................. 245
    impoverished by cost of transportation............................... 108
    in advance of England in the fourteenth century.................... 30
Indian, American, population, sparseness of in time of Wm. Penn...... 64
Indian tribes, infertility of, explained.. 82
Indians, American, a degenerate race.. 18

354 INDEX.

Individualism giving way to association	251
Inductive reasoning, its limits in natural science	76
Industries, diversified, sure defense against famine	59
Industries of savage tribes, but little diversified	16
Inebriate asylums	273
Inhabitation, slight modifications of the law of	33
Innovations in productive labor, false alarms of	96
Insurance in the State of New York, statistics of	257
Insurance, life, property, and maritime	257
Interest, difference between small and large capitals	285
Interest, money at, a hireling—interest or profits?	284
International labor league, opposed to coöperation	328
Inventions and discoveries of fifteenth century	31
Ireland, English policy of extermination avowed	244
Ireland, history of her manufactures	244
Iron, English, prices as affected by varied tariff rates	228
Iron, English prices of, fluctuations in	100
Iron of England, not one-eighth of her total exports	61
Iron, protection of, in English policy	100
Isothermal line of Mahommetan conquests	34
Israel goes into slavery for a supply of corn	65

J

Jackson, General, on farmer's foreign market	188

K

Knights of Pythias, German lodges	272
Knights of Pythias, origin, members, rate of growth, proportion of reliefs to receipts, law of climate	270
constitution, provision for casualties, trivial expenses	271
Knights of St. Crispin, their coöperative stores	317

L

Labor and capital, marriage of	293
Labor and capital, respective gains from increased productiveness	97
Labor, artificial, substituted for natural	63
Labor, choice in kinds of, how determined	216
Labor cost of gold and silver, difficult of estimation	114
Labor is capital	121
Labor and money, yokefellows in production	121
Labor is capital, but is usually treated as an associate	40
Labor, its improved forms, promise to secure adjustment of life to food	81
Labor, its kinds and varied rewards	216
Labor, its repugnance to association	26, 283
Labor, more and more demanded as supplies are drawn successively from the vegetable and mineral world	66

INDEX.

Labor-power measured by its actual products	50
Labor, skilled and unskilled	172
Labor remitted from low to high-priced work	96
Labor, rise in wages of, since abolition of villenage	90
Labor unions, difficulties and drift	330
Labor unions, do not aim to abolish the wages system	329
Labor unions, their universal prevalence, their justification; their policy requires a radical change	320
Labor, unskilled, favorable to fecundity	83
Labor value, Mr. Carey	87
Labor, value of, is the cost of its education and training	90
Labor value, tendency of, the law of, to equity in the distribution of wealth	88
Laborer, the, what he is in the system of production	292
Laborers, general improvement in their condition	102
Laborers, their better condition in United States	316, 317
Laissez faire	223, 224
Land and labor, only increase in value in progressive conditions	89
Land and labor, why their value increases	131
Land in itself valueless	126
Land, value of, is the cost of its improvement	90
Laws of nature tend to adjustment of man and earth	60
Laws of nature vindicate themselves	60
Lead, price rises as the duty falls	229
Libraries in the United States	255
Life, extension of, in the present century	62
Life, reproduction of, in inverse ratio to the power of maintaining it	77
Life, term of, lengthens, and fecundity diminishes, with improvement of the human race	78
Life, waste of, due to preponderance of the animal passions	83
Life, waste of, not a blunder of the Creator	83
List, Frederick, H. C. Carey and Stephen Colwell	5
Luxuries, not to be taxed as such	208

M

Macaulay, on bankers of the 17th century	135
Macaulay, on wages in England	91
Machinery, against weight and space	55
Machinery becomes bone and muscle to the brain and nerves of science	57
Machinery, ignorance scared by, as horses are at locomotives	63
Machinery, its velocity in work	56
Madison, on causes that induced the Federal Union	196
Malthus' corrective checks	42
Malthus' doctrine of disproportion of food to population	58

INDEX.

Malthus' formula of disproportion of food to population	42
Man, a, the type of a society	11
Man, not prices, the leading consideration in trade	179
Man regarded as a beast, not a safe basis for a philosophy of his relations and destiny	74
Mankind, collective, cosmopolitan, but the several families are bounded by their natal latitudes	33
Man's adjustment to his conditions, not a question of numerals, but of principles	75
Man's nature and destiny, philosophy of, rests on final causes	75
Manufactures, cheapen faster than the precious metals	114
Manufactures, Hamilton's report on, in 1791, great progress in	195
Manufactures, household, destroyed after peace of 1783	195
Manufacturing industry, new Era of, begins in 1814	99
Masses of matter, man's power over	56
Materalism in science	251
Material interests become social virtues	261
McCulloch and followers, their general maxim of trade falsified	214
McCulloch on territorial division of labor	158
McCulloch's doctrine of disproportion of man and food	43
Mediterranean border lands, exceptional races of	26
Merchant, a producer, the besetting sin	288
Merchant class supported by the consumers	298
Metallic money, estimated increase of	116
Metallic money, faults of	150
Metals, precious, effects of vast increase of	131
Metals, the precious, their qualities	110
Mexico, Cuba, and Spain, in the same belt of temperature	34
Middlemen, merchants, history and functions of	287
Middle States, east and west, the middle zone	38
MIGRATION AND OCCUPATION OF THE EARTH	33
Military system reformed	251
Mill bases his theory of political economy upon despair	45
Mill, corroborates Malthus	44
hopeless even of emigration as a remedy	44
Mill, John Stewart, scare at the exhaustion of English coal	63
Mill, population must overgrow provision of food	45
Millionaires' insignificance to the wealth of the millions	291
Mill's equivalence of money to values exchanged	123
Mineral kingdom, order of human control of	66
Money, a medium of exchange, but not a standard of value	90
Money as a producer of values	120
stimulous of its influx	121
Money as an exchanger of values	106
Money by excess cannot overstimulate industry	137

INDEX. 357

Money, change in the value of, since time of Henry VIII	112
Money demand affected by the credit system	117
Money early goes into association	283
Money, effect of abundance and scarcity of	124
Money, equivalence of to value of commodities in exchange	115
Money, fallacy of the doctrine that it is only an exchanger	129
Money in circulation, amount prior to 1860	123
Money increase, effects of	128
Money, par value of, defined	128
Money, increase of, cheapens commodities faster than its own exchange value declines	131
Money, increase of, effect upon value of debts	130
Money, its essential property is in its convenience	151
Money, its value is its labor cost	129
Money-lenders or partners	284
Money, metallic, without credit, is a low stage of barbaric barter	135
Money measured by its exchange equivalence	91
Money, mystery of	156
Money, not a standard of value, but of payment	112
Money is not dead capital	122
Money, not the equivalent of total exchanges	123
Money of account, dispenses with the money medium	118
Money of account, its equivalence to values in exchange	129
Money of all kinds, of East Indies, American Indians	109
Money, substantial, subject to the same law as other commodities	137
Money, supply of, not limited as in the case of food	117
Money, there never has been enough of it	130
Money, use of, diminishing relatively in England	118
Money values, not the directory in international trade	172
Monopolies, how fostered, and their overthrow	290
Moors superior to the Caucasian Spaniards in the thirteenth and fourteenth centuries	30
Moral improvement in restraint of fecundity	81
Morals, dependence of, upon industrial freedom	12
Mortality of the race in disordered conditions, extremely great	78

N

Napoleon, on political economy	191
Napoleon's popular loan	326
National banks, amount of deposits	259
National bank notes, amount in circulation	145
National banking system, requires amendment	153
National debt, how paid off	200
Nativities of people of the United States	35
Natural laws, adjustment of, to varied conditions	43

358   INDEX.

Nature has not the compound pulley, the screw, or the wheel and axle   54
Nature in rebellion against human authority..   16
Nature's resistance to man's control..   54
Negroes in the childhood of the race..   28
Negroes not to be judged by the present standard of rank..................   28
Negroes, the ballot their defense..   219
        only skilled labor can really emancipate them........................   220
Negroes, women and foreigners, excluded from O. U. A. M................   278
Nervous, and reproductive systems, antagonists...   79
Nervous system, relations of, to viability..   78
Net profits, per centage of, defect in principle and policy..................   320
New England and Canada, the northern zone...................................   38
Newspapers and books published in 1860..   255
Nineteenth century, prospects and promise of................................   31
Notes, in the rebellion, the only *American* money............................   147
Notes issued by government..   145
        amount issued...   145
Notes of the Federal Government, the work done by........................   146

O

Occupancy of unlike climates merely military and commercial...........   31
Odd Fellows, geographic distribution of, law of climate....................   268
Odd Fellows, proportion of, to the voters of the Union....................   269
Odd Fellows, political importance of, amount of funds......................   270
Odd Fellows, origin, success—negroes and women excluded; Rebekah
    degree, a female collateral branch..   265
Odd Fellows, statistics of the Order..   267
        expense of membership; rate of growth; death rate of............   267
        suspensions and expulsions; offenses of expelled members.......   268
Offences, capital, number in England, diminution of........................   256
Opinion, force of, in fixing wages..   96
Order, laws of, work through disorder...   293
Order of life, a true, will secure abundance..................................   84
Order of society, the true, delivers from evil..................................   12
Orders, the order of the day..   280
Organization, implies diversity in agreement................................   28
Organization of differences...   217
Overtrading in foreign imports, only, injures the national finances......   201
Over-population theory, protest of philosophy and philanthrophy........   73

P

Paper money...   133
Paper money, depreciation of...   115
Participation in profits as extra wages...   320, 321
Patriarchism, an unchecked despotism, and the type of all known
    despotisms..   19

INDEX.   359

Patriarchism, the family rule viciously extended	249
productive industry begins; property in the soil; money; commerce initiated; slavery of men and women, worse than the chattel slavery of modern times, and less favorable than barbaric bondage	23
Pauperism, provision for	255
People, the, safe against their oppressors	292
Periodical literature, growth of in ten years	255
Perry, professor, his labor market	328
Pennsylvania's political economists	5
Pennsylvania, representative State of the Union	4
Petroleum replaces turpentine	63
Philosophy, the inductive, compelled to assume provision of means for expectant ends	75
Political Economy, answers none of the demands of business	174
Political Economy, Daniel Webster and Napoleon, on	191
Political Economy, definition of	9
subjects of	9
Political Economy has not yet cut its wisdom teeth	62
Political Economy lacks the characteristics of a science	297
Political Economy, limits of its province; moral, political, and religious relations of	11
Political Economy, national as opposed to cosmopolitan	174, 177
Political Economy, its doctrines must vary with conditions	177
Political Economy, vicious generalizations of	32
Political Economy, Whately's, definition of—Carey's	163
Political unions, accommodate specialties of the various races	37
Population and products of France	47
Population, annual products and distributive average shares in United States, France, and Great Britain	52
Population, density of, in Europe and America	67
Population, density of, in Great Britain	49
Population, density of, in Middle States compared with that of France	48
Populations, enormous, of antiquity	78
Population, law of increase	71
rate of increase in the United States; in Great Britain, Prussia, and France	71
Popular loan in United States	325
Population of British West Indies	34
Population of Europe, but sixty-five to the square mile	62
Population of the United States, doubles in twenty-three and one-half years; wealth in eight and one-half years	49
Population, room enough in Europe and America for nineteen times their present number	62
Population, self-regulative	83

Population, varied rate of increase of, in nationalities nearly alike	71
Portugal, free trade in, and results	245
Potatoes, in France	48
Poverty, not commended by the Great Teacher	12
Precious metals, value of, is the cost of their production	114
Price, selling, of no consequence in coöperative stores	303
Prices at New York, not raised by influx of money	115
Prices, causes affecting	101
Prices, decline of, since 1817; and from 1855 to 1860	125
Prices, fall of, sixty per cent in English exports in thirty-five years	92
Prices, fluctuations of	100
Prices, how reduced by protective duties	226
Prices in England, reflected effect of on our crops	188
Prices of foreign goods regulated by domestic competition	225
Prices of land and labor rise; of products, decline	126
Produce, annual, the measure of provision for men	49
Production, definition of	107
Production in geometrical ratio to the money impulse	122
Production of food in the oldest countries increases	60
Products, domestic, proportion to foreign imports	169
Products, of 1860 over 1850, in detail	51
Products of manufactures, value of, in 1850 and 1860 in United States	93
Productive industry, its conditions	292
Productive industry, necessary to growth of man and of societies	17
Profits, larger, depend upon higher wages	89
Profits, net, in the ratio of sales	302
Progress in sixteenth and seventeenth centuries	31
Progress of the last five centuries, character and aim of	250
Property in United States, pro rata share in 1850 and 1860	49
Protective doctrine of our statesmen forty years ago; errors of	207
Protective duties hold prices down	226
Protection and free trade	190
Protection, distributes and adapts the industries to all capacities	223, 227
Protection, doctrine and policy of	204
Protection does not regard market values	211
Protection favors growth of trade in money value	215
Protection in Prussia, Belgium, France, Russia	239, 240, 241, 242
Protection in the historic nations	235
Protection is not arrayed against foreign trade, but promotes it	215
Protection, its influence in economic value of trade	215
Protection, means free domestic trade; its guiding rules	208
Protection, objections to	221
Protective policy in national history and destiny	246
Protection the reciprocal of allegiance	223
Protection unjustly classed with obsolete abuses	222

INDEX.

Protection, what it is	205
Protection aims at diversification of domestic industries	215
Protection secures and defends the opportunity of free labor	224
Proverbs concerning wealth and power, not true	290
Provisions, exports of, prices governed by quantities	188
Provision for human needs, moves faster than population	52
Pyramids and poor-houses	261

Q

Quantity of action of any of the functions not fixed	80

R

Races, laws of, regulating German, Italian and Austrian nationalities	37
Races, none of them cosmopolitan	32
Ramsay and Belknap	196
Rank and right of rule, determined	30
Railroads monopolize their traffic	288
Railroads of England, burdens and rapidity of transportation	56
Rails, steel, imported, price falls under increased duties	229
Rate of increase of production in United States, in decade 1850-60	50
Raw material, in manufactures, average value of	169
Raw materials, proportion of value of, to products	93
Reformed drunkards, proselytism	272
Reformers, knowledge necessary to	12
Religion and race will not account for the ruin of the nations that have adopted free trade	246
Remedies in history for monopoly of power	289
Republic, the great, its influences	253
Reproductive function, not a constant quantity	72
Reserved rights, the ruling aim of modern progress	250
Residents of United States, only seven per cent of, out of their natal climate	35
Retail stores, their cost and burden to the poor	298
Revenue from customs under our protective and unprotective tariffs	213
Revenue, only an incident to protection, but invariably follows it; proof, in the tables of customs' duties	213
Revenue reformers reduce themselves to $25,000,000 of revenue from customs	232
Revolution in political government, returning to order	251
Revolutions, intellectual and religious in the fifteenth century	31
Revulsions neither inevitable nor inexplicable	201
Revulsion, imminent in 1860, postponed and averted by the Rebellion and the Morrill tariff	203
Ricardo, on increasing sterility of the earth	44
Rights, not duties, the drift of modern democracy	250

Rochdale Pioneers; origin ; capital ; results in twenty-two years of trial ;
    financial history; details of a grand success; self-help......... 300, 301
Roman money, comparative value of.. 113
Romans, resided only in Italy.. 34
Rudiments of all the higher forms, in savage society...................... 18
Russia, communes described.. 311
        government of.. 312
Russian merchants, small proportion to the population..................... 312
Russian population, ninety per cent rural... 312
Russia, protective system, its results... 242

S

Saturn, reign of, on earth.. 15
Savagism, the earliest stage of society known to philosophy............... 16
Savage life, badly provided for... 64
Savage society, analogous to individual infancy............................... 18
Savage state, no capital, no wages, no division of labor................... 86
Savage tribes, limited industry of.. 16
Savages, the rule of the strongest... 17
Savings banks, in New England... 259
Savings banks in United States, history of....................................... 259
Savings banks, origin and extent of... 257
    amount of deposits held in England; depositors in 257
    parliamentary regulation of.. 258
    their excellent service.. 258
Schools, common, in the United States.. 254
    in Prussia.. 254
Schools, common, resistance of the House of Lords in 1839............... 254
Schultze, Herman... 306, 308
Sciences, the natural, built upon the harmonies of nature.................. 75
Scotland, banks of, excellence of the system..................................... 151
    principles upon which they are conducted............................. 152
    popularity of.. 152
Secret orders, almost innumerable ; list of those in the City of
    Philadelphia.. 276
Secret orders, differ from the religious sects in their relations to each
    other.. 278
    membership in them multiplied with proportionate benefits se-
        cured.. 278
Secret orders, immense extension of.. 265
Secret orders of colored people... 279
Secret orders, universal membership in, of the provident poor........... 279
Selfhood the basis of the Political Economy in vogue........................ 250
Service value, Frederick Bastiat... 87
Secret societies... 264

INDEX. 363

Slave trade, a hundred years ago, its abolition	253
Smith, Adam, on effect of influx of money	117
Smith, Adam, on service of paper representatives of money	135
Smith, Say, and Mill, their dogma of competition	327
Societary forces, three classes of	252
Societary growth, stages of	250
Societary movements, their characteristics	249
Sons of Temperance, beneficial provisions	273
Sons of Temperance, progress and decline of	274
Sophism of free traders, in respect to natural advantages of climate and soil	216
SOURCES OF ADVANCEMENT IN WEALTH	54
Space not conquered as time is by the telegraph	165
Spain, coöperation in	311
Spencer Herbert	84
Spiritualism in science	251
Springs, material and moral, in society	260, 282
Standard of value impossible	113
Statistical calculations and estimates	104
Statistics of trade and production, differences of the authorities	167
Steam and machinery, increase wages	99
Strike of workingmen in Lower Silesia	314
Substitution, instances of, vegetable for animal, and mineral for both	64
Substitution of the abundant and cheap, for the scarce and dear	63
Substitutions of cheaper and more abundant commodities, table of	67
Suffrage and idleness	219
Suffering not greater than sin, and orderly and necessary	60
Sugar, beet-root, in France	48
Super-natural, in the mechanical powers	54
"Supply and demand," abuse of the maxim	327

T

Tariff act, the first, preamble of	196
Tariff acts from 1789 to 1812	197
Tariff of 1824, compelled by universal distress	198
Tariffs of 1824 and 1828, errors of	198
Tariff of 1828, gave abundant revenue along with adequate protection	199
Tariff of 1842, imports under *per capita*	202
Tariff of 1842, modified in 1846	201
Tariff of 1846, its general character	201
Tariff of 1857, imports under *per capita*	202
Tariffs for revenue always fail of their intention	213
Tariff for revenue with incidental protection, absurdity of	210
Temperance pledge, in numerous secret orders	276
Temperance reform, origin and progress of	272

INDEX.

Temperance reform, origin and spread	253
Textile fabrics and metallic products unlimited	58
Theories, erroneous, of Political Economy, based upon facts in disorder	41
Thompson, George, picture of British rule in India	245
Tobacco, exports, value of	187
Trade between nations diversely situated	176
Trade disintegrates the man and the community	161, 162
Trade in natural products, should be across climates	173
Trade in artificial products	175
Trade, international, contributions to support of old countries	61
Trade legitimate, indicating its course	187
Trade maritime, not a peace-maker	163
Trade, must be complementary, not competitive	173
Trade of England, which imports no manufactures	215
Trade of France, which excludes manufactures	215
Trade reports, uncertainty and inaccuracy of	167
Trade unions, the insurrections that make revolutions	293
Trader's philosophy, a justification of the disorders of business	328
Transportation, consuming cost of	107
merchants of old	108
Transportation, defies and defeats competition	288
Transportation, exhaustive cost of	183
Transportation, rapidly growing into masterdom	289
Transportation, relative value of foreign and domestic goods	169
Treason, only a misdemeanor in the United States	256
Tropical products, duties on, enhance price to consumers	225
Turkey, debasement of the coin	244
history of her manufactures	243
Turkey, her free trade, and its results	243
Turkey, internal trade of, in the hands of foreign peddlers	243

U

Union of interests and efforts, force of	302
United American Mechanics, constitution and objects, members, growth, cost of reliefs	277
United States, capabilities and growth of; their work; their people, and their destiny	193
rapid and frequent changes in their commercial policy	194
repression of their manufactures when they were Colonies	194
United States, capital, wealth, and rate of increase of	49
United States, favorable conditions of	316, 317

V

Value, definition of	87, 89
Value, exchange standard of, impossible	113

INDEX.

Value, economic, of imports, distinguished from money value	166
Value of exports and imports, *per capita*	165
Value of products declines as land and labor rise	89
Velocity gained by steam-power and machinery	56
Viability and fecundity adjusted to each other	78

W

Wages	86
Wages, accumulations of, in United States, afford a sufficient capital to make the laborers self-employing	324
Wages and capital, proportions of, in the products	97
Wages and capital, proportion of profits on manufacture	93
Wages and food	102
Wages, comparative value, in 1814 and in 1860	103
Wages doubled in England in 112 years	92
Wages, English, in the 17th century	91
Wages, equitable increase in, under the law of distribution	88
Wages, growth of, governed by a general law	94
Wages, how affected by protection and free trade	227
Wages in the United States, increase fifteen per cent in ten years, double in forty-seven years	94
Wages, increase of, due to coöperating capital, but not at its loss	95
Wages keep pace with growth of general wealth	94
Wages, leveling tendency in rise of	99
Wages, nominal and real	90
Wages of men doubled in money, increased fourfold in purchasing power over their own products	102
Wages of skilled labor in 17th century, and rise of in 18th and 19th centuries	90
Wages of women have tripled, while those of men doubled	98
Wages outgrow the profits of coöperating capital	94
Wages, provision for increase of, traced to its source	95
Wages, proportion of, to value of products	93
Wages rise in proportion to productiveness of capital and labor	93
Wages rise in the inverse ratio of the cost of products	93
Wages rise with increase of money, why	125
Wages rise with profits	89
Wages, rise of, with decline of price in commodities	92
Wages system, its character	284
Wages, the index of productiveness	103
War, origin of, among savages	16
Washington's domestic coat	196
Washington on the happy results of the first tariff act	196
Waste of life not required to correct its excess	42
Water gas, an equalizer of national industries	68

INDEX.

Water gas, will replace England's exhausted coal	68
Wealth and population, relative growth of, in Great Britain	47
Wealth, answers to culture under natural laws	41
Wealth, British, how estimated	46
Weight carried on English railroads	56
Wealth, distribution of	86
Wealth, distribution of, in barbarism—in civilization	86
Wealth, distributive shares, double in England in twenty-five years	47
Wealth, growth of, accelerating in Great Britain	45
Wealth, growth of, according to Gladstone	46
Wealth, growth of English, since she used American cotton	62
Wealth, growth of, in Great Britain, according to Joseph Lowe	45
Wealth, growth of, in Great Britain, according to Leone Levi	45
Wealth, growth of, its indications	57
Wealth, growth of the general: power of capital over labor	290
Wealth, increases in England three and one-half per cent per annum, doubling once in twenty years, or two and a half times faster than population	46
Wealth, in United States, average share of inhabitants	49
Wealth is power at compound interest	41
Wealth of England, mode of estimating it	167
Wealth of the masses	325
Wealth of the people in contrast with that of the rich	291
WEALTH, THE LAWS AND CONDITIONS OF ITS GROWTH	40
Wealth, the measure of man's power over nature	41
Webster, Daniel, on Political Economy	191
Whale fisheries, conducted by coöperation	324
Wheat, grown in France	48
Wheat, home consumption of	185
Wheat, in England, quantity to the acre	61
Wheat in the United States, average crop of	61
Wheat, Mediterranean, grown on the oldest soil in Europe	61
Wheat, potatoes, and animal food, equivalents of	65
Wheat, price of in 1661, 1846, and 1865, in England	91
Wheat, unchanged in price in 170 years	92
Williamson and Marshall, on the distresses of the period preceding the Federal Union	195
Women and negroes, excluded by K. of P	272
Women and negroes excluded from Order of Odd Fellows	266
Women, being more and more admitted into secret orders	279
Women employed in manufactures, number and wages	218
Women excluded by S. of T., till lately	275
causes of decline of the Order	275
Women, improved condition of	101
wages, real, increased six times in 50 years	102

Women, statistics of their employments in 1860.............................. 219
Women, their dependence upon diversified industry........................... 217
Women, their interest in protection; must work if they would rule...... 218
Women, wages of, have tripled while those of men doubled................ 98
Women, wages of, proportion to those of men................................... 93
Women's wages, rise in purchasing power.. 101
Workingmen's union in Prussia, principles of.................................... 313

Y

Young, Arthur, estimate of relative increase of money and prices........ 124

Z

Zollverein, its happy adaptation to German industry......................... 211
Zollverein, principle of protection discarded valuations..................... 211
Zollverein, results of, in Germany... 212

CATALOGUE
OF
PRACTICAL AND SCIENTIFIC BOOKS,
PUBLISHED BY
HENRY CAREY BAIRD,
INDUSTRIAL PUBLISHER,
No. 406 WALNUT STREET,
PHILADELPHIA.

☞ Any of the Books comprised in this Catalogue will be sent by mail, free of postage, at the publication price.

☞ MY NEW AND ENLARGED CATALOGUE, 95 pages 8vo., with full descriptions of Books, will be sent, free of postage, to any one who will favor me with his address.

ARMENGAUD, AMOUROUX, AND JOHNSON.—THE PRACTICAL DRAUGHTSMAN'S BOOK OF INDUSTRIAL DESIGN, AND MACHINIST'S AND ENGINEER'S DRAWING COMPANION: Forming a complete course of Mechanical Engineering and Architectural Drawing. From the French of M. Armengaud the elder, Prof. of Design in the Conservatoire of Arts and Industry, Paris, and MM. Armengaud the younger and Amouroux, Civil Engineers. Rewritten and arranged, with additional matter and plates, selections from and examples of the most useful and generally employed mechanism of the day. By WILLIAM JOHNSON, Assoc. Inst. C. E., Editor of "The Practical Mechanic's Journal." Illustrated by 50 folio steel plates and 50 wood-cuts. A new edition, 4to. . $10 00

ARLOT.—A COMPLETE GUIDE FOR COACH PAINTERS. Translated from the French of M. ARLOT, Coach Painter; late Master Painter for eleven years with M. Ehrler, Coach Manufacturer, Paris. With important American additions . . $1 25

ARROWSMITH.—PAPER-HANGER'S COMPANION: A Treatise in which the Practical Operations of the Trade are Systematically laid down: with Copious Directions Preparatory to Papering; Preventives against the Effect of Damp on Walls; the Various Cements and Pastes adapted to the Several Purposes of the Trade; Observations and Directions for the Panelling and Ornamenting of Rooms, &c. By JAMES ARROWSMITH. 12mo., cloth $1 25

HENRY CAREY BAIRD'S CATALOGUE.

BAIRD.—THE AMERICAN COTTON SPINNER, AND MANAGER'S AND CARDER'S GUIDE:
A Practical Treatise on Cotton Spinning; giving the Dimensions and Speed of Machinery, Draught and Twist Calculations, etc.; with notices of recent Improvements: together with Rules and Examples for making changes in the sizes and numbers of Roving and Yarn. Compiled from the papers of the late ROBERT H. BAIRD. 12mo. . . . $1 50

BAKER.—LONG-SPAN RAILWAY BRIDGES:
Comprising Investigations of the Comparative Theoretical and Practical Advantages of the various Adopted or Proposed Type Systems of Construction; with numerous Formulæ and Tables. By B. Baker. 12mo. $2 00

BAKEWELL.—A MANUAL OF ELECTRICITY—PRACTICAL AND THEORETICAL:
By F. C. BAKEWELL, Inventor of the Copying Telegraph. Second Edition. Revised and enlarged. Illustrated by numerous engravings. 12mo. Cloth . . . .

BEANS.—A TREATISE ON RAILROAD CURVES AND THE LOCATION OF RAILROADS:
By E. W. BEANS, C. E. 12mo. . . . $2 00

BLENKARN.—PRACTICAL SPECIFICATIONS OF WORKS EXECUTED IN ARCHITECTURE, CIVIL AND MECHANICAL ENGINEERING, AND IN ROAD MAKING AND SEWERING:
To which are added a series of practically useful Agreements and Reports. By JOHN BLENKARN. Illustrated by fifteen large folding plates. 8vo. $9 00

BLINN.—A PRACTICAL WORKSHOP COMPANION FOR TIN, SHEET-IRON, AND COPPER-PLATE WORKERS:
Containing Rules for Describing various kinds of Patterns used by Tin, Sheet-iron, and Copper-plate Workers; Practical Geometry; Mensuration of Surfaces and Solids; Tables of the Weight of Metals, Lead Pipe, etc.; Tables of Areas and Circumferences of Circles; Japans, Varnishes, Lackers, Cements, Compositions, etc. etc. By LEROY J. BLINN, Master Mechanic. With over One Hundred Illustrations. 12mo. $2 50

BOOTH.—MARBLE WORKER'S MANUAL:
Containing Practical Information respecting Marbles in general, their Cutting, Working, and Polishing; Veneering of Marble; Mosaics; Composition and Use of Artificial Marble, Stuccos, Cements, Receipts, Secrets, etc. etc. Translated from the French by M. L. BOOTH. With an Appendix concerning American Marbles. 12mo., cloth . . $1 50

BOOTH AND MORFIT.—THE ENCYCLOPEDIA OF CHEMISTRY, PRACTICAL AND THEORETICAL:
Embracing its application to the Arts, Metallurgy, Mineralogy, Geology, Medicine, and Pharmacy. By JAMES C. BOOTH, Melter and Refiner in the United States Mint, Professor of Applied Chemistry in the Franklin Institute, etc., assisted by CAMPBELL MORFIT, author of "Chemical Manipulations," etc. Seventh edition. Complete in one volume, royal 8vo., 978 pages, with numerous wood-cuts and other illustrations. $5 00

BOWDITCH.—ANALYSIS, TECHNICAL VALUATION, PURIFICATION, AND USE OF COAL GAS:
By Rev. W. R. BOWDITCH. Illustrated with wood engravings. 8vo. $6 50

BOX.—PRACTICAL HYDRAULICS:
A Series of Rules and Tables for the use of Engineers, etc. By THOMAS BOX. 12mo. $2 50

BUCKMASTER.—THE ELEMENTS OF MECHANICAL PHYSICS:
By J. C. BUCKMASTER, late Student in the Government School of Mines; Certified Teacher of Science by the Department of Science and Art; Examiner in Chemistry and Physics in the Royal College of Preceptors; and late Lecturer in Chemistry and Physics of the Royal Polytechnic Institute. Illustrated with numerous engravings. In one vol. 12mo. . $1 50

BULLOCK.—THE AMERICAN COTTAGE BUILDER:
A Series of Designs, Plans, and Specifications, from $200 to to $20,000 for Homes for the People; together with Warming, Ventilation, Drainage, Painting, and Landscape Gardening. By JOHN BULLOCK, Architect, Civil Engineer, Mechanician, and Editor of "The Rudiments of Architecture and Building," etc. Illustrated by 75 engravings. In one vol. 8vo. $3 50

BULLOCK. — THE RUDIMENTS OF ARCHITECTURE AND BUILDING:
For the use of Architects, Builders, Draughtsmen, Machinists, Engineers, and Mechanics. Edited by JOHN BULLOCK, author of "The American Cottage Builder." Illustrated by 250 engravings. In one volume 8vo. . . . $3 50

BURGH.—PRACTICAL ILLUSTRATIONS OF LAND AND MARINE ENGINES:
Showing in detail the Modern Improvements of High and Low Pressure, Surface Condensation, and Super-heating, together with Land and Marine Boilers. By N. P. BURGH, Engineer. Illustrated by twenty plates, double elephant folio, with text. $21 00

BURGH.—PRACTICAL RULES FOR THE PROPORTIONS OF MODERN ENGINES AND BOILERS FOR LAND AND MARINE PURPOSES.
By N. P. BURGH, Engineer. 12mo. . . . $2 00

BURGH.—THE SLIDE-VALVE PRACTICALLY CONSIDERED:
By N. P. BURGH, author of "A Treatise on Sugar Machinery," "Practical Illustrations of Land and Marine Engines," "A Pocket-Book of Practical Rules for Designing Land and Marine Engines, Boilers," etc. etc. etc. Completely illustrated. 12mo. $2 00

BYRN.—THE COMPLETE PRACTICAL BREWER:
Or, Plain, Accurate, and Thorough Instructions in the Art of Brewing Beer, Ale, Porter, including the Process of making Bavarian Beer, all the Small Beers, such as Root-beer, Ginger-pop, Sarsaparilla-beer, Mead, Spruce beer, etc. etc. Adapted to the use of Public Brewers and Private Families. By M. LA FAYETTE BYRN, M. D. With illustrations. 12mo. $1 25

BYRN.—THE COMPLETE PRACTICAL DISTILLER:
Comprising the most perfect and exact Theoretical and Practical Description of the Art of Distillation and Rectification; including all of the most recent improvements in distilling apparatus; instructions for preparing spirits from the numerous vegetables, fruits, etc.; directions for the distillation and preparation of all kinds of brandies and other spirits, spirituous and other compounds, etc. etc.; all of which is so simplified that it is adapted not only to the use of extensive distillers, but for every farmer, or others who may wish to engage in the art of distilling. By M. LA FAYETTE BYRN, M. D. With numerous engravings. In one volume, 12mo. $1 50

BYRNE.—POCKET BOOK FOR RAILROAD AND CIVIL ENGINEERS:
Containing New, Exact, and Concise Methods for Laying out Railroad Curves, Switches, Frog Angles and Crossings; the Staking out of work; Levelling; the Calculation of Cuttings; Embankments; Earth-work, etc. By OLIVER BYRNE. Illustrated, 18mo., full bound $1 75

BYRNE.—THE HANDBOOK FOR THE ARTISAN, MECHANIC, AND ENGINEER:
By OLIVER BYRNE. Illustrated by 185 Wood Engravings. 8vo. $5 00

BYRNE.—THE ESSENTIAL ELEMENTS OF PRACTICAL MECHANICS:
For Engineering Students, based on the Principle of Work. By OLIVER BYRNE. Illustrated by Numerous Wood Engravings, 12mo. $3 63

BYRNE.—THE PRACTICAL METAL-WORKER'S ASSISTANT:
Comprising Metallurgic Chemistry; the Arts of Working all Metals and Alloys; Forging of Iron and Steel; Hardening and Tempering; Melting and Mixing; Casting and Founding; Works in Sheet Metal; the Processes Dependent on the Ductility of the Metals; Soldering; and the most Improved Processes and Tools employed by Metal-Workers. With the Application of the Art of Electro-Metallurgy to Manufacturing Processes; collected from Original Sources, and from the Works of Holtzapffel, Bergeron, Leupold, Plumier, Napier, and others. By OLIVER BYRNE. A New, Revised, and improved Edition, with Additions by John Scoffern, M. B , William Clay, Wm. Fairbairn, F. R. S., and James Napier. With Five Hundred and Ninety-two Engravings; Illustrating every Branch of the Subject. In one volume, 8vo. 652 pages . $7 00

BYRNE.—THE PRACTICAL MODEL CALCULATOR:
For the Engineer, Mechanic, Manufacturer of Engine Work, Naval Architect, Miner, and Millwright. By OLIVER BYRNE. 1 volume, 8vo., nearly 600 pages $4 50

BEMROSE.—MANUAL OF WOOD CARVING: With Practical Illustrations for Learners of the Art, and Original and Selected designs. By WILLIAM BEMROSE, Jr. With an Introduction by LLEWELLYN JEWITT, F. S. A., etc. With 128 Illustrations. 4to., cloth $3 00

BAIRD.—PROTECTION OF HOME LABOR AND HOME PRO-
DUCTIONS NECESSARY TO THE PROSPERITY OF THE
AMERICAN FARMER:
By HENRY CAREY BAIRD. 8vo., paper 10

BAIRD.—THE RIGHTS OF AMERICAN PRODUCERS, AND THE
WRONGS OF BRITISH FREE TRADE REVENUE REFORM.
By HENRY CAREY BAIRD. (1870) 5

BAIRD.—SOME OF THE FALLACIES OF BRITISH-FREE-TRADE
REVENUE-REFORM.
Two Letters to Prof. A. L. Perry, of Williams College, Mass. By
HENRY CAREY BAIRD. (1871.) Paper 5

BAIRD.—STANDARD WAGES COMPUTING TABLES:
An Improvement in all former Methods of Computation, so arranged that wages for days, hours, or fractions of hours, at a spe-
cified rate per day or hour, may be ascertained at a glance. By
T. SPANGLER BAIRD. Oblong folio $5 00

BAUERMAN.—TREATISE ON THE METALLURGY OF IRON.
Illustrated. 12mo. $2 50

BICKNELL'S VILLAGE BUILDER.
55 large plates. 4to. $10 00

BISHOP.—A HISTORY OF AMERICAN MANUFACTURES:
From 1608 to 1866; exhibiting the Origin and Growth of the Prin-
cipal Mechanic Arts and Manufactures, from the Earliest Colonial
Period to the Present Time; By J. LEANDER BISHOP, M. D., ED-
WARD YOUNG, and EDWIN T. FREEDLEY. Three vols. 8vo.,
$10 00

BOX.—A PRACTICAL TREATISE ON HEAT AS APPLIED TO
THE USEFUL ARTS:
For the use of Engineers, Architects, etc. By THOMAS BOX, author of "Practical Hydraulics." Illustrated by 14 plates, containing 114 figures. 12mo. $4 25

CABINET MAKER'S ALBUM OF FURNITURE:
Comprising a Collection of Designs for the Newest and Most
Elegant Styles of Furniture. Illustrated by Forty-eight Large
and Beautifully Engraved Plates. In one volume, oblong
$5 00

CHAPMAN.—A TREATISE ON ROPE-MAKING:
As practised in private and public Rope-yards, with a Description
of the Manufacture, Rules, Tables of Weights, etc., adapted to the
Trade; Shipping, Mining, Railways, Builders, etc. By ROBERT
CHAPMAN. 24mo. $1 50

CRAIK.—THE PRACTICAL AMERICAN MILLWRIGHT AND MILLER.

Comprising the Elementary Principles of Mechanics, Mechanism, and Motive Power, Hydraulics and Hydraulic Motors, Mill-dams, Saw Mills, Grist Mills, the Oat Meal Mill, the Barley Mill, Wool Carding, and Cloth Fulling and Dressing, Wind Mills, Steam Power, &c. By DAVID CRAIK, Millwright. Illustrated by numerous wood engravings, and five folding plates. 1 vol. 8vo. $5 00

CAMPIN.—A PRACTICAL TREATISE ON MECHANICAL ENGINEERING:

Comprising Metallurgy, Moulding, Casting, Forging, Tools, Workshop Machinery, Mechanical Manipulation, Manufacture of Steam-engines, etc. etc. With an Appendix on the Analysis of Iron and Iron Ores. By FRANCIS CAMPIN, C. E. To which are added, Observations on the Construction of Steam Boilers, and Remarks upon Furnaces used for Smoke Prevention; with a Chapter on Explosions. By R. Armstrong, C. E., and John Bourne. Rules for Calculating the Change Wheels for Screws on a Turning Lathe, and for a Wheel-cutting Machine. By J. LA NICCA. Management of Steel, including Forging, Hardening, Tempering, Annealing, Shrinking, and Expansion. And the Case-hardening of Iron. By G. EDE. 8vo. Illustrated with 29 plates and 100 wood engravings.
$6 00

CAMPIN.—THE PRACTICE OF HAND-TURNING IN WOOD, IVORY, SHELL, ETC.:

With Instructions for Turning such works in Metal as may be required in the Practice of Turning Wood, Ivory, etc. Also an Appendix on Ornamental Turning. By FRANCIS CAMPIN, with Numerous Illustrations, 12mo., cloth . . $3 00

CAPRON DE DOLE.—DUSSAUCE.—BLUES AND CARMINES OF INDIGO.

A Practical Treatise on the Fabrication of every Commercial Product derived from Indigo. By FELICIEN CAPRON DE DOLE. Translated, with important additions, by Professor H. DUSSAUCE. 12mo.

CAREY.—THE WORKS OF HENRY C. CAREY:

CONTRACTION OR EXPANSION? REPUDIATION OR RESUMPTION? Letters to Hon. Hugh McCulloch. 8vo. 38

FINANCIAL CRISES, their Causes and Effects. 8vo. paper 25

HARMONY OF INTERESTS; Agricultural, Manufacturing, and Commercial. 8vo., paper $1 00
  Do.   do.   cloth   . . . $1 50

LETTERS TO THE PRESIDENT OF THE UNITED STATES. Paper $1 00

MANUAL OF SOCIAL SCIENCE. Condensed from Carey's "Principles of Social Science." By KATE McKEAN. 1 vol. 12mo. $2 25

MISCELLANEOUS WORKS: comprising "Harmony of Interests," "Money," "Letters to the President," "French and American Tariffs," "Financial Crises," "The Way to Outdo England without Fighting Her," "Resources of the Union," "The Public Debt," "Contraction or Expansion," "Review of the Decade 1857—'67," "Reconstruction," etc. etc. 1 vol. 8vo., cloth $4 50

MONEY: A LECTURE before the N. Y. Geographical and Statistical Society. 8vo., paper 25

PAST, PRESENT, AND FUTURE. 8vo. . . . $2 50

PRINCIPLES OF SOCIAL SCIENCE. 3 volumes 8vo., cloth
  $10 00

REVIEW OF THE DECADE 1857—'67. 8vo., paper   50

RECONSTRUCTION: INDUSTRIAL, FINANCIAL, AND POLITICAL. Letters to the Hon. Henry Wilson, U. S. S. 8vo. paper 50

THE PUBLIC DEBT, LOCAL AND NATIONAL. How to provide for its discharge while lessening the burden of Taxation. Letter to David A. Wells, Esq., U. S. Revenue Commission. 8vo., paper 25

THE RESOURCES OF THE UNION. A Lecture read, Dec. 1865, before the American Geographical and Statistical Society, N. Y., and before the American Association for the Advancement of Social Science, Boston . . . 50

THE SLAVE TRADE, DOMESTIC AND FOREIGN; Why it Exists, and How it may be Extinguished. 12mo., cloth $1 50

LETTERS ON INTERNATIONAL COPYRIGHT. (1867.)
  Paper   50
REVIEW OF THE FARMERS' QUESTION. (1870.) Paper 25
RESUMPTION! HOW IT MAY PROFITABLY BE BROUGHT
  ABOUT. (1869.) 8vo., paper   50
REVIEW OF THE REPORT OF HON. D. A. WELLS, Special
  Commissioner of the Revenue. (1869.) 8vo., paper   50
SHALL WE HAVE PEACE? Peace Financial and Peace Political. Letters to the President Elect. (1868.) 8vo., paper 50
THE FINANCE MINISTER AND THE CURRENCY, AND
  THE PUBLIC DEBT. (1868.) 8vo., paper . .   50
THE WAY TO OUTDO ENGLAND WITHOUT FIGHTING
  HER. Letters to Hon. Schuyler Colfax. (1865.) 8vo., paper
                                                       $1 00
WEALTH! OF WHAT DOES IT CONSIST? (1870.) Paper 25

CAMUS.—A TREATISE ON THE TEETH OF WHEELS:
Demonstrating the best forms which can be given to them for the purposes of Machinery, such as Mill-work and Clock-work. Translated from the French of M. CAMUS. By JOHN I. HAWKINS. Illustrated by 40 plates. 8vo. $3 00

COXE.—MINING LEGISLATION.
A paper read before the Am. Social Science Association. By ECKLEY B. COXE. Paper 20

COLBURN.—THE GAS-WORKS OF LONDON:
Comprising a sketch of the Gas-works of the city, Process of Manufacture, Quantity Produced, Cost, Profit, etc. By ZERAH COLBURN. 8vo., cloth 75

COLBURN.—THE LOCOMOTIVE ENGINE:
Including a Description of its Structure, Rules for Estimating its Capabilities, and Practical Observations on its Construction and Management. By ZERAH COLBURN. Illustrated. A new edition. 12mo. $1 25

COLBURN AND MAW.—THE WATER-WORKS OF LONDON:
Together with a Series of Articles on various other Waterworks. By ZERAH COLBURN and W. MAW. Reprinted from "Engineering." In one volume, 8vo. . . $4 00

DAGUERREOTYPIST AND PHOTOGRAPHER'S COMPANION:
12mo., cloth $1 25

DIRCKS.—PERPETUAL MOTION:
Or Search for Self-Motive Power during the 17th, 18th, and 19th centuries. Illustrated from various authentic sources in Papers, Essays, Letters, Paragraphs, and numerous Patent Specifications, with an Introductory Essay by HENRY DIRCKS, C. E. Illustrated by numerous engravings of machines. 12mo., cloth $3 50

DIXON.—THE PRACTICAL MILLWRIGHT'S AND ENGINEER'S GUIDE:
Or Tables for Finding the Diameter and Power of Cogwheels; Diameter, Weight, and Power of Shafts; Diameter and Strength of Bolts, etc. etc. By THOMAS DIXON. 12mo., cloth. $1 50

DUNCAN.—PRACTICAL SURVEYOR'S GUIDE:
Containing the necessary information to make any person, of common capacity, a finished land surveyor without the aid of a teacher. By ANDREW DUNCAN. Illustrated. 12mo., cloth.
$1 25

DUSSAUCE.—A NEW AND COMPLETE TREATISE ON THE ARTS OF TANNING, CURRYING, AND LEATHER DRESSING:
Comprising all the Discoveries and Improvements made in France, Great Britain, and the United States. Edited from Notes and Documents of Messrs. Sallerou, Grouvelle, Duval, Dessables, Labarraque, Payen, René, De Fontenelle, Malapeyre, etc. etc. By Prof. H. DUSSAUCE, Chemist. Illustrated by 212 wood engravings. 8vo. $10 00

DUSSAUCE.—A GENERAL TREATISE ON THE MANUFACTURE OF SOAP, THEORETICAL AND PRACTICAL:
Comprising the Chemistry of the Art, a Description of all the Raw Materials and their Uses. Directions for the Establishment of a Soap Factory, with the necessary Apparatus, Instructions in the Manufacture of every variety of Soap, the Assay and Determination of the Value of Alkalies, Fatty Substances, Soaps, etc. etc. By PROFESSOR H. DUSSAUCE. With an Appendix, containing Extracts from the Reports of the International Jury on Soaps, as exhibited in the Paris Universal Exposition, 1867, numerous Tables, etc. etc. Illustrated by engravings. In one volume 8vo. of over 800 pages $10 00

DUSSAUCE.—PRACTICAL TREATISE ON THE FABRICATION OF MATCHES, GUN COTTON, AND FULMINATING POWDERS.
By Professor H. DUSSAUCE. 12mo. . . . $3 00

DUSSAUCE.—A PRACTICAL GUIDE FOR THE PERFUMER:
Being a New Treatise on Perfumery the most favorable to the Beauty without being injurious to the Health, comprising a Description of the substances used in Perfumery, the Formulæ of more than one thousand Preparations, such as Cosmetics, Perfumed Oils, Tooth Powders, Waters, Extracts, Tinctures, Infusions, Vinaigres, Essential Oils, Pastels, Creams, Soaps, and many new Hygienic Products not hitherto described. Edited from Notes and Documents of Messrs. Debay, Lunel, etc. With additions by Professor H. Dussauce, Chemist. 12mo.
$3 00

DUSSAUCE.—A GENERAL TREATISE ON THE MANUFACTURE OF VINEGAR, THEORETICAL AND PRACTICAL.
Comprising the various methods, by the slow and the quick processes, with Alcohol, Wine, Grain, Cider, and Molasses, as well as the Fabrication of Wood Vinegar, etc. By Prof. H. Dussauce. 12mo. $5 00

DUPLAIS.—A COMPLETE TREATISE ON THE DISTILLATION AND MANUFACTURE OF ALCOHOLIC LIQUORS:
From the French of M. Duplais. Translated and Edited by M. McKennie, M D. Illustrated by numerous large plates and wood engravings of the best apparatus calculated for producing the finest products. In one vol. royal 8vo. $10 00
☞ This is a treatise of the highest scientific merit and of the greatest practical value, surpassing in these respects, as well as in the variety of its contents, any similar volume in the English language.

DE GRAFF.—THE GEOMETRICAL STAIR-BUILDERS' GUIDE:
Being a Plain Practical System of Hand-Railing, embracing all its necessary Details, and Geometrically Illustrated by 22 Steel Engravings; together with the use of the most approved principles of Practical Geometry. By Simon De Graff, Architect. 4to. $5 00

DYER AND COLOR-MAKER'S COMPANION :
Containing upwards of two hundred Receipts for making Colors, on the most approved principles, for all the various styles and fabrics now in existence; with the Scouring Process, and plain Directions for Preparing, Washing-off, and Finishing the Goods. In one vol. 12mo. $1 25

EASTON.—A PRACTICAL TREATISE ON STREET OR HORSE-POWER RAILWAYS:

Their Location, Construction, and Management; with General Plans and Rules for their Organization and Operation; together with Examinations as to their Comparative Advantages over the Omnibus System, and Inquiries as to their Value for Investment; including Copies of Municipal Ordinances relating thereto. By ALEXANDER EASTON, C. E. Illustrated by 23 plates, 8vo., cloth $2 00

FORSYTH.—BOOK OF DESIGNS FOR HEAD-STONES, MURAL, AND OTHER MONUMENTS:

Containing 78 Elaborate and Exquisite Designs. By FORSYTH.

4to., cloth $5 00

⁂ This volume, for the beauty and variety of its designs, has never been surpassed by any publication of the kind, and should be in the hands of every marble-worker who does fine monumental work.

FAIRBAIRN.—THE PRINCIPLES OF MECHANISM AND MACHINERY OF TRANSMISSION:

Comprising the Principles of Mechanism, Wheels, and Pulleys, Strength and Proportions of Shafts, Couplings of Shafts, and Engaging and Disengaging Gear. By WILLIAM FAIRBAIRN, Esq., C. E., LL. D., F. R. S., F. G. S., Corresponding Member of the National Institute of France, and of the Royal Academy of Turin; Chevalier of the Legion of Honor, etc. etc. Beautifully illustrated by over 150 wood-cuts. In one volume 12mo.
$2 50

FAIRBAIRN.—PRIME-MOVERS:

Comprising the Accumulation of Water-power; the Construction of Water-wheels and Turbines; the Properties of Steam; the Varieties of Steam-engines and Boilers and Wind-mills. By WILLIAM FAIRBAIRN, C. E , LL. D., F. R. S., F. G. S. Author of "Principles of Mechanism and the Machinery of Transmission." With Numerous Illustrations. In one volume. (In press.)

GILBART.—A PRACTICAL TREATISE ON BANKING:

By JAMES WILLIAM GILBART. To which is added: THE NATIONAL BANK ACT AS NOW IN FORCE. 8vo. . . $4 50

GESNER.—A PRACTICAL TREATISE ON COAL, PETROLEUM, AND OTHER DISTILLED OILS.

By ABRAHAM GESNER, M. D., F. G. S. Second edition, revised and enlarged. By GEORGE WELTDEN GESNER, Consulting Chemist and Engineer. Illustrated. 8vo. . . $3 50

GOTHIC ALBUM FOR CABINET MAKERS:
Comprising a Collection of Designs for Gothic Furniture. Illustrated by twenty-three large and beautifully engraved plates. Oblong $3 00

GRANT.—BEET-ROOT SUGAR AND CULTIVATION OF THE BEET:
By E. B. GRANT. 12mo. $1 25

GREGORY.—MATHEMATICS FOR PRACTICAL MEN:
Adapted to the Pursuits of Surveyors, Architects, Mechanics, and Civil Engineers. By OLINTHUS GREGORY. 8vo., plates, cloth $3 00

GRISWOLD.—RAILROAD ENGINEER'S POCKET COMPANION.
Comprising Rules for Calculating Deflection Distances and Angles, Tangential Distances and Angles, and all Necessary Tables for Engineers; also the art of Levelling from Preliminary Survey to the Construction of Railroads, intended Expressly for the Young Engineer, together with Numerous Valuable Rules and Examples. By W. GRISWOLD. 12mo., tucks. $1 75

GUETTIER.—METALLIC ALLOYS:
Being a Practical Guide to their Chemical and Physical Properties, their Preparation, Composition, and Uses. Translated from the French of A. GUETTIER, Engineer and Director of Founderies, author of "La Fouderie en France," etc. etc. By A. A. FESQUET, Chemist and Engineer. In one volume, 12mo. $3 00

HATS AND FELTING:
A Practical Treatise on their Manufacture. By a Practical Hatter. Illustrated by Drawings of Machinery, &c., 8vo. $1 25

HAY.—THE INTERIOR DECORATOR:
The Laws of Harmonious Coloring adapted to Interior Decorations: with a Practical Treatise on House-Painting. By D. R. HAY, House-Painter and Decorator. Illustrated by a Diagram of the Primary, Secondary, and Tertiary Colors. 12mo. $2 25

HUGHES.—AMERICAN MILLER AND MILLWRIGHT'S ASSISTANT:
By WM. CARTER HUGHES. A new edition. In one volume, 12mo. $1 50

HUNT.—THE PRACTICE OF PHOTOGRAPHY.
By ROBERT HUNT, Vice-President of the Photographic Society, London. With numerous illustrations. 12mo., cloth . 75

HURST.—A HAND-BOOK FOR ARCHITECTURAL SURVEYORS:
Comprising Formulæ useful in Designing Builders' work, Table of Weights, of the materials used in Building, Memoranda connected with Builders' work, Mensuration, the Practice of Builders' Measurement, Contracts of Labor, Valuation of Property, Summary of the Practice in Dilapidation, etc. etc. By J. F. HURST, C. E. 2d edition, pocket-book form, full bound $2 50

JERVIS.—RAILWAY PROPERTY:
A Treatise on the Construction and Management of Railways; designed to afford useful knowledge, in the popular style, to the holders of this class of property; as well as Railway Managers, Officers, and Agents. By JOHN B. JERVIS, late Chief Engineer of the Hudson River Railroad, Croton Aqueduct, &c. One vol. 12mo., cloth $2 00

JOHNSON.—A REPORT TO THE NAVY DEPARTMENT OF THE UNITED STATES ON AMERICAN COALS:
Applicable to Steam Navigation and to other purposes. By WALTER R. JOHNSON. With numerous illustrations. 607 pp. 8vo., ... $10 00

JOHNSTON.—INSTRUCTIONS FOR THE ANALYSIS OF SOILS, LIMESTONES, AND MANURES.
By J. W. F. JOHNSTON. 12mo. 35

KEENE.—A HAND-BOOK OF PRACTICAL GAUGING,
For the Use of Beginners, to which is added a Chapter on Distillation, describing the process in operation at the Custom House for ascertaining the strength of wines. By JAMES B. KEENE, of H. M. Customs. 8vo. . . . $1 25

KENTISH.—A TREATISE ON A BOX OF INSTRUMENTS,

And the Slide Rule; with the Theory of Trigonometry and Logarithms, including Practical Geometry, Surveying, Measuring of Timber, Cask and Malt Gauging, Heights, and Distances. By THOMAS KENTISH. In one volume. 12mo. . . $1 25

KOBELL.—ERNI.—MINERALOGY SIMPLIFIED:

A short method of Determining and Classifying Minerals, by means of simple Chemical Experiments in the Wet Way. Translated from the last German Edition of F. VON KOBELL, with an Introduction to Blowpipe Analysis and other additions. By HENRI ERNI, M. D., Chief Chemist, Department of Agriculture, author of "Coal Oil and Petroleum." In one volume. 12mo. $2 50

LANDRIN.—A TREATISE ON STEEL:

Comprising its Theory, Metallurgy, Properties, Practical Working, and Use. By M. H. C. LANDRIN, Jr., Civil Engineer. Translated from the French, with Notes, by A. A. FESQUET, Chemist and Engineer. With an Appendix on the Bessemer and the Martin Processes for Manufacturing Steel, from the Report of ABRAM S. HEWITT, United States Commissioner to the Universal Exposition, Paris, 1867. 12mo. . . $3 00

LARKIN.—THE PRACTICAL BRASS AND IRON FOUNDER'S GUIDE.

A Concise Treatise on Brass Founding, Moulding, the Metals and their Alloys, etc.; to which are added Recent Improvements in the Manufacture of Iron, Steel by the Bessemer Process, etc. etc. By JAMES LARKIN, late Conductor of the Brass Foundry Department in Reany, Neafie & Co.'s Penn Works, Philadelphia. Fifth edition, revised, with extensive Additions. In one volume. 12mo. $2 25

LEAVITT.—FACTS ABOUT PEAT AS AN ARTICLE OF FUEL:
With Remarks upon its Origin and Composition, the Localities in which it is found, the Methods of Preparation and Manufacture, and the various Uses to which it is applicable; together with many other matters of Practical and Scientific Interest. To which is added a chapter on the Utilization of Coal Dust with Peat for the Production of an Excellent Fuel at Moderate Cost, especially adapted for Steam Service. By H. T. LEAVITT. Third edition. 12mo. . . . $1 75

LEROUX.—A PRACTICAL TREATISE ON THE MANUFACTURE OF WORSTEDS AND CARDED YARNS:
Translated from the French of CHARLES LEROUX, Mechanical Engineer, and Superintendent of a Spinning Mill. By Dr. H. PAINE, and A. A. FESQUET. Illustrated by 12 large plates. In one volume 8vo. $5 00

LESLIE (MISS).—COMPLETE COOKERY:
Directions for Cookery in its Various Branches. By Miss LESLIE. 60th edition. Thoroughly revised, with the addition of New Receipts. In 1 vol. 12mo., cloth . . $1 50

LESLIE (MISS). LADIES' HOUSE BOOK:
a Manual of Domestic Economy. 20th revised edition. 12mo., cloth $1 25

LESLIE (MISS).—TWO HUNDRED RECEIPTS IN FRENCH COOKERY.
12mo. 50

LIEBER.—ASSAYER'S GUIDE:
Or, Practical Directions to Assayers, Miners, and Smelters, for the Tests and Assays, by Heat and by Wet Processes, for the Ores of all the principal Metals, of Gold and Silver Coins and Alloys, and of Coal, etc. By OSCAR M. LIEBER. 12mo., cloth $1 25

LOVE.—THE ART OF DYEING, CLEANING, SCOURING, AND FINISHING:
On the most approved English and French methods; being Practical Instructions in Dyeing Silks, Woollens, and Cottons, Feathers, Chips, Straw, etc.; Scouring and Cleaning Bed and Window Curtains, Carpets, Rugs, etc.; French and English Cleaning, etc. By THOMAS LOVE. Second American Edition, to which are added General Instructions for the Use of Aniline Colors. 8vo. 5 00

MAIN AND BROWN.—QUESTIONS ON SUBJECTS CONNECTED WITH THE MARINE STEAM-ENGINE:
And Examination Papers; with Hints for their Solution. By THOMAS J. MAIN, Professor of Mathematics, Royal Naval College, and THOMAS BROWN, Chief Engineer, R. N. 12mo., cloth $1 50

MAIN AND BROWN.—THE INDICATOR AND DYNAMOMETER:
With their Practical Applications to the Steam-Engine. By THOMAS J. MAIN, M. A. F. R., Ass't Prof. Royal Naval College, Portsmouth, and THOMAS BROWN, Assoc. Inst. C. E., Chief Engineer, R. N., attached to the R. N. College. Illustrated. From the Fourth London Edition. 8vo. $1 50

MAIN AND BROWN.—THE MARINE STEAM-ENGINE.
By THOMAS J. MAIN, F. R. Ass't S. Mathematical Professor at Royal Naval College, and THOMAS BROWN, Assoc. Inst. C. E. Chief Engineer, R. N. Attached to the Royal Naval College. Authors of "Questions Connected with the Marine Steam-Engine," and the "Indicator and Dynamometer." With numerous Illustrations. In one volume 8vo. $5 00

MARTIN.—SCREW-CUTTING TABLES, FOR THE USE OF MECHANICAL ENGINEERS:
Showing the Proper Arrangement of Wheels for Cutting the Threads of Screws of any required Pitch; with a Table for Making the Universal Gas-Pipe Thread and Taps. By W. A. MARTIN, Engineer. 8vo. 50

MILES—A PLAIN TREATISE ON HORSE-SHOEING.
With Illustrations. By WILLIAM MILES, author of "The Horse's Foot"

MOLESWORTH.—POCKET-BOOK OF USEFUL FORMULÆ AND MEMORANDA FOR CIVIL AND MECHANICAL ENGINEERS.
By GUILFORD L. MOLESWORTH, Member of the Institution of Civil Engineers, Chief Resident Engineer of the Ceylon Railway. Second American from the Tenth London Edition. In one volume, full bound in pocket-book form $2 00

MOORE.—THE INVENTOR'S GUIDE:
Patent Office and Patent Laws: or, a Guide to Inventors, and a Book of Reference for Judges, Lawyers, Magistrates, and others. By J. G. MOORE. 12mo., cloth $1 25

NAPIER.—A MANUAL OF ELECTRO-METALLURGY:
Including the Application of the Art to Manufacturing Processes. By JAMES NAPIER. Fourth American, from the Fourth London edition, revised and enlarged. Illustrated by engravings. In one volume, 8vo. $2 00

NAPIER.—A SYSTEM OF CHEMISTRY APPLIED TO DYEING:
By JAMES NAPIER, F. C. S. A New and Thoroughly Revised Edition, completely brought up to the present state of the Science, including the Chemistry of Coal Tar Colors. By A. A. FESQUET, Chemist and Engineer. With an Appendix on Dyeing and Calico Printing, as shown at the Paris Universal Exposition of 1867, from the Reports of the International Jury, etc. Illustrated. In one volume 8vo., 400 pages $5 00

NEWBERY.— GLEANINGS FROM ORNAMENTAL ART OF EVERY STYLE;
Drawn from Examples in the British, South Kensington, Indian, Crystal Palace, and other Museums, the Exhibitions of 1851 and 1862, and the best English and Foreign works. In a series of one hundred exquisitely drawn Plates, containing many hundred examples. By ROBERT NEWBERY. 4to. $15 00

NICHOLSON.—A MANUAL OF THE ART OF BOOK-BINDING:
Containing full instructions in the different Branches of Forwarding, Gilding, and Finishing. Also, the Art of Marbling Book-edges and Paper. By JAMES B. NICHOLSON. Illustrated. 12mo. cloth $2 25

NORRIS.—A HAND-BOOK FOR LOCOMOTIVE ENGINEERS AND MACHINISTS:
Comprising the Proportions and Calculations for Constructing Locomotives; Manner of Setting Valves; Tables of Squares, Cubes, Areas, etc. etc. By SEPTIMUS NORRIS, Civil and Mechanical Engineer. New edition. Illustrated, 12mo., cloth
$2 00

NYSTROM. — ON TECHNOLOGICAL EDUCATION AND THE CONSTRUCTION OF SHIPS AND SCREW PROPELLERS:
For Naval and Marine Engineers. By JOHN W. NYSTROM, late Acting Chief Engineer U. S. N. Second edition, revised with additional matter. Illustrated by seven engravings. 12mo.
$2 50

O'NEILL.—A DICTIONARY OF DYEING AND CALICO PRINTING:
Containing a brief account of all the Substances and Processes in use in the Art of Dyeing and Printing Textile Fabrics: with Practical Receipts and Scientific Information. By CHARLES O'NEILL, Analytical Chemist; Fellow of the Chemical Society of London; Member of the Literary and Philosophical Society of Manchester; Author of "Chemistry of Calico Printing and Dyeing." To which is added An Essay on Coal Tar Colors and their Application to

Dyeing and Calico Printing. By A. A. FESQUET, Chemist and Engineer. With an Appendix on Dyeing and Calico Printing, as shown at the Exposition of 1867, from the Reports of the International Jury, etc. In one volume 8vo., 491 pages . . $6 00

OSBORN.—THE METALLURGY OF IRON AND STEEL:
Theoretical and Practical: In all its Branches; With Special Reference to American Materials and Processes. By H. S. OSBORN, LL. D., Professor of Mining and Metallurgy in Lafayette College, Easton, Pa. Illustrated by 230 Engravings on Wood, and 6 Folding Plates. 8vo., 972 pages $10 00

OSBORN.—AMERICAN MINES AND MINING:
Theoretically and Practically Considered. By Prof. H. S. OSBORN, Illustrated by numerous engravings. 8vo. (*In preparation*.)

PAINTER, GILDER, AND VARNISHER'S COMPANION:
Containing Rules and Regulations in everything relating to the Arts of Painting, Gilding, Varnishing, and Glass Staining, with numerous useful and valuable Receipts; Tests for the Detection of Adulterations in Oils and Colors, and a statement of the Diseases and Accidents to which Painters, Gilders, and Varnishers are particularly liable, with the simplest methods of Prevention and Remedy. With Directions for Graining, Marbling, Sign Writing, and Gilding on Glass. To which are added COMPLETE INSTRUCTIONS FOR COACH PAINTING AND VARNISHING. 12mo., cloth, $1 50

PALLETT.—THE MILLER'S, MILLWRIGHT'S, AND ENGINEER'S GUIDE.
By HENRY PALLETT. Illustrated. In one vol. 12mo. . $3 00

PERKINS.—GAS AND VENTILATION.
Practical Treatise on Gas and Ventilation. With Special Relation to Illuminating, Heating, and Cooking by Gas. Including Scientific Helps to Engineer-students and others. With illustrated Diagrams. By E. E. PERKINS. 12mo., cloth . . . $1 25

PERKINS AND STOWE.—A NEW GUIDE TO THE SHEET-IRON AND BOILER PLATE ROLLER:
Containing a Series of Tables showing the Weight of Slabs and Piles to Produce Boiler Plates, and of the Weight of Piles and the Sizes of Bars to Produce Sheet-iron; the Thickness of the Bar Gauge in Decimals; the Weight per foot, and the Thickness on the Bar or Wire Gauge of the fractional parts of an inch; the Weight per sheet, and the Thickness on the Wire Gauge of Sheet-iron of various dimensions to weigh 112 lbs. per bundle; and the conversion of Short Weight into Long Weight, and Long Weight into Short. Estimated and collected by G. H. PERKINS and J. G. STOWE $2 50

PHILLIPS AND DARLINGTON.—RECORDS OF MINING AND METALLURGY:
Or, Facts and Memoranda for the use of the Mine Agent and Smelter. By J. ARTHUR PHILLIPS, Mining Engineer, Graduate of the Imperial School of Mines, France, etc., and JOHN DARLINGTON. Illustrated by numerous engravings. In one vol. 12mo. . $2 00

PRADAL, MALEPEYRE, AND DUSSAUCE.—A COMPLETE TREATISE ON PERFUMERY:
Containing notices of the Raw Material used in the Art, and the Best Formulæ. According to the most approved Methods followed in France, England, and the United States. By M. P. PRADAL, Perfumer-Chemist, and M. F. MALEPEYRE. Translated from the French, with extensive additions, by Prof. H. DUSSAUCE. 8vo. $10

PROTEAUX.—PRACTICAL GUIDE FOR THE MANUFACTURE OF PAPER AND BOARDS.
By A. PROTEAUX, Civil Engineer, and Graduate of the School of Arts and Manufactures, Director of Thiers's Paper Mill, 'Puy-de-Dôme. With additions, by L. S. LE NORMAND. Translated from the French, with Notes, by HORATIO PAINE, A. B., M. D. To which is added a Chapter on the Manufacture of Paper from Wood in the United States, by HENRY T. BROWN, of the "American Artisan." Illustrated by six plates, containing Drawings of Raw Materials, Machinery, Plans of Paper-Mills, etc. etc. 8vo. $5 00

REGNAULT.—ELEMENTS OF CHEMISTRY.
By M. V. REGNAULT. Translated from the French by T. FORREST BENTON, M. B., and edited, with notes, by JAMES C. BOOTH, Melter and Refiner U. S. Mint, and WM. L. FABER, Metallurgist and Mining Engineer. Illustrated by nearly 700 wood engravings. Comprising nearly 1500 pages. In two vols. 8vo., cloth $10 00

REID.—A PRACTICAL TREATISE ON THE MANUFACTURE OF PORTLAND CEMENT:
By HENRY REID, C. E. To which is added a Translation of M. A. Lipowitz's Work, describing a new method adopted in Germany of Manufacturing that Cement. By W. F. REID. Illustrated by plates and wood engravings. 8vo. $7 00

RIFFAULT, VERGNAUD, AND TOUSSAINT.—A PRACTICAL TREATISE ON THE MANUFACTURE OF COLORS FOR PAINTING:
Containing the best Formulæ and the Processes the Newest and in most General Use. By MM. RIFFAULT, VERGNAUD, and TOUSSAINT. Revised and Edited by M. F. MALEPEYRE and Dr. EMIL WINCKLER. Illustrated by Engravings. In one vol. 8vo. (*In preparation.*)

RIFFAULT, VERGNAUD, AND TOUSSAINT.—A PRACTICAL TREATISE ON THE MANUFACTURE OF VARNISHES:
By MM. RIFFAULT, VERGNAUD, and TOUSSAINT. Revised and Edited by M. F. MALEPEYRE and Dr. EMIL WINCKLER. Illustrated. In one vol. 8vo. (*In preparation.*)

SHUNK.—A PRACTICAL TREATISE ON RAILWAY CURVES AND LOCATION, FOR YOUNG ENGINEERS.
By WM. F. SHUNK, Civil Engineer. 12mo., tucks . . $2 00

SMEATON.—BUILDER'S POCKET COMPANION:
Containing the Elements of Building, Surveying, and Architecture; with Practical Rules and Instructions connected with the subject. By A. C. SMEATON, Civil Engineer, etc. In one volume, 12mo. $1 50

SMITH.—THE DYER'S INSTRUCTOR:
Comprising Practical Instructions in the Art of Dyeing Silk, Cotton, Wool, and Worsted, and Woollen Goods: containing nearly 800 Receipts. To which is added a Treatise on the Art of Padding; and the Printing of Silk Warps, Skeins, and Handkerchiefs, and the various Mordants and Colors for the different styles of such work. By DAVID SMITH, Pattern Dyer, 12mo., cloth
$3 00

SMITH.—THE PRACTICAL DYER'S GUIDE:
Comprising Practical Instructions in the Dyeing of Shot Cobourgs, Silk Striped Orleans, Colored Orleans from Black Warps, ditto from White Warps, Colored Cobourgs from White Warps, Merinos, Yarns, Woollen Cloths, etc. Containing nearly 300 Receipts, to most of which a Dyed Pattern is annexed. Also, a Treatise on the Art of Padding. By DAVID SMITH. In one vol. 8vo. $25 00

SHAW.—CIVIL ARCHITECTURE:
Being a Complete Theoretical and Practical System of Building, containing the Fundamental Principles of the Art. By EDWARD SHAW, Architect. To which is added a Treatise on Gothic Architecture, &c. By THOMAS W. SILLOWAY and GEORGE M. HARDING, Architects. The whole illustrated by 102 quarto plates finely engraved on copper. Eleventh Edition. 4to. Cloth. $10 00

SLOAN.—AMERICAN HOUSES:
A variety of Original Designs for Rural Buildings. Illustrated by 26 colored Engravings, with Descriptive References. By SAMUEL SLOAN, Architect, author of the "Model Architect," etc. etc. 8vo.
$2 50

SCHINZ.—RESEARCHES ON THE ACTION OF THE BLAST-FURNACE.
By CHAS. SCHINZ. Seven plates. 12mo. . . . $4 25

SMITH.—PARKS AND PLEASURE GROUNDS:
Or, Practical Notes on Country Residences, Villas, Public Parks, and Gardens. By CHARLES H. J. SMITH, Landscape Gardener and Garden Architect, etc. etc. 12mo. $2 25

STOKES.—CABINET-MAKER'S AND UPHOLSTERER'S COMPANION:
Comprising the Rudiments and Principles of Cabinet-making and Upholstery, with Familiar Instructions, Illustrated by Examples for attaining a Proficiency in the Art of Drawing, as applicable to Cabinet-work; The Processes of Veneering, Inlaying, and Buhl-work; the Art of Dyeing and Staining Wood, Bone, Tortoise Shell, etc. Directions for Lackering, Japanning, and Varnishing; to make French Polish; to prepare the Best Glues, Cements, and Compositions, and a number of Receipts, particularly for workmen generally. By J. STOKES. In one vol. 12mo. With illustrations
$1 25

STRENGTH AND OTHER PROPERTIES OF METALS.
Reports of Experiments on the Strength and other Properties of Metals for Cannon. With a Description of the Machines for Testing Metals, and of the Classification of Cannon in service. By Officers of the Ordnance Department U. S. Army. By authority of the Secretary of War. Illustrated by 25 large steel plates. In 1 vol. quarto $10 00

SULLIVAN.—PROTECTION TO NATIVE INDUSTRY.
By Sir EDWARD SULLIVAN, Baronet. (1870.) 8vo. . $1 50

TABLES SHOWING THE WEIGHT OF ROUND, SQUARE, AND FLAT BAR IRON, STEEL, ETC.
By Measurement. Cloth 63

TAYLOR.—STATISTICS OF COAL:
Including Mineral Bituminous Substances employed in Arts and Manufactures; with their Geographical, Geological, and Commercial Distribution and amount of Production and Consumption on the American Continent. With Incidental Statistics of the Iron Manufacture. By R. C. TAYLOR. Second edition, revised by S. S. HALDEMAN. Illustrated by five Maps and many wood engravings. 8vo., cloth $6 00

TEMPLETON.—THE PRACTICAL EXAMINATOR ON STEAM AND THE STEAM-ENGINE:
With Instructive References relative thereto, for the Use of Engineers, Students, and others. By WM. TEMPLETON, Engineer 12mo.
$1 25

THOMAS.—THE MODERN PRACTICE OF PHOTOGRAPHY.
By R. W. Thomas, F. C. S. 8vo., cloth 75

THOMSON.—FREIGHT CHARGES CALCULATOR.
By Andrew Thomson, Freight Agent $1 25

TURNING: SPECIMENS OF FANCY TURNING EXECUTED ON THE HAND OR FOOT LATHE:
With Geometric, Oval, and Eccentric Chucks, and Elliptical Cutting Frame. By an Amateur. Illustrated by 30 exquisite Photographs. 4to. $3 00

TURNER'S (THE) COMPANION:
Containing Instructions in Concentric, Elliptic, and Eccentric Turning; also various Plates of Chucks, Tools, and Instruments; and Directions for using the Eccentric Cutter, Drill, Vertical Cutter, and Circular Rest; with Patterns and Instructions for working them. A new edition in 1 vol. 12mo. $1 50

URBIN—BRULL.—A PRACTICAL GUIDE FOR PUDDLING IRON AND STEEL.
By Ed. Urbin, Engineer of Arts and Manufactures. A Prize Essay read before the Association of Engineers, Graduate of the School of Mines, of Liege, Belgium, at the Meeting of 1865-6. To which is added a Comparison of the Resisting Properties of Iron and Steel. By A. Brull. Translated from the French by A. A. Fesquet, Chemist and Engineer. In one volume, 8vo.
$1 00

VOGDES.—THE ARCHITECT'S AND BUILDER'S POCKET COMPANION AND PRICE BOOK.
By F. W. Vogdes, Architect. Illustrated. Full bound in pocketbook form. $2 00
In book form, 18mo., muslin 1 50

WARN.—THE SHEET METAL WORKER'S INSTRUCTOR, FOR ZINC, SHEET-IRON, COPPER AND TIN PLATE WORKERS, &c.
By Reuben Henry Warn, Practical Tin Plate Worker. Illustrated by 32 plates and 37 wood engravings. 8vo. . . $3 00

WATSON.—A MANUAL OF THE HAND-LATHE.
By Egbert P. Watson, Late of the "Scientific American," Author of "Modern Practice of American Machinists and Engineers," In one volume, 12mo. $1 50

WATSON.—THE MODERN PRACTICE OF AMERICAN MACHINISTS AND ENGINEERS:
Including the Construction, Application, and Use of Drills, Lathe Tools, Cutters for Boring Cylinders, and Hollow Work Generally, with the most Economical Speed of the same, the Results verified by Actual Practice at the Lathe, the Vice, and on the Floor. Together with Workshop management, Economy of Manufacture, the Steam-Engine, Boilers, Gears, Belting, etc. etc. By EGBERT P. WATSON, late of the "Scientific American." Illustrated by eighty-six engravings. 12mo. $2 50

WATSON.—THE THEORY AND PRACTICE OF THE ART OF WEAVING BY HAND AND POWER:
With Calculations and Tables for the use of those connected with the Trade. By JOHN WATSON, Manufacturer and Practical Machine Maker. Illustrated by large drawings of the best Power-Looms. 8vo. $10 00

WEATHERLY.—TREATISE ON THE ART OF BOILING SUGAR, CRYSTALLIZING, LOZENGE-MAKING, COMFITS, GUM GOODS,
And other processes for Confectionery, &c. In which are explained, in an easy and familiar manner, the various Methods of Manufacturing every description of Raw and Refined Sugar Goods, as sold by Confectioners and others . . . $2 00

WILL.—TABLES FOR QUALITATIVE CHEMICAL ANALYSIS.
By Prof. HEINRICH WILL, of Giessen, Germany. Seventh edition. Translated by CHARLES F. HIMES, Ph. D., Professor of Natural Science, Dickinson College, Carlisle, Pa. . . $1 25

WILLIAMS.—ON HEAT AND STEAM:
Embracing New Views of Vaporization, Condensation, and Expansion. By CHARLES WYE WILLIAMS, A. I. C. E. Illustrated. 8vo.
$3 50

WORSSAM.—ON MECHANICAL SAWS:
From the Transactions of the Society of Engineers, 1867. By S. W. WORSSAM, Jr. Illustrated by 18 large folding plates. 8vo.
$5 00

WÖHLER.—A HAND-BOOK OF MINERAL ANALYSIS.
By F. WÖHLER. Edited by H. B. NASON, Professor of Chemistry, Rensselaer Institute, Troy, N. Y. With numerous Illustrations. 12mo. $3 00

Printed in Dunstable, United Kingdom